PETERSON FIELD GUIDE TO
WEATHER

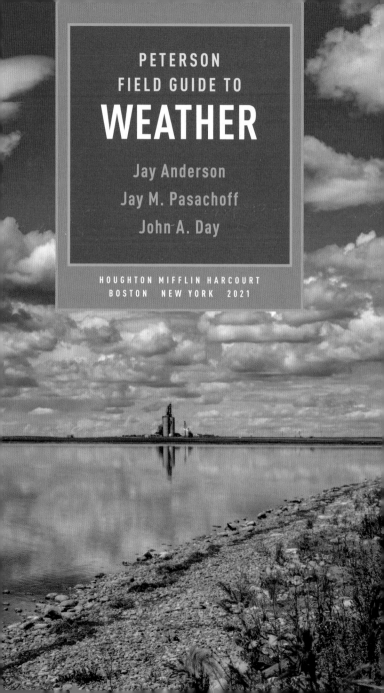

PETERSON
FIELD GUIDE TO
WEATHER

Jay Anderson

Jay M. Pasachoff

John A. Day

HOUGHTON MIFFLIN HARCOURT
BOSTON   NEW YORK   2021

For information about permission to reproduce selections from this book,
write to Permissions, Houghton Mifflin Harcourt Company,
3 Park Avenue, 19th Floor, New York, New York 10016.

www.hmhbooks.com

PETERSON FIELD GUIDES and PETERSON FIELD GUIDE SERIES
are registered trademarks of
Houghton Mifflin Harcourt Publishing Company.

Library of Congress Cataloging-in-Publication Data
is available.

Book design by Eugenie S. Delaney

Printed in Thailand

IMO 10 9 8 7 6 5 4 3 2 1

DEDICATION

We dedicate this *Field Guide to Weather* to our predecessor and coauthor, the late John Day. John, with coauthor Vince Schaefer, wrote the *Peterson Field Guide to the Atmosphere* and the *Peterson First Guide to Clouds and Weather.*

John grew up in Colorado and graduated in airline meteorology from the Boeing School of Aeronautics in 1937. About ten years later, he resigned as a forecaster for Pan American World Airlines (only terrestrial weather then, no space weather forecasting yet) and went back to university at Oregon State, where he got his Ph.D. He long taught in the physics department at Linfield College in McMinnville, Oregon, where one of us (Jay Pasachoff) had the privilege of meeting him and his wife, Mary, when John was in his nineties.

John, starting with his work on forecasting clouds for Pan Am flights, became Cloudman, eventually creating the website cloudman .com. *The Book of Clouds,* which includes many of his photos, is available through various online booksellers.

John was enthusiastic about this new edition, and we are sorry that he couldn't survive to work on it with us. We are glad to try to carry on John Day's work in bringing atmospheric science to the general public.

—Jay Anderson and Jay Pasachoff

ROGER TORY PETERSON INSTITUTE
OF NATURAL HISTORY
Jamestown, New York

Continuing the work of Roger Tory Peterson through Art, Education, and Conservation

In 1984, the Roger Tory Peterson Institute of Natural History (RTPI) was founded in Peterson's hometown of Jamestown, New York, as an educational institution charged by Peterson with preserving his lifetime body of work and making it available to the world for educational purposes.

RTPI is the only official institutional steward of Roger Tory Peterson's body of work and his enduring legacy. It is our mission to foster understanding, appreciation, and protection of the natural world. By providing people with opportunities to engage in nature-focused art, education, and conservation projects, we promote the study of natural history and its connections to human health and economic prosperity.

Art—Using Art to Inspire Appreciation of Nature
The RTPI Archives contains the largest collection of Peterson's art in the world—iconic images that continue to inspire an awareness of and appreciation for nature.

Education—Explaining the Importance of Studying Natural History
We need to study, firsthand, the workings of the natural world and its importance to human life. Local surroundings can provide an engaging context for the study of natural history and its relationship to other disciplines such as math, science, and language. Environmental literacy is everybody's responsibility—not just experts and special interests.

Conservation—Sustaining and Restoring the Natural World
RTPI works to inspire people to choose action over inaction, and engages in meaningful conservation research and actions that transcend political and other boundaries. Our goal is to increase awareness and understanding of the natural connections between species, habitats, and people—connections that are critical to effective conservation.

For more information, and to support RTPI, please visit rtpi.org.

CONTENTS

ACKNOWLEDGMENTS

We thank John Day for beginning us on this book, and for the original encouragement also from his wife, Mary Day, as well as continuing liaison with his daughter Patti Day.

We are grateful for the support of Lisa White, editor of Peterson Field Guides at Houghton Mifflin Harcourt, for seeing this book through to publication.

Jay Pasachoff thanks Naomi Pasachoff, as well as his daughters/sons-in-law/grandchildren Eloise/Tom/Sam/Jessica and Deborah/Ian/Lily/Jacob/Xander. At Williams College, he thanks especially Madeline Kennedy for her continued assistance on a wide variety of matters dealing with this book.

We also wish to acknowledge the contributions of Lisa White and Beth Burleigh Fuller, editors with Houghton Mifflin Harcourt, who, over many years and fruitful discussions, encouraged, cajoled, and supervised this work into production.

Jay Anderson thanks his wife, Judy, whose love and encouragement over more than five decades gave him time to watch the sky.

AUTHORS' COMMENTS

We are pleased to bring the *Peterson Field Guide to Weather* to your attention. It is an entirely new work, brought into the twenty-first century, and extending the original *Peterson Field Guide to the Atmosphere* (1981) and *Peterson First Guide to Clouds and Weather* (1991), both by Vincent Schaefer and John Day. It is an honor to have the opportunity to write this new book to replace the earlier editions in the distinguished Peterson Field Guide series.

The contents of this field guide are based primarily on the field, forecasting, research, and training experiences of the authors, and benefit from many years of observation, measurement, study, and photography. One of us, Jay Pasachoff, as long-time author of the *Peterson Field Guide to the Stars and Planets*, was privileged to work with John Day in beginning the preparations for the new book. Jay Anderson, during his early years as a meteorologist, had the pleasure of learning from Vince Schaefer's expertise in satellite meteorology. The two of us have long worked together in arranging for observations of total solar eclipses from various locations around the globe.

We hope this *Field Guide to Weather* is an interesting, readable, and useful book to you.

FROM THE SERIES EDITOR'S NOTE FOR *FIELD GUIDE TO THE ATMOSPHERE* (1981)

If there were not so many people interested in birds, other wildlife, and plants, we would not have the environmental movement as we know it today. The Field Guide Series, now in its fifth decade, has played no small part in laying the groundwork for this philosophical revolution, this new ecological awareness.

The *Field Guides* offer a visual approach to nature study. Although they make a bow to formal systematics by using its accepted nomenclature, they keep scientific jargon and terminology to a minimum. They rely strongly on their illustrations.

This book, the 26th in the series, deals with a part of the environment that affects every one of us—as well as every bird, mammal, fish, insect, and plant—daily. The atmosphere is that dynamic sea of air that bathes all living things and affects their survival. We see its ever-changing cloud forms, its kaleidoscopic sky coloration, its evanescent rainbows, mists, and fogs. We feel its winds, its rains, and its snows; its heat and its cold. Yet how many of us can interpret its moods and patterns, understand clearly what they mean, or make weather predictions on the basis of them?

Dr. Vincent Schaefer and Dr. John Day, who have never lost their sense of wonder and curiosity about atmospheric phenomena, have spent a large part of their lives observing the drama of the sky. They have recorded, measured, and photographed clouds and other meteorological manifestations, not only from ground level but also from aloft, from aircraft. Their purpose in this *Field Guide* is to instill a greater awareness, so that we will think more about what goes on and take the moods of the weather less for granted.

The birder who learns to read a weather map will know when to expect a flight of raptors at Hawk Mountain or at Cape May. The atmospheric pressure and wind flow will tell him. In much the same way he can decide whether Point Pelee on Lake Erie or one of the other migration points is a good bet for warblers on a particular weekend in May or September. And, of course, if a tropical storm or a nor'easter moves in, he knows that rare seabirds are always a possibility. In a similar fashion the lepidopterist can guess with fair accuracy when certain butterflies and moths will emerge. Indeed, weather patterns affect the fortunes of many animals and plants, at times contributing to their successful reproduction, at other times condemning them to failure.

Quite aside from all the practical as well as the peripheral advantages of knowing something about the atmosphere, the nature-oriented person will find the recognition and interpretation of its signs and symbols fascinating. So study this *Field Guide* at home. And when you travel, by all means take it with you in your backpack, in your briefcase, or in the glove compartment of your car.

Roger Tory Peterson

PETERSON FIELD GUIDE TO
WEATHER

INTRODUCTION

Go outside and look up.

Above you is a laboratory and a canvas—a laboratory to demonstrate the physics of gases and the dynamic behavior of the wind; a canvas for Nature to show off her atmospheric landscapes of cloud and light. It is a place for artists and scientists, for the photographer and the forecaster; it is the abode of birds and pilots. It is a training ground in which to learn to interpret the signs in the sky, a skill that we hope you will acquire from this *Peterson Field Guide to Weather*.

This is a field guide, but you will find that much of it seems unrelated to what you see in your upward glance. For an avid weather watcher, "field" has a much broader meaning than just the outdoors. It includes the evening display of satellite images on television and the graphic depictions of fronts and highs and lows moving across the continent that lurk on a map behind the TV presenter. It includes the description on the radio about the latest hurricane track, the forecast for a coming snowstorm, and the radar display of dangerous thunderstorms on the internet. In our content-rich society, "weather" goes much further than the view out the window, though we are very much entranced by that outdoor experience ourselves and want you to wade in our enthusiasm.

Some—probably most—of the sky's treats that we have witnessed and describe here were unexpected and all the more pleasing for it. A commonplace rainbow on a cross-country drive, the soft mist of a fog, or a looming storm with lightning and thunder: all spark a moment of pleasure and an appreciation of Nature's capacity to entertain or threaten. It may be a private moment for you, secretly appreciated because only you have noticed and understood the phenomenon in the sky. It may be a public moment—perhaps to instruct a child, impress a friend or partner, teach a crowd, or run for cover.

Seven Basic Facts About the Atmosphere

If you want to understand the phenomena that you see in the sky, you cannot avoid bumping into the physical laws that govern the behavior of gases, the transmission of light, the transfer of energy, and several other natural rules. Some are complex relationships; others are almost trivial in their simplicity. To start you off, here are seven things about the atmosphere that will shape your understanding.

1. Air pressure falls as you go upward in the atmosphere.

Air pressure is simply the weight of the atmosphere. It changes from place to place on the globe, but is always high at the ground and lower as you go upward as there is less air above you as you ascend (Figure I-1).

At sea level, the average weight of the atmosphere is 14.7 pounds per square inch (1.03 kg per square cm), which would amount to a force of over 25,000 pounds (11,300 kg) on a 3-foot by 4-foot (0.9 × 1.2 m) desk. Fortunately, this pressure pushes in all directions, upward and downward, outward and inward, so we and the table don't have to bear the weight of all of that atmosphere. At 18,000 feet (5,500 m) altitude, average air pressure falls to half of the sea-level value, 7.3 pounds per square inch. Our hypothetical desk now has to bear a weight of only 12,500 pounds.

FIG. I-1. *A simple home barometer displays the pressure in both inches of mercury and millibars.*

2. Air moves from high pressures to lower pressures.

Just as water flows downhill, air flows from higher pressures to lower pressures. Air rushes out of a tire when the valve is released; it pops out of a soft-drink can when the cap is opened; your lungs inhale with every breath; and your lips can blow outward or pull air inward depending on the pressure you create within your cheeks. In the atmosphere, air flowing from high- to low-pressure areas is responsible for the wind (Figure I-2). Because of the rotation of our planet, wind does not usually flow directly from high to low but instead follows a spiraling path as it leaves the high and moves into the low (Figure I-3).

Sea-breeze winds, familiar to those who live along the margins of an ocean or large lake, are caused when the pressure falls over land, drawing in air from higher pressure regions over water. Winds at high altitudes in the atmosphere flow in response to pressure differences that exist at those levels. Winds from thunderstorms arise from rain-cooled air that has a higher pressure because of its cooler temperature. Mountain winds are caused by air flowing up or down the terrain in response to temperature-based pressure differences along the valley.

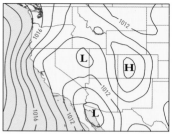

FIG. I-2. *This map shows contours of pressure with centers of high and low values. Over the Pacific Ocean, pressure lines are tightly packed, creating a strong pressure gradient. The gradient is generally much weaker over land, where the lines spread out to circle the highs and lows.*

There is one exception to the flow from high to low: higher pressures at the surface of the Earth do not cause air to flow upward into lower-pressure levels aloft. A good thing, too, as our atmosphere would disappear into space in an instant. In this case, gravity, which pulls the atmosphere down toward the ground, is able to overcome pressure forces that are trying to push

FIG. I-3. *Two low-pressure storm systems are outlined by a spiral of cloud that maps the flow of air into the lows. The spiral is caused by the Coriolis force.*

it away. The two are usually in equilibrium, but when that balance is upset, some very interesting weather can occur as the atmosphere makes corrections.

3. When air rises upward, it cools. Conversely, when it sinks downward, it warms.

When a sample of air rises, it ascends into a region of lower pressure, so it expands outward until its own pressure matches the pressures of its surroundings. That expansion requires energy—it is a form of "work" as a physicist would understand it. The energy to do that work is stolen from the internal energy of the expanding volume, so its temperature falls.

Conversely, when a sample of air sinks downward in the atmosphere, it is compressed as it moves into higher-pressure surroundings and is warmed. The process of both warming and cooling is called "adiabatic," and amounts to a temperature change of 5.4°F for every 1,000 feet (1°C for every 100 m) of ascent or descent, provided the air remains dry.

Adiabatic expansion and contraction might seem rather esoteric, but you encounter them frequently in your daily routine. Compressed cans of air or spray paint may form frost around the outlet as the contents expand into the atmosphere. A manual bicycle pump will heat up from repeated compression as a tire is inflated. A more extreme form of compression heating is found in diesel engines, where the air is compressed to $\frac{1}{15}$ to $\frac{1}{25}$ of its original volume, raising cylinder temperatures to more than 400°F (200°C) to ignite the fuel.

Adiabatic expansion and compression become more complicated when the air contains moisture, a subject we'll discuss in later chapters.

4. Water vapor is the most important "weather" gas in the atmosphere.

To be sure, oxygen is probably more important to you, but from your sky-watcher viewpoint, water vapor is what makes the clouds, hail, rain, and snow, the colors in halos and rainbows, fogs, dew, frost, and so on—a congregation of landscapes and skyscapes. Without water vapor, the Earth would be a much less interesting place.

FIG. 1-4. *This map shows the global concentration of water vapor in the atmosphere. Red shows the highest concentration of vapor, green the least. Most water vapor is found in warm, tropical climates.*

FIG. I-5. *Cool, saturated air near the ground has condensed into cloud droplets and formed this slightly elevated fog bank in eastern Arizona. The flow of wind, toward the Chiricahua Mountains in the background, is gradually lifting and cooling the air as it rises along the terrain.*

Water is a molecule with unique characteristics that make it especially suited for manufacturing weather. It is found everywhere in the universe, but on Earth, we have it in great abundance at temperatures at which it can exist in gaseous, liquid, and solid form (Figure I-4). If life is discovered on other worlds, it is likely that those planets will also harbor temperatures that allow water vapor to exist in those three states. Because of its special status, we'll have a bit more to say about water in the first chapter.

5. When air cools, its moisture content may reach saturation.
Moisture, in the form of water vapor, is always present in the atmosphere and usually referred to as humidity. There is no completely dry airmass anywhere on the Earth since even the harshest desert or coldest ice cap has at least a little water in suspension as a vapor. The atmosphere does have a limit on the maximum amount of water vapor that it can hold, and that limit depends on temperature. Warm air can hold much larger amounts of moisture than cold, but once that limit is reached, the air is said to be saturated and any additional moisture will usually condense into droplets or ice crystals or settle on the ground

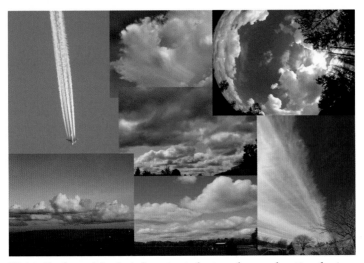

FIG. I-6. *Clouds reveal the physical processes in the atmosphere: condensation of moisture, air currents, saturation, winds and jet streams, aerosols, cooling rates, and turbulence, for instance.*

as dew and frost. At 68°F (20°C) air can hold more than 13 times as much water vapor as at 0°F (−18°C) before it becomes saturated.

If we cool a parcel of air, its water-holding capacity will decline. Eventually, with enough cooling, the air will become saturated or even supersaturated, and the vapor will begin to condense (Figure I-5). Conversely, when the air is warmed, the moisture-holding capacity increases, so the air will become drier and drier. Cooling and heating mechanisms are important processes in forming and dissipating clouds and precipitation.

If you string together the five important points we've already discussed about the atmosphere, you will recognize how clouds might form: rising air, cooling as it expands into lower pressures aloft, will eventually reach saturation and condense into cloud water droplets. This is the essence of all cloud formation (Figure I-6), though we'll have more to say on that subject in Chapter 2.

6. When water changes phase from gas to liquid to solid (condensation and freezing), heat is released. When it goes in the opposite direction, from solid to liquid to gas (melting and evaporation), heat is required.

Water molecules (or any molecule) contain energy that is a consequence of their internal and external motions, which can be in the form of vibration, rotation, and translation (movement). When in a solid form as ice, the water molecule is linked strongly to neighboring molecules by electrical bonds and is free only to vibrate. When ice melts and turns to a liquid state, all three motions become possible, but they are limited by the influence of nearby molecules with which they still maintain weak bonds. When water evaporates to become a vapor, it separates from its neighbors, molecular bonds all but disappear, and the molecules may move freely.

To change a solid to a liquid or a liquid to a gas requires heat, as the bonds between molecules must be given energy to break them apart. This energy goes into storage within the liquid or gas molecules and is known as "latent heat." When water changes phase in the opposite direction, condensing from a vapor to a liquid or freezing from a liquid to a solid, latent energy is given back to the environment in the form of heat and surrounding temperatures will rise.

Latent heat absorption and release are tremendously important in the atmosphere, as they may lower or increase temperatures according to the direction of the phase change. Evaporation and melting cool the surrounding environment because of the heat they require to set molecules free from their liquid or solid state. Condensation and freezing release heat back to the environment. The phase changes between gas and liquid release or require 7.5 times as much energy as those between liquid and solid.

7. Stability connects the upper and lower atmosphere.

In meteorology, stability is closely related to the concept of buoyancy and whether air will drift upward or sink back to its original position if it's given a push. If the atmosphere is forced to rise by some process (such as a cold front or the flow over a mountain) and then sinks back to where it started, conditions are said to be stable. If the displaced air continues to rise on its own after the initial forcing, then the environment is unstable, at least until the rising air reaches a higher stable layer.

We are all familiar with the phrase "hot air rises," and we experience it in many ways in day-to-day activities. In the same fashion, air that becomes heated will also rise, provided that it is warmer than its unheated surroundings. This rising air is buoyant because its higher temperature causes it to expand, giving it a lower density; it floats

FIG. I-7. *Strong thunderstorms carry enormous amounts of moisture and heat from surface levels into the upper atmosphere. In contrast, open spaces between the clouds show where air is sinking back toward the ground, bringing cool, dry air from aloft to lower levels.*

upward. The same process also applies in the reverse direction, so that a cold parcel may sink from higher levels until it either reaches the ground or meets a colder atmospheric layer (Figure I-7).

The up-and-down motions caused by instability mix water vapor, heat, dust, and pollutants through the depth of the atmosphere. When air moves upward, a downward motion must develop to compensate, so there is a continuous overturning of the atmosphere brought on by surface heating and instability. Without this instability-driven transport, clouds and precipitation would occur much less frequently, and the weather would be much less interesting.

As any storm chaser can testify, the assessment of atmospheric instability is a complex procedure that involves consideration of moisture, solar heating, movement of warm and cold fronts, cloudiness, and a collection of other difficult-to-measure parameters. Fortunately, buoyancy in the atmosphere also gives rise to clouds that develop vertically in distinctive shapes that will allow you to assess and even predict the local instability in considerable detail.

What Is in This Guide?

In Chapter 1, we disassemble the Earth's atmosphere. We begin by describing the physical structure and the characteristics of the atmosphere's five layers, particularly the lowest layer, the troposphere, which is the source of most of our weather and the one in which we live. We pay special attention to the most important part of the troposphere—the boundary layer that lies against the ground and exchanges energy, moisture, and particulates with the surface. We also spend a little time describing interesting atmospheric layers, called inversions, in which the temperatures misbehave a bit by getting warmer as we go upward instead of colder.

Water is at once a familiar object that attracts little attention but also a marvelously complex molecule whose physical and chemical behavior is critical for both life and meteorology. We discuss the personality quirks of a water molecule and then follow up with a description of how meteorologists quantify the water content of the atmosphere. Most importantly, Chapter 1 explores the role of water in the environment and the characteristics that make it so important to weather and climate. Finally, we touch on the Earth's hydrological cycle and how water moves through the global environment.

In the final section of Chapter 1, we discuss the role of solar energy in the atmosphere. Though we bask continuously in the glow of the Sun's warmth, not all of the energy that falls on our planet remains here. Only around half is retained; the rest is returned to space in one form or another. That fraction that the Earth keeps is itself divided among several reservoirs, and we discuss how the energy is partitioned among them and how it changes with the seasons.

In Chapter 2, we introduce a precipitation ladder—a description of the sequence of events that leads from vapor in the atmosphere to cloud and precipitation. Along the way, we encounter topics such as evaporation, condensation, cooling, and droplet growth. Chapter 2 closes with an introduction to the types of precipitation: rain and snow, of course, but also others such as sleet, freezing rain, graupel, ice pellets, and hail.

In Chapters 3 and 4, we look at clouds. In Chapter 3, we discuss the "ordinary" clouds and how they are recognized and classified. Chapter 4 introduces unusual clouds—that is, those clouds that are rare or unfamiliar in form. Here is where the artistic part of a meteorologist's personality resides, for many of the structures in Chapter 4 are strikingly beautiful, colorful, or even ominous. Chapters 3 and 4 are for the cloud watchers, an amusement that resides in all of us, at least part of the time.

Chapters 5 and 6 are for those who delight in viewing clouds and weather from above. First, we describe and show examples of cloud images from the air, passing on some tips for photography and seating. There are many photos of clouds taken from the air in this book, and Chapter 5 will explain how we acquired them. In Chapter 6, we move to a satellite perspective, and while most of us will never have the opportunity to personally view clouds from space, satellite images are everywhere on the internet and on television. Instead of following the brief descriptions provided by TV announcers, you will be able to interpret the cloud patterns for yourself and pass judgment on the forecast reliability.

Chapter 7 deals with winds. To begin with, we outline the global winds that control the climates of the world. Next, our focus will shift to some regional and local flows that have more day-to-day impact. Some of these winds are personal: they bring cool air in the heat of the day, damaging gusts in mountains, heavy snow in winter, or a dry and warm chinook. Some come with the seasons, bringing monsoons with wet or dry weather. And, since the atmosphere is more than just a surface layer, we have to consider winds aloft and how the weather is controlled.

Fronts and frontal systems are the subject of Chapter 8, but we begin with a description of airmasses, where frontal boundaries have their origin. North America is home to five or more airmasses (depending on the season and how airmasses are defined), and all have their characteristic weather. We go on to the subject of warm and cold fronts and their characteristics and then to the large-scale storm systems that are defined by warm and cold fronts. Here we learn about comma clouds, storm evolution, satellite-based observations, and the way winds flow through these systems. If you understand these storms, the TV weather forecasts—especially in winter—will make a lot more sense.

Severe weather events of all types and seasons make their debut in Chapter 9, and we must admit to a special fondness for severe thunderstorms and the threats and spectacles that they pose. This chapter won't teach you to chase storms—that requires a book in itself—but it will make you more aware of some of the hazards that might be coming your way when the summer heat is building. To balance our discussion, we leave much of the second half of the chapter for winter storms: the Colorado low, Texas hooker, Hatteras low, and the nor'easter. We end Chapter 9 with hurricanes and tropical storms, the bad boys of the tropics.

Chapter 10 was perhaps the most fun to write, for it deals with the play of light in the atmosphere. It is here that we introduce some of the most spectacular forms that the sky and its clouds can produce: rainbows, halos, sundogs, coronas, glories, rays and shadows, sunsets and the green flash, and the aurora. Some of these displays are uncommon and found primarily, but not exclusively, in cold climates and seasons. Others are daily events, though often overlooked. A few are very rare and all the more appealing if you can recognize them and identify their cause.

In Chapter 11, we go back to the beginning, turning to the history of meteorology and introducing the characters who built the science, from the time of ancient Babylon to the present. We use history to show how weather-measuring instruments evolved, though for several instruments, that story is far from clear. Along the way we meet many familiar faces—Aristotle, Galileo, Pascal, Celsius—but also those less well known, such as Santorio, Berti, Howard, and Gay-Lussac. The history of meteorological instruments is the history of the science itself, as the insights gained during the earlier centuries were almost entirely thanks to ever-better instrumentation.

In the Appendix, we discuss the atmospheres on other planets within our and other solar systems, as well as some especially interesting moons and a spectacular comet.

The atmosphere, with all of its signs and secrets, is a wonderful amphitheater for the knowledgeable weather watcher and an inspiration to the artist. We hope you relish exploring the coming chapters and find that our explanations and examples contribute to your enjoyment of the atmosphere.

CHAPTER 1

THE ATMOSPHERE

Structure of the Earth's Atmosphere

Examine a color satellite image of the Earth (Figure 1-1) and one unique character of our planet captures your attention: it's blue. It's blue because of the atmosphere and because of the oceans. Embedded in this blue mantle of gases are clumps of white clouds, circulating slowly across the planet, never ending and never the same from one moment to another.

Within the solar system, the Earth's atmosphere has a very special status. Its mixture of gases—primarily nitrogen and oxygen in the form of the molecules N_2 and O_2—is unique, allowing life to develop and spread across its surface. Together these two gases comprise 99 percent of the atmosphere (Table 1-1) but play almost no role in the daily weather of the planet, as they are well mixed and always gaseous. The most important weather role belongs instead to a minor constit-uent—water vapor—that not only varies considerably from place to place and season to season, but is able to switch between vapor, liquid, and solid phases. Carbon dioxide goes through a small annual cycle in response to the seasons (Figure 1-2), but it too always remains in a vapor state.

FIG. 1-1. *The Earth is blue in this GOES-17 weather satellite image—a consequence of the water vapor in its atmosphere and its liquid water oceans.*

The blanket of air that envelops our planet can be conveniently divided into five layers (Figure 1-3) based mostly on how temperatures behave through the layer. In order, from the ground, these layers are the troposphere, stratosphere, mesosphere, thermosphere, and exosphere. The boundary between each layer is given a name based on

GAS	PERCENT BY VOLUME
nitrogen (N_2)	78.08
oxygen (O_2)	20.95
water vapor (H_2O)	0.4 generally, but typically 1–4% in the lower atmosphere
argon (Ar)	0.93
carbon dioxide (CO_2)	0.04

TABLE 1-1. *The most important gases in the Earth's troposphere*

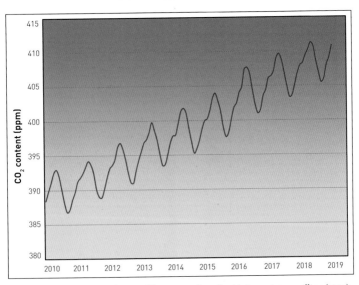

FIG. 1-2. *A graph showing the monthly mean carbon dioxide in parts per million (ppm) from 2010 to 2019 measured at Mauna Loa in Hawaii. The up-and-down cycle in the graph reflects global variations in the uptake of carbon dioxide from the atmosphere by plant photosynthesis. Minimum values occur in September or October, at the end of the northern summer. The rising trend goes back more than 60 years.*

the lower layer and the suffix "pause," so that the boundary between the troposphere and stratosphere is known as the tropopause; between the stratosphere and mesosphere, we have the stratopause, and so on. While each layer has unique characteristics in addition to its temperature profile, it will come as no surprise that the troposphere is the most important, as most of the weather we experience is created there.

The Troposphere

The troposphere (Figure 1-4) contains about three-quarters of the atmosphere's mass and nearly all of its water vapor. It is the region where clouds and precipitation form, where pollutants lurk in highest

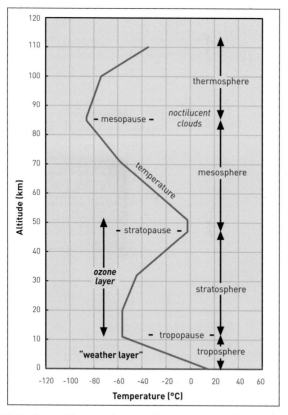

FIG. 1-3. *The layers of the atmosphere according to temperature. The exosphere lies above the thermosphere.*

FIG. 1-4. *This photo, taken from the International Space Station in 2013, shows the thin crescent of the moon rising over the limb and atmosphere of the Earth. The troposphere is the orange-red glow near the horizon, topped by the brownish tropopause. Directly above the tropopause is the grayish stratosphere, above which lie the blue-toned mesosphere and thermosphere and, eventually, the blackness of space.*

concentration, and where humans have their main connection with the atmospheric environment. In the cold air over the Arctic and Antarctic, the troposphere has an average depth of about 4.3 miles (7 km). Over middle latitudes, this rises to around 11 miles (17 km), and in tropical regions, to around 12.5 miles (20 km). The troposphere is divided into two layers: a lower region in which interaction with the surface is most important and an upper region where the air is able to flow freely.

THE PLANETARY BOUNDARY LAYER

The lowest layer of the troposphere is known as the planetary boundary layer—a region where the Earth's surface interacts with the atmosphere, exchanging heat, water vapor, and aerosols. This is the layer where heat is passed back and forth between the ground and the air and where water evaporates to add humidity to the atmosphere. It is a region where winds feel the friction of the underlying ground, where aerosols and pollutants arise, and where humans have their greatest impact.

The depth of the boundary layer is highly variable as it depends on

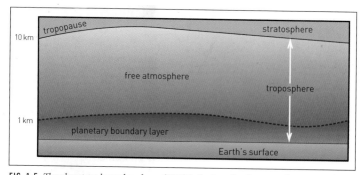

FIG. 1-5. *The planetary boundary layer (PBL) is the interface between the ground and the atmosphere. Above the PBL lies the free atmosphere, where the influence of the surface is much reduced.*

FIG. 1-6. *Taken on descent into Cairo, this photo shows the top of the planetary boundary layer. The dust, humidity, and pollution of the PBL make it readily apparent from an aircraft when seen at an oblique angle from just above the layer. The convective white clouds show where the entrainment zone is most active, mixing the moist, boundary-layer air with the pristine air above.*

latitude, the roughness and character of the ground beneath, the time of day, and the season. On a summer afternoon, the boundary layer typically ranges between ¾ and 2 miles over North America, but at night it is much lower, generally below one-half mile and occasionally nearly at the surface. The boundary layer is lowest at higher latitudes and in the winter; over oceans it has little variability from day to night or from season to season.

At the top of the boundary layer, surface influences—particularly friction—come to an end and the free atmosphere begins (Figure 1-5). The divide between the free atmosphere and the boundary layer is often visible from a descending aircraft (Figure 1-6) as a distinct transition between hazy, particle-laden, low-level air and the pristine skies above.

The atmosphere is largely transparent to solar radiation, so most of the troposphere's heating comes from the Sun-warmed ground; at higher levels, it is cooled by infrared (heat) radiation that escapes to space. This combination of low-level heating and upper-level cooling gives the troposphere an average temperature that declines with altitude (Figure 1-3) though there are many temporary local, diurnal, and seasonal variations in this pattern. The temperature decline is often interrupted by inversions, at the ground or in a layer aloft, where temperature rises instead of falling with height.

In the early morning hours after a clear or lightly clouded night with light winds, the lower atmosphere becomes stratified into a number of layers. Because the ground is an efficient emitter of infrared radiation, it has cooled steadily overnight, reaching its lowest temperature just

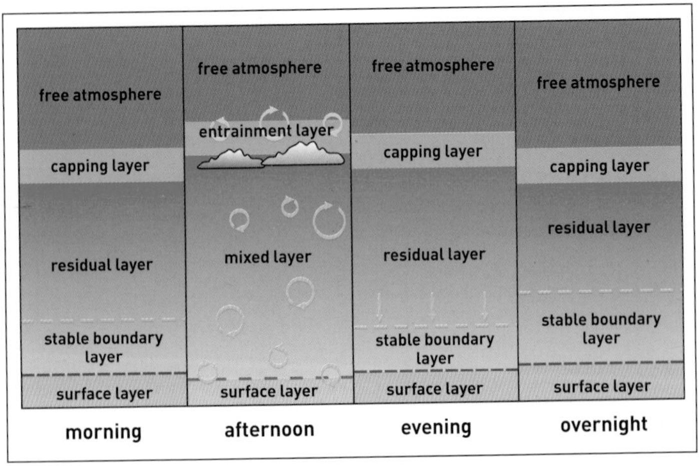

FIG. 1-7. *The evolution of the planetary boundary layer through the day. Morning insolation heats the surface layer, after which turbulent mixing distributes the heat through the lower atmosphere, creating a well-mixed zone that is topped by an entrainment layer. The entrainment zone mixes boundary layer air with air from the free atmosphere above. As night returns, a stable boundary layer re-forms, leaving a residual layer aloft that is topped by a capping inversion.*

FIG. 1-8. *A plume of smoke spreads out beneath a temperature inversion that marks the top of the planetary boundary layer on this early morning. The small convective "bumps" in the cloud above the smoke stacks mark where the warmest part of the plume attempts to break through the inversion.*

after daybreak. The cold surface temperatures are passed to a thin skin of adjacent atmosphere (known as the surface layer), and as the night progresses, the ground-based cooling spreads upward, helped by a slow mixing of the lower atmosphere by turbulence or light winds (Figure 1-7).

Because the coldest temperatures are at the surface and gradually warmer temperatures are above, the morning boundary layer forms an inversion—a layer in which temperatures rise with altitude rather than decline. Instrumented balloons sent aloft around sunrise to measure temperature will reveal that this boundary layer inversion has reached a few tens or hundreds of feet above the surface. The top of the boundary layer is often marked by spreading, flat-topped chimney plumes (Figure 1-8), especially in winter. Still higher, above the nighttime surface-based inversion, are the remains of the previous day's boundary layer, known as the residual layer. In this layer, temperatures follow the normal trend, gradually falling with height.

The residual layer is topped by a second inversion, called the capping layer, that marks the transition to the free atmosphere. The capping layer inversion is usually much weaker than the surface inversion formed at the cold ground.

Shortly after dawn, the rising Sun begins to heat the ground, quickly erasing the cold surface-based inversion and sending warm bubbles of air upward to raise the temperature of the lower troposphere. The turbulent, rising thermals increase in intensity during the day, mixing the atmosphere throughout the lower troposphere and erasing the distinction between the surface, boundary, and residual layers. This deeper mixed layer becomes the daytime planetary boundary layer, still topped by a capping inversion where thermals lose their upward momentum and come to a stop. The capping layer is fairly porous and allows a modest exchange of heat and moisture between the planetary boundary layer and the free atmosphere; this region of exchange is often referred to as the entrainment zone or entrainment layer.

As night falls, the ground cools, winds decline, and turbulence becomes sporadic. The ground and lower atmosphere cool again and the stable boundary layer with its inversion rebuilds. The cold surface air beneath the inversion may deposit frost or dew, or condense into a thin ground fog (Figure 1-9) if temperatures fall low enough. Above the surface-based inversion, the afternoon mixed layer is cut off from the ground, and returns to its previous identity as the overnight residual layer.

FIG. 1-9. *Light winds and clear autumn nights allow the air near the ground to cool to the saturation point, forming a thin fog that hugs the grass.*

In the real world, cloud cover, winds, seasonal changes, instability, and a host of other factors influence this daily cycle, complicating the simple picture outlined in Figure 1-7. In the most extreme cases, when daytime surface heating and humidity are sufficient, strong updrafts will punch through the entrainment layer, carrying large quantities of boundary layer air upward in thunderstorms to mix into the free atmosphere (Chapter 9).

The daily cycle of changes in the boundary layer leaves visible traces that become obvious to the interested weather watcher. A thermometer shows that grass temperatures are typically 5°F to 8°F colder than the air at chest height after a clear summer night. By midmorning, the cold air has disappeared and the grass is now warmer than the layers above. Frost forms overnight in the lowest spots where the coldest air collects. Chimney plumes rise only a short distance in the morning before turning sideways to drift downwind, but in the afternoon they rise upward and dissipate. Smog is heaviest and visibilities lowest in the morning hours, but largely gone in the afternoon, except for a lighter-colored haze in the sky. Birds—eagles in particular—perch until midmorning on a cool day and then depart abruptly to soar upward, floating on the first thermals as they rise. If the day is humid, cloud watchers will be rewarded as well, catching the early cumulus puffs before they grow to larger buildups.

INVERSIONS

An important part of the planetary boundary layer's diurnal cycle is the formation and dissipation of the surface-based inversion. The name "inversion" comes from the upside-down temperature pattern within the layer, where warmer air lies on top of cooler air. Inversions are very common and are a crucial factor in controlling the upward and downward movements in the atmosphere. They may form at any level in the atmosphere (the tropopause is at an inversion) but the most common is the boundary layer inversion that forms overnight against the ground when skies are clear and winds are light.

On windy nights, especially over rough terrain, the skin of cold air that forms along the ground is mixed with higher, warmer layers, and inversions will be weak or will not form at all. Long winter nights are great inversion producers, particularly because snow is a good infrared emitter and cools quickly once the Sun has set. When the daylight returns, the bright white snow cover reflects the morning sunlight back to space and the ground cannot warm enough to break

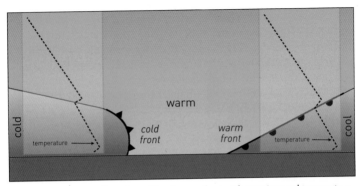

FIG. 1-10. *Cross section through a cold and warm front with superimposed temperature profiles. Two frontal inversions are depicted in each frontal zone: one near the surface and another aloft where the cold air transitions to a warmer layer above.*

the inversion. In cold Arctic airmasses, formed under the continuous night of a snow-covered surface, the inversion is a semipermanent feature of winter, sometimes extending through most or even all of the troposphere.

Cold fronts spread low-temperature air along the ground, under-cutting and lifting warmer air, forming an inversion above the surface where the two layers meet. Warm fronts spread high-temperature air over the top of the surface cold air, again creating an inversion (Figure 1-10) at the interface between the two airmasses. High-pressure systems (Chapter 7) also create inversions, so regions of the globe underlying the semipermanent, tropical anticyclones (highs) have strong inversions that suppress the formation of clouds, giving us sunny Mediterranean and Caribbean holiday climates that provide escape from winter. This type of inversion is a dominant factor in San Francisco's weather, where cold marine air over the ocean is overlain by an inversion created by the Hawaiian anticyclone in the mid-Pacific. Moisture trapped under the inversion forms extensive fog and low cloud along the California coast, which, on flowing inland across the city, burns off as the cool air is warmed over the land.

Inversions suppress the vertical mixing of the atmosphere by impeding the upward motion of air parcels from lower layers (as in the smoke plume of Figure 1-8). On an otherwise unsettled day, thunderstorms have a more difficult or even impossible time under an inversion; moisture and cloud may accumulate under inversions and winds may have unique directions and strengths. For a storm chaser,

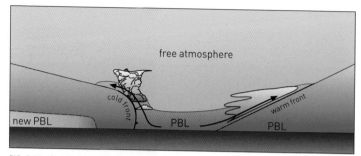

FIG. 1-11. *Ventilation of the boundary layer by warm- and cold-frontal systems. On the left, a moving cold front slides under the warmer air in front, lifting it to higher levels. On the right, warm air pushing against the cold is compelled instead to rise above it. By lifting the boundary layer upward, the fronts will introduce surface-layer air into the free atmosphere. Convective clouds generated by frontal lifting will augment the venting.*

an inversion at an altitude of 1 or 2 miles (1½ to 3 km) allows heat and moisture to "cook" in the lower levels of the atmosphere and acquire enough energy to explode upward into giant severe thunderstorms late in the day.

We encounter inversions almost daily in the patterns formed by the clouds. In the middle atmosphere an inversion is a kind of "lid," and clouds that press up against the lid adopt a smooth-topped appearance, often in complex and almost mysterious-looking shapes. In particular, lenticular clouds, named for their lenslike shapes, rely on inversions for their formation.

THE FREE ATMOSPHERE

The free atmosphere is the part of the troposphere above the planetary boundary layer. It is not entirely independent of lower parts of the atmosphere, as air from lower down does mix into upper levels by a process known as "venting." Deep convective clouds such as thunderstorms carry moisture, heat, and other constituents into the free atmosphere, sometimes in very large quantities. Cold fronts (Chapter 8) operate in a more relaxed fashion, undercutting low-level air and lifting it upward until it pushes into the free atmosphere (Figure 1-11). The heating of mountain slopes during the day and cooling at night give birth to complex mountain flows in which sun-warmed air rises during the day and mountain-cooled air sinks at night, blending the boundary layer and upper tropospheric atmospheres. More vigorous stirring occurs when strong upper-level winds flow more or less perpendicularly across a mountain barrier. On reaching the lee side, the winds drop sharply downward to lower altitudes, often generating moderate to intense turbulence in waves and eddies that quickly mix air through the depth of the troposphere.

The Stratosphere

The transition to the stratosphere, on average about 6 miles (11 km) above sea level, is marked by an inversion where falling temperatures in the tropopause evolve to a region where temperatures first stop falling and then, a little higher, begin to rise with height (Figure 1-3). In effect, the stratosphere is a 24-mile (38-km) deep inversion, with temperatures near –72°F (–58°C) at the bottom and near freezing at the top. Such a profile makes the atmosphere extremely stable, so there is very little vertical mixing in the stratosphere.

The stratosphere's higher temperature comes courtesy of the ozone molecules that are present at high altitudes, primarily between 10 and 15 miles (15–25 km) altitude (Figure 1-12). Ozone is a molecule made up of three oxygen atoms, and it's very efficient at absorbing high-energy ultraviolet radiation from the Sun and then using it to warm the surrounding atmosphere. A very good thing, too, as ultraviolet

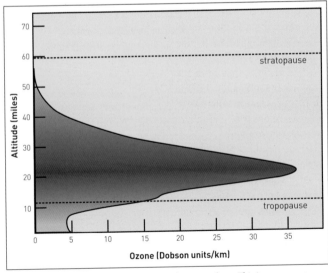

FIG. 1-12. *Vertical distribution of ozone in the atmosphere. This is an average distribution; in reality, ozone concentration varies widely around the globe.*

FIG. 1-13. *Noctilucent clouds over Manitoba, Canada. The name is derived from the Latin words for "night shining."*

radiation is harmful to most life forms, and even the little bit that makes it through to the ground will give a sunburn to the unwary.

The combination of warm (well, relatively warm) temperatures and low humidity makes clouds very unlikely in the stratosphere, but on occasion, strikingly colorful nacreous or mother-of-pearl clouds can be seen. Composed of ice crystals or exotic combinations of water ice and acid crystals, they form in the coldest, lower part of the stratosphere, between 10 and 16 miles (15–25 km) above the surface. Nacreous clouds (Chapter 4) are very rare, and when you spot them with their marvelous colors, you will have a very special moment to store away in your mind.

The Mesosphere

If cold is what you want, the mesosphere is where you will find it. From the stratopause at 31 miles (50 km) to the mesopause at 50 or 56 miles (80 or 90 km), temperatures decline steadily, reaching a minimum around –148°F (–100°C) at about 52 miles (85 km). The cooling is caused by the emission of longwave radiation to space, mostly from carbon dioxide molecules.

In spite of its altitude, low density, and extreme cold, the mesosphere has some interesting meteorological features. Chief among these are noctilucent clouds (Figure 1-13), the highest clouds visible in the Earth's atmosphere. Composed of water-ice crystals that form directly from the vapor phase, noctilucent clouds are most often visible from latitudes above 50° in the summer when the nighttime sun is less than about 16° below the horizon. At their high altitude, the clouds remain illuminated above the northern horizon when the rest of the sky is in darkness. They have a beautiful pearly, lacy appearance; time-lapse photography shows that the clouds sometimes occur in layers, moving in different directions.

The Thermosphere and Exosphere

Two more layers complete our survey of the atmosphere, but both are so high that they have almost no meteorological importance. The thermosphere, extending to a height of 300 to 620 miles (500 to 1,000 km) above the mesopause, is the realm of low-orbiting satellites such as the International Space Station and so is more a part of the space environment than the Earth's atmosphere. Perhaps the most distinguishing feature of the thermosphere is that it is the home to most of the aurorae. The excitation and ionization of molecules and atoms by solar particles causes them to fluoresce in the greens and purples characteristic of a strong auroral display (Chapter 10). The thermosphere is also the region that absorbs the most energetic x-ray and ultraviolet radiation from the Sun, a function that greatly protects the life forms on the Earth below.

Above the thermosphere is the exosphere, a region where the gases of the Earth's atmosphere escape into space. Though the Earth's gravitational field dominates until about halfway to the Moon (118,000 miles, 190,000 km), most researchers would probably put 6,200 miles (10,000 km) as the upper limit of our atmosphere.

Water in the Atmosphere

Our Unique Planet

The Earth is well endowed with water, but it is not unique in the solar system in that respect. Some of the moons of Jupiter and Saturn have large amounts of water ice, and Mars has water in its thin atmosphere and locked away underground. Earth is unique in that water can exist here in three states—gas, liquid, and solid—sometimes simultaneously. The "Blue Planet" nickname we have hung on our world is a reflection of the very prominent amount of liquid water in our oceans

FIG. 1-14. *The water vapor content of the atmosphere in May 2018.*

and lakes. Strangely, in spite of tremendous liquid reservoirs, water vapor is not evenly mixed around the globe but varies tremendously from day to day, season to season, and place to place (Figure 1-14).

It is estimated that there are 332 million cubic miles (1,386 million cubic km) of water on Earth with 95 percent contained in the oceans. Of the total, 2.6 million cu. mi. (10.6 million cu km) is fresh water and almost all of that is locked away as groundwater. Only 0.001 percent of the Earth's water resides in the atmosphere but its presence there, and its transition between solid, liquid, and gas, lies at the heart of Earth's weather.

The Properties of Water

Water is a small molecule formed from two hydrogen atoms and one oxygen atom (H_2O or HOH), held together by strong electrochemical bonds. The molecule is V-shaped, with the oxygen atom at the point of the V and the two hydrogens lying at the ends of the arms (Figure 1-15). This lopsided arrangement prevents the negative charges on the oxygen atom from completely canceling the positive charges on the hydrogen. As a result, the water molecule is a "polar molecule," with a weak posi-

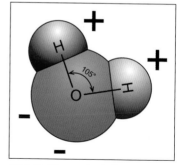

FIG. 1-15. *Water molecules have a net positive charge on one side and a negative charge on the other because of the oxygen atom's greater affinity for electrons.*

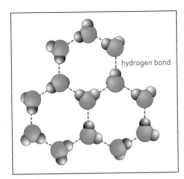

FIG. 1-16. *When water freezes, molecules organize into a six-sided lattice joined by weak electrical bonds between the positive side of one molecule and the negative side of a neighbor. These hydrogen bonds, shown here as red dashed lines, give water many of its unusual characteristics.*

tive charge on one side and a weak negative charge on the other.

This polar nature of the water molecule causes neighboring molecules to attract each other, with the negative side of one forming a weak attachment with the positive side of another (Figure 1-16). This connection is known as a hydrogen bond, and gives water one of its most useful characteristics—the ability to remain a liquid at typical Earth temperatures. Without the cohesion of hydrogen bonding, the low molecular weight of water would cause it to form a gas at ordinary temperatures. Water's small molecular size and the hydrogen bonds that it forms also give it other unusual properties, many of which are fundamental to meteorological processes.

Melting and Boiling Points of Water

When water takes the form of an ice crystal, individual molecules share adjacent hydrogen bonds, causing the molecules to be arranged tightly in a static position (Figure 1-16). Later, when the ice is warmed, the applied heat disrupts the bonds and causes the water to turn to a liquid. The energy required to break the bonds is relatively large, so water has an uncharacteristically high melting point temperature of 32°F (0°C). Even as a liquid, water molecules still retain a modest level of polar bonding and as a consequence, the molecules do not readily evaporate from a liquid surface. This lingering attraction gives water a comparatively high boiling point of 212°F (100°C), above which the remaining bonds are overcome and the liquid turns to a gas.

The Density of Water and Ice

Most liquids become denser as they cool and would sink to the bottom of a container if poured into warmer liquid. Water is no different—until its temperature falls below 39.18°F (3.989°C). At that point, hydrogen bonds begin to assert their presence and cause the polar molecules to organize into a quasi-crystalline structure that takes up

FIG. 1-17. *Ice floats because its density as a solid is less than its density as a liquid.*

more space than the jumbled disorganization of warmer molecules. This semicrystalline organization gives cold water a lower density than warm, so water colder than 39°F will float to the top of a lake or ocean. If you go swimming in the spring, after the ice has melted on a lake, the top layers will be very cold, while a deep dive will reveal warmer water below. By midsummer, when all of the lake temperatures are above 39°F, it is the warm layer that floats on top while the colder water has settled to the bottom.

As water further cools toward the freezing point, density continues to decline until the crystalline structure is frozen in, forming ice with a volume that is about 9 percent larger than an equivalent amount of liquid water. This is quite at odds with most substances, which have solid phases that are denser than their liquid states. It's an absolutely critical property, too, for it means that ice floats on top of liquid water (Figure 1-17) instead of

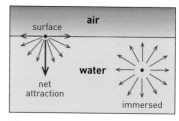

FIG. 1-18. *Water molecules on the surface of a droplet feel a force pulling them back into the liquid body because of the combined attraction of their neighboring molecules. Those molecules deeper within the liquid body are tugged in all directions and have no net force acting. The uneven forces at the top of the liquid are the cause of surface tension.*

FIG. 1-19. *Surface tension causes the water drops on this leaf to adopt a spherical shape.*

FIG. 1-20. *Surface tension allows this paper clip to float on the surface of a cup of water.*

sinking to the bottom. If ice sank, all of the fish and life in a pond or lake would be forced to the surface or entombed in winter.

Surface Tension

Within a body of water, the attractive force of hydrogen bonds between molecules tugs in all directions and there is no net force on an individual water molecule (Figure 1-18). Molecules at the surface, however, feel only a downward pull from the molecules beside and below. The result is a net inward and lateral force called surface tension that causes molecules on the outside of a drop to resist stretching and breaking, making the liquid surface behave as a thin elastic sheet. Surface tension controls the shape of raindrops, the beading of water drops on a surface (Figure 1-19), and gives insects and other small objects the ability to "float" on a water surface (Figure 1-20).

How Much Water Vapor Can the Atmosphere Hold?

The atmosphere around and above us does not have an unlimited capacity to hold water—there is a limit that depends on temperature and when that limit is reached, the air is said to be saturated. It's a bit of a fuzzy limit, as it is not uncommon for air to achieve supersaturation, sometimes by a large amount, when other physical conditions are absent, a subject we'll address in Chapter 9.

Water moves into the atmosphere by evaporation and leaves it by condensation and precipitation, typically when it becomes saturated. The most visible form of condensation is cloud, which is formed from tiny droplets that condense out of atmospheric water vapor. Condensation is also visible as frost or dew when the air near the ground becomes saturated after cooling overnight. What exactly, then, is saturation?

In a closed container half-filled with water, molecules will evaporate from the liquid into the air above (Figure 1-21). At the same time, some of the water vapor molecules will come into contact with the liquid surface and condense back into the water reservoir. Eventually a balance will be reached between evaporation and condensation in which the number of molecules returning to the water surface equals those leaving. At that point, the atmosphere is said to be saturated.

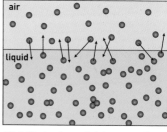

FIG. 1-21. *A volume of air is saturated when the number of molecules leaving the water body is balanced by an equal number captured at the surface.*

If we were to perform the same experiment with ice in the container, we would find that the number of molecules needed to attain saturation over ice is slightly lower than over water. Molecules are bound more tightly in ice crystals than in liquid water and so escape less readily. When water and ice coexist in the atmosphere, which they can do quite easily at temperatures below zero, molecules will evaporate from the water drop and condense on the ice crystal—an important process in making rain and snow (Chapter 2).

The amount of saturated water vapor that an atmosphere can hold depends on temperature. Molecules move more quickly at higher temperatures and so evaporate more readily from the water surface—a relationship we exploit when we place a shirt over a radiator to dry it out or hang laundry in the sun. Conversely, we can convince moist air to reach saturation by cooling, a process that happens nearly every warm and humid day when beads of water collect on a soft drink can removed from the refrigerator or on a glass of cold water (Figure 1-22).

In the atmosphere, saturation is reached by adding moisture or by cooling. Moisture can be added from many sources: evaporation from raindrops falling from a higher level, airflow over a lake or

FIG. 1-22. *Water vapor condenses and forms droplets on a glass of ice water whose surface temperature is lower than the dewpoint of the surrounding air.*

ocean, evaporation from crops and forests, and from wet ground or melting snow. Cooling comes from events such as an overnight temperature decline, from the passage of cold fronts, and from the lifting of air to higher levels in the atmosphere.

Measuring Humidity

We use the word "humidity" as a general term to talk about water in our atmosphere. To say that the air is humid is to say that there is water vapor in it, not that the day is necessarily muggy or uncomfortable. There is no absolutely dry atmosphere anywhere on the Earth, though the cold, upper troposphere and the stratosphere have very low humidity.

Most of us are familiar with "relative humidity" from its use in our day-to-day weather forecasts, but relative humidity is not always the best measurement of water content. In both winter and summer, morning relative humidities are often over 90 percent, but the amount of moisture in the air is very different in the two seasons. As you might suspect, there are several ways of measuring water content, each one with its own special advantages and limitations.

Vapor Pressure and Saturation Vapor Pressure

Our atmosphere is composed of a number of gases that collectively exert a force that we know of as air pressure. That pressure is made up of the individual contributions of each one of the gases, so we can speak of and measure the "partial pressure due to oxygen" or the "partial pressure due to nitrogen" or that of any of the constituent gases. From this, we come to the first measurement of water content— the partial pressure due to water vapor, or "vapor pressure," as it is most commonly known. For example, air at sea level with a temperature of 68°F (20°C) might have a vapor pressure of 15 millibars (mb), a small number compared to the average atmospheric pressure of 1,013 mb. This would be a comfortable, dry day with about an ounce of water vapor suspended in 100 cubic feet of air (9.5 g/cu m).

While the vapor pressure in a sample of air is a useful parameter in engineering and air conditioning, a more important measure is the vapor pressure if the sample were saturated. The partial pressure of water at saturation is called the "saturated vapor pressure." In the graph of Figure 1-23, we see that the saturation vapor pressure is low at cold temperatures and climbs slowly and then more rapidly as temperature increases. Using the same temperature as the example in the

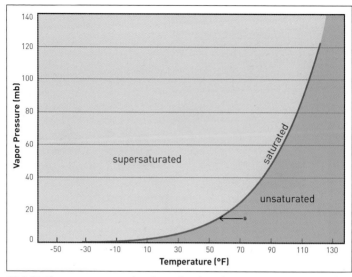

FIG. 1-23. *The saturation point of a volume of air depends on its temperature, as seen by the curve in this graph of vapor pressure versus temperature. Under most circumstances, moisture in the air will condense to water droplets at the saturation curve, but in some special settings, the atmosphere may hold a small amount of water vapor in excess of the saturated limit.*

paragraph above, at sea level and 68°F (20°C), the saturated vapor pressure is 23 mb, equivalent to 1.7 ounces of water vapor in 100 cubic feet of air (17.3 g/cu m).

Relative Humidity

Relative humidity, commonly called RH, is a measure of how much moisture is in the air compared to how much it could hold if saturated, expressed as a percentage. A relative humidity of 70 percent then means that the air holds 70 percent of the amount of vapor that would bring it to saturation at that temperature. Saturated air then has a relative humidity of 100 percent. When the atmosphere is supersaturated (by a sudden cooling, for instance), the RH will be over 100 percent. Relative humidity is usually calculated as the ratio of the actual vapor pressure to the saturated vapor pressure (which, in our example above, would be 1/1.7 or about 59 percent).

Though relative humidity is the most common expression of atmospheric humidity, it has one big flaw—it depends on temperature.

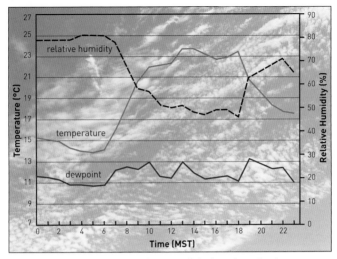

FIG. 1-24. *A graph of temperature, dewpoint, and relative humidity during a summer afternoon in Toronto. While the dewpoint remained relatively constant, the relative humidity rose and fell in response to the trend in the temperature.*

An air sample that is saturated with water at 40°F and a sample that is saturated at 78°F both have a relative humidity of 100 percent, but the warmer air is holding 3½ times as much moisture as the colder. When the atmosphere cools overnight, the temperature falls but the amount of moisture in the air remains relatively constant. As a result, the relative humidity rises, so nearly every morning the radio will announce a value of 80, 90, or even 100 percent. The graph in Figure 1-24 shows the changes in temperature, moisture (expressed as dewpoint), and relative humidity during the course of a clear day at Toronto, Ontario.

In spite of its limitations, relative humidity is an extremely useful measure of many aspects of atmospheric moisture, because it tells us how close the air is to saturation. It and the dewpoint temperature, discussed next, are the two best descriptions of atmospheric moisture for daily use.

Dewpoint Temperature

While vapor pressure is important for industry and scientific uses, it isn't an easy unit to use in daily conversation. We need a measurement that tells us how comfortable the day will be: dry or humid;

pleasant or oppressive? Meteorologists prefer a more direct measure of atmospheric moisture that doesn't respond strongly to temperature changes—the dewpoint temperature. The name says it all: if we cool a sample of air, eventually the moisture within will reach saturation and liquid droplets will condense onto the surrounding landscape. The dewpoint temperature (usually just "dewpoint") is the temperature at which dew will form. When temperatures are below freezing, the dewpoint is called the frost point (Figure 1-25).

If the air sample in our example above (a vapor pressure of 15 mb at 68°F, as shown by the red dot) were cooled to about 56°F (13°C), it would become saturated with water vapor. Cool it any further and the water vapor will condense into droplets, forming dew, fog, or rain-drops. The difference between the dewpoint temperature (56°F) and the actual temperature (68°F) in the air is known as the "spread" and is equal to 12°F (6.5°C) in our example. Dewpoints don't go up and down between day and night as much as temperatures (Figure 1-24), so if the overnight low is forecast to fall to 55°F in our example above, then dew can be anticipated.

You see evidence of the dewpoint all around you every day: a drinking glass has droplets of water on the surface (Figure 1-22) because the temperature of the glass is lower than the dewpoint of

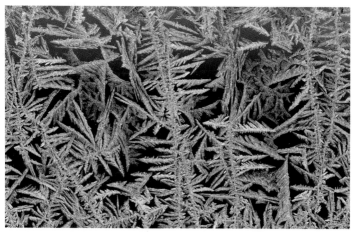

FIG. 1-25. *Frost forms on a window when moist air inside the house comes in contact with below-freezing temperatures on the glass during a cold winter day. The temperature of the window glass is below the condensation point (the frost point) of the inside air.*

the surrounding air. Morning dew collects on the grass because the lawn cooled below the air's dewpoint temperature overnight. Moisture or frost collects on a window during the winter because humid inside air is touching the cold glass (Figure 1-25). Your car window forms mist or frost when you get into it on a cold day because your breath raises the moisture content inside the car until the interior dewpoint rises to the temperature of the windshield.

Dewpoint is a very good indicator of how comfortable the day will be. A dewpoint of 55°F (13°C) is comfortable on a summer day. Dewpoints of 64°F (18°C) might feel a touch uncomfortable, while those above 73°F (23°C) will make the day feel downright miserable, though people in humid climates are better adapted to high dewpoints than those in drier regions. In winter, when the dewpoint (actually the frost point) is below zero, the humidity will have only a slight impact on how the day feels because there is so little moisture in the air to begin with.

In Minnesota or Manitoba, a typical winter dewpoint might be –8°F (–22°C) with a temperature of 5°F (–15°C), giving a spread of 13°F (7°C). Take that outdoor air into a house and heat it to 72°F (22°C), and the spread increases dramatically to 80°F (27°C). Suddenly the house is full of very dry air, the cat goes into hiding because every pat comes with a spark of static electricity, skin dries out, throats are dry in the morning, and plants need watering every other day. Because we see its effects in day-to-day life, dewpoint is probably the most useful measure of how the water content in the air will affect your day.

In our discussion of humidity, you may have noted how important are the concepts of saturation and the "distance" of a particular humidity measurement from saturation. When saturation is reached, the various humidity measures adopt particular values:

- The relative humidity is 100 percent.
- Vapor pressure equals saturation vapor pressure.
- Temperature equals dewpoint.
- The spread is zero.

The Hydrological Cycle

Water links the atmosphere, ground, subsurface, oceans, lakes, ice caps, and rivers in a complex and ever-changing relationship that coincidentally provides a habitat for the life on this planet. While this book is concerned mostly with water in the atmosphere, it is worthwhile to take a look at the flow of the elixir that makes our world so comfortable. The

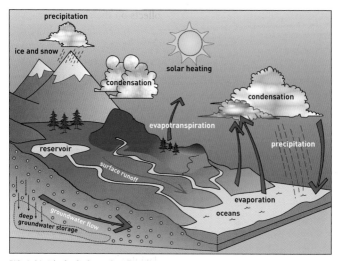

FIG. 1-26. *The hydrological cycle connects water in the oceans with vapor in the air, precipitation, storage in reservoirs, groundwater flow, and deep storage.*

movement of water from oceans to atmosphere to lakes and rivers and back by precipitation is known as the hydrological cycle (Figure 1-26).

The concept of the hydrological cycle seems to have begun around 350 BCE with Aristotle, who compiled his theories about natural philosophy in his treatise *Meteora*, or *Meteorology*. In Aristotle's times, meteorology dealt with all aspects of earth sciences, or, in his words, "all the affections we may call common to air and water, and the kinds and parts of the earth and the affections of its parts," not the more limited atmospheric role to which we confine it in this era. Aristotle's summary of hydrology is just as succinct:

> Now the sun, moving as it does, sets up processes of change and becoming and decay, and by its agency the finest and sweetest water is every day carried up and is dissolved into vapour and rises to the upper region, where it is condensed again by the cold and so returns to the earth.

Oceans cover nearly 71 percent of the surface of the Earth. In the Northern Hemisphere, land constitutes 40 percent of the surface area, while in the Southern Hemisphere, land makes up only half that amount. The larger proportion of water in the Southern Hemisphere gives it lower maximum temperatures in the summer and warmer winter temperatures (neglecting Antarctica) because of water's great heat capacity.

The oceans are the source of 86 percent of the global evaporation, with the largest part of that coming from the tropical waters of the Indian and Pacific Oceans. The average annual evaporation from the sea surface ranges from 11 to 16 inches (30–40 cm) in cold, high latitudes to over 79 inches (200 cm) in the tropics. Wind is a large part of the evaporation process, as moving air removes high-humidity air from near the surface and replaces it with drier air that can then be filled with more vapor. A large portion of the evaporation loss—90 percent, in fact—is returned to the oceans almost immediately by precipitation. The rest is caught up in atmospheric circulations and carried over the land and to other latitudes.

Water vapor flows from tropical climates to temperate and polar regions to join atmospheric water that originated locally in those regions. This flow, carried around the globe, represents an enormous heat transfer, as latent heat contained within the water vapor is given back when the vapor condenses to form clouds and precipitation. Without the moist air from the south, winter temperatures in Arctic regions would be considerably colder than they are now—akin to the bitter winter temperatures over Siberia, where mountains block the flow of southerly and oceanic winds.

Precipitation brings water onto the land, but rainfall is highly variable around the globe, as testified by the presence of deserts and jungles at various latitudes. Convective weather systems (Chapter 9) provide the bulk of the year-round rainfall in equatorial and tropical regions and in the summer in temperate zones between 30° and 60° north and south latitude. In other seasons, mid-latitude rain and snowfall come from migrating low-pressure systems (Chapter 8). Around the poles, precipitation is light and comes from a mixture of low-pressure storms and thin clouds formed in moist flows from the south.

Water on the ground has one of three fates. It can run off overland into streams, rivers, and lakes; it can percolate into the subsurface to flow downhill through the soil or be captured by plants and sent back into the atmosphere; or it can filter into deep reservoirs, where some of it may languish for centuries and even millennia. A portion of the moisture is caught up in glaciers and polar caps, where it may remain for a million years or more, but these reservoirs account for only a small part of the global supply.

Plant roots pull water from the upper levels of the soil, carry it by osmotic processes to the leaves, and evaporate it into the air through the pores or stomata on leaf surfaces. This is called evapotranspiration, because a transport mechanism (transpiration) and evaporation are involved in the process. Both evaporation and transpiration are highly variable processes, but in general, under the best circumstances, evapotranspiration may move two to three times as much water into the atmosphere as simple evaporation.

Much of the moisture evaporated into the atmosphere is returned in a few days as rainfall. It has been estimated that one-quarter to one-third of the thunderstorm precipitation that falls on the Great Plains in summer is recycled moisture. The balance of the rainfall comes from moisture that is advected (carried by winds) into the region, primarily from the Gulf of Mexico. Rivers and lakes first store and then transport precipitation back to the oceans, where the hydrological cycle begins anew.

The hydrological cycle is a bit like a river. Some parts of it move along quickly, while others meander slowly, and still others are nearly stagnant. The rate of movement through the parts can be gauged by "residence time"—a kind of overall average length of time that a water molecule might spend in a certain reservoir. Table 1-2 gives some of

RESERVOIR	RESIDENCE TIME
Antarctic ice cap	20,000 years
glaciers	20–100 years
oceans	3,200 years
winter snowpack	2–6 months
soil moisture	1–2 months
groundwater (shallow)	100–200 years
groundwater (deep)	10,000 years
lakes	50–100 years
rivers	2–6 months
sea ice	2–8 years
atmosphere	9 days

TABLE 1-2. *Reservoir residence times in the hydrological cycle*

these times; you will notice that the shortest time is the time spent in the atmosphere—a mere nine days. This rapid recycling of water gives the atmosphere its dynamic variability and challenges the skill of the forecaster.

Energy in the Atmosphere

Energy is a surprisingly vague scientific concept in spite of its common use in day-to-day life and research. In 1964, Nobel laureate Richard Feynman said, ". . . in physics today, we have no knowledge of what energy is. We do not have a picture that energy comes in little blobs of a definite amount." Faced with an ambiguous definition, we opt to describe energy as an intrinsic property of matter that has the capability to cause changes within a physical system. Fortunately, meteorologists are mostly concerned about only two types: electromagnetic radiation and thermal energy.

Virtually all of the energy that drives the world's weather comes from the Sun in the form of electromagnetic radiation—light in all its forms. Thermal energy is energy contained in the internal motion and vibration of atoms and molecules. The part of thermal energy related to the motion of individual molecules (translation) is often treated separately and called kinetic energy.

Energy is transferred by only two processes—heat or work. Heat is the flow of energy from a warmer body to a cooler one that causes a change in temperature. Work is a mechanical process that results in a displacement or movement of an object. To a weather watcher, work consists of processes that cause changes in atmospheric motion. Energy in storage that can be made available by moving—cold air on a hillside, for instance—is known as potential energy.

Molecules move and vibrate, and we feel and measure this microscopic kinetic energy as temperature. Heating a gas or liquid causes the average speed of the molecules to increase (Figure 1-27), whereas in a solid, where the molecules are bound to each other, raising the temperature causes the intermolecular vibrations to increase. There are limits to the amount of heating in a solid or liquid, however, as the vibrations may become so intense that the bonds between molecules are overcome, and a change in state takes place: water boils to become steam or ice melts into a liquid. During the time that a change in state is taking place, heat does not cause a rise in temperature, but instead goes into breaking the chemical bonds between the molecules.

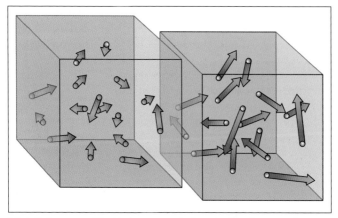

FIG. 1-27. *In gases and liquids, heat content is determined by the average kinetic energy of the constituent atoms and molecules. In this schematic, the volume on the right has a higher temperature than that on the left by virtue of the greater speed of its atoms. Because the volumes are the same, the container on the right also has a larger internal pressure caused by the greater kinetic energy of the atoms striking the surface and each other.*

The first law of thermodynamics tells us that energy can be neither created nor destroyed—it has to go somewhere or do something and the accounting system is absolutely precise. Energy never goes missing, so there are no leftovers or shortfalls when balancing the energy budget. However, energy is readily converted back and forth among its various forms and can move in and out of storage. Solar radiation heats the ground and overlying air; pressure differences cause air to move; heavy, cold air slides down a mountain slope converting gravitational potential energy to kinetic energy. When water vapor condenses into liquid droplets in a cloud, heat is released that contributes to the upward growth of the cloud. To a large extent, weather is energy on the move.

When most substances are heated (water is a prominent exception), they expand to occupy a larger space, and their density subsequently decreases. Conversely, when materials are cooled, density increases. Density differences are tremendously important in the atmosphere because they are one of the major causes of rising and falling motions. Turn on a stove, and the hot air above the element will float upward because heating has given it a lower density. Pour cold milk carefully into hot coffee, and the milk will sink to the bottom of the cup and stay there (for a time) because a cold liquid has a higher density than a warm one. Pour in more hot coffee, and the cold milk will come to the surface, buoyed by the hot liquid that mixed with it at the bottom of the cup.

Forecasters take advantage of the ready association between heating and buoyancy by adopting the concept of imaginary "parcels" to help assess the vertical movement of air in the environment. These parcels are virtual volumes of air that move in response to different physical conditions imposed upon them, usually changes in temperature, pressure, and moisture content. This so-called parcel meteorology is hugely useful for understanding thunderstorms and other forms of convective cloud and has broad application throughout the science of meteorology. In terms of energy, parcel meteorology is used to evaluate the conversion of thermal energy into kinetic energy and the consequences of that conversion.

Solar Energy in the Atmosphere

The Sun (Figure 1-28) has a predictable personality, providing a dependable supply of energy to its planets as it passes through a comfortable middle age in the course of stellar evolution. The unsteady rise and fall of the 11-year solar cycle, occasional violent flares, and the ejection of charged particles do little to disturb this equilibrium, so the Earth enjoys a stable environment in which to go about its daily chore of producing weather.

If the Earth were without an atmosphere, our planet's average surface temperature (the equilibrium temperature) would range between 4.1°F and –3.6°F (–15.5°C and –19.8°C), according to whether we were at the closest or farthest distance from the Sun in our orbit. Fortunately, the equilibrium temperature is boosted to about 59°F (15°C) by the insulating qualities of the gases in the atmosphere, a feature commonly known (and misnamed) as the greenhouse effect.

The Earth's orbit is nearly circular, so the amount of energy received from the Sun at our closest point (*perihelion*) in January is only

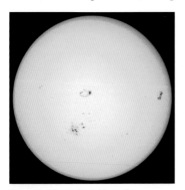

FIG. 1-28. *The Sun's visible surface (photosphere) with several sunspots.*

slightly greater than that received in July at the most distant point (*aphelion*). At perihelion, the Earth is moving most rapidly in its orbit, so the seasons go by more quickly than when at aphelion. This makes Northern Hemisphere summers slightly longer and winters a little shorter than corresponding seasons in the Southern Hemisphere. Presently, summers in the north are 4.7 days longer than winters but this is only temporary, as orbital parameters change over the centuries, and eventually the circumstances will be reversed.

When averaged over a year, the Earth receives a relatively constant supply of energy from the Sun. Spread that energy across our globe-shaped planet, however, and the regions directly under the Sun—the tropics—will receive a greater amount of energy than those partly "around the curve." At those high latitudes, sunlight is more dilute compared to tropical and equatorial regions because it is spread out across a larger area on the surface (Figure 1-29).

FIG. 1-29. *Even in summer months, sunlight strikes higher latitudes at an angle, diluting the amount of energy per unit area compared to that at a location that is directly beneath the Sun in the tropics. This decrease in available energy is partly compensated by the longer daylight in summer, but in winter, the shorter days (or even 24 hours of darkness) contribute substantially to a deficit in solar energy.*

The Earth rotates as well as revolves, and the axis of rotation is tilted at an angle of 23.4° (Figure 1-30) with respect to its orbital plane. At one position in the orbit (Figure 1-30, right side) the Northern Hemisphere is tipped toward the Sun; on the opposite side (the left), it is the Southern Hemisphere that will get the benefit of more direct sunshine. The hemisphere tilted toward the Sun is rewarded by longer hours of daylight and a higher intensity of solar radiation; the opposite hemisphere has long nights and a diluted energy supply. The changeable cycle of solar energy received in each hemisphere in the course of an orbit is the cause of the seasons.

The tilt of the Earth's rotation axis and the seasonal movement of the Sun in the sky have a great influence on our climate and weather. In higher northern latitudes, summer is announced by a gradual increase in the altitude of the Sun each day as the Earth marches around its orbit. With the approach of the solstice in late June, when the Sun

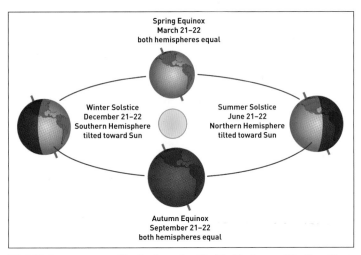

FIG. 1-30. *Seasons are caused by the alternating tilt of the Northern and Southern Hemispheres toward the Sun as the Earth proceeds in its orbit. On the right, the North Pole is tilted toward the Sun, giving long hours of daylight and a large flux of solar radiation. On the left, it is the Southern Hemisphere that gets the benefit of a summer sun, while short nights (or complete darkness) and a low Sun without much warming power cool the North.*

reaches its highest point in the northern sky, the daylight hours get longer, and temperatures soar (Figure 1-31). After reaching its maximum northward position around June 21, the solar altitude turns southward, sinking lower each day until reaching its most southerly point around December 21. In tropical regions, between 23.4° north and south latitude, the Sun is always close to overhead, so seasons are muted and temperatures high all through the year. In the Southern Hemisphere, the cycle, though reversed in the months, is an exact counterpart of that in the North.

At Minneapolis, the last day of June basks in 14½ hours of sunshine, while New Year's Day can manage only 9¾ hours. In contrast, on the equator at the mouth of the Amazon River, Belém (Brazil), has 12 hours of daylight in June and the same 12 hours in December. At the end of June, a noontime sun at Minneapolis can deliver only 70 percent of the energy that falls on Belem; at Anchorage, the solar energy supplied drops to only 48 percent. The ascent of the Sun in spring and summer and the descent in fall and winter have been a part of human experience going back to the evolution of our species and are celebrated in human-made monuments such as Stonehenge at least back to Neolithic times.

The flow of energy from the Sun into the atmosphere must be balanced by a cooling mechanism; otherwise the temperature of the Earth would quickly rise to lethal levels. That cooling is accomplished by the emission of long-wavelength infrared radiation to space. In effect, the Earth glows in infrared light.

Radiation

Electromagnetic radiation from the Sun can be described by wavelength, frequency, or energy. We use wavelength in this book, and stick to units based on the metric system. As we show in Figure 1-32, the range of wavelengths for electromagnetic radiation extends from several kilometers (thousands of meters) on the longwave side to less than a nanometer (nm; one-billionth of a meter) on the short-wave side.

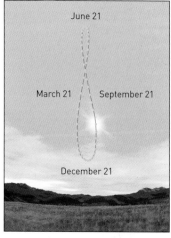

FIG. 1-31. *The Sun's noontime path at weekly intervals in its annual cycle from a location at 50° north latitude. The Sun traces out a figure-eight pattern, known as an analemma, from its lowest point in the sky at the winter solstice on December 21 to its highest point on June 21. The up-and-down part of the figure is a consequence of the Earth's inclination to the Sun; the back-and-forth part is due to changes in the planet's orbital speed.*

Along the way, we pass meters, centimeters, millimeters, and micrometers (one-millionth of a meter, denoted as μm and usually called microns). The whole spectrum is divided into parts and given common names such as radio, infrared (IR), visible, ultraviolet (UV), microwave, and so on. Humans see wavelengths from violet (390 nm) to deep red (740 nm); birds see a little wider range with vision that extends from the ultraviolet to deep red.

Our Sun, a pretty ordinary star with a balmy surface temperature of 10,000°F (5,500°C), emits at all wavelengths from gamma rays to radio waves, but by far the largest part of its light is concentrated in visible and infrared wavelengths with a peak in the green part of the visible spectrum (Figure 1-33). This electromagnetic radiation floods the solar system with energy, a tiny fraction of which lands on the daylight side of the Earth. Meteorologists refer to the important part of this energy—

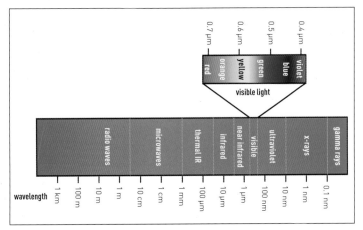

FIG. 1-32. *The electromagnetic spectrum spans the wavelength range from gamma rays with a wavelength less than 0.1 nm to radio waves that are many kilometers in length. Visible wavelengths occupy a very small part of the range but play the most important role in the transfer of energy from the Sun to the Earth.*

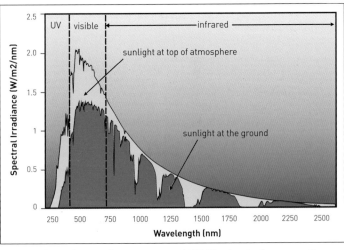

FIG. 1-33. *The Sun has a surface temperature of 5778 K and emits electromagnetic radiation across a range of energies, peaking in visible wavelengths. In this graph, the yellow area shows the intensity of radiation received from the Sun at the top of the atmosphere. The radiation that manages to reach the surface after passing through the atmosphere (called atmospheric windows) is shown in red. The gaps in the red curve are areas where solar radiation is absorbed.*

near-ultraviolet, visible, and near-infrared wavelengths—as shortwave radiation. Longer solar wavelengths, in the infrared, donate a small amount of energy to the atmosphere but are much more important in cooling the planet, as we will see. The rest of the incoming solar radiation is largely unimportant, since the energy in those regions is tiny and has almost no role to play in driving the Earth's weather, though ultraviolet radiation is important in the stratosphere and mesosphere.

Once the Sun's energy reaches the Earth, it must make a final journey through the atmosphere to arrive at the surface. About half of the incoming solar radiation is captured by atmospheric gases or reflected back to space by particles suspended in the air (Figure 1-34). Ultraviolet radiation is largely absorbed high in the stratosphere by ozone. Around 25 percent of visible light is reflected by suspended particulates or absorbed by gases. At long-wavelength infrared frequencies (longwave radiation), the atmosphere acts more like a picket

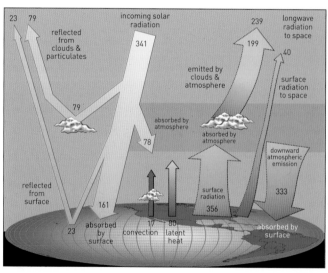

FIG. 1-34. *Shortwave radiation from the Sun is absorbed and reflected as it makes its passage through the atmosphere to the ground. The solar energy captured at the surface and in the atmosphere then participates in a complex cycle of re-radiation and absorption as it makes its way back to space, leaving behind a portion to warm the Earth and provide energy that creates the conditions that support life. Over a long period of time, the balance is nearly exact (otherwise the Earth would warm or cool), but in the short term, imbalances between heating and cooling are the cause of day-to-day weather.*

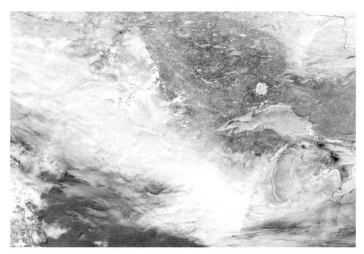

FIG. 1-35. *In this wintertime satellite image, bright white snow covers a broad swath of the Canadian Prairies, reflecting sunlight back to space and reducing the energy available for warming the ground and atmosphere. Over the forests around and north of Lake Superior and over the snow-free terrain in the lower left of the image, the darker albedo absorbs solar energy more effectively, and daytime temperatures are higher than those on the plains.*

fence: some wavelengths are partly absorbed, some completely, and for the rest, the atmosphere is almost transparent. Those wavelengths at which longwave radiation can penetrate to the ground are called window regions.

Once incoming solar radiation has passed through the atmospheric gauntlet and reaches the surface, a portion is reflected back into space and the balance is absorbed and converted to heat. The proportion that is reflected depends on the brightness of the ground, a measure called albedo. Figure 1-34 illustrates that, globally, about one-third of the energy coming from the Sun is reflected by clouds and the surface. Locally, however, the albedo is highly variable, and this variation has significant impacts on regional weather, as albedo moderates solar heating, a consequence that is evident when you wear dark clothing on a sunny day.

Fresh snow has a high albedo, reflecting 80 to 90 percent of the incident sunlight (Table 1-3). Oceans are dark, reflecting only about 7 percent of the arriving radiation, as are coniferous forests, which have albedos ranging up to only about 15 percent (Figure 1-35). The albedo

SURFACE	ALBEDO (REFLECTIVITY)
ocean	4–10%
coniferous forest	8–15%
grass	25%
desert sand	30–50%
new snow	80–88%
asphalt roads	2–10%

TABLE 1-3. *Albedo of a sample of ground surfaces*

of clouds varies depending on type, opacity, and thickness. Birds that overwinter have a significant advantage if they are dark colored or inhabit coniferous forests instead of more reflective open fields. Ultimately, about 45 percent of the shortwave energy arriving from the Sun is absorbed at the ground (Figure 1-34); the balance is sent back into space and no longer contributes to global heating.

The large disparity in solar insolation at the tropics and the poles is the driving force that powers global weather systems and ocean currents, which together strive to reduce those differences by transporting heat and moisture from warm, moist latitudes to cool, dry regions. In a complicated fashion, tropical heat and moisture are carried northward, while polar and arctic air flow back to the south. In the oceans, global-scale currents transport tropical water northward and polar water to the equator. It is a never-ending circulation designed to even out temperatures around the globe, a goal that is never achieved because the Sun keeps adding energy into the mix.

Longwave Radiation from the Earth

The Earth can't continuously absorb shortwave radiation, or we'd warm up to very high temperatures that would cook the planet. We have to cool off somehow, and that cooling is accomplished by emitting radiation back to space at much longer wavelengths, primarily in the infrared. At an average temperature of 288 K (59°F), our planet "glows" in the wavelength band from about 3 to 50 micrometers with a peak at 10 micrometers, a region called the thermal infrared. There is considerable local variation according to the temperature and nature of the underlying surface—cloud, ground, ocean, ice, city—so that the planet shines in a complex pattern of infrared light, day and night.

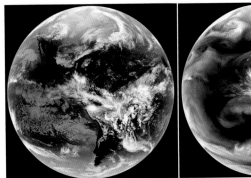

FIG. 1-36. *The Earth in thermal infrared wavelengths as seen by a* GOES *weather satellite. The left-hand image is taken in the 11-µm window region and captures infrared wavelengths that arise from the surface and from clouds. The image on the right, which shows the water vapor distribution in the upper atmosphere, utilizes the 6-µm band that is strongly absorbed and re-emitted by moisture in the atmosphere. Only radiation from the higher layers of the atmosphere can escape to space (and reach the satellite) at 6 µm.*

The flow of thermal infrared radiation to space is regulated by the gases in the atmosphere and by clouds. Radiation in window regions can flow directly to space. Those wavelengths in more opaque parts of the spectrum can emit to space only from high altitudes, where the atmospheric gases are thin enough that they no longer form a barrier to the flow of long-wavelength light.

The opacity of our atmosphere to infrared light is a consequence of its constituent molecules, especially oxygen, ozone, water vapor, and carbon dioxide. The radiation leaving the ground is captured by these atmospheric gases and by clouds before it can make it all the way to space. The captured energy is then re-emitted in all directions, only to be captured and re-emitted again. Eventually the cascade of blocked infrared radiation makes it all the way to the upper atmosphere, where it can escape to space. Spacecraft cameras that operate at thermal infrared wavelengths can capture these wavelengths as "heat" images that show ground and clouds (in a window region) or structures higher in the atmosphere (Figure 1-36). Because the Earth emits longwave radiation day and night, these satellite images are the ones that you see on a television or online weather report.

Clouds have a special role to play in the energy balance of the Earth. During daylight, they reflect solar radiation and cool the underlying surface. At the same time, clouds also trap longwave energy coming from the ground and then re-emit it to their surroundings. This capture and emission process is most important at night as the effect on the temperature balance in the daytime is swamped by solar radiation. Thick liquid-water clouds are largely opaque to thermal radiation, forming very effective atmospheric blankets that trap longwave emissions and re-radiate energy back to the ground. Cold, high-level ice clouds are less efficient, sending only a modest amount of longwave radiation back to the surface, usually with only a degree or two of warming on the ground below. The heat that is trapped by clouds will eventually work its way out to space, usually by a slow overturning that carries warm air from cloud base to cloud top, where it can radiate to higher levels.

It's not only clouds that block infrared radiation. On a chilly morning in fall when the lawn has a beard of white ice crystals or a carpet of dew, areas under and near the trees will be dry because the outgoing radiation has been trapped by the foliage and emitted back to the ground. In the fall, flowers and vegetables that lie under or close to trees and houses will also be spared a nip of frost by infrared heat trapped and re-emitted, allowing a knowledgeable gardener a few more days or weeks before harvest must be completed.

The stability of the Earth's climate is evidence that incoming shortwave energy is in balance with the cooling outflow of longwave radiation over extended periods of time (decades and beyond). On short time scales—hours, days, months—the complex factors that police the flow of energy in the atmosphere give the planet an uneven distribution of heating (Figure 1-37). The atmosphere and oceans

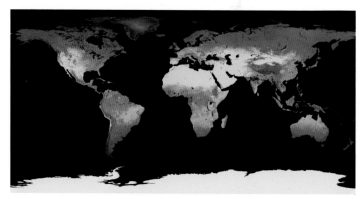

FIG. 1-37. *The average monthly temperature at the ground in August 2018.*

respond by developing weather systems and currents that redistribute warm and cold air and water. These circulations take the form of high- and low-pressure systems in mid-latitudes, hurricanes in the tropics, thunderstorms at the equator, dust storms in the deserts of Africa, the Gulf Stream current, and a myriad of other mechanisms of energy exchange. In all cases, heat is being passed from one location to another; cold is being mixed with warm; and the Earth's oceans and atmosphere are striving toward equilibrium. The constant influx of sunlight prevents that equilibrium from being established, and so weather has gone on and will go on for billions more years.

The Fate of Solar Energy at the Ground

Solar energy that reaches the ground has three possible destinies: it may raise the temperature of the ground; it may evaporate water or melt snow; or it may be used for photosynthesis (Figure 1-38). The first process is called sensible heating—heat that we sense or feel as a rise in temperature. The second is a phase change in which liquid water is converted to a vapor, or snow to a liquid and perhaps to vapor as well. Phase changes soak up a substantial amount of energy (known as latent heat), which is stored in the vibration of the water molecule

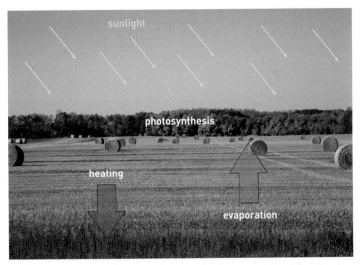

FIG. 1-38. *Solar energy reaching the ground has three fates: warming the ground, evaporating moisture, or capture for photosynthesis. In each case, the energy deposited goes on to participate in other energy-exchange reactions.*

SPECIFIC HEAT OF COMMON SUBSTANCES

SUBSTANCE	SPECIFIC HEAT (CAL/GM°C)
water (liquid)	1.00
water (ice or snow)	0.50
water (vapor)	0.47
wet mud	0.60
wood	0.42
wet soil	0.35
dry soil	0.19
sand	0.19
air	0.24

TABLE 1-4. *Specific heat of common substances expressed as the number of calories of heat energy needed to raise the temperature of 1 gram by 1° Celsius*

and is only given up when the vapor changes back to a droplet or the droplet to ice. Photosynthesis, while fundamental to life, is a relatively small consumer of solar energy.

Ground surfaces don't all heat up or cool down at the same rate; each one has a distinctive response to solar energy that is characterized by a measurement known as specific heat or heat capacity, some of which are shown in Table 1-4. A calorie of heat will warm water by 1°C (1.8°F), but the same amount of heat will warm mud by almost twice as much and sand by more than 5°C (8°F). Lakes and oceans change temperature slowly compared to land, remaining relatively cool during the daytime, while the surrounding terrain, which has a much lower specific heat, warms strongly during the day and cools as quickly at night. That's one reason why lakeside cottages are popular.

Latent Heat

It takes energy to boil water, melt ice, and evaporate sweat; the energy is used to break the bonds between water molecules. Conversely, when water condenses or freezes, that energy is released back to the environment as the bonds are re-formed (Figure 1-39). Changes from ice to water to water vapor and back again are known as phase changes, and the heat required or given up is known as latent heat (the Latin root of "latent" means "lie hidden"). Sunlight falling on wet soil will expend

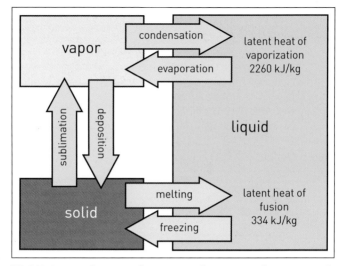

FIG. 1-39. *Processes that cause a change in state release or capture large amounts of energy, particularly between liquid and vapor phases. When water changes from liquid to vapor or solid to liquid forms, the energy acquired from the environment is captured in the internal motion of the molecule and is designated as "latent." This energy is released back to the environment when the phase transition moves in the opposite direction.*

most of its energy evaporating moisture, leaving a smaller amount for warming the ground and air. Over a lake or ocean, as much as 90 percent of incoming solar energy may be diverted to evaporation. Globally, the energy passed to the atmosphere in the form of latent heat is almost three times that accomplished by sensible heating.

Very dry soils have little or no moisture to evaporate, so the full energy of sunlight goes into raising the temperature. The same dry soil and atmosphere favor strong overnight cooling, so deserts have a deserved reputation for heat in the afternoon and coolness in the morning. Snow surfaces are very reluctant to warm during the day, as the high albedo and large amounts of latent heat required to melt and vaporize the ice crystals leave very little solar energy to raise the temperature. The first day of snow cover at the start of winter guarantees a much lower maximum temperature in the days to follow.

Warming triggered by the release of latent heat is pervasive in the atmosphere wherever clouds form, dew condenses, fog thickens, or ice freezes. When moist, rising air condenses into cloud droplets at the bottom of a thunderstorm, the latent heat set loose will give the storm a fresh injection of energy that hugely accelerates its rising updraft. Latent heat carried in moist air may be transported far from its source by atmospheric circulations and then released when the vapor condenses to rain or snow. Arctic regions, which have no sunlight during the dark of winter, are warmed instead by warm southerly winds (sensible heat) and by the latent heat carried in water vapor. The flow of latent heat works vertically, too. Upper levels of the atmosphere are warmed by clouds condensing out of vapor lifted from below. The capture and release of latent heat is a critical process in driving the world's weather.

Energy Transfer: Conduction and Convection

In addition to radiation, two other processes help to move energy around in the Earth-atmosphere system. One is conduction—the transfer of heat when fast-moving molecules collide with and transfer some of their kinetic energy to slower molecules. The companion of conduction is convection—a transfer of heat by the flow of a liquid or gas, almost always vertically in the atmosphere. Conduction transfers the Sun's heat both downward into the ground and upward into the atmosphere. It is an inefficient process, so the conductive layer in the atmosphere is only a few inches thick at best—the surface layer that anchors the planetary boundary layer. Once conduction has warmed this thin layer of air, convection spreads it upward into the troposphere.

Convection comes in two forms: free and forced. Free convection arises from buoyancy, when a heated layer of air begins to rise upward because of its lower density. In effect, the buoyant air is floating upward in the atmosphere and is replaced by nearby downward convective drafts that are a little cooler. On a hot afternoon in summer, convective plumes of warm air (thermals) begin to rise upward, first as tiny bubbles and later as large columns, spreading the heat through an ever-greater depth of the atmosphere. By the end of the day, the depth of the convection-heated lower atmosphere—the planetary boundary layer—may reach several miles. Puffy low-level clouds such as those in Figure 1-40 are a sign that convection is occurring and warm plumes are rising, even though the day may be bright and rain-free.

Birds and glider pilots search out rising convective plumes, using them to soar to higher altitudes with a minimum expenditure of

FIG. 1-40. *Solar energy that reaches the ground will warm the surface. The warm ground will in turn heat a small layer of the atmosphere (the boundary layer) by conduction. As the boundary layer is heated, bubbles of warm air (thermals) will rise upward in a process known as convection, spreading the heat through a greater depth of the atmosphere. The rising thermals may condense into cumulus clouds like these if the rising plumes rise enough to reach the condensation level. In the adjacent clear-sky areas, compensating downward flows will balance the upward transfer of mass.*

energy. Why pay for altitude when you can get it for nothing? The world record holder for soaring on these updrafts has to be the great frigatebird (*Fregata minor*) of the Indian Ocean, which has been recorded floating continuously for over two months on convective updrafts, sometimes reaching altitudes over 12,000 feet (4,000 m).

As we've seen in our discussion of the boundary layer, nighttime brings falling temperatures at the surface as infrared radiation flows to space. The air against the ground then is cooled by conduction; the cooling spreads gradually upward during the night, driven by a slow-moving up-and-down convective circulation that may chill the lowest layers of the atmosphere to a depth of tens or hundreds of feet before sunrise. Convection is much less active at night, so the cooling of the lower atmosphere proceeds at a much lower rate once the Sun has set.

Forced convection arises from winds and the turbulent vortices they create as they flow across the ground, mixing warm air from the surface with cooler air brought down from a higher layer. The size of

FIG. 1-41. *Longwave radiation flowing to space is already cooling the lower atmosphere in this evening scene. The amount of cooling will depend on the cloud cover and the nature of the underlying surface.*

the turbulent eddies depends on the smoothness of the surface and the speed of the wind. Air may also be spread up and downward by the flow over mountains and by frontal systems, where the rising and falling air currents take place on a much larger scale. On a typical afternoon, both turbulence and buoyancy work together to distribute heat from the ground into the higher parts of the atmosphere. The net result of this conduction and convection is to take heat (latent and sensible) from the lower parts of the atmosphere and dump it at a higher level, sometimes very quickly, as in thunderstorms. The heat deposited at upper levels will radiate to space more effectively than in the lower levels, helping to maintain the overall energy balance of the atmosphere when radiation by itself cannot accomplish the task.

All three of the energy-transfer processes—radiation, conduction, convection—are important in the atmosphere, and all are happening constantly, day and night. They define the structure of our atmosphere, the movement of storm systems, the formation of clouds, and the short- and long-range climate of the Earth.

CHAPTER 2

CLOUDS AND PRECIPITATION

Cloudscapes

Have you looked at the sky and wondered how clouds form and what controls their infinite variety of shapes? At one glance, we might see puffy cumulus pillows outlined against fibers of thin cirrus, or a spreading mid-level cloud that brings promise of a change in the weather. Another day will bring a heavy overcast from advancing thunderstorms, visible on the horizon as a somber darkness punctuated by lightning. Waves and streaks, smooth-topped or ragged, thick or thin—clouds tell us about the state of the sky, hint at the upcoming weather, and provide endless entertainment and occasional thrills for those who care to watch (Figure 2-1).

Clouds form when water vapor becomes visible as liquid droplets or ice crystals. The process is a complex one and some parts of it still resist understanding; it becomes even more tangled when we go from making clouds to making precipitation. As water in the atmosphere changes from gas to liquid to solid, major exchanges of heat energy take place with widespread implications for the eventual shape of the cloud and the type of precipitation that might fall.

Making clouds and rain is a step-by-step process that lends itself to illustration by means of a set of stairs (Figure 2-2)—a scheme for

OPPOSITE, FIG. 2-1. *A towering white thunderstorm anvil cloud in the background and dark, vigorous buildups in front threaten rain and perhaps even large hail as an unstable weather system moves off to the right. Heavy rain is already falling in the distant lower right from two previous storms. The spindly towers on the left are not so threatening, lacking the energy to build higher into the atmosphere; they will likely dissipate within the next half-hour.*

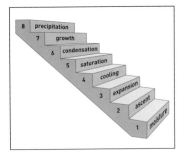

FIG. 2-2. *The process of converting water vapor to rain and snow is an eight-step process, as depicted in this staircase. Each step represents one stage in the formation of clouds and precipitation.*

organizing the sequence of events that leads from water vapor to the fall of precipitation. The stair has eight treads, some more important than others, but all are critical for the production of our daily weather. Let us look at those steps.

The First Step: Moisture

Water enters the atmosphere by evaporation, a process regulated by the temperature of the evaporating liquid, the temperature of the atmosphere, and the humidity in the air immediately above the water surface. Air temperature has a role, because warm air can hold more moisture than colder air can. At the water surface, molecules are in continuous motion, but those with the largest amounts of energy are most likely to break free from the liquid and escape into the air. Since molecular energy increases with temperature, warm water will have a higher rate of evaporation than cold, so the most humid atmospheres are found in tropical and equatorial regions (Figure 2-3) where both air and water are warm. However, even over the most desiccated deserts, air is never completely without moisture.

The amount of water vapor that can be held in the air has a limit. When that capacity is reached, the air is saturated and cannot accept any more vapor. Consequently, an atmosphere that contains only a small amount of vapor and is far from saturation is much more efficient at taking up molecules from a lake or ocean. The rate of evaporation is also helped by wind, which mixes the atmosphere near the surface with air from higher up, continually introducing a fresh supply of drier air to gather up water molecules while carrying away the moisture-rich surface layer.

With so much liquid water on the Earth's surface, you might wonder why the atmosphere is not saturated with vapor and the whole of the planet covered in a blanket of cloud. Fortunately, this depressing scenario is avoided by the efficiency with which water is removed from the atmosphere, largely by precipitation. The Earth has a range of wet and dry climates that owe their persistence to such features as

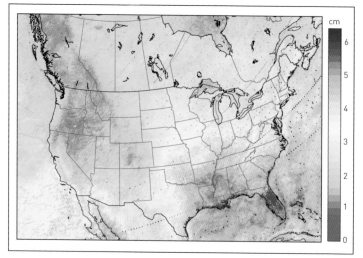

FIG. 2-3. *A map showing the average amount of water vapor in the atmosphere in May 2018 over North America. The measurement is of precipitable water—the amount of water in centimeters that would cover the ground if all of the moisture in the air were condensed onto the surface.*

the proximity to moisture sources, the amount of solar energy available, and wind-driven processes in the atmosphere that cause air to sink downward and rise upward. As a result, the globe has a complex mixture of dry and humid regions not only from place to place, but also at various levels within the atmosphere (Figure 2-4).

In cold climates, oceans and lakes are frozen and water is locked away as ice and snow for the winter season, depriving the atmosphere of much of its moisture resources. Clouds are still present however, especially in the Arctic, but the moisture usually comes with southerly winds that carry water vapor from warmer regions.

The Second Step: Ascent

The atmosphere is restless, continuously stirring heat, moisture, pollutants, and other constituents at all scales, from very small eddies a few inches deep to updrafts that reach through the depth of the troposphere. Since moisture in the atmosphere originates at the ground, the most important of the various stirrings are those that carry water vapor upward, where it can turn into clouds and rain. As noted in

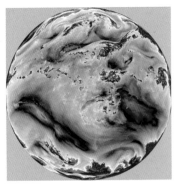

FIG. 2-4. *A GOES-16 satellite image, collected on September 22, 2019, showing the distribution of water vapor in the atmosphere between 500 and 200 mb. The image utilizes wavelengths around 6.5 μm emitted by water molecules. Orange shades outline warmer temperatures where water vapor is low. Colors from gray through blue to red show increasing amounts of water vapor in the upper atmosphere. The flowing patterns are formed by mid-level winds.*

Chapter 1, the stirring mechanisms can be separated into two broad categories: forced ascent, in which the air is pushed or pulled upward, and buoyant ascent, in which it rises on its own.

Forced ascent takes many complex forms. Mountain barriers are particularly important, compelling prevailing winds to rise on the windward side and descend on the leeward (Figure 2-5), mixing low-level air into the middle and upper troposphere. Those of us living in mountain environments will be very familiar with this process, visible as cloud patches that form and dissipate as they flow around and over the terrain. In flatter landscapes, the flow of air across the ground on a windy day creates turbulence that is very effective at

FIG. 2-5. *Moisture in the air condenses into water droplets and a visible cloud as it is forced to rise over a mountain peak.*

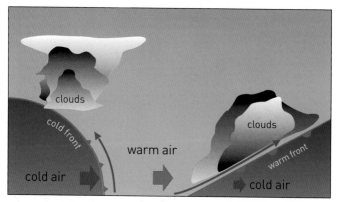

FIG. 2-6. *Warm air is lighter than cold and gives way when the two types of air collide. On the left side, an incoming cold front pushes under the warmer air, lifting it upward to form clouds and precipitation. On the right, advancing warm air cannot easily dislodge the entrenched colder atmosphere and instead rises over it, forming layers of cloud in the process.*

mixing surface heat, humidity, and pollutants to higher levels. Frontal systems, lying at the boundary between warm and cold air, force air upward over large areas and through large depths as they advance across the landscape (Figure 2-6).

Probably the most important of the mechanisms that cause air to rise is that due to the pattern and changes in upper-level winds. High-level wind streams are in a constant state of flux, twisting and turning to compensate for imbalances in energy and mass in the atmosphere. These twists and turns create regions where air rises slowly upward and or sinks downward, moving energy in the form of heat and moisture through the depth of the atmosphere in an attempt to restore equilibrium. It's a never-ending process, as just as one atmospheric problem is repaired, another inequity develops somewhere else, and the upper-level winds must adjust anew to bring the next one under control.

The cause of the imbalances in the atmosphere is the Sun itself, which heats different parts of the Earth at uneven rates. The tropics and equator are much warmer than the poles, continents warmer than oceans, and sunny climates warmer than cloudy. Winds at both low and high levels respond in a never-ending effort to smooth out the temperature differences. These ongoing adjustments are responsible for our changeable daily weather, bringing clouds, rain, and sunny

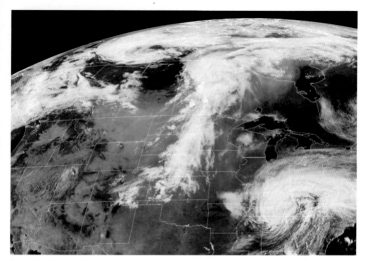

FIG. 2-7. *This satellite image shows a large storm stretching from northern Canada through the Central Plains.*

skies in their turn. Wherever you see a cloud, you can be sure that the air is rising in that part of the atmosphere to sustain the cloud; if not, it will soon dissipate.

In winter, when the difference in temperature between pole and equator is strongest, large 800-mile-wide (1,300 km) storms (Figure 2-7) grow and die on a weekly basis across temperate latitudes, stirring the atmosphere as they mix polar and tropical air. On a smaller but very intense scale, hurricanes (and their typhoon and cyclone cousins) form at tropical latitudes to relieve unsustainable temperature buildup in the subtropical ocean and atmosphere.

On a smaller scale, local imbalances in atmospheric temperature and moisture in the vertical dimension are brought back into balance by a process called buoyancy. On a typical summer day, the Sun warms the ground, and temperatures rise in the air immediately above the surface. As the popular maxim tells us, "Warm air rises," so the heated air near the ground will want to float upward, carrying heat and humidity to higher levels. The rising bubbles of air may be invisible, marked only by soaring birds, or may turn into puffy cumulus clouds and towering thunderstorms. Convective clouds—the name given to those powered by this buoyancy—are a daily feature of the mid-latitude summers and the year-round weather of the tropics. Buoyancy

FIG. 2-8. *Convective turrets bubble upward as warm air rises and condenses into clouds.*

is an important part of summer weather, and we'll have a lot more to say about it in Chapter 3.

Buoyancy comes at every possible scale, so convection can have a huge range of influence. It may be a few inches in depth, as, for instance, when that warm bubble of air next to the ground first begins to float upward. Conversely, an afternoon convective bubble may rise over 10 miles (16 km) to form a towering thunderstorm (Figure 2-8) before it loses its buoyancy and comes to a halt. Some of the most impressive and threatening weather comes from convective clouds and convective processes, but that little bubble at the surface and its millions of companions are the start of it all.

A discussion of ascent in the atmosphere would not be complete without mentioning its opposite—descent. As one region of the atmosphere rises, another must descend in compensation at both large and small scales. On a windy day, every gust is a sign that air from aloft has reached down to the surface, carrying a little momentum from higher up where winds flow more strongly. This descending air also brings lower humidities, cooler temperatures, and cleaner air.

The Third Step: Expansion

When a gas expands on its own without outside sources of energy, it cools. Though not intuitively obvious, expansion is a form of work (as a physicist would define it), so energy is required. If there is no external source of energy available, then the expansion process takes heat from the internal energy of the gas, causing the temperature of the gas to decline. This process is called "adiabatic expansion" and is a critical feature of the Earth's weather. When air ascends to higher altitudes where the pressure is lower, it expands to remain in balance with its new surroundings and so the rising air will cool.

While it seems odd that a "free" expansion would cost energy, we encounter this phenomenon quite often in daily life. Air released from a tire feels (and is) cool from adiabatic expansion. The contents of a soft-drink container may abruptly turn to ice when the cap is popped and the high-pressure contents are suddenly exposed to lower atmospheric pressure. Twirling cloud vortices seen at the wingtips of an aircraft form when the air flowing past the wing is suddenly reduced in pressure and cooled adiabatically to saturation. While the actual processes in the atmosphere are not completely adiabatic, the approximation is close enough that it provides a very useful description of how clouds form, as we'll see in the fourth level of our staircase.

The Fourth Step: Cooling

Rising, unsaturated air cools at a rate of 5.5°F per 1,000 feet (9.8°C per kilometer), a value known as the "dry adiabatic lapse rate" (DALR). The DALR is the same for every type of air, at every altitude, and for any amount of lifting—but only as long as the air is unsaturated. And, because adiabatic processes are completely reversible, air that descends and is compressed warms at the same rate. You will find the effects of adiabatic warming wherever air is compressed—in a bicycle pump, for instance, which heats at the bottom end where the air is compressed to force it into the tire. Adiabatic cooling and warming is an important feature of the atmosphere, as it determines the altitude at which clouds will form and dissipate.

Air can also be cooled by contact with cold ground, by mixing with colder air, or by emitting infrared radiation to the sky and space. The first of these is often called "advection cooling" because it occurs when warm air is carried by the winds (that is, advected) into a colder environment. Warm-air advection provides the moisture for the later formation of fog and low clouds on dry, clear nights; cold-air advection, on the other hand, frequently brings clearing skies to an otherwise cloudy day. On cloud-free nights, long-wavelength infrared radiation is emitted from the surface to the sky and space, cooling the ground, which in turn cools the air in contact (Figure 2-9). Infrared

FIG. 2-9. *Early morning sunlight illuminates a thin fog formed above a cold ground. Clear skies overnight allowed the ground to radiate infrared energy to space, lowering the surface temperature. The lower temperatures were transferred to the overlying atmosphere, cooling it to the saturation point.*

emission to space may also lower temperatures at the tops of clouds, causing them to grow deeper overnight. All of these cooling mechanisms are "diabatic," as the energy gained or lost is exchanged with another source.

The Fifth Step: Saturation

To make clouds, the air must become saturated with moisture. There are two main ways to achieve this: by cooling the air column or by adding moisture into it. The atmosphere can hold only so much moisture, a quantity that depends on the air temperature. Warm air can hold more water vapor than cold air can, so if air is cooled, its moisture-holding capacity will decline.

In a typical atmosphere, the moisture content of the air is a "conserved" property, meaning that it doesn't change very easily. In practical terms, this means that the dewpoint remains constant or changes very slowly. Temperature is not conserved, so when a sample of air is cooled, the temperature falls while the dewpoint remains largely unchanged. With continued cooling, the air temperature will decline

FIG. 2-10. *A rising parcel of air moves into lower pressures aloft and expands to keep in balance with its surroundings. This expansion requires energy, which is extracted from the rising parcel and so its temperature falls; the moisture in the parcel, represented by the dewpoint temperature, changes only slightly. If, at some higher elevation, the temperature falls to the dewpoint, moisture in the parcel will condense and a visible cloud will form.*

until it reaches the dewpoint temperature, at which point the atmosphere is at its saturation point, just able to hold its moisture. The relative humidity, which has been rising as the temperature falls, reaches a value of 100 percent. Further cooling will cause the air sample to become slightly supersaturated, an unstable situation that is usually relieved by removing water vapor from the sample by condensation, first into cloud droplets and later in the formation of precipitation.

In a moist ascending atmosphere that is cooling at the dry adiabatic lapse rate (Figure 2-10), saturation will be reached at some level above the starting point (air doesn't have to start rising from the ground). It doesn't necessarily form clouds when it becomes saturated—as we'll see, one other condition is required—but saturation or near-saturation is certainly a requirement for clouds to form.

In contrast, when moisture is added to the air, usually by evaporation, it is the dewpoint that rises until the saturation point is reached. Evaporation tends to be a much slower process than cooling, but given

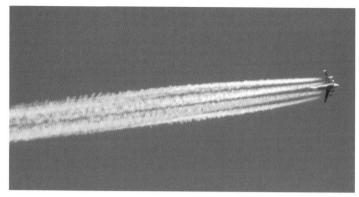

FIG. 2-11. *A contrail forms behind a high-altitude aircraft as moisture and exhaust particles mix with cold surrounding air. The mixture of engine and atmospheric air reduces the temperature of the exhaust below the condensation point of the moisture.*

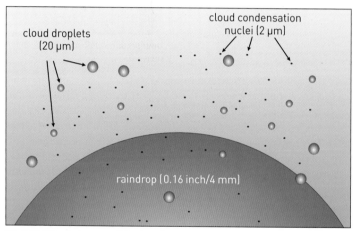

cloud condensation
nuclei (2 µm)

cloud droplets
(20 µm)

raindrop (0.16 inch/4 mm)

FIG. 2-12. *The relative sizes of cloud condensation nuclei (CCN), cloud droplets, and a raindrop. Each cloud droplet contains at least one CCN, and the raindrop contains many thousands, as it forms from the amalgamation of many droplets.*

enough time, a source of moisture, and light winds to avoid mixing drier air with the humid, the dewpoint will rise to the higher saturation temperature. Wet ground, melting snow, or water bodies are generous moisture sources, but the fastest humidification comes on a rainy day when falling raindrops evaporate into and saturate drier air below.

In a more complicated fashion, saturation can also be achieved by the mixing of air samples with different temperatures and humidities, most often when warm, moist air mixes with dry, cold air. You've probably seen this process many times without recognizing it, as it's one of the ways that contrails can form behind an aircraft (Figure 2-11).

The Sixth Step: Condensation

Water molecules are generally too tiny and too widely dispersed in the atmosphere to merge spontaneously to form liquid droplets even when the humidity has reached or even exceeded the saturation point. Another factor must be involved—something that will bring the water molecules together to encourage their coalescence. That missing factor is provided by microscopic solid particles, called "cloud condensation nuclei" (CCN). Cloud condensation nuclei offer a substrate on which molecules can gather, greatly increasing the frequency at which they merge to form a droplet. Without these nuclei, water vapor would only condense spontaneously when the atmosphere became highly supersaturated. A measure of their importance is that every cloud droplet, in their uncountable trillions, will host one or more of these tiny condensation nuclei at its core (Figure 2-12).

A common feature of these CCN is that they must be hygroscopic—that is, able to attract water vapor from the surrounding environment. There are many candidates, both natural and man-made: sea spray, clay, meteoritic dust, soot from forest and agricultural fires, emissions from industry and automobiles, and sulfates from volcanic eruptions. One of the most common sources comes from volatile organic compounds that combine with oxygen in the atmosphere to first become sticky and then to grow into sizes typical of CCN. These organic compounds are frequently natural in origin—for instance, pinene, a constituent of pine resin that helps to give coniferous forests their distinctive smell. Some nuclei, such as salt particles, are so effective that they begin to absorb water at relative humidities around 70 percent. In contrast, most other CCN candidates require a slight supersaturation, up to a few percent above 100, to promote condensation.

CCN concentrations typically range from 800 to 16,000 or more per cubic inch (50 to 1,000 per cubic centimeter) and sometimes reach as high as 250,000 per cubic inch (15,000 per cc) in highly polluted airmasses (Figure 2-13), so in most environments, there are plenty

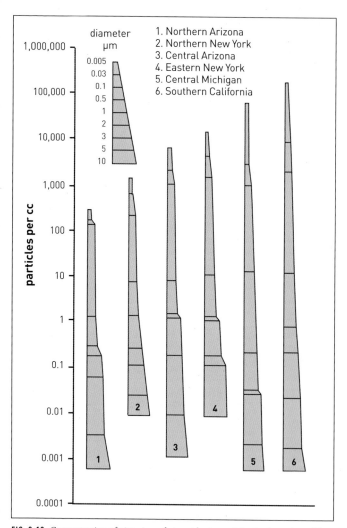

FIG. 2-13. *Concentration of nine sizes of atmospheric particles in clean air and in air with increasing amounts of pollution.*

of nuclei to go around. Too many condensation nuclei will suppress precipitation, as the numerous particles will compete for the available moisture, forming countless tiny cloud droplets that remain suspended in the atmosphere. This is the principle behind cloud seeding for hail suppression, which introduces an artificial condensation nucleus in the form of silver iodide crystals into a thunderstorm environment to promote the growth of many small hailstones instead of fewer and larger stones.

Ice Nuclei

Cloud condensation nuclei are required to form water clouds, but many clouds are also formed from ice crystals and, just as with water clouds, a form of "starter particle" is needed to get the ice crystals growing. Such particles, called ice nuclei, are relatively large atmospheric specks, few in number, and typically ranging in size from 5 to 50 microns at concentrations from 3 to 300 per cubic foot (0.1 to 10 per liter). In contrast to cloud condensation nuclei, ice nuclei are hydrophobic (literally, "water-fearing"). These nuclei can be minuscule bits of sea salt, clay, soot, organic matter, or dust, but in recent years, mineral dust and bacteria have been identified as playing a significant role in ice crystal initiation. Nucleating bacteria become coated with a protein template that aligns water molecules into a lattice that matches that of an ice crystal, greatly reducing the energy required to begin the freezing process.

The water-ice composition of clouds depends mostly on temperature. Observations in natural clouds show that ice formation begins at temperatures as warm as 23°F (–5°C) and perhaps as high as 28°F (–2°C) but is most effective at temperatures of 10°F (–12°C) and colder. Liquid water droplets can prevail in clouds down to a temperature of around 14°F (–10°C), becoming a mixture of ice and water from there to –4°F (–20°C) and then turning completely to ice. In winter climates, all clouds will be composed of either ice or a mixture of ice and supercooled water, but in summer, ice crystals will not begin to dominate cloud composition until altitudes above 10,000 feet (3,000 m) or thereabouts. Clouds that are made up primarily of ice crystals tend to be thin and fibrous, while those with water droplets are more opaque and solid-looking.

At approximately –38°F (–39°C), supercooled water droplets freeze spontaneously without the need for a nucleus. At warmer temperatures, but below the freezing point, other mechanisms conspire to form crystals. For instance, existing ice crystals might scavenge water molecules from the vapor state and grow slowly by deposition. More dramatically, a free-floating ice nucleus may run into a supercooled liquid globule, almost instantly converting the entire droplet to ice. The most common method, however, occurs when an ice nucleus that is already embedded in a warm water droplet gradually turns the droplet to ice as temperatures cool below the freezing point.

Latent Heat and Buoyancy

When water changes state from a gas to a liquid or a liquid to a solid, a considerable amount of latent energy is returned to the atmosphere as heat, and the temperature will rise in the surrounding air. This energy was placed into storage in the molecular vibrations of the water molecule when it first evaporated and is given back when it returns to a liquid or icy state. Its name, "latent heat," comes from the Latin word *latens,* which means "to lie hidden."

In the atmosphere, latent heat release is most important when a rising parcel of air, reaching saturation after cooling at the dry adiabatic lapse rate, suddenly acquires an internal heat source as its water vapor begins to condense (Figure 2-14). The release of latent heat would be akin to turning on the gas burner in a hot-air balloon. Because of the added heat, the cooling rate of 5.5°F per 1,000 feet now becomes much less—perhaps as low as only 1° per 1,000 feet in very warm air. The onset of the latent heat release begins at the base of the clouds but does not end there. It will continue throughout the depth of the cloud as long as there is water vapor available to convert to droplets, or droplets to ice.

The amount of latent heat released in a cloud depends on the amount of moisture in the rising air column, which in turn hinges primarily on temperature and a little bit on pressure. Moist, warm air at saturation will release large amounts of latent heat. When the air is cold, however, it holds much less moisture and the heat contribution from condensation is much less. That's one reason why cumulus clouds are uncommon in winter months across the northern states and Canada: the amount of moisture in the air is so low that rising plumes of air cool quickly and sink back. The latent heat set free is not enough to contribute significantly to their buoyancy.

To view the role of latent heat in its most energetic form, we need only take a close look at the mechanics of a thunderstorm. These convective storms are formed from a very rapid updraft in the atmosphere, fueled almost entirely by buoyancy. Convection begins in pools of heated, unsaturated air near the surface, perhaps formed when sunlight falls on a dark field or forest. The heated air floats upward—a rising plume, invisible except for the birds that soar on its

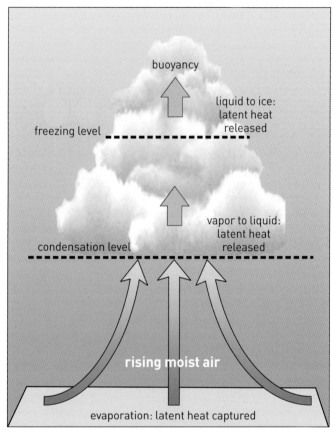

FIG. 2-14. *Air cools as it rises. If a parcel of moist air rises far enough, its temperature will decline to the saturation point and moisture will condense into visible cloud droplets. The condensation process releases latent heat; the added energy will give the rising air additional buoyancy and allow the cloud to continue rising. More latent heat is released if the water droplets rise high enough to freeze at some higher level.*

buoyancy. As the plume rises, it cools, though it still remains warmer than its surroundings.

At some higher level, the rising plume eventually cools to its saturation point. Water vapor turns into water droplets, collecting on always-present cloud condensation nuclei. Latent heat is dumped into the plume and upward motion takes off, now fed by the new supply of energy. A once-timid cumulus cloud becomes a towering cumulus and then a thunderstorm as the new energy supply adds to the buoyancy of the rising plume of air. The growing storm pulls in low-level air from below the cloud—air that provides an ongoing supply of latent heat to the updraft as it condenses in turn within the storm. Eventually, somewhere in the middle of the storm, cloud droplets grow to become raindrops or freeze into ice crystals and perhaps hail. They begin to fall back toward the ground, eventually cutting off the supply of moist air from the surface and bringing the storm to an end.

The release of latent heat has enormous consequences in the atmosphere and in the overall climatology of the Earth. Any weather process in which water freezes or condenses will donate heat to the surrounding environment—heat that increases upward movement, changes the form of precipitation, deepens a low, fuels a hurricane, strengthens or weakens a jet stream—in short, just about every atmospheric process. Thunderstorms would find it impossible to grow without the heating provided by the conversion of thousands of tons of water vapor into rain, ice, and hail. Latent heat drives updrafts in convective storms that range from about 30 mph (48 km/h) in a mature non-severe thundershower to 80 to 150 mph (130 to 240 km/h) in a tornado-producing thunderstorm.

For a strawberry farmer or the owner of an orange grove in Florida, the release of latent heat can save a threatened crop. When temperatures fall below the freezing point overnight, a light mist of water sprayed on the crops will turn to ice and release latent heat into the fruit. The morning may find the crop covered in a coating of glaze, but the heat released from freezing will have protected the fruit from damage. And while we don't suggest you do this, passing your hand slowly through the steam from a kettle can cause a serious burn as the vapor condenses on your skin and gives up its latent heat. On a global scale, latent heat trapped in moist tropical air is a major factor in the redistribution of heat on the Earth as it is carried toward the poles by the winds, eventually giving up its energy when it turns to cloud in some distant weather system.

The counterpart to latent heat release during condensation and freezing is the cooling of the air during melting and evaporation. Precipitation often falls into dry air at lower levels, evaporating or melting and cooling the level below until the layer becomes saturated. The falling raindrops and ice crystals are often visible as streaks of evaporating rain (virga) beneath the clouds (Figure 2-15), and even

FIG. 2-15. *Tendrils of virga descend below a developing storm, evaporating just before reaching the ground. In a few more minutes, the sub-cloud environment will be saturated by the descending precipitation and rain will reach the surface. The evaporating water will also cool the air beneath the storm.*

though no precipitation reaches the ground, you may feel a refreshing breeze spreading outward from the cloud above as the cooled air reaches the surface.

All clouds have some contribution to their buoyancy from condensation and latent heat release, but most don't have the drama of a thunderstorm. In large low-pressure weather systems, the rising air is much gentler and is spread over hundreds of square miles. With this ongoing ascent, more and more air reaches saturation, creating thicker and deeper clouds, and eventually precipitation. Large winter storms deposit enormous amounts of heat into the middle atmosphere, changing the flow of jet streams and initiating both warm and cold spells as the upper-level winds adjust to the heating. In essence, every cloud puts at least a little bit of latent heat into the atmosphere.

The Seventh Step: Droplet and Ice Crystal Growth

At the seventh step, we reach the point where clouds have begun to form on our staircase. In previous steps, moist air, created by evaporation from a surface water source, has cooled by ascent and reached its saturation point. Condensation nuclei and ice nuclei have provided a

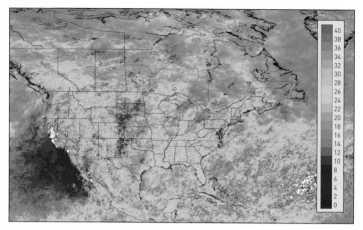

FIG. 2-16. *Cloud droplets have a wide range of sizes according to their type and environment. In this image, visible and infrared observations from satellite have been used to calculate droplet sizes in North American clouds. The largest droplets (red and orange) are found in convective clouds that form over subtropical latitudes where moisture is abundant. Blue tones over the Pacific west of California and Mexico are low stratus clouds, which have smaller droplet sizes, a consequence of the small amount of moisture and their gentle rising motions. The scattered red speckles across the continent come from the large cloud droplets in thunderstorms where updrafts are strong and condensation nuclei plentiful.*

substrate on which water molecules can align, release latent energy, and begin to behave like a cloud droplet or an ice crystal. At this stage, a cloud droplet has a diameter of about 0.0008 inches (20 microns). This tiny particle's diameter must then grow 200 times larger in a period of about 10 to 20 minutes in order to form a raindrop.

Cloud droplets grow in a competitive environment. Supersaturated humidities provide a supply of water molecules, but the growth of the droplets themselves scavenges moisture from the air and reduces that humidity. To continue growing, the amount of in-cloud water vapor must be replenished, a process that is usually accomplished by a continuing ascent in the atmosphere that feeds fresh vapor into the cloud as condensation removes it. Small droplets grow rapidly with the addition of each water molecule, but as the droplet size increases, growth rates decline, eventually tending to level off at diameters of about 10 to 20 microns (around 1/1000 of an inch). Two other processes now have to take over to grow droplets to precipitation size: collision and coalescence.

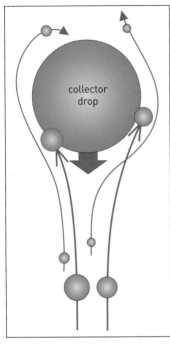

A 20-micron droplet has a fall velocity of 0.5 inches per second (1.2 cm/second), too slow to overcome the typical updraft velocities of ascending air. In contrast, a 40-micron droplet has a fall velocity of 2 inches per second (4.8 cm/second). Every cloud will have a mix of droplet sizes (Figure 2-16) according to the concentration of condensation nuclei, cloud age, and updraft velocity and so will contain drops with very different up and down velocities. Collisions between drops are inevitable, leading to a steady growth in droplet size as time passes. While a particular cloud can have a wide range of droplet sizes dictated by local conditions, measurements from aircraft and from satellite (Figure 2-16) show that convective clouds tend to be made of larger cloud particles while low-level stable clouds are composed of smaller ones.

FIG. 2-17. *Large collector drops, falling through a collection of smaller water droplets, will tend to capture the medium-sized drops in their path while sweeping the smallest out of the way. Turbulence in the wake of the collector drop, however, may catch the smallest particles if they pass by close enough.*

The biggest cloud drops enlarge by scooping up smaller particles in their path, growing rapidly at first, and then more slowly. The tiniest globules are swept out of the way of the faster-falling drops, but medium-sized cloud particles (Figure 2-17) collide and become a part of the growing raindrop. The larger falling drops also create a turbulent wake that scoops up smaller drops as they pass, much like the grime that collects on the back window of a van as it drives down a wet street. Once the falling drops grow larger than about 0.08 inch (2 mm), air resistance causes their spherical shape to become flattened (Figure 2-20), and, if growth continues, the drop may become so big that it shatters to create a new supply of smaller drops.

In clouds with both supersaturated water droplets and ice crystals, the crystals will grow at the expense of water droplets because of the lower

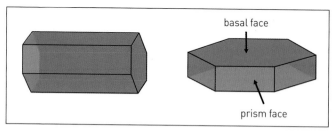

FIG. 2-18. *Columnar ice crystals with their principal planes.*

basal face

prism face

saturation vapor pressure over an ice surface. This is analogous to having a high-pressure region around a water drop and low-pressure above the ice, so that as molecules migrate from high to low pressures, the water drops evaporate and the ice crystals grow. Called the Bergeron-Findeisen process, it is a very effective way of scavenging water vapor from the air to form ice. Even more dramatic is the conversion of a supercooled water droplet to ice that occurs almost instantaneously if the droplet contacts an already-formed ice crystal.

Ice crystals come in many shapes, but the basic form is a six-sided hexagon that can be plate-like or columnar (Figure 2-18). As they grow, branches sprout from the corners of the hexagons where the interception of water molecules is more efficient, and the familiar snowflake shape takes form. The shape of snowflakes is temperature- and saturation-dependent, with simple plates and hexagons forming at low supersaturation across a wide range of temperatures, while complex snowflakes form at high supersaturation and cold temperatures (around 5°F/–15°C). Those fluffy snowflakes that bring enchanted winter evenings are likely formed somewhere aloft at temperatures between 15° and –8°F (–10 to –22°C) in high-humidity surroundings.

The Eighth Step: Precipitation

Rain. Snow. Sleet. Freezing rain. Drizzle. Snow pellets. Virga. Showers. Ice pellets. Snow grains. Hail. Graupel. Freezing drizzle.

The list of precipitation types is a long one and seems to defy easy classification, though an obvious start is a three-category scheme that meteorologists often use: liquid, freezing, or frozen. It is not a very useful classification, as it puts hail in with snow, for instance, and the two are very different in formation, the season of occurrence, and impact. Another classifying system might be to relate the precipitation type to the cloud type. Stratus clouds produce tiny drizzle drops because their ascent rates are usually so slow that the growing precipitation drop falls out of the cloud before it has had a chance to achieve a decent size. Showers, with their larger raindrops, come from moderate-sized cumulus clouds and from thunderstorms. Hail usually signals a thundercloud, while graupel suggests cumulus. This scheme, too, is not a very discriminating categorization.

Atmospheric meteors (yes, that is the name given to things that are "high in the sky" and why we are called meteorologists) are spawned as water or ice, but they may undergo considerable modification by temperature and humidity environments that they encounter on the way to the ground. Ice crystals may melt and then freeze again as they first pass through a layer with above-freezing temperatures and then into a lower colder layer. Simple ice crystals often coalesce with others to form complex snowflakes, or encounter water drops that promptly freeze. Raindrops may freeze in lower cold layers to form icy balls, sometimes mixed with snow. Hail may make several trips up and down through a thunderstorm, growing in size and complexity with each circuit. Some forms of ice crystals seem to fall from clear skies. The relatively simple process of forming ice crystals and water drops becomes much more complicated in the fall from the cloud to the ground. We will now turn to that subject.

Rain

Rain is, of course, liquid water droplets that usually range from 0.04 to 0.15 inch (1–4 mm) in size. Record-setting 0.34-inch (8.6-mm) raindrops were measured in tropical airmasses in Brazil and the Marshall Islands, and scientists could not rule out half-inch-sized drops. Any larger than that and the droplets would break apart into smaller pieces. Both of these record-setting drops were detected beneath towering cumulus clouds; those in Brazil probably coalesced around smoke particles, while those from the Marshall Islands likely used sea salt particles as condensation nuclei.

Raindrops fall at a speed that is a balance between gravity and atmospheric drag, with the largest (and heaviest) drops falling most rapidly. Light stratiform-cloud rain has a terminal velocity of 4–9 mph (2–4 m/s), while the largest thunderstorm drops reach 16–20 mph (7–9 m/s) (Figure 2-19). Only the smallest and slowest-falling drops are round. As size and fall velocity increase, drops flatten on the bottom (Figure 2-20). By the time they reach 1/10 inch (2 mm) in size

FIG. 2-19. *A schematic diagram showing the distribution of different sized raindrops within a mature thunderstorm. Blues and greens represent raindrops between 0.5–3 mm in size and yellows, oranges, and reds represent raindrops between 4–6 mm in size. Raindrop sizes increase toward the lower parts of the storm as drops increase in diameter by collision and coalescence.*

and a fall speed of 13 mph (6 m/s), a small concavity begins to form on the flattened underside. The concavity grows as drop size increases until the raindrop has the appearance of a tiny parachute, 0.2 inches (5 mm) across. This is an unstable configuration, and the drop usually breaks at this point.

Once precipitation leaves the cloud base, it enters an environment that is no longer saturated and thus, it begins to evaporate. Rain clouds often have hanging gray tails of virga (Figure 2-15), while ice clouds have trailing wisps of ephemeral crystals that in one cloud form gives the name "mare's tail cirrus."

Snow

"No two snowflakes are the same."

True—and no surprise either, given the factors that control the assembly of water molecules into a crystal. As the nascent snowflake travels through a cloud, it encounters ever-changing environments that control its morphology. Temperature and the degree of super-saturation are the major controls, but to decipher the details, we have to zoom in on the surface of the building crystal and examine events on an atomic scale.

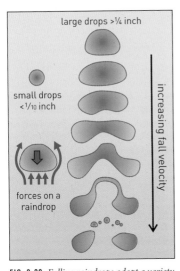

large drops >¼ inch

small drops
<¹/₁₀ inch

forces on a
raindrop

increasing fall velocity

FIG. 2-20. *Falling raindrops adopt a variety of shapes depending on their size and fall velocity. Only the smallest drops are round; larger drops become pancake-shaped and then fracture if too large.*

As the temperature of the ascending air cools to around 14°F (–10°C), supercooled water droplets will begin to freeze around available ice nuclei. Not all of the droplets will freeze at once, and the first-born crystals will attract water vapor from the air by the Bergeron-Findeisen process. As these early crystals grow, they will tend to adopt the shape of simple hexagonal plates or columns (Figure 2-21).

At temperatures to just below freezing, and to between 14°F and –4°F (–10° C and –20°C), water vapor deposits most rapidly on the prism faces, especially where the corners of the hexagonal crystal project farthest into the supersaturated air. This leads to the branching, six-sided, dendritic shape of the

FIG. 2-21. *Six-sided columnar ice crystals that formed overnight in a thick fog.*

classic snowflake (Figure 2-22). At intermediate temperatures, particularly around the 14°F point, growth accumulates in the center of the crystal and spreads outward, forming columnar and plate-like crystals. Complex snowflakes form at high supersaturation and cold temperatures (around 5°F/–15°C). Plates and columns are also favored in the very coldest air where the atmospheric moisture is very low. In the end, however, very few snowflakes are "perfect" symmetric

FIG. 2-22. *A nearly perfect snow crystal, formed at a temperature of 16°F (–10°C). Several small imperfections in the crystal symmetry are caused by supercooled droplets that have frozen onto the original crystal and begun to grow on their own.*

crystals, as they agglomerate with other crystals, often of different forms, to make up the snowflake cluster that we see by eye.

The beautiful intricacy of snowflakes (Figure 2-23) is a reflection of the complex environments that the growing crystals follow through the cloud. Since no two crystals assemble molecules in the same way, snowflakes are infinitely variable, so that we end up with innumerable complex, symmetric patterns that entrance the viewer and the scientist. Ukichiro Nakaya, a pioneer in the classification of snowflakes, was often quoted by his colleagues as stating, "Snow crystals are the hieroglyphs sent from the sky" (Bender 1962).

Sleet

The definition of sleet depends on where you live. To the National Weather Service in the United States, sleet is "generally transparent, globular, solid grains of ice . . ." or, in other words, frozen raindrops or ice pellets. If you live in Michigan, sleet is a mixture of rain and snow. British meteorologists use the latter definition, though sleet is also used to refer to wet snow. In western Canada, meteorologists avoid the term altogether, using "a mix of rain and snow" or "wet snow" in official forecasts, though public use is drifting toward the Michigan meaning.

Ice Pellets

Ice pellets are frozen raindrops or partly melted and refrozen snowflakes. They are small, semitransparent, hard balls of ice that bounce when they strike the ground. Ice pellets are formed when snowflakes

FIG. 2-23. *Plate XVII of "Studies among the Snow Crystals During the Winter of 1901– 2," by Wilson Bentley, "The Snowflake Man." From* Annual Summary of the Monthly Weather Review *for 1902. Bentley was an American meteorologist whose passion was photographing snowflakes.*

fall into an above-freezing warm layer lying about 1 to 2 miles (1½–3 km) aboveground and then back into a subfreezing layer below (Figure 2-24). The flakes melt in the warm layer and then refreeze into ice pellets in the cold. Sometimes they are confused with hail, but ice pellets are a cold-season precipitation type. As noted above, ice pellets are also known as sleet in the United States.

Freezing Rain

Ice pellets and freezing rain are first cousins. If the depth of the under-lying cold layer is too shallow, or temperatures are only slightly below freezing, then melted snowflakes falling through the warm layer aloft will reach the surface as raindrops instead of ice pellets. If the surface temperature is below the freezing point (Figure 2-24), the already-cold raindrops will freeze on contact, covering trees, roads, sidewalks, and anything else they encounter with a coating of semitransparent ice (Figure 2-25). Ice storms of freezing rain are one of the most destructive forms of winter weather. The North American ice storm of 1998 painted southern Ontario, southern Quebec, Maine, and upper New York with a massive amount of ice, bringing long-term power outages and the destruction of millions of trees.

Freezing rain is either translucent or clear in appearance, depend-ing on how rapidly it freezes on the surface. With colder surface

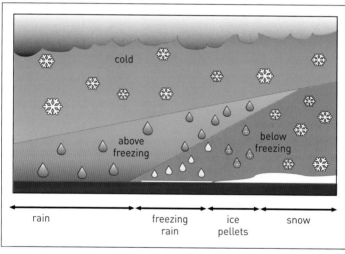

FIG. 2-24. *Above- and below-freezing temperature layers in the atmosphere determine many of the types of winter precipitation. At the cloud layer, precipitation falls as snow, but if the flakes encounter a melting layer, the snow will turn to rain. If a second layer of cold air lies against the ground, the type of precipitation will depend on the depth of each of the warm and cold layers. If the warm layer aloft is shallow or the surface cold layer deep, then ice pellets will tend to form. If the surface layer is cold but relatively shallow, then the raindrops will become supercooled and freeze on contact to form freez-ing rain. Rain may also freeze on contact with a very cold surface even if the air tem-perature is above zero.*

FIG. 2-25. *Freezing rain has coated this bush with a layer of heavy ice.*

temperatures or with small drops, rain will freeze quickly, trapping air in the ice crystal, and giving the resulting ice a milky white appearance. In warmer temperatures—those only a few degrees below freezing—the raindrops freeze more slowly, allowing time for the air to diffuse from the developing crystal, leaving a nearly transparent icy layer in its place.

One of the more insidious forms of freezing rain occurs when a road surface is wetted by a light misty rain, dense fog, or melting snow. As temperatures fall below the freezing point, or if the pavement is already cold, a very thin layer of ice, known as "black ice," may form. Because the pavement is barely wetted, air bubbles can easily escape from the water film as it freezes, leaving a transparent coating that is virtually impossible to distinguish from the underlying road. Bridges are particularly prone to black ice because they allow the road to be cooled from below as well as above, so highway departments usually warn of especially slippery conditions on the approach to overpasses. Heavier rainfall and gusty winds will not form black ice, as they stir up the freezing water, mixing air into the ice and turning it a translucent white color.

While it's not thought of as freezing rain, there are circumstances in which ice can deposit directly onto a surface without precipitation.

This occurs when warm, often melting, temperatures arrive after a long and deep cold spell in which temperatures may have fallen to 0°F (–18°C) or lower. Though the new air temperature may be above the freezing point, the cold ground will be below the dewpoint temperature of the newly arrived airmass. Water vapor in the warm air will condense and freeze onto the ground, even under clear skies. This is typically described as "the frost coming out of the ground." Such conditions are also extremely hazardous for highway travel, as the warming temperatures bring a sense of safety, while the ice deposited is typically black ice. Such conditions are particularly dangerous at night.

Snow Pellets and Graupel

Snow pellets are an uncommon form of winter precipitation that results when falling snow crystals encounter supercooled water droplets in the lower parts of a cloud. The snowflake acts as an ice nucleation site, and the water droplets freeze onto the surface of the crystal. The crystal is then said to be "rimed." If the water droplets accumulate to the extent that the shape of the original snowflake is only partly visible, the resulting particle is called graupel (Figure 2-26) or, colloquially, soft hail.

Graupel, easily broken by fingers, has an opaque white appearance and a crumbly texture caused by air that is entrained into the crystal

FIG. 2-26. *Graupel, with a coin for scale.*

as it freezes. It forms most often in cumulus or towering cumulus clouds in the late fall when surface temperatures are close to the freezing point, but when the Sun still has enough oomph to manufacture convective clouds.

Snow Grains

Snow grains are very like snow pellets, except that they are smaller (0.04 inch/1 mm) and come from stable clouds such as stratus or fog. Their physical structure is quite variable: they may be bundles of rime ice, rime ice with a glaze coating, tiny clusters of snow crystals, or just simple ice crystals.

Drizzle

Drizzle is uniform liquid precipitation composed of droplets about 0.02 inches (0.5 mm) in diameter. Light drizzle barely has the capacity to wet a surface, leaving clothing dry even in extended periods of exposure. This precipitation originates in overcast stratus clouds that have weak rising currents, high water content, and a depth of around 1,600 feet (500 m). In these clouds, turbulence plays a critical role in promoting the collision and coalescence of the water droplets until they reach a size large enough to fall.

Showers

Showers are short-duration rainfalls that come from larger convective clouds such as towering cumulus, or thundershowers (Figure 2-27). The main difference between simple showers and thundershowers is usually the size of the parent cloud and the intensity and duration of the precipitation. Continuous rain can have a showery character if embedded convective clouds bring occasional bouts of heavier rainfall. Showers can be composed of snow when the season is late or if nearby open lakes provide moisture and heat toward the production of convective clouds during the winter months. Less common is the notorious "thundersnow" that brings huge accumulations of snow in a very short period—think of converting the rainfall from a moderately intense thunderstorm to its equivalent in snow (the normal ratio is 10:1). Many a forecast has gone dangerously wrong when thundersnow developed unexpectedly on a cold fall day.

As most storm chasers can testify, extremely heavy showers are the hallmark of an intense thunderstorm. Mix that heavy rain with tornado-strength wind, and the precipitation becomes "aerosolized," a

FIG. 2-27. *Heavy rain from a distant storm obscures the landscape.*

term of uncertain origin and possibly incorrect. Visibility in such rainfall drops nearly to zero—perhaps one or two feet at best—and precipitation accumulation approaches several inches per hour, though only for a short time. Though theoretically extremely hazardous, the visibility is so low that a vehicle has no choice but to stop and wait it out, so accidents are rare.

Hail

Hail may not be the most dangerous form of precipitation (see Chapter 9), but it is certainly a contender for one of the most damaging. Hail consists of lumps or pieces of ice, sometimes agglomerated, that fall with considerable force from thunderstorms. They begin as small ice crystals that then grow rapidly as they accumulate supercooled water droplets from the surrounding high-humidity air in the updraft region of a storm. The extreme updrafts inside a thunderstorm are capable of suspending precipitation particles until they grow to considerable size. Stones may make several trips up and down in the updraft core until they become too large to remain suspended, or until ejected from the updraft.

When cut in half, large hailstones show alternating layers of transparent and opaque ice several millimeters thick (Figure 2-28). The

FIG. 2-28. *A small hailstone, showing layers of both transparent and opaque ice.*

opaque white layers consist of ice with entrapped air bubbles—a sign that freezing has been rapid. Semitransparent layers form when ice is slower to freeze, usually aided by a large release of latent heat. The extra time taken to solidify provides the air bubbles with an opportunity to escape.

Freezing Drizzle

Freezing drizzle is a bit of a strange bird—liquid precipitation that can form without any above-freezing temperatures. In central and northern Canada, freezing drizzle can form and fall at temperatures as cold as 10°F (–12°C), although warmer temperatures are more common. Under such conditions, the droplets must be supercooled and have condensed on cloud condensation nuclei without turning to ice, likely because of the lack of ice nuclei. It is extremely dangerous to aircraft when it contacts wings and other control structures, as the airframe provides the template on which the droplets can freeze, which it does very quickly. For those of us on the ground, freezing drizzle is not as dangerous, as it seldom accumulates enough mass to affect power lines and trees, although an extended period of precipitation can make

FIG. 2-29. *Hoarfrost bejewels a grove of trees after a cold winter night with fog.*

roads and sidewalks slippery and hazardous, especially if it contributes to the formation of black ice.

Hoarfrost

Hoarfrost forms on clear, freezing nights when solid objects emit infrared radiation to space and cool to a temperature that is below the dewpoint temperature of the air. Water vapor will condense on the surface—usually tree branches, fences, and buildings—and ice crystals will be deposited on every exposed surface (Figure 2-29). Nights with fog are especially favored for hoarfrost formation. Ice crystals are usually deposited more heavily on the upwind side of a branch or fence, even though the wind is very light. In the morning light, hoarfrost usually brings marvelously ethereal scenes for the photographer.

Ice Crystals

Ice crystals are the only type of precipitation that can fall from a clear sky, though thin clouds are often present. Colloquially described as "diamond dust," they consist of tiny unbranched ice needles, columns, or plates that have formed in temperatures of 14°F (−10°C) or colder by vapor deposition on ice nuclei. They are visible as glittering motes, often suspended against intense blue skies, but may occasionally be seen superimposed against nearby buildings when a fall is particularly heavy. Typically, ice crystals are found after the passage of a cold front, while temperatures are falling rapidly. They are frequently associated with marvelous halos and sun pillars.

Complexity

The formation of clouds and rain is a complex process that involves far more than just raising the humidity to saturation. Cloud condensation and ice nuclei, cooling processes, layers of humidity and temperature in the atmosphere, buoyancy, residence time in the cloud environment, and other factors all contribute to what seems to be a simple and straightforward development. Computer models used for weather forecasting have difficulties with the process and must substitute approximations and guesses in order to mimic the steps in our staircase that nature generates so easily.

When you encounter precipitation in one of its many forms, take time to examine it closely. While raindrops may seem mundane, their pattern on the ground will give you clues to their size, and their temperature a hint about their origin aloft. When snow or ice falls, examine the crystal structures, the pattern of riming and crystal organization, and the presence of entrained air and other inclusions such as dust or tiny condensation nuclei. Even the ordinary can take on an unfamiliar pose.

Hoarfrost crystals are formed when water vapor condenses directly into ice, usually under clear, cold skies with temperatures a few degrees below the freezing point. If winds are light, a steady supply of moisture is provided to the growing crystals, causing them to develop most aggressively in the direction of the wind.

Over the course of a winter, successive snowfalls may assemble into layers, packed by the wind and compressed by overlying deposits. The hardness of individual layers will vary according to water content, the passage of time, the strength of the wind, temperature, and the type of snow crystal. In this image, erosion of the snow layers by the wind has exposed a half-dozen or more layers.

Water vapor collects most efficiently on the edges of a developing ice crystal, leading to the formation of snowflakes with a six-sided symmetry. In this example, the molecules of water in the cloud have formed a beautiful star-shaped crystal, interrupted only by another passing crystal that has hitched on for the ride to the ground.

Strong thunderstorms produce dense columns of heavy rain and, frequently, large or small hail. In this image, the white column in the foreground may be heavy rain appropriately illuminated by the Sun, but more likely is a swath of hail superimposed on darker curtains of heavy rainfall in the background.

These vertical ice crystals formed on flat surfaces overnight, when clear skies allowed ground temperatures to drop below the freezing point while a light fog drifted inland from a nearby water body.

Storm chasers follow in the wake of a hail-producing storm that left a trail of white roads and fields over a distance of more than 30 miles (50 km). While the hail in this location was only nickel-sized, stones in other parts of the storm were large enough to break car windscreens.

CHAPTER 3

AN ATLAS OF CLOUDS

Naming Clouds

"There's a cloud that looks like a cat."

"That one looks like a car."

"That looks like cirrus *uncinus*."

Cirrus *uncinus*?

What causes the wide, wild diversity of cloud types and forms? Why do they have the shapes that they do? What makes a cloud spread across the sky, or build up in heaps? Why are some of them thin, others thick?

Clouds are composed of water droplets or ice crystals, so their presence tells us that the atmosphere must be filled with enough water vapor at cloud level to make those droplets and crystals. That alone is useful information, but to a sky-watcher, much more can be gleaned from the character of those white sentinels. Cloud opacity speaks to us about the density of cloud droplets, the depth of the cloud, and whether they are composed of ice crystals or water droplets. Cloud form may advise us of the speed and direction of winds aloft. Vertically growing clouds tell of atmospheric instability—the tendency of air to rise or sink according to its temperature and buoyancy—and may give warning of impending severe weather. Colors in the clouds give clues about the size of droplets and crystals and their concentrations. Shadows reveal the extent of atmospheric pollution. Best of all, clouds provide us with an entertaining and entrancing sky that reveals secrets to the interested observer.

Thanks primarily to English meteorologist Luke Howard (1772–1864), clouds are classified by two criteria: their appearance to an

FIG. 3-1. *In spite of their usually semitransparent nature, cirrus clouds are often found precipitating, such as these clouds. The wispy tails are known as "fall streaks" and are composed of ice crystals that have fallen from the thicker, higher clumps into a lower region of lighter winds, where they stream out behind the faster-moving parent clouds. Clouds such as these are referred to as cirrus* uncinus, *meaning "hook shaped."*

observer and the height of their base above the ground. In Howard's scheme, low-level clouds are those whose bases lie below 6,500 feet (2,000 m); mid-level cloud bases extend from 6,500 to 20,000 feet (2,000 to 6,000 m); and high clouds are those with bases above 20,000 feet (Table 3-1). Low clouds are graced with the prefix "strato" or simply called "stratus," Latin for "layer." Mid-level clouds have the prefix "alto" added to the cloud name to indicate their relative position in the troposphere. "Cirrus" or the prefix "cirro" designates high-level clouds (Figure 3-1). The meaning of cirrus—"curl of hair"—is an apt metaphor, as these ice clouds often adopt a swirling shape in the winds of the upper atmosphere. Clouds that build upward because of buoyant instability are given names derived from the word "cumulus," Latin for "heap" or "pile" (Table 3-1). If the buoyancy is small and mixed into one of the layers, then the suffix "cumulus" is added to the layer name to show that it is composed, at least partly, of small, embedded buildups of cloud.

LEVEL	LAYERED	HEAPED	PRECIPITATING
low: <6,500 feet	stratus	stratocumulus	nimbostratus
mid: 6,500–20,000 feet	altostratus	altocumulus	
high: >20,000 feet	cirrus or cirrostratus	cirrocumulus	
vertical	cumulus	towering cumulus	cumulonimbus

TABLE 3-1. *Luke Howard's classification scheme for cloud types.*

FIG. 3-2. *A classic example of broken stratocumulus clouds, spreading from the right. The weak convective nature of the cloud is revealed by the lumpy appearance with bright intervening breaks between the individual elements. Dark cloud bases reveal the position of the deeper convective elements where the air is rising, while the lighter patches are regions where the air is descending. This cloud is too thin to produce precipitation. A cirrostratus or altostratus layer can be seen in the gaps in the low cloud.*

Classification of a cloud as low, middle, or high does not guarantee its composition—each may be made up of water droplets or ice crystals or both, according to the season and temperature. In winter we may see cirrus-looking types at mid-levels and sometimes even at low levels, but the name given to the cloud type is based on altitude alone.

Low-level clouds have names that reflect their layered or heaped nature, or both. Stratus is flat; cumulus builds upward and is heaped.

FIG. 3-3. *Soft-edged altocumulus clouds punctuate a deep blue sky, telling of a small layer of modest instability in the mid-levels of the atmosphere. The tufted appearance of the cumulus elements identifies this as altocumulus* floccus, *from the Latin for "lock of wool."*

Stratocumulus is a little of both—embedded heaped bits in a generally flat layer (Figure 3-2).

Mid-level clouds have the most rational naming convention, as the prefix "alto" is added to their names to give an indication of their height. Altostratus is simply flat, banded, or featureless cloud above 6,500 feet (2 km). Altocumulus has a bumpy appearance, sometimes over quite a depth (Figure 3-3). However, thunderstorms that have a base at mid-levels, as they do occasionally, are not given the alto prefix but instead retain just their cumulonimbus name.

The highest clouds are all part of the cirrus group and have a variable appearance. Because they are composed of ice crystals, they tend to be thin and semitransparent unless they have considerable depth (Figure 3-4). Cirrus stands alone as a cloud name, but cirrocumulus and cirrostratus are also widely used. Generally, cirrus will be used to describe a sky that is fairly open between the cloud elements, while cirrostratus describes a solid overcast, at least over a part of the sky. Cirrocumulus is a collection of ice clouds in small tufts or buildups. Generically, the term cirrus can be used for all of the high-level types when simplicity is required.

FIG. 3-4. *Cirrostratus clouds are known for the halos formed by their constituent ice crystals, such as this display on a warm, wintery afternoon. Ice-crystal formations within cirrus clouds can become amazingly complex when crystals are just the right size and alignment as in these high-altitude clouds.*

Cirrus clouds are responsible for some of the sky's most attractive phenomena—the halos, arcs, parhelia, rings, and other optical phenomena (Chapter 10) that result as light is refracted and reflected from their ice-crystal constituents (Figure 3-4). Altostratus and altocumulus clouds have their own optical phenomena as well, often producing colored rings around the Sun or Moon, but are probably better known for the marvelous sunsets they can produce.

Cumulus clouds are the familiar popcorn puffs of small vertical development that mark a fine summer day. They may have a base at any level, but their main characteristic is that they are vertically growing clouds that result from instability in the atmosphere. Once a cumulus cloud has grown to a size where its vertical depth is greater than its height above ground, it is most often called towering cumulus. When a growing towering cumulus cloud begins to produce lightning (and thunder), it becomes a cumulonimbus (Figure 3-5), more commonly called a thunderstorm. All clouds that grow vertically through buoyancy are called convective clouds in recognition of the fact that they are transferring heat from lower parts of the atmosphere to higher levels (Chapter 1).

Nimbus clouds are the odd ones; just about any of the kinds of clouds can produce rainfall, but only two cloud types are distinguished with the nimbus name: cumulonimbus (a thunderstorm) and nimbostratus (a low, dark raincloud). Thunderstorms frequently have no precipitation at all at the start of their life cycle, though it usually comes with time. A very thick, dark stratus layer with rain—one that extends upward through the mid- and upper levels—is called nimbostratus, but if it produces snow, it will likely be called stratus alone, named only for its flat appearance and low altitude. Towering cumulus, which produces showers, is not graced with a nimbus prefix. It's not an entirely logical naming system.

Looking back across the cloud-naming scheme, you can see that clouds develop either in stable airmasses (the stratiform types) or in unstable conditions (the cumuliform types). For mixed types such as stratocumulus, we have a little bit of instability that produces small amounts of upward growth, but not enough to destroy the overall layered character of the cloud.

Cloud names are simple, but the word "altocumulus" doesn't say very much about the detailed appearance of the cloud. Is it made of small or large elements? Does it have a banded or wavelike appearance? Are the cumulus buildups fairly deep or are they little more than small puffs? Is it approaching, or does it cover most of the sky? Over the years, a host of common names and Latin appendages have been developed to add more descriptive information, but they are not in widespread use.

Cirrus *uncinus* is a type that you would recognize easily, as the word "*uncinus*" means "curly hooks," but it also has a common name: mare's tail cirrus, and sometimes horsetail cirrus. Cumulus *humilis* (Figure 3-6) should be easy to decipher, given the resemblance of *humilis* to humility, but in this case, it means "of small size." These are the fair-weather, puffy clouds that are about as high as they are wide. Slightly taller and more widespread cumulus clouds are called (if you want) cumulus *mediocris*. Cumulus *castellanus* are tall, thin cumulus clouds that are perhaps a little smaller than towering cumulus (or not, depending on the eye of the beholder), and the resemblance of the word *castellanus* to castle provides a clue about their shape. At mid-levels, altocumulus *castellanus* is a valuable clue to storm chasers that the day might be very exciting around 4 or 5 P.M. (Figure 3-7). We have cumulus *radiatus* for clouds arranged in parallel lines, cumulus *fractus* (fractured) for wispy leftover bits of cumulus on the way to

FIG. 3-5. *A powerful thunderstorm at maturity, just as precipitation begins and after the anvil has formed. The cauliflower buildups on its closest flank are cells that will be drawn into the main cell to feed the already powerful updraft, but this storm does not have a long lifetime. The circular anvil reveals relatively weak winds aloft that will prevent its development into a long-lived multicell or a supercell storm.*

FIG. 3-6. *In this scene, fair-weather cumulus cloud is gradually increasing across the landscape as an invading altostratus layer spreads in above, possibly spelling a change in the weather. As the higher layer thickens, the Sun will become hidden and ground heating will decline, bringing an end to the rising warm-air plumes that are the source of the cumulus buildups.*

FIG. 3-7. *Sometimes the reason for a particular patch of cloud defies explanation. This line of isolated altocumulus* castellanus *drifts alone in the mid-level winds, perhaps supported by a small wave in the atmosphere generated by the distant hills. The cloud maintained its integrity during more than an hour of observation.*

evaporation, and cumulus *pannus* for fast-moving scud clouds found beneath mature thunderstorms. There are many more (some examples are shown in Table 3-2), but you won't usually encounter them except in textbooks.

Beyond the Latinized formal names, there are many common names for cloud patterns. Mares' tails is one we've encountered above. Some other cloud metaphors include mackerel sky, shelf cloud, scud, rotor cloud, lee wave cloud, beaver tail, wall cloud, anvil—the list can become very long, as different regions have evolved their own cloud lexicon. No wonder cloud-appreciation websites have popped up to celebrate the infinite variety of beautiful cloud forms in our atmosphere.

The Role of Stability

Humidity and ascent play critical roles in the creation of clouds, but instability also has a significant part to play in a cloud's appearance. In order to appreciate this sculptural mechanism, we must come to an understanding of what is meant by "instability." To do this, meteorologists invent a fictitious "parcel" of air that can be endowed with a

LATIN APPENDAGE TO CLOUD TYPE	MEANING
uncinus	hooked
castellanus	castlelike; like fortifications
radiatus	radiating
fractus	broken, fractured
pannus	shredded; ragged
fibratus	fibrous, filamented
spissatus	thickened; condensed
congestus	piled up, heaped, accumulated
mediocris	medium
volutus	rolled
undulatus	having waves; undulating
lacunosus	having holes
humilis	near the ground; low; of small size
translucidus	transparent; diaphanous
intortus	twisted; tangled

TABLE 3-2. *A sample of Latin adjectives that may be attached to the primary cloud name to better describe its appearance. There are many more.*

set of characteristics (such as warm or cold, humid or dry) and then set it loose within a larger environment to see what will happen if it is pushed upward or downward. Since the parcel is a virtual bundle of air and not a real one, its behavior is usually predicted by mathematical calculation or by the use of specialized graphs. The use of parcel theory is an important part of severe-weather forecasting, as every storm chaser can attest.

Warm air rises. In fact, any sample of a liquid or gas (that is, a fluid) that is warmer than its surroundings will attempt to float upward, as higher temperatures cause the sample to expand, giving it a lower density and making it buoyant. Conversely, a cold liquid or gas embedded in warmer surroundings will sink downward, pulled by its higher density. Examples of positive (upward) and negative (downward) buoyancy in day-to-day life are abundant: cold milk sinks in hot coffee, hot-air balloons rise upward when propane heaters are turned on, upper floors are warmer than lower ones in a heated building, and cold air sinks and rushes along the floor when a freezer door is opened.

The tendency of warm fluids to rise and colder ones to sink is related to the concept of stability. If a parcel of air is forced upward, it will keep on rising as long as it is warmer than its environment. If, for one reason or another, it becomes colder than the environment, it will lose its buoyancy, come to rest, and then begin to sink, eventually settling at some level where the parcel's internal temperature matches that of its surroundings. If that's not possible, the parcel will sink back to where it started, usually the ground (Figure 3-8). An atmosphere is said to be unstable if an air parcel is buoyant and rising, and stable if it's sinking. When the air parcel is at rest, in equilibrium with its surroundings, it is said to have neutral buoyancy or stability.

In some sense, instability is a fuzzy concept, as any atmosphere can be described as unstable if a sufficiently warm sample of air is placed in its midst. In midwinter, when atmospheres are usually very stable, the hot plume from a chimney is unstable until the rising air cools and comes to equilibrium with its surroundings, usually fairly quickly. Forest fires may generate their own thunderstorms from the large amounts of heat given off by burning. Realistically, atmospheric stability should be determined from physically reasonable processes such as the heating of the ground by the Sun each day if you are to use it to predict afternoon weather.

In the real atmosphere, a parcel of air cools adiabatically as it rises, as we saw in Chapter 2. Typically, though not always, the atmosphere also cools with altitude, so the presence of instability will be determined by which cools most quickly: the rising air parcel or the surrounding atmosphere. All rising air eventually slows and stops, though sometimes the upward motion may continue to the stratosphere. More commonly, instability ends where the rising parcel encounters warmer environmental temperatures at some level aloft. Quite often, the atmosphere contains an inversion—a layer where temperatures actually rise with height. When it encounters an inversion, the rising parcel is stabilized very quickly, even if the temperature inversion is very small.

One complication that enters the calculation of instability is the release of heat into the rising sample parcel as it begins to condense into clouds. Adiabatic cooling causes the relative humidity in the ascending air to increase until, at some point, the air becomes saturated and cloud droplets or ice crystals begin to form. As we've seen

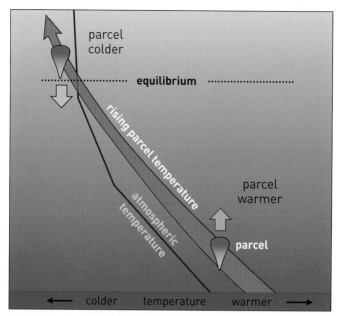

FIG. 3-8. *A buoyant parcel of air will rise upward as long as it is warmer than its surroundings, even though it cools as it rises; as long as this continues, the atmosphere is said to be unstable within that region of rising air. At some higher point, when the parcel encounters a warmer layer and becomes negatively buoyant, the layer is now said to be stable and the parcel will come to a halt or sink back until it is at equilibrium with its surroundings. Stable and unstable layers may be found at any altitude in the atmosphere.*

earlier, water's change in phase from vapor to liquid and from liquid to ice releases latent heat, which increases the temperature of the rising parcel. Using a hot-air balloon analogy, the release of latent heat is akin to turning on the heater to cause the balloon to rise even more quickly. The additional heat helps maintain the instability, and the parcel may rise considerably farther upward until coming to a stop. As long as the air remains warmer than its surrounding environment, it will continue to ascend, converting ever more water vapor to droplets and crystals and releasing heat. For this reason, humidity is as important as temperature in determining the stability of an atmosphere. Meteorologists have to evaluate both to accurately predict the amount of instability in an air column.

The depth of the instability can be quite small, from a few inches (when the ground first begins to warm in the morning) to many thousands of feet, often reaching to the top of the troposphere. Small amounts of instability are frequently observed mixed in stratus-type clouds, giving them a lumpy appearance or opening clear spots between the elements. Instability is not restricted to the surface layers, but can occur at any layer within the tropopause. Instability also changes: the Sun warms the ground; warm and cold fronts approach and pass; or upper-atmosphere winds bring changing temperatures aloft.

Convective Clouds

Convective clouds are those that arise from instability. All such clouds have a limited lifetime, from minutes in cumulus updrafts to as much as several hours for large, severe thunderstorms in a very unstable environment. Humble cumulus clouds are usually stopped by a temperature inversion that traps the climbing updraft. Towering cumulus clouds (Figure 3-9) encounter stable conditions at a higher level, usually by cooling as they rise until the atmosphere around them becomes too warm to support a buoyant updraft. Cumulonimbus clouds suffer the same fate, but the largest such storms can rise to the tropopause (Figure 3-10) and for a short distance into the stratosphere, before the inversion at the tropopause brings them to a stop.

Temperature inversions, because they stop or reduce the upward motion of buoyant air currents, act as a kind of "lid" on the atmosphere. Clouds and air pollution can be trapped near the ground beneath a low-level inversion, low and high clouds may take on distinctive smooth-topped shapes when they form beneath a mid-level inversion, and thunderstorms usually send out a long shelf of high-level cloud that is topped by inversions at the top of the troposphere. We'll have a look at these types of clouds and many others in the sections that follow.

The Sky's Armada

Low-Level Clouds

STRATUS

In its most common form, stratus is a flat, opaque, medium-white to gray, mostly featureless cloud that masks the Sun and Moon (Figure 3-11), producing a shadowless landscape. Subtle shades of light and

FIG. 3-9. *A towering cumulus cloud (often called cumulus* congestus*) is a strong convective cloud that may extend anywhere from 2,000 to 20,000 feet vertically. Though the larger towers can produce heavy rain, they are not considered hazardous.*

FIG. 3-10. *Cumulonimbus clouds are often called thunderstorms, though they do not have to produce lightning to be given the name—appearance is enough. This cumulonimbus is a thunderstorm and a severe one at that. In this example, a flat anvil cloud can be found near the top of the buildup, where the storm is in stable equilibrium with its surroundings.*

FIG. 3-11. *A layer of stratus cloud across a winter scene tells of slow updrafts and stable conditions.*

dark in the cloud deck betray unevenness on its top side or a variable opacity within the layer. Its formless base often defies estimates of its height, creating a two-dimensional canvas out of the normally dynamic sky. Thinner stratus will give an outline to the Sun or Moon but often only as a vague bright patch in the sky.

The word "stratus" comes from the Latin "to spread out" or "layer." Stratus forms in extensive regions of slow uplift, where the air cools sufficiently for its water vapor to condense into small cloud droplets. The lifting may be caused by flow across a gradually rising terrain or by a gentle ascent over a slightly colder layer of air that lies along the ground. Stratus often forms in precipitation, when lower layers of the atmosphere are humidified by evaporating rain falling from higher levels. Because of their diminutive size, droplets in stratus clouds are readily held in suspension, so that, at best, the cloud by itself can only manage precipitation in the form of misty drizzle. In the cold of winter, stratus often comes with tenuous, drifting, tiny snowflakes that do little more than dust the ground.

In California, early summer is often given the nickname "May Gray" or "June Gloom" for the frequent incursions of marine stratus over coastal cities. San Francisco in particular is famous for its stratus, which provides a never-ending visual treat as it flows over the coastal hills into the bay, much like water over a waterfall. The cloud is usually brought up short against the inland hills and mountains and erodes readily under the afternoon Sun.

FOG AND MIST

Fog is cloud that lies against the ground or just above. It is a personal kind of cloudiness—mysterious, where stratus is depressing. Fog is the stuff of lurching zombies and ominous smugglers. Aviation forecasters distinguish fog from mist according to visibility: fog reduces visibility to less than ⅝ mile (1 km); mist applies to higher visibilities, up to 5 miles (8 km).

There are half-a-dozen processes that create fog, but the two most likely are radiation and advection. Radiation fog forms at night over ground that has been cooled by the emission of thermal infrared radiation under a clear sky (Figure 3-12). The first sign that fog may be forming is a heavy dewfall followed shortly thereafter by wispy tendrils of cloud that drift almost imperceptibly along the ground. Low-lying areas are particularly prone to radiation fog, as the cool air collects in valley bottoms and topographic hollows before condensing into fog (Figure 3-13). As the night continues, the fog layer grows thicker and deeper as heat is lost to space by longwave radiation escaping from the

FIG. 3-12. *After a day of melting temperatures that loaded the air with moisture, a clear night brings falling temperatures and the formation of a thin radiation fog. While the depth of the fog is barely above the streetlights in this evening picture, by morning it will have built considerably higher and will take several hours to dissipate.*

FIG. 3-13. *Cool air draining down the hillsides has reduced the temperature to the dewpoint in the valley below, forming a dense fog that is just beginning to dissipate in this image, taken in the early morning. The edges of the fog are spreading across the sunny fields, attracted by the initial warming of the grassy surface under the clear skies above. The warming ground generates small convective currents that rise upward; the rising air must be replaced, and so draws the fog upward along the slopes, where it will also be warmed and dissipated. The small protruding tops in the overcast are also a sign of mixing along the top of the fog bank.*

top of the fog layer. This radiation cooling is aided by a slow turbulent mixing that spreads the cooling through the rest of the layer. It's a very sensitive process, and only a slight wind coming along at the start of the night may be enough to dissipate the fog altogether.

Once a relatively thick layer of fog has formed, radiation upwelling from below is partly captured by the cloudy air, raising the temperature near the ground. The fog may lift a few feet (a meter or two) off of the ground, forming a kind of "tunnel" of good visibility under a ceiling of semitransparent or opaque cloud. The effect is enchanting, putting the observer in a "room" of his or her own, manufactured by nature for private enjoyment. Radiation fog is magical stuff, but devilishly difficult to forecast. On many a clear night, measurements of temperature and moisture tell the meteorologist that the relative humidity has reached 100 percent, but the expected fog never materializes. Instead, only a heavy dew is deposited to thumb its nose at the forecaster.

Advection fog occurs when moist air, pushed by the wind, moves over an already-cold surface and is cooled to the saturation point. This fog is often found with the approach of spring and fall warm fronts, where saturated air becomes trapped beneath a frontal inversion. In the springtime, snow-covered ground is a favorite setting for producing advection fogs, as the melting snow provides the atmospheric moisture and the snow surface contributes to the cooling. One of the world's foggiest locations lies over the waters off Newfoundland and Labrador, where the mingling of warm air and cold ocean currents provides the perfect conditions for a persistent fog—the kind that befell the *Titanic*.

Fog erodes inward from the edges once the Sun climbs above the morning horizon. After an hour or two, thin spots in the middle of the fog bank begin to open, and from there, the rest of the fog bank dissipates from both outside and inside as holes grow bigger and the perimeter shrinks. Those thin spots often lie over urban areas where city temperatures are higher than the surrounding countryside, or over hills where the ground lies closer to the top of the fog layer. In the autumn, advection fogs can be difficult to dissipate, as they have a tendency to lift off the ground and form a solid stratus layer, much to the detriment of the forecast.

Because cold air collects in low spots in the terrain, mountain valleys in fall and winter are favorite collecting points for fog, particularly in the Canadian Rockies and the Appalachians, where nights are long and the daytime Sun hangs low in the sky (Figure 3-14). This valley fog sometimes persists for days, almost clearing in the afternoon before thickening again later that night. When the fog does finally dissipate, it will come with strong winds ahead of an incoming weather system or an outbreak of much colder air that robs the atmosphere of its moisture.

Because of its local nature, it is not surprising that there are special names for kinds of fog. One is sea smoke (or steam fog), which is created when cold winter air passes over warm water. On rivers and ponds, the smoke never thickens enough to rise more than a small distance above the water, forming twisting snakes of water vapor that dangle in the air (Figure 3-15). Ice fog is made up of tiny ice crystals suspended in the air, but the name is also given to the mist created by automobile exhaust on winter days when temperatures decline to the −20°F (−28°C) mark or colder. Upslope fog forms when moist air is forced to rise over terrain and cools adiabatically. Precipitation fog

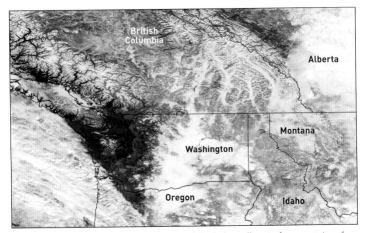

FIG. 3-14. *Early morning satellite images reveal fog-laden valleys in the mountains of British Columbia, Washington, and Oregon in this January 3, 2013, image. Fog is easily identified by its bright, flat appearance and its tendency to outline the contours of the terrain.*

FIG. 3-15. *A cool autumn night, light winds, and moisture supplied by a warm lake combine to saturate the air just above the lake surface, forming a thin mist called "steam fog." Though neither the cold air nor the lake air is saturated, the mixture of the two elevates the humidity to 100 percent and beyond, condensing and forming tendrils of fog along the lake surface. A lake or pond is not even necessary, as dew-soaked grass or wet soil are often suitable for the task.*

forms under steady rainfall, when falling drops evaporate, causing the air near the ground to become saturated. This type of fog is typically associated with approaching warm fronts and may persist for a considerable time.

Perhaps the most beautiful of fogs is the freezing fog that brings brilliant hoarfrosts to make the landscape glow in the morning light (Figure 2-29). In this case, fog forms at temperatures below the freezing point, producing supercooled water droplets that freeze on every exposed branch, blade of grass, pole, or wire, coating them in feathery ice-crystal jewelry.

STRATOCUMULUS

Stratocumulus is stratus with a promise of a brighter day. It is a convective layer cloud that forms in conditions of weak, shallow instability, usually below a drier layer that prevents significant upward growth (Figure 3-16). Stratocumulus layers are generally fairly thin, extending over a depth of several hundred feet (a few hundred meters) in the lower atmosphere. They are typically topped by a surprisingly strong but very shallow stable inversion. Stratocumulus is the most common

FIG. 3-16. *Stratocumulus clouds are formed and maintained by slow lifting processes in the low-level atmosphere and typically produce only light precipitation—usually drizzle or snow flurries. In this example, the stratocumulus has deeper convective clouds embedded that bring the gray curtain of rainfall in the left background. This stratocumulus deck probably formed from low-level cloud left behind by previous deep convection.*

type of cloud, covering nearly a quarter of the Earth's surface on average, with twice as much lying over the oceans as over the land.

Stratocumulus may appear as a fairly solid layer or as patches of dark rounded clouds, often loosely organized into waves and rolls. While it forms under conditions similar to stratus, it is more inclined to bring light rain or snow than its flatter cousin because of its embedded convection. The two low cloud types often coexist, with patches of stratocumulus embedded in larger areas of stratus. The convective part of stratocumulus—the "cumulus" part of the name—comes from the slow overturning of the layer when the cloud top cools by the emission of radiation and sinks downward, to be replaced by small convective turrets that rise to protrude above the top of the layer.

Stratocumulus (and sometimes stratus) can develop from cumulus clouds that are capped by a moderate to strong warm layer in the atmosphere. As the cumulus grows, upper layers of the cloud encounter the temperature inversion and spread out horizontally until the sky is largely covered in cloud. Strong winds will also often generate stratocumulus clouds by vigorously stirring the lower atmosphere as they flow over the terrain. The turbulence in the wind carries moist surface air upward, where it cools adiabatically to form a cloudy layer. In such cases, the stratocumulus is usually formed in rolls or billows aligned along the wind, with clear spaces between, where the air dries in descending currents (Figure 3-17). Stratocumulus billows come with unpleasant cool and windy weather, sometimes with a light drizzle to add to the misery, but the cloud formations themselves may be surprisingly attractive.

In winter, stratocumulus comes with high-pressure systems and stable weather behind a cold front, usually with little or no precipitation. After the front moves away, expanding blue-sky gaps between the cloud elements indicate an improvement in the weather and a return to sunshine. In summer, intense thunderstorms will often leave behind a large pool of rain-cooled air topped with stratocumulus that may persist through the night and into the following morning.

When cold winter air flows over warmer open water, stratocumulus clouds may take the form of long curving lines of cloud, best seen in satellite images. These "cloud streets" build in an environment that is more unstable than usual because of the juxtaposition of a warm surface with a very cold airmass above it. Stratocumulus clouds that form over the Great Lakes in winter give rise to "lake-effect snowstorms" on the downwind shore that may drop prodigious amounts of snow.

FIG. 3-17. *These bands of stratocumulus cloud are referred to as "cloud streets" and form in horizontal rolls that line up along the wind direction in the boundary layer. The clouds mark the position where the roll is rising, while the clear skies between the streets mark areas of descending air. The top of the roll is marked by a stable inversion.*

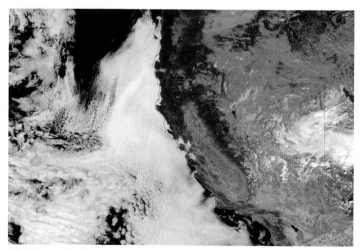

FIG. 3-18. *Low-level marine stratocumulus hugs the California coast in this image from the* Terra *satellite on October 21, 2018. Marine stratus forms in moist air trapped beneath the subsidence inversions associated with the Earth's semipermanent subtropical anticyclones (highs).*

Persistent fields of stratus and stratocumulus can be found in the subtropics, located over cold ocean currents along the west sides of the continents (Figure 3-18). The cloud is trapped beneath temperature inversions created by the semipermanent anticyclones (high-pressure areas) that lie along the 30th parallel in both north and south latitudes. These large areas of marine cloudiness play an important role in regulating the Earth's temperature by reflecting a large amount of sunlight during the day and emitting longwave radiation at night. Collectively, these low-level clouds tend to cool the globe, in contrast to higher-level clouds, which have the opposite effect.

Stratocumulus clouds in Arctic airmasses often bring light freezing drizzle, illustrating that supercooled liquid droplets are present in the cloud, even though temperatures may lie in the –5 to –12°F (20 to –25°C) range. The droplets are slow to convert to ice particles because of a shortage of ice nuclei in pristine Arctic air (Chapter 2). These precipitating stratus clouds are frustratingly difficult to anticipate, and the forecaster can only wait for their occurrence and amend the forecast.

Mid-Level Clouds

Mid-level clouds form and dissipate as a result of rising and sinking motions in the atmosphere. Low-level clouds do this as well, but low clouds are influenced by surface conditions and the flux of energy and moisture from below. Stratus clouds have their feet on the ground, whereas altostratus and altocumulus float in the wind currents aloft. Mid-level clouds may be composed of water droplets or ice crystals (or both) depending on the season and altitude.

ALTOSTRATUS

Altostratus is characterized by a uniform gray to bright white color with little texture except for the occasional ripple on its underside. It is often observed in layers, especially with incoming weather systems. Thin altostratus will show the Sun and Moon, but thicker, more opaque clouds will obscure the sky (Figure 3-19). Altostratus tends to form as approaching warm fronts lift the mid-level air to condensation, usually starting with a cirrostratus layer that thickens and descends to mid-levels of the troposphere. Because of their association with incoming weather systems, altostratus clouds can spread over thousands of square miles. In the tropics, but less so in temperate zones, altostratus can also form from the spreading of upper clouds from thunderstorms.

FIG. 3-19. *Altostratus, showing a barely visible Sun.*

In contrast to its low-level stratus cousin, altostratus can acquire a large vertical depth, from several hundred to several thousand feet. This large vertical extent gives the cloud a distinctive composition, with ice crystals at the colder top, a mixture of ice and supercooled water droplets in the middle, and supercooled or ordinary water droplets at the bottom. Altostratus may produce light precipitation on its own, or seed lower layers of stratus and stratocumulus to produce heavier snowfalls on the ground, but for the most part, rain or snow from mid-levels alone will evaporate before it reaches the ground. If precipitation is persistent, however, the falling moisture will humidify layers below, eventually building the cloud layer downward to form nimbostratus when the precipitation reaches the ground.

ALTOCUMULUS

Altocumulus is a mid-level cloud that forms in discrete bundles, painting the sky in an infinitely variable canvas. Its cumulus nature gives it a bumpy appearance, often in the form of elongated patches or in regularly spaced waves. In a busy sky, several wavelengths may be apparent, crossing each other at small angles according to the height of each cloud. Cloud elements have a well-defined edge and are mostly opaque, features of their largely water-droplet constitution, though in colder atmospheres, altocumulus elements will be composed wholly or partially of ice crystals. This mix of water phases gives altocumulus clouds the ability to form several kinds of cloud halos and colored displays that greatly add to their appeal.

Forms of altocumulus have many popular names. One of the more common wave patterns, "mackerel sky," is a pattern of clumps and rolls (Figure 3-20) that resemble the striping on a mackerel fish (obviously from an era when mackerel didn't come in a tin can). Mackerel skies appear in some common weather lore, such as this old mariner's rhyme:

> *Mackerel sky, mackerel sky,*
> *Never long wet and never long dry.*
> *Mares' tails and mackerel scales*
> *Make tall ships carry low sails.*

Altocumulus clouds are the most varied of all of the cloud types and often bring beautiful cloudscapes, especially in the magical glow of sunrise and sunset (Figure 3-21). Because of its convective nature, altocumulus often produces precipitation, forming a long, descending tail of wispy, evaporating raindrops called virga.

ALTOCUMULUS *CASTELLANUS*

Altocumulus *castellanus* (Figure 3-7) is a more unstable type of mid-level cloud that forms deeper convective turrets ("castles") than the small billows typical of most altocumulus. In appearance, it is similar to moderate-sized cumulus, but at a higher altitude and with more fibrous tops and sides, often tilted over in the upper-level winds. Storm chasers pay considerable attention to the presence of altocumulus *castellanus,* as it indicates instability in the mid-levels that offers the possibility of severe thunderstorms later in the day.

ALTOCUMULUS *LENTICULARIS*

Lenticular clouds are among the most beautiful of cloud formations and may occur at any level, but those formed from altocumulus are often the most spectacular. Lenticular means "lenslike" and refers to the smooth-topped, curved appearance of this type of cloud (Figure 3-22). Lenticulars form in wavelike undulations beneath inversions and give the appearance of being "trapped" against some higher barrier. The most visually stunning altocumulus *lenticularis* are formed in the flow downwind of a mountain range or over single peaks, where they are often described as "UFO-like." Because they are linked to the terrain that creates the wave, the cloud is stationary,

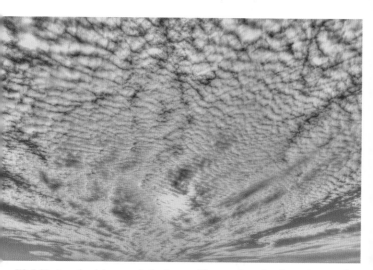

FIG. 3-20. *A mackerel sky, named after its resemblance to the scales of a mackerel fish. A mackerel sky can form from altocumulus (this example) or cirrocumulus clouds and is the term for a sky with irregular waves with open blue patches between.*

FIG. 3-21. *A brilliant red sunset reflecting off of an altocumulus layer.*

FIG. 3-22. *Wispy lenticular wave clouds arc above the Andes Mountains in Chile.*

FIG. 3-23. *Stacked lenticular clouds drift across a winter prairie landscape. These lenticulars are not fixed to some feature in the terrain but are moving along with a slow westerly flow.*

leading to the technical name "altocumulus standing lenticular." The lenslike clouds may be stacked in layers for a considerable depth, stuck in place as the air flows up and through them.

Lenticular clouds do not have to be attached to the terrain, and they are quite common on the Great Plains at both low and mid-levels, trapped in waves that form beneath an inversion, just like their mountain siblings. In this case, the lenticulars will move with the flow, often in the company of many other similarly shaped clouds (Figure 3-23).

High-Level Clouds

CIRRUS

Cirrus clouds (Figure 3-24) are feathery ice-crystal clouds that dwell at 4 to 8 miles (6 to 13 km) above the surface and are usually transparent or semitransparent unless their depth exceeds a half mile (1 km). The name "cirrus" is a catch-all descriptor that is applied to all high-level forms that are not obviously cirrocumulus or cirrostratus. These common high-level clouds are shaped by the winds, tracing out the flow of the air aloft in the alignment of their strands. Because of their icy composition, they are the whitest of the clouds, showing off colors in the morning and evening when they are illuminated by the Sun.

Cirrus forms when high-level moisture condenses from vapor to ice crystal without first changing to liquid water. Because they are largely transparent to sunlight, they have little effect in cooling the globe, but at night, ice-crystal clouds are effective at trapping the outgoing infrared radiation that cools the planet. As such, they are important moderators of the Earth's climate.

Changes in cirrus cloudiness are often useful in making a short-range forecast. If high-level cloudiness is increasing from the west, usually blending into cirrostratus, it may be a sign of an approaching warm front as the air at high levels is lifted to saturation. The approach of a distant warm front may also be indicated by clumps of cirrus with long hairlike striations moving slowly from the west. The position of the jet stream, which carries storms from west to east, may be marked by a long band of cirrus with well-defined edges, sometimes cross-banded by waves of thicker cloud. Thunderstorm cirrus, in large sheets, will have an obvious source in the upstream direction, though the storm may be out of sight beyond the horizon. High mountains may form cirrus clouds in the wind flow over their tops, usually in concert with lower altostratus layers. But most of all, cirrus forms the

FIG. 3-24. *Feathery cirrus clouds.*

wispy strands that decorate the sky on quiet days, evidence of weak ascent and moisture in upper levels of the atmosphere. It's a mischievous kind of cloud, producing occasional surprises of colored halos and streaks from its ice-crystal nature.

CIRROCUMULUS

Add a little instability to the upper levels of the atmosphere, and small white or pale blue clouds arranged in waves, ripples, or globular patterns emerge. They form in thin semitransparent layers and show almost no shading (Figure 3-25). Cirrocumulus are the only high-level clouds where supercooled water droplets are found, though their composition is largely of ice crystals. When the liquid drops contact an ice crystal, they freeze rapidly, causing an ice-crystal precipitation (virga) that appears as descending curved streamers that evaporate a short distance below the cloud. In concert with the other cirriform clouds, cirrocumulus that is thickening from a westerly direction may herald the approach of a warm front and associated weather system.

From the ground, cirrocumulus cloudlets appear as fleecy elements no larger than a finger held at arm's length. Like altocumulus, cirrocumulus regularly organizes in rows, forming a high-altitude version of a mackerel sky. Unlike lower clouds, it is always broken up into ripples and patches and is often accompanied by sheets of cirrostratus. Cirro-

FIG. 3-25. *Cirrocumulus clouds can be identified by the small size of the individual cumulus elements. In this image, the cirrocumulus is mixed with a small patch of cirrostratus (behind the building) that displays a faint iridescence.*

cumulus is a sign of upper-level instability that might be an indication of thunderstorms later in the day, though normally these icy cloud patches are a sign of a good-weather day. Their height makes them the last of the clouds to be illuminated by the Sun in the evening or the first in the morning, lending an especially colorful ending to the day.

CIRROSTRATUS

Thin, hazy, uniform, and featureless cirrostratus clouds bring a whitish, semitransparent veil to the sky. This cloud type is more opaque than cirrus, but still often thin enough to allow sunlight to reach the ground except when accompanied by altostratus. The edges of cirrostratus cloud tend to be ragged and outlined by wispy cirrus forms. When thin, it is a frequent halo producer (Figure 3-26), especially when it covers a large part of the sky.

Cirrostratus arises from the gradual lifting of air high in the troposphere under stable conditions, a situation often fashioned by approaching weather systems. The stable nature of the cloud allows it to form ripples and waves as it responds to the wind at cloud level. If the cirrus layer forms a uniform and thickening veil-like covering,

FIG. 3-26. *Cirrostratus clouds are often accompanied by halos because of their ice-crystal composition.*

it is likely that an approaching warm front will bring rain within the day. Cirrostratus also forms in concert with low-pressure storms and in the debris cloud thrown up by distant thunderstorms.

CONVECTIVE CLOUDS

Clouds formed by rising plumes of warm and moist air in an unstable environment are called convective clouds and have a derivative of the word "cumulus" somewhere in their name. They are most often surface-based with their roots at the ground where the warm plumes of air began ascending. While other clouds build in layers, convective clouds build vertically, sometimes to great depths. The buildups don't have to have their feet on the ground; they can begin from any level in the atmosphere, as long as there is a mechanism to start the air rising to trigger vertical growth. For this reason, we have cumulus-type clouds at all levels in the atmosphere. For most of us, the best-known form of a convective cloud is the ubiquitous "fair-weather" cumulus—puffy cauliflower clouds that dot the sky on a warm and sunny day (Figure 3-27).

Heat and moisture are required to initiate the instability on which convective clouds are formed, so buildups usually wait until the afternoon when temperatures are reaching their maximum for the day. On the more humid days, clouds may begin building around midmorning, but this is usually a sign that the more extreme forms of convection—thunderstorms—are less likely. Storm chasers prefer to have a late start to deep convection, usually after 4 p.m., as that gives the atmosphere time to build up the low-level heat and humidity before beginning explosive upward growth. Convection can also be initiated by a number of "triggers" that push the surface air upward to the condensation point without waiting for temperatures to peak. Among these triggers are cold and warm fronts, colliding wind flows along lakes and coastlines, low-pressure troughs, and even the winds generated by other thunderstorms.

A typical convective day will begin with cumulus clouds in the early afternoon that grow into towering cumulus later in the day if the instability stretches into the mid-layers of the atmosphere. These early clouds tend to make the air column more stable by depositing moisture and heat into the middle atmosphere. Cloud watchers will quickly notice that small surface-based convective clouds have a very short lifetime, measured in minutes. These are the clouds of childhood that change from cats to foxes, to elephants, to trucks, and then wisp away. When first formed, cloud tops are solid and the sides are crisp and bumpy with cauliflower-like shapes. When upward motion stops, the tops become fibrous, and wispy bits begin to blow off in the wind.

FIG. 3-27. *An aerial view of modest cumulus clouds speaks to low-level instability capped by a dry stable layer that prevents deeper buildups.*

FIG. 3-28. *A weak towering cumulus cloud has no future as it succumbs to stronger winds aloft. Leaning convective buildups such as this are referred to as "turkey towers" by storm chasers.*

Sides lose their shapes a little more slowly, but only a few minutes after decay starts, nothing remains but a few transparent fibers that drift away in the wind. Dissipation is caused in part by the loss of upward velocity as the rising air parcel encounters warmer, stable layers aloft, and in part by the mixing of drier surrounding air with the rising cloud.

Large cumulus clouds—towering cumulus and cumulonimbus—have a somewhat different behavior. Time-lapse photography shows that the convective towers grow by hundreds or thousands of successive smaller updrafts and not by the giant upward motion of one warm parcel of air. Each one of these contributing updrafts surges skyward for a short time and then slows and stops, merging with the existing cloud mass to become part of the overall convective cell. If convective clouds grow into towering cumulus and cumulonimbus, updrafts blend into a single, stronger, rising core in the middle of the storm (Figure 3-29). Updraft velocities are greatest in the center of the cloud under the top of the growing towers, reaching a maximum just before precipitation begins.

Plumes of air will cool as they rise, and eventually temperatures will fall to the saturation point where the first tiny cloud particles condense. These nascent cloud droplets will grow to raindrop size if the ascent is continuous and deep enough. If and when the ascending air cools to the freezing point, the suspended drops then turn to ice. The change from vapor to water droplets and from droplets to ice releases latent heat into the rising updraft, further driving the upward growth of the convective cells.

Growing convective cells will eventually encounter warmer surrounding temperatures at some higher level, a point known as the equilibrium level. At this point, the parcel begins to decelerate, but upward motion doesn't end until the momentum acquired at lower levels is eroded by the warmer environment. At the equilibrium level, rising air spreads out to form the large flat-topped anvil cloud that is characteristic of thunderstorms. The anvil subsequently blows downstream with the upper-level winds (Figure 3-28). A mature non-severe thunderstorm will have a lifetime of only an hour or so before dissipating, but organized lines and clusters of storms, or the severe-weather-producing supercell storm, may continue well into the evening and overnight before gradually dying away.

FIG. 3-29. *A prominent anvil cloud sits atop a cumulonimbus storm, with smaller cumulus and towering cumulus in the foreground. The cumulonimbus has reached maturity and is beginning to decay, as shown by the feathery edges of its anvil.*

Cumulonimbus clouds have a distinctive shape and behavior that identifies them even without their signature thunder and lightning. They are tall white convective towers, usually vertical or slightly leaning downwind, with a dark veil of rain hanging from the base once precipitation begins. At maturity, a spreading, flat-topped altocumulus and cirrus anvil cloud stretches downwind from the storm top, pointing in the direction of the upper-level winds. The core of the updraft on stronger storms may be visible as a small bump protruding above the anvil, known as an overshooting top. As storm chasers quickly learn, the strongest thunderstorms, called supercell storms, have several distinctive appearances, and much more will be said of them in Chapter 9.

In Praise of Clouds

Clouds have beauty and grandeur that appeals to the artistic side of human nature: a red-tinged sunset; a magnificent, distant thunderstorm; a brooding, gray overcast; or the promise of better weather in a spot of blue embedded in a wet sky. Poetry uses clouds as metaphors to set the mood, from Wordsworth's pensive "I wandered lonely as a cloud . . ." to the drama of "The thick black cloud was cleft, and still . . ." in Coleridge's *Rime of the Ancient Mariner*. Clouds dominate the scene in the world's galleries: glorious, rich landscapes by John Constable and brooding hillsides by Andrew Wyeth; stylized clouds by Vincent van Gogh, photographs by Ansel Adams. Joni Mitchell's clouds "got in my way." For Bob Dylan, it was the ominous ". . . long black cloud is coming down."

Clouds are the "indicator species" of the atmosphere. Where clouds are present, moisture and upward-moving air can be inferred. Patterns, shapes, colors, and the evolution of clouds reveal the presence of fronts, jet streams, radiation processes, instability, temperatures, and cloud composition. Knowledgeable cloud watchers are rewarded not only by the visual treat of an ever-changing skyscape but also by the quiet, personal pleasure of deciphering a part of the secret workings of the atmosphere.

In this chapter, we've sketched the outlines of ordinary clouds. In the next, we'll discuss the spectacular.

These regularly spaced lines of stratocumulus are called "billow" or "wave" clouds, where billow means "organized in parallel lines." The more scientific name for these clouds is stratocumulus undulatus or "undulating." The bands of cloud are formed by small waves in the atmosphere confined beneath a low-level temperature inversion. The cloud outlines the ascending part of the wave, where water vapor condenses; clear zones represent the wave trough, where the air is descending, warming, and evaporating.

In this morning scene, cold air has pooled in the valley to the left overnight, condensing into a fog and stratus layer. The smooth wavelike tops to the stratus layer provide evidence of a slow flow of air out of the valley into the more open spaces on the right. As it emerges onto the flatter ground, the air spreads horizontally, creating a slow downdraft that helps to dissipate the stratus tendrils.

In winter, fall, and spring, cold air pools in mountain valleys, trapping moisture under a difficult-to-remove inversion. This view, in the Bridgeport Valley, California, shows the top of an inversion-trapped stratus layer lapping against the mountain slopes. The heavy cloud cover restricts the amount of sunlight that reaches the ground beneath the cloud deck, helping to preserve the inversion. The cloud can be removed by moderate to strong winds that mix the underlying layer with the drier atmosphere above, by the arrival of a fresh cold front, or by the gradual mixing of moist and dry air along the cloud edges over a period of several days.

Extensive fields of overcast stratocumulus clouds in this early morning view bring a somber mood to a city. The mixture of dark and bright cloud bases indicates the presence of both deep and shallow sections in the cloud deck. Rain is falling in the right background, creating a hazy veil over the distant buildings. Though the base of these clouds is at the stratus level, the presence of rain indicates that cloud tops extend well into middle cloud levels.

Clouds frequently occur in layers with a distinct separation between the levels, as illustrated by this image of stratocumulus underlying a similar pattern of altocumulus. The higher altocumulus level is distinguished by brighter clouds, still illuminated by the setting Sun, but the apparent size of the elements at each level also provides a clue as to their altitude. The spreading sunbeams in the distance are known as crepuscular rays.

The smooth lens-shaped formations in the middle are lenticular clouds, a common species at higher levels, but less frequent at stratocumulus heights. They are most common on the lee side of higher terrain, where they remain nearly stationary, but in this scene, over northwestern Ontario, there is no upstream orographic influence and so these stratocumulus lenticularis move slowly in the upper flow. Their outlines are less distinct than typical mid-level examples and the stacked layers tend to blend together, suggesting that the formation will be relatively short lived. At higher layers, spreading altocumulus and altostratus and an overcast layer of cirrostratus suggest an approaching warm front.

The California coast, with its cold offshore current, is a frequent host to fog and low stratus clouds, where the overlying atmosphere is cooled to saturation by the underlying ocean. In this view, from La Jolla, California, the fog is both shallow and dense in response to available moisture and the lack of wind. The fog retreats offshore during the afternoon when the Sun warms the land, but slips in again overnight as inland temperatures fall.

This turbulent mix of low-level cloud suggests the form known as asperitas, a type of cloud recently recognized by the World Meteorological Organization. The word comes from the Latin aspero meaning "to make rough." Stratocumulus asperitas has the appearance of a form of mammatus that has been sheared off by winds at the cloud's base.

Table Mountain, in Cape Town, South Africa, is noted for its "tablecloth" of orographic cloud, formed when moist southeast winds are directed over the mountain's slopes, causing the atmosphere to cool and condense into clouds as it rises. Here we see stratocumulus clouds on the nearby flank where rising currents encounter a modest instability. In the background, a flatter stratus cloud layer reveals a more stable atmosphere and mid-level moisture.

Developing thunderstorms are great consumers of air and moisture, scavenging the surrounding heat and moisture to feed their updrafts. The air drawn into the storm often forms stratus "tags" that can be used to trace the flow into the convective storm. In this example, tails of ragged stratus mark the location of the inflow air beneath the growing turrets above.

Steady precipitation saturates the air, building cloud bases downward until they reach the ground. In this scene, a misty view of the Great Wall of China suggests that the steady drizzle will soon complete the saturation of the atmosphere and form a more opaque layer of stratus and fog.

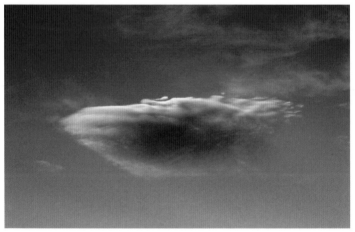

Like some strange fish in the sky, this patch of altocumulus cloud has lenticular characteristics, remaining stationary in the sky as the air currents flow through the cloud mass. The central body of the cloud is made up of two or three layers stacked one atop the other. Rising air enters the cloud from the left, condenses, and then dissipates as it sinks on the right edge.

A view of overcast altostratus with patchy lower-level cumulus and stratocumulus in the middle distance. The fuzzy, descending, dark gray patches on the right side are early signs of the start of precipitation, possibly from convective elements embedded within the altostratus layer. These clouds will likely turn into a nimbostratus layer in a few hours.

Classic altocumulus clouds form in shallow, unstable layers in the middle atmosphere, where the air is rising. The intervening spaces between the cloud elements are created where the surrounding air sinks to compensate for the rising motions.

A dramatic patch of altocumulus billow clouds, caught in the shadows of the setting Sun. Above, a thick layer of cirrostratus marks an approaching front, while below, in the distance, lower-level altocumulus marks a small layer of instability in the atmosphere. Such winter-season clouds usually herald the approach of warmer weather and precipitation.

The evening sun illuminates bands of vigorous altocumulus castellanus, *a name derived from the turretlike appearance of the cloud towers. While no precipitation is evident from these clouds, the wispy nature of the cloud base in the upper right shows that rain is falling from beneath the bigger turrets and evaporating a short distance below the cloud base.*

Dissipating cumulus clouds below and altocumulus clouds aloft give evidence of two instability regimes in the atmosphere. The lower cumulus clouds derive their energy from the warm land and sea surface, building upward according to the temperature and low-level instability. Altocumulus clouds do not have an underlying energy source and so rely on the amount of instability aloft and the presence of large-scale ascent in the middle atmosphere.

A line of altocumulus lenticularis *clouds maps the crest of an otherwise invisible atmospheric wave. As air flows through the wave structure, it rises toward the crests and sinks in the troughs. Rising air cools and condenses into visible clouds; sinking air warms and dissipates, making the wave visible as a series of equally spaced cloud elements. Waves are stable only in conditions where there is a weak inversion aloft. In this example, the inversion gives the cloud tops their smooth profile.*

Altocumulus floccus *clouds stand silhouetted against the sunset, showing a fibrous appearance that predicts early dissipation.*

Fibrous cirrus tufts, known as cirrus floccus, *show evidence of a modest uplift and instability in the upper atmosphere that causes moisture to condense into ice-crystal clouds. The wispy streaks are produced by crystals that become heavy enough to begin to settle out, forming delicate tails when stretched by lower-level winds. Ragged cumulus clouds on the bottom and right of the scene complete the image, testifying to a similarly unstable atmosphere at lower levels.*

This evening image from Arizona shows a band of cirrocumulus clouds associated with the subtropical jet stream, which runs along the left edge of the clouds. The asymmetrical appearance of the cloud suggests a descending motion to the left of the jet stream axis and a rising motion to the right. The clumpy and banded structures in the cloud are formed by turbulence in the atmosphere at that level.

Streamers of cirrus fibratus clouds mark the flow of jet-stream winds. Thin layers of cirrus fibratus usually indicate fair weather ahead.

These cirrus billow or undulatus *clouds have formed beneath the stratosphere in a jet-stream flow. Several different wavelengths at different levels in the atmosphere can be identified in the image. The wavelength of these billows is a reflection of the wind speed at altitude.*

Cirrostratus wave clouds, formed in the lee of a topographical barrier, trace out the wavy shape of the high-level flow. These streamers have characteristics that resemble mid-level lenticular clouds. Their smooth tops indicate a stable atmosphere aloft, in contrast to the moderately unstable conditions at lower levels shown by the ragged cumulus cloud.

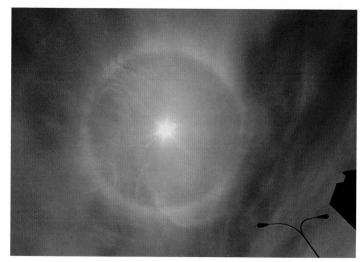

A sky full of thin cirrostratus nebulosus provides the backdrop for a dramatic 22° halo around the Sun. Halos such as this can form only in thin ice-crystal clouds. The nebulosus form is the most common of cirrus clouds. It has been estimated that cirrus clouds cover about 25 percent of the globe at any time.

At least two levels of cirrus cloud can be seen in this image. One is a feathery cirrus fibratus species; the other, a lower cirrocumulus (left of center). In the fibratus layer, ice crystals are falling slowly and aligning with the wind; after a short fall, the crystals evaporate. Feathery cirrus clouds usually indicate fair weather, though if thick enough, they may herald an approaching warm front.

CHAPTER 4

UNUSUAL CLOUDS

Clouds are the offspring of atmospheric physics, so they become a science classroom in the sky as well as visual treat. In this chapter, we will explore some of the more unusual forms of cloud structure. Some of these may be familiar to you, only to become special once you understand the mechanisms that created them. Best of all, unusual clouds are often the most stunning of creatures, sometimes incredibly rare, so if you go cloud hunting, a camera is an essential accessory.

Nacreous Clouds

Lucky indeed is the observer who stumbles upon these strikingly colored waves of mother-of-pearl or nacreous clouds silhouetted against deep, blue-black skies of evening. These gorgeous clouds (Figure 4-1) appear in the twilight hours after sunrise or before dawn, when the light from the Sun illuminates them from below the horizon. They take the form of translucent waves and undulations with unforgettable iridescent pastel shades that glow magically against the background sky.

Nacreous clouds, or polar stratospheric clouds (PSCs), are wave clouds that form at altitudes of 10 to 15 miles (16 to 24 km) in the lower and middle stratosphere at temperatures below −108°F (−78°C). Their composition is complex—usually mixtures of water and nitric acid sometimes blended with sulfuric acid. They are most often seen in winter months when the stratosphere experiences its lowest temperatures. Stratospheric clouds play an important role in the destruction of the ozone layer. The crystals that compose these clouds offer a surface on which man-made chlorine can be arranged to destroy ozone molecules.

FIG. 4-1. *Nacreous or polar stratospheric clouds photographed from a NASA research aircraft.*

Noctilucent Clouds

Live far enough north—at latitudes between 50° and 60°—and the short summer nights may reveal the highest clouds of all: noctilucent or "night-shining" clouds that form in the ultra-cold layers of the mesosphere, about 47 to 53 miles (75 to 85 km) high. These mesospheric clouds become visible when the Sun has set to between 6° and 16° below the horizon and illuminates only the upper layers of the atmosphere. Unlike the lower nacreous clouds, which are found in the winter months, noctilucent clouds are summer visitors, taking advantage of colder seasonal temperatures in the mesosphere and the Sun's high elevation in June, July, and August.

Noctilucent clouds are composed of tiny ice crystals that form in temperatures below about −184°F (−120°C), a frigid environment that allows water vapor to condense directly into ice. They are most often seen in the 50° to 60° latitude band across Canada and northern Europe, where short nights provide the best conditions for visibility, though reports have been received as far south as Utah in North America and Austria in Europe. Locations farther north have too much summer daylight to see the clouds, while southern latitudes have only brief evening and morning twilight hours for illumination. While present, they are less often seen in the Southern Hemisphere, where the continents tend to lie farther from the poles.

FIG. 4-2. *Noctilucent clouds, photographed from La Ronge, Saskatchewan.*

Noctilucent clouds have a form much like cirrus but with more feathery structures (Figure 4-2). Time-lapse photography sometimes reveals that the clouds lie at several distinct layers, sometimes moving in separate directions. Colors are subtle but definitely on the blue side, except when low against the horizon, where they are cast in red shades from the twilight color of the below-the-horizon Sun (Figure 4-3). When the Sun is only a small distance below the northern horizon—around 6° or 8°—noctilucent clouds may cover most of the sky, but as the night progresses, the cloud-illumination zone moves toward the horizon. Though mostly seen when the Sun is setting, they are also visible in the morning twilight as the sky brightens.

Wave Clouds and Mountain Clouds

Toss a stone into a pond and a ripple will spread out along the surface of the water. Gravity will pull the ripple back to its original level, but as the wave sinks, it overshoots, and so sets up a further series of undulations that gradually decay away. Such ripples are called gravity waves—waves that form at the boundary between two fluids of different densities and gradually decay as they succumb to the force of gravity. In the case of atmospheric gravity waves, buoyancy pushes the air upward and gravity pulls it down, making an up-and-down

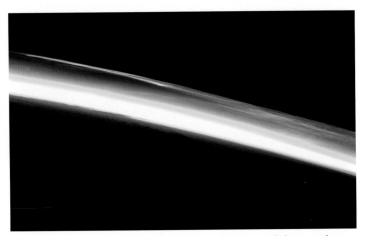

FIG. 4-3. *Taken from the International Space Station, this photograph shows noctilucent clouds illuminated by the setting Sun and glowing as light blue ribbons stretching across the arc of the Earth. Low clouds on the horizon appear yellow and orange, while higher tropospheric clouds and aerosols (dust and pollution) shine a brilliant white.*

oscillation in the atmosphere. A water wave forms at the boundary between air and water; in the atmosphere, that boundary is a temperature inversion—the border between cooler low-level air and warmer air above.

An atmospheric wave can be triggered by several events: wind flow over mountains, thunderstorm updrafts, jet-stream winds, and frontal systems. Waves are ubiquitous and so there is almost always an oscillation of some sort present in the sky to be revealed by clouds.

Mountain or Lee Waves

When moving air meets a mountain barrier, it first rises to cross the peaks and then sinks back on the lee side, forming an up-and-down ripple that may propagate for hundreds of miles downwind (Figure 4-4). The ripples are stationary, locked in place by their connection to the topography. The air flowing through the wave rises up and down to follow the crests and valleys, adopting different wavelengths and intensities according to the shape of the terrain, the speed and direction of the wind, the humidity, and the stability of the atmosphere.

The best-formed mountain waves are created when the air column is stable and where winds blow directly across the topographic bar-

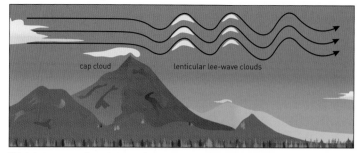

FIG. 4-4. *Lee waves form downwind of a topographic barrier. As air rises to the peak of the wave, adiabatic cooling causes moisture to condense and form clouds. On descent into the wave trough, the clouds dissipate, leaving a series of regularly spaced clouds to mark the position of the undulations. The lee waves may be in the form of lenticular clouds or longwave trains of altocumulus.*

rier at moderate to strong velocities (over 22 mph, 35 km/h), increasing slowly with altitude. Waves may have amplitudes that extend through most of the troposphere or be confined to a shallow layer that oscillates through a depth of several hundred feet. They may be as small as the width of a single mountain or extend for hundreds of miles downstream and parallel to the axis of a mountain range. The spacing from crest to crest depends on the strength of the airflow, with larger wavelengths associated with stronger winds. In Rocky Mountain and Appalachian flows, wavelengths typically range from 2 to 25 miles (3 to 40 km) and average around 8 miles (13 km). Because they form on the downwind side of mountain ranges, they are frequently called lee waves.

If moisture is present, the mountain wave becomes visible when air

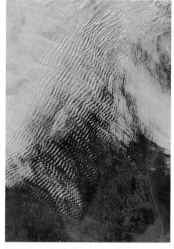

FIG. 4-5. *A field of wave clouds generated by flow over the Appalachian Mountains is captured in this* Terra *satellite image from December 27, 2012. On the left side of the image, the waves are embedded in, or on top of, a lower cloud layer, but on the Atlantic side of the mountains, the low cloud is blocked by the terrain and the waves stand out against the darker ground.*

FIG. 4-6. *These altocumulus billows (altostratus* undulatus*) have formed in the flow over the Chiricahua Mountains in eastern Arizona. Waves such as these are stable only if topped by a warmer layer or inversion above the cloud tops. The waves are oriented perpendicular to the wind at altitude.*

rising in the wave crest cools to saturation and forms a cloud. As the flow descends into the following trough, the air is warmed and the cloud dissipates (Figure 4-4). The rise and fall of the atmospheric wave then appears as a series of cloud lines, especially in satellite images, with each line marking the position of the crest (Figure 4-5). Because of their easy visibility over large distances, altocumulus and cirrocumulus clouds form the most obvious waves for ground observers (Figure 4-6).

In rare circumstances, the trough of a mountain wave can reach down to the surface, causing sudden, violent windstorms along the lee slopes that may last for only a few minutes. This phenomenon is occasionally visited on Boulder, Colorado, and the surrounding area, where brief wind speeds in excess of 100 mph (160 km/h) have been recorded. Lee waves also create turbulence that can be a hazard for aircraft, though glider pilots seek them out in order to climb to extremely high altitudes. On August 6, 2006, an unpowered glider rose to over 50,000 feet (15 km) over Argentina using the lift generated by large-amplitude lee waves.

Lenticular Clouds

Lenticular clouds are among the most beautiful clouds in the sky and can be found just about anywhere, wherever waves, moisture, and stability come together. The most spectacular examples are usually found above or slightly downstream of isolated mountain peaks, where they can build upward to resemble an otherworldly stack of lopsided pancakes and invite comparisons to UFOs (Figure 4-7). Mountain lenticulars don't move, forming continuously on the upwind side and dissipating on the downwind as air flows through the lee wave; for this reason, they are called standing lenticular clouds. Standing lenticulars can persist for hours until the upper flow changes or the humidity declines.

Lenticulars are identified by their smooth tops and their high degree of symmetry, standing out among ordinary instability and layer clouds (Figure 4-8). The name comes from their similarity to a lens, with smooth tops that arise because they are "pressed up" against the inversion that traps the gravity wave. There may be several in a stack or a single cloud of small dimension, usually in a sky that contains other lenticulars of similar shape. A form of cumulus cloud, they may be found at any level in the troposphere.

FIG. 4-7. *Airflow over the hills and mountains of the South Island of New Zealand has created these cone-shaped lenticular clouds. Though the formation's round appearance suggests rotation, the clouds are stationary. Air is flowing through the lenticular clouds from the right.*

FIG. 4-8. *A small line of standing (stationary) lenticular clouds marks the presence of a wave crest in this skyscape from western New Mexico.*

FIG. 4-9. *A small pileus or cap cloud forms atop a growing towering cumulus. The pileus persisted for only a half-minute before merging with the updraft rising from below.*

Away from mountains, lenticulars are created by thunderstorm outflows, the flow over small hills, and frontal systems—in fact, any place where gravity waves and stability combine with a supply of moisture. Because these lenticulars aren't attached to the terrain, they move with the wind, forming and dissipating as they drift across the land-

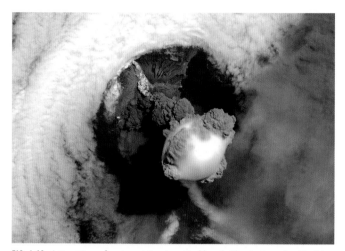

FIG. 4-10. *A towering volcanic eruption is capped by a brilliant pileus cloud in this view from the International Space Station. The dust from the eruption is just beginning to break through the cloud cap.*

scape. Lenticulars like company and usually occur in a group that may cover a significant part of the sky.

A somewhat unique form of a lenticular cloud is frequently seen at the top of growing thunderstorms and towering cumulus (Figure 4-9). They are called pileus (PIE-lee-us), from the Latin for "cap," and tend to have a translucent appearance because of their relative thinness and ice-crystal composition. Time-lapse movies of pileus show that they have short lifetimes, forming in the rising updraft and dissipating when the upward growth of the thunderstorm ceases. In unusual circumstances, a pileus can be much larger than the diameter of the thunderstorm over which it forms, but the usual dimension is much smaller than the top of the storm (Figure 4-10).

Undular Bores

An undular bore is a unique form of gravity wave caused when a wave disturbance is created in a low-level stable layer. The initial impetus can come from a variety of sources: a thunderstorm outflow, a cold front, or a sea-breeze circulation. As the disturbance moves through the cold, surface-based air, it initiates one or more waves. Under the right circumstances, only a single wave will form, traveling outward as a smooth-edged, rolling, horizontal cloud that seems to have no rational reason for existence (Figure 4-11).

The most famous of the undular bores is nicknamed the "Morning Glory," and is found in northern Australia along the southern shores of the Gulf of Carpentaria near the town of Burketown. These are truly the granddaddies of roll clouds, as they can be more than 60 miles (100 km) long, appearing as long tubes from a satellite or aircraft (Figure 4-12). The Morning Glory is typically 0.6 to 1.2 miles (1 to 2 km) in width and depth. Its overhead passage is usually marked by an abrupt wind squall and a small pressure jump. Sometimes there is only one roll; at other times, there may be as many as eight, moving at speeds up to 40 mph (65 km/h). Strong updrafts make them a favorite of glider pilots, who gather in northern Australia from September to mid-November to take advantage of the rolls.

Cap Clouds and Banner Clouds

Cap clouds are the "hats" that form over mountain peaks as the air is forced upward and lifted to saturation (Figure 4-13). They usually wrap over the peak, lower on the upwind side and higher on the downwind, so that it resembles a cape draped over the mountaintop. If the air is stable above the peak, cap clouds may take a lenticular form, trapped atop the peak instead of in the downwind wave train.

FIG. 4-11. *This approaching roll cloud marks the position of a single gravity wave propagating outward from thunderstorms in the distance.*

FIG. 4-12. *A Terra satellite image of a 16-wave undular bore over the Gulf of Mexico on March 15, 2008.*

FIG. 4-13. *A cap cloud hangs over a peak in the New Zealand Alps, created by the condensation of air flowing over the mountain peak. The weak circulation aloft allows the cloud in this example to have a ragged instead of smooth appearance.*

Banner clouds, on the other hand, form on the lee side of mountain flanks, where the air flows around the peak rather than over it. As the flow splits to go around the mountain, the spreading of the winds forms a low-pressure region that draws air upward from lower levels

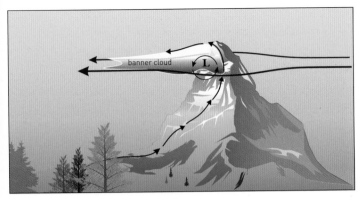

FIG. 4-14. *Banner clouds are formed in the lee of isolated mountain peaks when low-level air is drawn upward by pressure changes induced by splitting in the upper-level flow.*

along the downwind flank (Figure 4-14). The rising air condenses to form a cloud plume that blows downwind, gradually dissipating as it mixes with the surrounding atmosphere. While the plume often resembles snow blowing off the peak, the dynamical explanation is supported by time-lapse movies that show cloud tags flowing upward along the lee side of the slope before being caught in the high-level wind. In most cases of banner clouds, the mountain peak itself remains cloud free.

Banner clouds form most readily on the sides of steep pyramidal peaks that are relatively isolated from their neighbors. Of the world's mountains, Mount Everest and the Matterhorn are probably best known for their prominent banners (Figure 4-15).

Clouds Associated with Thunderstorms

Mammatus

Mammatus clouds (the name comes from the Latin for "having breasts") are an atmospheric enigma, largely benign in character and studied only sporadically by the meteorological community, but beautiful and occasionally ominous-looking to the casual observer. They appear as smooth-sided pouches hanging on the underside of a cloud, resembling a collection of cloudy udders. When illuminated in the glow of morning or evening light, they become one of the most attractive of clouds as attested by their many images on the internet.

Mammatus are most often spotted hanging under the anvil on

both the upwind and downwind side of a thunderstorm (Figure 4-16), though they can also be found beneath almost any type of cloud, including stratocumulus, altocumulus, and even cirrus. In a thunderstorm, they may be present as disorganized clumps covering a small part of the underside of the anvil or spread out over hundreds of miles. When mammatus are semitransparent, their edges can sometimes be seen to be curling upward, a visual clue that the air in the pouch is descending into drier air.

On average, mammatus clouds have a horizontal dimension of 0.4 to 1.8 miles (250 m to 3 km), and a vertical extent below the cloud base that ranges from 1,000 to 3,600 feet (300 to 1,100 m) with most around 1,600 feet (0.5 km). The typical lifetime of an individual pouch is on the order of 10 minutes, but large fields of mammatus may last for a few hours. In spite of their appearance, mammatus pouches are not necessarily a harbinger of severe weather, though they tend to be associated with stronger thunderstorms. Most often, the protuberances are seen as a storm is departing and any threat to the observer is over.

While many theories have been advanced to explain these unusual formations, none has yet received wide acceptance, and even the composition of mammatus—ice, water, or a mixture of the two—is open

FIG. 4-15. *A banner cloud attached to the downwind side of the Matterhorn. Nearly saturated low-level air is rising up the lee side (left) of the mountain in response to an upward pressure force created by the flow around the mountain peak.*

FIG. 4-16. *Mammatus clouds, hanging beneath the anvil of a departing thunderstorm, mark the passing of unstable weather and the return to quieter conditions.*

FIG. 4-17. *Evening shadows illuminate the pouches of mammatus clouds.*

to discussion. However, there are two characteristics that seem to be present in their environment: the presence of warm, dry air beneath cool, saturated clouds; and the conversion of ice crystals directly to water vapor that further cools the cloudy air and causes it to sink. In some studies, mammatus clouds are described as forming in a highly turbulent layer in the atmosphere, while other measurements place them in a quiet, light-wind environment. Temperature measurements from balloons sometimes show a stable temperature inversion below the cloud base, and at other times a very unstable lapse rate. Perhaps the single unifying characteristic of mammatus clouds is their unique and intriguing appearance (Figure 4-17).

The mysterious character of mammatus is not solved by flying through them, as this account from American meteorologist C. J. Hlad (1944) indicates:

> At 13,000 feet [3,962 m] we entered the actual mammatus cloud deck, although it didn't appear to be a cloud deck from a technical standpoint. There were vast openings where the visibilities were very good, below we could see trails of very heavy drops, yet there was no rain striking the plane. The turbulence was very light in these openings. Seeking an explanation, we went down to 12,000 feet [3,658 m] and passed under the rain trails. There was no rain striking the plane at this level either, although looking above us we could see the large drops. Next, we entered this "ball" of rain which appeared to be suspended in the air. Inside, the rain drops were very heavy and the turbulence was moderate to heavy. After flying under, over, and through several of these rain "balls," the conclusion was reached that they were the actual "sacks" that gave the cloud deck above its mammatus appearance. These rain "sacks" extended as much as 1,000 feet [305 m] downward from the main deck and yet no rain fell from any of those that we passed under.

Asperitas Clouds

Asperitas clouds (Figure 4-18) are the newest addition to the panoply of cloud types, receiving formal recognition by the World Meteorological Organization (WMO) in 2017. Asperitas are rare clouds, seen most often above the Great Plains of the United States in the company

FIG. 4-18. *Dramatic and somewhat ominous asperitas clouds flow across the Great Plains behind a departing line of showers and thundershowers.*

of thunderstorms, though that is not a necessary requirement. The name comes from the Latin *aspero,* meaning rough or uneven, but that barely begins to describe the appearance of these unusual formations.

Asperitas clouds were first identified from images submitted to the United Kingdom–based Cloud Appreciation Society, which provides an online forum for observers from around the world to submit their favorite cloud pictures. Among the many thousands submitted, a few were noticed to be an unusual and unrecognized type, and a campaign was begun to acquire official recognition of the new form from the WMO. The flowing waves on the underside of clouds will be what first catches your attention when asperitas is present, but their movement is best captured in time-lapse photos, as it is not particularly obvious to the eye. They tend to be smooth-bottomed, and often have a menacing appearance though they're not associated with severe weather. They may be related in some form to mammatus clouds, but that kinship is also uncertain.

Asperitas forms in an unstable atmospheric region that lies above a surface-based stable layer. Turbulence in the higher layer creates waves that move along the cloud base, giving it some of the personality of stratiform clouds. Observations and modeling experiments suggest that the cloud forms below the freezing level and so is composed of water droplets. Wind shear, convection, gravity waves, and mountain waves may be involved, but as yet the true character of asperitas has not been deciphered.

Shelf Clouds

It is an unsettled summer day. The Sun is shining for now, but in the west, dark clouds punctuated by a faintly audible lightning display promise a change to thunderstorms and wet weather. As the clouds approach, ominous, gloomy skies promise a heavy dump of rain, and thoughts of severe weather and running for cover enter the mind.

A long line of spreading, low-based clouds intrudes on your consciousness—a strange-looking horizontal cloud that resembles a step or series of steps flowing across the landscape, just in advance of the approaching storms. It's a fast-moving cloud line that forms a broad arc from south to north, smoother on the top than on the bottom, and built up in a series of layers parallel to the ground. The lowest layer is the most ragged, a little in front of the rest, and slightly chisel-shaped, skimming through the atmosphere several hundred feet above the surface (Figure 4-19). Within minutes, the line of cloud moves overhead, darkening the sky. A ripple of air disturbs the fields across the road, and then the squall hits. A shelf cloud has arrived, and along with it, a cool, often-damaging wind.

FIG. 4-19. *Outflow or shelf clouds form along the leading edge of a thunderstorm gust front when rain-cooled air spreading outward from the storm lifts the surrounding warm and moist air up and over the cold outflow.*

FIG. 4-20. *In this diagram, shelf clouds form above a cold outflow (blue arrows), where the warm and humid environmental air (yellow arrow) is lifted above the denser surface flow. As the outflow advances, the shelf cloud may become detached from the thunderstorm and change into a roll cloud. The depth and form of shelf and roll clouds is usually a reflection of the strength of the outflow wind.*

Precipitating convective clouds almost always produce a cold outflow wind in the middle age of their life cycle. The winds are formed by the descent of rain- and evaporation-cooled air that spreads outward beneath the parent cloud as it reaches the ground (Figure 4-20). In weaker storms, the outflow is a gentle zephyr, welcomed as a temporary cool breeze on a hot and humid day, but in bigger storms, the outflow is much more assertive, spreading across the landscape in advance of the storm in a "take-note" blast of wind. As the cold, high-density winds move out from the storm, they lift the moist air ahead, carrying it upward to saturation and turning it into the characteristic shape of a shelf cloud. The upward flow is made obvious by ragged stratus cloud tags on the leading edges that trace out the rapid motion of the rising air.

Outflow winds eventually decay away as the associated shelf cloud becomes ragged and fragmented. Even in that dissipating stage, the shelf tends to be relatively easy to identify, mostly from its linear form and its association with a dying storm. The line will eventually slow, break into parts, and finally come to a halt, dissipating into small stratus clouds of indeterminate origin.

Wall Clouds

A wall cloud is a large, circular, and sometimes rotating appendage that hangs beneath a severe supercell thunderstorm in the rain-free area toward the back of the storm (Figure 4-21). This usually distinctive cloud marks the low-level position of the core of the cumulonimbus where the primary updraft is entering into the storm. Wall clouds are formed from the ingestion and condensation of moist, rain-cooled air that comes from the precipitation area on the front side of the storm. Rotating wall clouds are dear to the heart of storm chasers, as they indicate that the environment is rich in rotation, a necessary condition for the formation of the biggest and strongest tornadoes. Most strong tornadoes form beneath or in close proximity to a wall cloud.

Wall clouds range in width from about 800 feet to 5 miles (250 m to 8 km), typically with ragged edges and bases. In the most intense storms, the wall cloud may almost touch the surface as it moves across the landscape with the thunderstorm (Chapter 9). When moisture is abundant in the boundary layer, low-level cloud fragments can often be seen moving toward and joining the wall cloud. These tags curl around the outer rim of the wall cloud before merging and then rising into the core of the storm. In other circumstances, the wall cloud

FIG. 4-21. *It looks ominous, and it is. This wall cloud marks the inflow region of a severe thunderstorm, a location that often forms tornadoes. Air flowing into the storm from the right, marked by a stubby tail cloud, is turning sharply upward to feed the growing thunderstorm with moisture and heat. A collar cloud circles the top of the wall cloud.*

forms simply by a lowering of a portion of the storm base, usually on the south or southwest side of the thunderstorm. The wall cloud itself often slopes downward toward the ground in the direction of the heavy precipitation at the front flank of the storm.

Tail Clouds and Beaver Tails

Tail clouds and beaver tails are types of cloud bands that mark the inflow of air into the updraft of a severe thunderstorm. While both are well known to experienced storm chasers, the distinction between the two is a bit arcane. The visibility of these inflow bands will depend on the storm's distance and the direction from which you are viewing it.

A tail cloud is a horizontal, linear cloud that merges into the wall cloud beneath a severe thunderstorm. This interaction is a diagnostic feature, as other inflow bands intercept the main body of the storm at a level above the wall cloud. With enough time to watch from a safe location, the tail cloud can sometimes be observed flowing toward the wall cloud and wrapping around it as it gets caught up in the storm's rotation. In Figure 4-21, the tail cloud appears as a pointed projection to the lower right of the wall cloud. Typically (and in this example) the tail cloud points slightly downward in a direction toward the heavy precipitation area ahead of the storm. Tail clouds come in many shapes and sizes, often forming and dissipating in the life cycle of a severe storm as the strength of the updraft changes.

Beaver tails (or beaver's tail) is storm chaser slang for a different form of inflow cloud band—one with a broad, flat appearance, though it takes some imagination to make the connection between the cloud's shape and a real beaver tail (Figure 4-22). In contrast to the wall cloud, the beaver tail merges with the body of the storm at the level of the storm's base. It forms along the boundary between the rain-cooled air in the front of the thunderstorm and the warm, moist inflow from the storm's right side.

Kelvin-Helmholtz Billows

The atmosphere has a love affair with waves, continuously forming and dissolving a host of vertical undulations at all scales whenever air is set into motion. Most of these clouds are formed from gravity waves, but there is one unique form that is driven by a different mechanism: the Kelvin-Helmholtz (K-H) shearing instability, named for Lord Kelvin and Hermann von Helmholtz, who studied the properties of wave

FIG. 4-22. *A pointed "beaver tail" cloud moves toward the updraft in this view from beneath a developing severe thunderstorm.*

FIG. 4-23. *Kelvin-Helmholtz instability clouds east of the Continental Divide near Fort Collins, Colorado.*

disturbances in fluids of different density. A shearing instability occurs when sharp changes in wind speed across a layer in the atmosphere generate turbulence that forms a wave. On the ocean, its counterpart is simply the wind blowing across the water that creates waves.

A Kelvin-Helmholtz wave is easy to recognize, for it looks like a classical breaking ocean wave, evenly spaced, across the top of a band of cloud (Figure 4-23). If you are lucky, once in a while when all of the parameters align, you may be treated to a rare view of this most perfect of wave clouds. K-H waves form when the wind speed at the top of the cloud is stronger than the wind within the cloud. They can be formed at any layer, from surface-based fogs up to cirrus level. K-H instability may be found in the vicinity of jet streams or along a warm front, usually displayed in short segments that fade away rapidly, a measure of the energy-dissipating efficiency of turbulence. Kelvin-Helmholtz instabilities are thought to be responsible for much of the clear-air turbulence experienced by aircraft, especially when no visible clouds warn of the presence of the shear.

Virga

Virga is precipitation that evaporates before it reaches the ground. Perhaps it doesn't belong in a chapter on clouds, but virga can form very attractive and strange-looking shapes. You have probably noticed it under convective clouds, where the first descending rain showers appear silhouetted against the sky for a few moments before reaching the ground. In small developing thunderstorms and towering cumulus, virga is the first sign that downdrafts are beginning in the storm and that the storm will soon begin to weaken.

Sometimes virga develops in surprising places, such as from tiny pieces of cirrocumulus (Figure 4-24) that don't seem deep enough and thick enough to maintain their own existence, much less produce ice- and snow-crystal precipitation. The hooked cirrus tufts known as mares' tails are formed when a high-speed wind captures ice particles falling from a higher cloud and stretches them out into long hairlike filaments. Such cirrus is often a sign of an approaching warm front with more substantial precipitation to follow.

Virga falling from altocumulus or cirrocumulus usually adopts a curved shape as it falls through the atmosphere. This may be due to changes in wind speed in the atmosphere below the parent clouds, or to the gradually declining size of the raindrops or snow crystals as they evaporate, which eventually stops their fall and leaves them drifting in the winds.

Precipitation falling from higher levels into a lower cloud deck will often "seed" a lower layer by supplying it with ice nuclei around which

FIG. 4-24. *Two small altocumulus clouds mark their presence in the sky with a streak of ice-crystal virga that evaporates after falling about half the distance to the ground. The curve traced by the falling ice crystals shows that evaporation is relatively slow below the cloud base, but increases rapidly in the lower part of the streak where the virga curves to the left.*

droplets can collect and build into larger raindrops or snowflakes. In particular, ice particles from the anvil of a thunderstorm can "seed" smaller developing convective clouds, providing them with a supply of nucleation particles for their own condensation and growth.

Fallstreak Holes or Hole-Punch Clouds

Fallstreak holes have been called "crop circles in the sky" in recognition of their shape and rarity, but their cause has a mundane explanation. These "hole-punch clouds" are created in mid- and high-level clouds that contain supercooled water droplets. If some of the water droplets can be induced to freeze, the newly formed ice nuclei will initiate a cascade of freezing within the cloud body as each new crystal provides a condensation nucleus on which the remaining water droplets can gather and solidify. As the number of ice crystals grows, they scavenge water droplets from the cloud, leaving a hole centered on the site of the original disturbance (Figure 4-25).

Once initiated, the ice crystals grow by the Bergeron-Findeisen process inside the cloud until they are large enough to fall (Chapter 2).

FIG. 4-25. *A fallstreak hole with ice-crystal virga, caught near Salem, Oregon.*

This gives the hole-punch cloud its second distinguishing characteristic: a funnel-shaped streak of ice-crystal virga centered in the middle of the hole and tapering to a point some distance below.

For more than half a century, meteorologists have suspected that aircraft played a role in creating fallstreak holes, but this was not confirmed until 2007, when a series of openings appeared in clouds over Colorado at the same time that a C-130 Hercules aircraft, instrumented to study cloud ice particles, was in the area. As the aircraft flew below the hole, onboard radar detected an unusual vertical precipitation band stretching to the ground that was associated with a gap in the solid altocumulus cloud cover. Later investigation revealed that two turboprop aircraft had flown along the path a little earlier, on a heading that would have taken them through the hole.

The fast-moving tips of propellers on an aircraft create an area of rapid expansion and cooling that likely causes the supercooled water droplets to freeze into ice particles. Data collected by instruments aboard the aircraft showed that the parent cloud was composed of water droplets, but the ice particles falling from the cloud were composed of ice and were heavily rimed—coated with frozen water droplets—a sign that supercooled droplets had frozen suddenly on a suitable nucleus.

Fallstreak holes are also thought to originate when virga from a higher-level cloud falls on a lower layer, providing ice nuclei to accelerate the precipitation process. The latent heat released during the freezing process also plays a role in drying and opening the cloud deck when fallstreaks are forming.

Contrails

Contrails (a contraction of "condensation trails") are a familiar part of our world—linear ice clouds stretching out behind high-flying aircraft when conditions in the upper atmosphere are favorable (Figure 4-26). After their formation, a short distance behind the aircraft engine, they may grow in width and length, or dissipate quickly, leaving only a short streak to briefly mark their passage. Contrails form when temperatures at flight level are –40°F (–40°C) or colder. At those temperatures, the atmosphere can hold very little water vapor and is often close to being supersaturated from the little moisture that is available. Even when the high-altitude air is saturated, the vapor can't condense into ice-crystal clouds because of a shortage of nucleating particles on which to freeze.

Contrails can form when the blend of hot, moist exhaust gases and cold, dry ambient air results in a supersaturated mixture at an intermediate temperature. Soot particles emitted in the exhaust along with

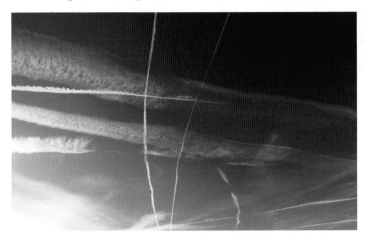

FIG. 4-26. *New and old cloud threads crisscross the sky in this image of spreading, long-duration contrails. High humidity at flight level allows the contrails to maintain their presence for an extended period of time.*

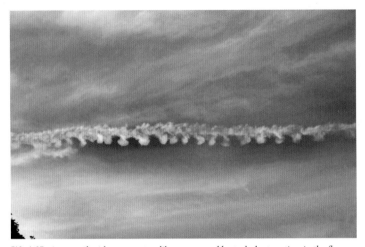

FIG. 4-27. *A contrail with mammatus-like sacs caused by turbulent vortices in the flow behind an aircraft.*

condensation nuclei already present in the atmosphere provide a condensation surface on which the supersaturated air can collect, forming water droplets that quickly turn to ice. The process is very similar to the icy cloud that your warm breath forms on a cold winter day.

Contrails are usually pretty ordinary cloud lines, but the dedicated cloud observer will take considerable interest in some of the odd shapes that occasionally present themselves. If the atmosphere at flight level has a high relative humidity to begin with, contrails may persist for a considerable time, or even spread out across the sky, joining with other contrails to form a thin overcast. If contrails get gradually longer during the day, it is a sign that humidity is rising and an increase in cloudiness is likely to follow—a useful relationship for amateur astronomers who are trying to decide whether the night will be clear. One common form has a shape that evokes memories of mammatus (Figure 4-27).

The shape and evolution of contrails are also dictated by the wind speed and wind shear aloft, with additional twists and turns introduced by the vortices that form behind the aircraft. One of the more interesting and rarer forms is a contrail that evolves from narrow wavy cloud lines into sinusoidal shapes that merge and form a series of high-altitude cloud "smoke rings," a phenomenon known as Crow instability.

Satellite Images of Unusual Clouds

Von Kármán Vortices

The next time you have an opportunity to watch water flow in a shallow stream, take note of the whirlpools that curl behind a stone that is embedded in the current. As each whirlpool is formed, it is caught up by the passing current and whisked away, only to have another form in its place. A chain of small whirlpools stretches away downstream from the stone, each circulation gradually dissipating as it travels, but always replaced by another.

In regions with an extensive sheet of marine stratus, the flow of the wind is made apparent by a similar chain of vortices stretching downwind in the flow. These cloud vortices (and the water ones) are von Kármán vortices, named after Theodore von Kármán (1881–1963), the Hungarian-born American engineer and scientist who first described them. In the case of our atmospheric whirlpools, the "rock" in the stream is usually a small, flat island. The disturbance flows downwind in a series of paired spirals, turning in opposite directions, one after the other (Figure 4-28). Such vortices are common in satellite images, especially in mid-latitudes and polar regions, where extensive stratus and stratocumulus clouds are available to trace out the twisting of the winds.

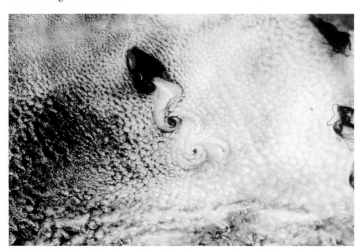

FIG. 4-28. *MODIS satellite image of von Kármán vortices downwind from Guadalupe Island, west of Baja, Mexico.*

Ship Trails

When the first satellite pictures appeared on the desktops of operational meteorologists in the 1970s, nearly every image revealed some new mystery to decipher. One of the strangest of the mysteries was the appearance of long curving lines of clouds that crisscrossed the centers of high-pressure systems off the west coast of North America like a giant game of tic-tac-toe (Figure 4-29). The lines often persisted for days, drifting slowly with the low-level winds. Infrared images showed that the cloud lines were relatively warm and so located only a small distance above the surface.

Initial speculation about the tracks was that they had to be man-made, as their linearity could not be explained by any meteorological theory. Because they were at such low levels in the atmosphere, the most rational explanation was that they had to be a consequence of ship movement. In short order thereafter, individual tracks were correlated with the movement of individual vessels. In effect, the lines are the marine equivalent of the contrails left by aircraft. What was left to explain was why they formed.

Ship trails form in clean atmospheres (typically of Arctic origin) beneath a strong inversion, usually in the midst of thin broken or scattered stratocumulus clouds—conditions often found beneath large, oceanic, high-pressure systems. The natural clouds have scavenged

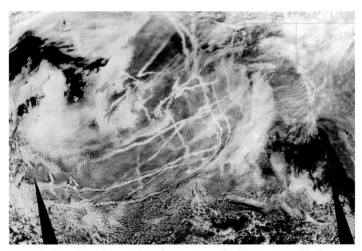

FIG. 4-29. *Ship trails in the central Pacific Ocean west of California captured by the* MODIS *imager on board the* Aqua *satellite on February 12, 2012.*

FIG. 4-30. *A cold Arctic outbreak cloaks the Great Lakes in streamers of cloud on February 7, 2011. The dry, cold airmass acquires moisture during its trajectory over the warmer water. The cloud lines curve to follow the wind direction. Heavy snow is falling beneath the streamers where they reach the lee shore, especially where higher terrain along the shore provides additional lift to the air stream.*

most of the cloud condensation nuclei (Chapter 2) and so the moisture contained within the airmass is doomed to remain in vapor form until a suitable substrate can be found. Ship exhaust provides a source of sulfur dioxide aerosols and other condensation nuclei, which quickly promote the growth of new clouds along the track of the vessel. In satellite photos, ship-trail clouds are brighter than the surrounding natural clouds, because the generous supply of condensation particles leads to the formation of smaller but brighter cloud droplets within the exhaust plume. The trails are found more often along the west coast of a continent, logically because the east sides already have a ready supply of condensation nuclei of continental origin.

Cloud Streets and Streamers

Blow frigid air across open water and the result will be long strings of small convective clouds that line up approximately along the wind direction, gradually widening as their overwater trajectory lengthens (Figure 4-30). Such cloud lines, or cloud streets, are common in the winter season when lakes are unfrozen or when continental Arctic

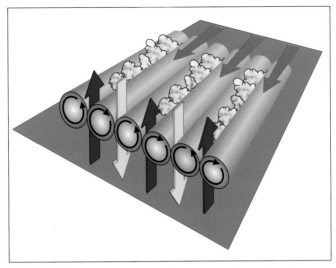

FIG. 4-31. *Cloud streets form in cold air above a warm surface, usually under an inversion where winds are relatively constant. In such circumstances, lines of parallel, oppositely rotating longitudinal rolls organize to shape the convection into long lines of cloud divided by clear skies. For each roll, air will be moving upward on one side and downward on the other, reinforced by interactions with the neighboring roll. Individual cloud streets form along the rising portion of the rolls while cloud-free skies develop in the sinking air. The separation of the cloud streets is about two to three times the depth of the inversion.*

air blows out to sea. There is little pleasant that can be said about cloud streets, as they come with biting winds, Arctic temperatures, heavy snowfalls or icy drizzle, and, for sailors, the risk of dangerous icing on a ship's superstructure. They do, however, produce interesting satellite images.

The combination of strong winds, cold air, lake moisture, and underlying instability causes the low-level circulation to form a series of side-by-side rotating vortex "tubes" of wind. Adjacent vortex tubes turn in opposite directions, so that between them, on one side, the air is compelled to rise, while on the other it sinks downward (Figure 4-31). Vigorous cumulus clouds form on the rising air side and dissipate on the descending side, forming long lines of convection that outline the flow of the wind.

Cold-air outbreaks over the oceans on the east sides of continents make especially prominent cloud lines, but the biggest impact to humans comes on land, where the flow over open lakes in winter brings the legendary "lake-effect" snowstorm. Any open lake is capable of producing downwind snowstorms in cold Arctic air, at least until the lake freezes, but the best streamers come when the wind is oriented along the long axis of the lake so that there is a significant overwater trajectory before the streamer reaches land again on the opposite windward shore. For pure ornery winter weather, there are few lakes that can hold a candle to the Great Lakes of North America. Northerly Arctic blasts bring heavy snowfalls to the south shore of Lakes Superior and Huron, while westerly winds that blow along the axis of Lake Erie can bury Buffalo, New York, in several feet of drifted snow. Even diminutive Lake Winnipeg, in the center of the continent, has its fall season of annoying lake streamers until freeze-up brings an end to the process.

Not the Last Word on Clouds

Mother Nature paints her skies with wonderful cloudscapes. The clouds may be impaled on the topography, bounce rhythmically against an invisible inversion ceiling, bubble up to tropopause heights, spread across the plains in a great gust of wind, or hang ponderously from the underside of thunderstorm anvils. Each formation has a story to tell, of physics, chemistry, stability, humidity, and other natural processes. For many, the final explanation is still waiting.

We've covered only a few of the intriguing formations that perform on the sky's stage; there are hundreds more for you to discover, as clouds are the symptoms of the atmosphere's daily personality. Keep an eye on the sky and carry a camera or use your smartphone. Every cloud has a secret to reveal.

Outflow shelf clouds come in many shapes and sizes, but this example is especially dramatic in the fading evening light. Winds were relatively sedate in the spreading outflow, coming from heavy thunderstorms out of the photo to the right. The air was very moist and so able to form this stately, long-lived cloud with its multiple layers in spite of the modest outflow speed.

In a thunderstorm, air is gathered from the surrounding environment and turned into the storm's updraft. For stronger storms and especially for supercell thunderstorms, the updraft region is marked by a cylindrical lowering in the cloud base such as this, known as a wall cloud. The wall cloud forms beneath the storm base when rain-cooled air in the updraft condenses, usually only a short distance above the surface. If the wall cloud is rotating, it is a sign that the parent thunderstorm is a supercell, and a tornado may be imminent.

Mountains are marvelous cloud makers and shapers, as they deflect the wind or cause the air to ascend and descend. In this image, cap clouds provide a morning shroud over two peaks in Bora Bora in French Polynesia. The cap cloud on the left forms on the broad shoulders of the mountain rather than on its sharp-pointed peak. Both of these clouds dissipated a few minutes after the photo was taken as the rising Sun warmed and dried the atmosphere.

Mammatus (from the Latin for "having breasts") is most spectacular at sunset when the orange glow of the Sun strikes the hanging cloud pouches at an oblique angle. While usually associated with cumulonimbus anvils, mammatus clouds can also be found less frequently on the underside of many other cloud types. The striking appearance and smooth edges make them one of the most noted cloud formations. Mammatus clouds may persist for a considerable amount of time if the precipitation particles are large or the cloud water content is very high.

An unusual form of mammatus ahead of an approaching line of multicell thunderstorms. The pouches have formed from a thick anvil cloud that is visible above the lobes and has its own cellular patterns.

Blowing sand, dust, and dirt are important components of the world's weather. Dust and sand from the Sahara blows regularly into the equatorial Atlantic, where some hypotheses suggest that it may reduce the frequency of hurricanes, even though other factors may be favorable. This image shows a short-lived Egyptian sandstorm west of El Alamein in 2005 that formed on winds that reached about 40 mph. Such storms were used tactically to launch and hide infantry attacks during World War II.

When the Sun is high, smoke usually forms a hazy obscuring layer in the atmosphere that shows little structure. However, as twilight develops, layers and waves may become prominent, such as those seen in this image taken over Oregon in 2013, when forest fires were particularly heavy. Smoke aloft can usually be identified by the pink color that it imparts to the Sun or by the soft-sided and lacy pattern that it adopts.

The dynamic environment of thunderstorm outflows is mirrored in the great variety of cloud shapes they are able to produce, such as these lenticular and roll clouds. These clouds have formed just beneath the top of the cool surface air, confined to lower levels by the temperature inversion above the outflow.

Dust devils are frequent events in the American Southwest and many other places in the world, usually persisting for only a minute or so before dissipating. Usually harmless, they can become big enough to lift small objects and cause minor damage to structures. Dust devils range in size from a few feet to more than 35 feet (10 m) and can reach heights of 1½ miles (2,414 m) in the strongest cases. They are formed when the air near the surface acquires a spin, often in the turbulence as it flows past a small bush or other obstruction. The spinning sun-warmed air rises, stretches, and builds upward. Surrounding hot air spirals in toward the spinning tube, carrying dust and sand to make it visible. When the supply of warm air is exhausted, the devil collapses rapidly.

It looks like an ordinary fog bank, but it's actually a late-afternoon roll cloud moving across this South Dakota landscape, over hills and above the ground, without dissipating. Such clouds are an atmospheric version of a soliton—a single wave that keeps its shape while moving at a constant speed. This cloud was a few hundred feet wide, and rolled over the photographer a few minutes later.

This onrushing shelf cloud forms at the leading edge of a cold outflow generated by the heavy rain in the background. A few moments after this image was taken, winds surged to over 40 mph (65 km/h), followed quickly by a driving rain. In the right background, tendrils of dark stratus are lined up to mark the inflow winds feeding the storm.

Dramatic lenticular cap clouds have formed above the growing convective turrets in the feeder line alongside a large, severe thunderstorm.

A twisting funnel cloud emerges from the trailing side of a thunderstorm. A funnel cloud becomes a tornado when it begins to raise dust and debris on the ground, even though it may not be visible all the way to the surface. This funnel cloud, though rotating rapidly, dissipated after two or three minutes and never touched the surface.

Diaphanous cirrus-level Kelvin-Helmholtz billow clouds advertise the presence of wind shear in the upper-level atmosphere.

Even humble cumulus clouds can develop an enigmatic pileus cap if atmospheric conditions are right.

This rope cloud signals the end of a tornado as the rotating funnel withdraws into the clouds. Rope clouds often adopt contorted shapes as the rotation declines.

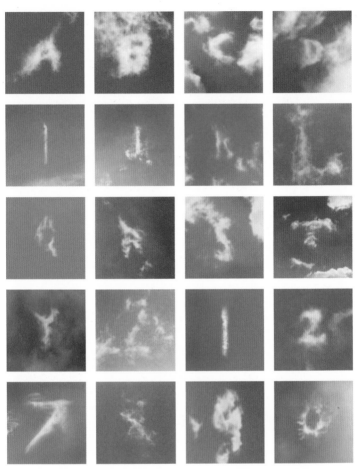

A cloud keyboard: alphabet, numbers, and punctuation by Susan Eder and Craig Dennis. The unusual nature of some clouds is derived from chance rather than from physical processes.

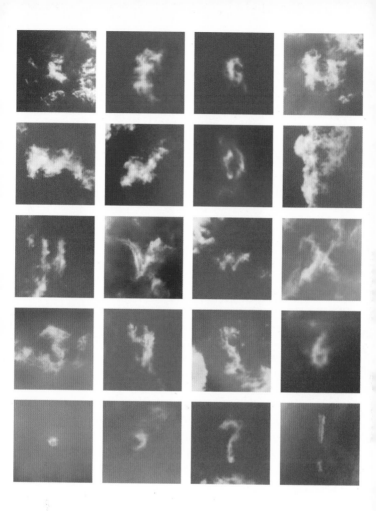

CHAPTER 5

A VIEW FROM THE AIR

Clouds are just as fascinating from the air as from the ground, but the high-altitude perspective presents the atmosphere and its processes in a fresh light, if for no other reason than that the observer's area of view is so much larger. Cloud-making processes that are difficult to fathom from the ground are often clearer from above.

Successful cloud watching from an aircraft requires a little advance planning. Which flight, which seat, which side of the aircraft, what time of day: all are important in getting the best views and photographs. The choice seats are undoubtedly those several rows ahead of the wing, where the view to the ground is unimpeded. Second choice would be those behind the wing, but at that location, the exhaust from the engines introduces distortion into the line of sight and spoils the view a little bit. If rear-cabin seats are unavoidable, sit well to the rear where the exhaust has smoothed out somewhat.

Ground views are best when the Sun is behind the observer, but cloud views may benefit from either side. Optical treats such as a sub-sun are seen only on the sunward side of the aircraft, but glories are visible only from the shadowed side. If the flight takes place in the evening, the setting Sun may display a marvelous set of crepuscular rays, but the opposite side may show equally impressive but less common anti-crepuscular shadows. You could be lucky, traveling on a flight with an empty row of seats on the opposite side, but that is a rare occurrence indeed. For the most part, you will have to accept your fate, but the best approach is just to take time to look.

Time of day is important, if you have the luxury of choosing. Morning, evening, midday—all have their attractions, though a low Sun has more color appeal. A night flight with a bright Moon can present nearly the same opportunity as a daylight Sun, but camera exposures will have to be longer. If there is no Moon, there is an opportunity to watch for aurorae on high-latitude flights, provided you are on the north side of the aircraft. Aurorae viewed from aloft give an incredible feeling of being embedded in the dancing lights.

Photography from the cabin involves some special adaptations. One of the bigger problems, especially at night, is reflection from the window glass. To overcome this, press the camera lens against the glass and surround the lens with a towel or blanket to subdue the intruding light. Dirty windows are usually cleaner toward the corners and edges, though the framing of the photo might be compromised. Because the atmosphere absorbs blue light, scenes of the ground often look washed out. Professional aerial photography uses red filters to map the ground and get past the problem of blue-light absorption, but this is not an option for most photographers unless they are fortunate to own one of the very few camera models that have an extended red sensitivity or an infrared capability. Blue-light absorption is not a critical factor for cloud photography, however, unless the clouds are low against the ground.

In the daytime, sunlight striking the window will scatter across the scene, reducing contrast and ruining any photos that you might try. Sometimes, however, the window is only partly in the sunlight and photos can be taken without glare by crowding into the part of the window that is in shadow. Zooming out a bit will help. If the window is a bit grubby, try cleaning with a little water and a page from a newspaper (or the airline magazine).

Wide-angle lenses fit best with the rapid passage of scenery in a typical flight as there are few circumstances in which a telephoto is required, though distant cloudscapes may be helped by a little magnification. Don't be reluctant to put a bit of wing into the scene, as it gives a sense of scale and perspective. For night scenes, exposures can be relatively long, up to a minute for an aurora if the plane is flying on a steady course. Ground detail will be smudged, but the aurora, many hundreds of miles distant, will reproduce with considerable detail. Noctilucent clouds are always a treat from the air and will photograph as easily as the aurora.

Thunderstorms are probably the most appealing clouds to photograph from the air, particularly if you are at cloud-top level and close by. Perhaps fortunately, pilots are reluctant to fly close to thunderstorms, so the opportunity to catch a pileus cloud directly out the window may come only once in a lifetime. Instead, flights under the anvil, above a lenticular cloud, through a field of stratocumulus, or above a fog bank will have to do, but all can have a great appeal, especially under low-light angles that enhance cloud textures. Clouds from aircraft are a "target of opportunity," so the best approach is to always be prepared.

A sun-lit wall of towering cumulus clouds marks the back edge of a cold front, moving to the east (left) across the Great Plains.

A classic example of a thunderstorm's growing updraft, with its cauliflower sides and tops that are just beginning to glaciate (turn to ice). A gray mid-level collar cloud is visible under the aircraft wing; such collars are formed where the airflow is forced to divert around the convective turret.

Clouds, especially convective clouds, take on a three-dimensional character when seen from aloft. In this view, the cumulus clouds are growing in an atmosphere with a modest amount of instability, as seen in the soft edges of the top and sides of the individual turrets. The edges of the cloud on the right are mixing or "entraining" with the surrounding environmental air. Entrainment brings drier air into the main mass of the cloud, evaporating the cloud droplets and robbing the growing cell of heat as the water droplets and ice particles are returned to the vapor state. Rising air columns must be balanced by descending air in order to preserve the mass balance of the atmosphere. The "valleys" in this cloud field are regions around the edges of the larger cells where the air is sinking, warming the air column and suppressing the growth of convection on the perimeter of the main cloud masses.

A dark anvil cloud from a distant thunderstorm blankets the sky above, while dying cumulus clouds below provide an epitaph for the day in this late afternoon scene. Anvil clouds are formed from the moisture carried upward and deposited under the tropopause by strong thunderstorms. In the distance, sunlight still illuminates the thunderstorm tops.

The golden evening Sun illuminates layers of altocumulus and stratocumulus clouds. Because of the Sun's angle, the higher clouds are in shadow and have bluer tones while the low clouds take on a golden hue. The size and character of the cloud elements is similar in the two levels, but from the ground, the higher cloud level would appear to be composed of smaller cumulus heaps. The smoother clouds at the upper level reveal a small-amplitude wave flowing through the cloud field.

A field of stratocumulus clouds have formed in a moist, slightly unstable airmass in response to a gentle upward lift forced by large-scale air motions. A temperature inversion at the cloud tops restrains their upward growth. Stratocumulus clouds are common in the cool flow behind cold fronts in the fall season, when the ground is still relatively warm. These clouds have a quasi-linear arrangement oriented at right angles to the flow.

Cumulus cloud "streets" or lines form within the lowest 1 to 2 miles (1.6 to 3 km) of the atmosphere when winds are approximately constant with height and the boundary layer is topped by an inversion. The streets are oriented roughly along the wind with a separation that is two or three times their height aboveground. The individual cells tend to grow in size with distance downwind along the cloud line.

An aircraft passing below the photographer casts a dark contrail against the underlying clouds. The photographer's vantage point reveals both the vertical and horizontal deflections of the contrail. The contrail is dark because the low Sun is illuminating its underside.

The hard tops of this towering cumulus tell of a storm that is still building upward, driven by heat extracted from the conversion of water vapor to droplets and droplets to ice. The rising column of air is composed of numerous smaller updrafts, seen here as individual cauliflower bumps in the main mass of cloud.

Beneath a gray cirrostratus ceiling, a small cirrocumulus cloud dissipates into ice crystals that evaporate after falling a short distance. Cirrocumulus clouds do not achieve a great depth, as the air aloft contains too little moisture to provide a large latent heat release. In the background, lower cumulus and towering cumulus clouds tell of a more unstable and humid airmass that, nevertheless, is about to dissipate as solar heating fades away with the sunset.

A sunny day over the Altai Mountains between China and Russia reveals striated glaciers in the valleys and a cap of cumulus clouds over the higher peaks. The clouds form over the peaks from air that rises along the heated slopes. The clear skies above the valleys are promoted by air descending in the middle of the valley to replace that drawn upslope.

A low Sun reveals several scales of waves generated by the flow over elevated terrain. In the foreground, smooth-topped stratus formed in the flow over a mountain ridge evolves into a short-wavelength corrugation on the downward side of the flow. In the middle distance, longwave ripples spread downwind in two directions—toward the upper left and lower left—in a more complex interaction between wind and terrain. Cumulus clouds, building from below, break up the wave pattern though some traces of the wave are visible for several wavelengths into the cumulus field.

A field of cumulus clouds decorates the land but avoids the cooler ocean surfaces in this image from Papua New Guinea. Clear skies above indicate the presence of a high-pressure system with dry, descending air throughout the region. The subsiding air creates a temperature inversion at cloud-top level, causing the cumulus buildups to have a sharp upper limit. The clouds are nearly vertical because of the small amount of wind shear.

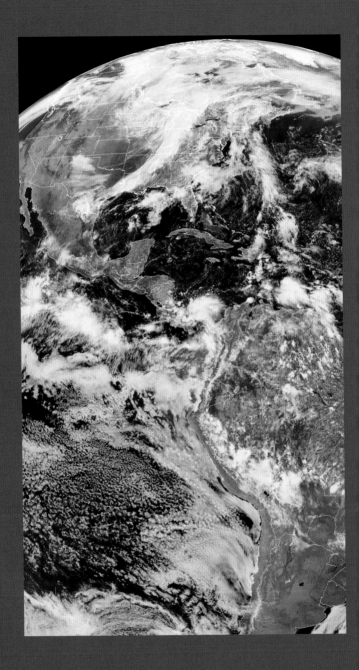

CHAPTER 6

WEATHER SATELLITES

Satellite pictures of the Earth's clouds and surface are omnipresent in our modern media world. Every television weather broadcast serves up a standard menu of images, almost always animated and usually strangely colored. Explanations of events are usually cursory in the limited time allotted for the weather report, and the images swirl past so quickly that fine details leave us with only vague impressions.

Explore weather satellite offerings on the internet, however, and a rich panoply of wavelengths, scenes, and science will spread out across your viewing screen. Thunderstorms will burst upward; wind-driven cloud lines will rush across the landscape; large, synoptic-scale storms will twist in complex circulations; and the weather outside will take on a new dimension, revealed as a small part of a much-larger circulation. This view of the world was almost impossible until the 1970s, and in the half-century since, the science of meteorology has evolved in accuracy and precision as the information from those scenes was incorporated into mental and numerical models. It would be fair to say that you cannot completely understand the view outside your window until you've seen it from space.

Weather satellites come in two flavors—those that pass overhead in low orbits, transmitting images of the scene below, and those that orbit over one spot high above the Earth, sending images of the entire globe to ground stations (Figure 6-1). Each has played a major role in understanding the way our weather works.

OPPOSITE. GOES-16 *is a geostationary satellite positioned to observe North and South America from an altitude of 22,236 miles (35,786 km) over the equator. At that altitude, its 24-hour orbit keeps it above the same point on the Earth.*

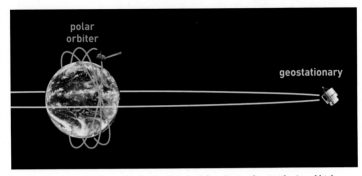

FIG. 6-1. *Weather satellites orbit the Earth in both low (510 miles; 820 km) and high (22,230 miles; 35,780 km) orbits, each with its own advantages and disadvantages. Polar-orbiting Operational Environmental Satellites (POES) occupy the low-orbit position, covering the planet on a path that passes over the poles. The higher geostationary satellites have an orbital period of 24 hours, which allows them to maintain a fixed position above the equator over the rotating Earth.*

History

The history of weather observations from orbit is as much a story of technology as of meteorology. The first spacecraft carried very simple instruments, which quickly evolved into more and more sophisticated sensors as each launch built on the lessons of the one before. Visible-light imagers, useful only in daylight, were quickly joined by infrared sensors that allowed day-and-night observations. In turn, the infrared sensors became more versatile, expanding into many wavelengths across the longwave spectrum. In contrast, visible-wavelength sensors were deliberately limited to the red end of the spectrum where the longer wavelengths were able to better penetrate the atmosphere and give a clearer view of the clouds and ground below.

The first weather satellite, *Vanguard 2,* was launched by the United States on February 17, 1959. Instruments on board were designed to observe cloud-cover patterns over the daylight part of its orbit from an altitude that varied between 350 and 1,800 miles (560–3,000 km). There were no cameras on board; instead, observations were carried out by a pair of photocells that measured the intensity of reflected sunlight in the scene below from which the proportion of cloudy and clear skies could be determined.

Just over a year later, on April 1, 1960, *TIROS-1* (Television Infrared Observation Satellite) was launched into a 400-mile-high (650 km) orbit carrying two cameras for photography in the visible spectrum (Figure 6-2). Because of these cameras, which returned images that could be used directly in forecasting, *TIROS* rather than *Vanguard* is considered to be the first successful weather satellite. By today's standards, the images relayed to Earth were of modest quality, with resolutions of 1.5 miles (2.4 km) in one camera and 1,000 feet (300 m) in another. *TIROS* also carried two radiometers that were sensitive to infrared wavelengths to measure the water vapor content in the atmosphere.

FIG. 6-2. TIROS-1 *undergoes vibration testing at the Astro-Electronic Products Division of RCA in Princeton, New Jersey, prior to launch.*

In the first orbit, *TIROS-1* revealed that weather systems could be readily identified; later orbits revealed structures that had not been noted before or were known only in rough detail. *TIROS-1* was followed by nine others in the TIROS series, providing a valuable palette of operational weather observations from orbit until 1967 (Figure 6-3). Storm systems, particularly hurricanes, could be tracked from day to day, jet streams could be positioned from cloud lines, and the movement of comma cloud systems and fronts could be used for the daily forecasts.

The TIROS series served more as an engineering test platform than as a meteorological observing system, and so successive launches brought ongoing changes in such elements as camera design, optical layout, orbital configurations, and communication. Early spacecraft stored images on magnetic tape until they were in range of a receiving station and could download a sequence of scenes from around the Earth. With *TIROS-8* in late 1963, images could be transmitted directly to ground receiving stations as the scene from space was being recorded. The first complete mosaic of the Earth's weather was assembled in February 1965 by *TIROS-9*. The last two TIROS satellites, 9 and 10, were put into polar orbits, giving them the ability to view

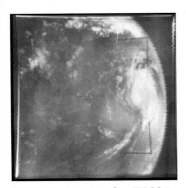

FIG. 6-3. *Hurricane Betsy from TIROS-7 on August 30, 1965.*

the entire planet as they circumnavigated the Earth. That orbit was further amended to a "sun-synchronous" orbit in *TIROS-10,* causing it to pass over each part of the globe at approximately the same time each day, a characteristic that has been adopted by nearly all low-orbit weather satellites to this day. These orbital characteristics have been incorporated into the general name for all low-orbit weather satellites: POES, for Polar-orbiting Operational Environmental Satellite.

In February 1966, the TIROS series was replaced by a second generation of polar-orbiting satellites named ESSA, after the sponsoring agency (the Environmental Science Services Administration). The ESSA spacecraft were the first fully operational weather satellites, providing consistent and routine global images through the latter half of the 1960s. Odd-numbered satellites retained the tape recorders and occasional data downloads of the TIROS series, but even-numbered satellites delivered a real-time broadcast of their television images to stations scattered around the globe. A total of nine ESSA satellites were successfully launched between 1966 and 1969.

At the same time that the TIROS satellites were providing routine observations from space, a second constellation of seven spacecraft, called Nimbus, was built and placed into orbit. Nimbus was not a dedicated meteorology satellite, but instead a technology development platform. From 1964 to 1978, the Nimbus spacecraft were the test bed for instruments that later made their way onto other satellites. The original Nimbus launches carried early versions of instruments that later evolved into the sophisticated devices that today routinely survey the Earth's environment from orbit. These include devices that measure the temperature profile of the atmosphere, monitor the ozone layer, map sea ice, measure the flow of incoming and outgoing radiation from the Sun and Earth, and use microwave frequencies to collect meteorological data in and through clouds. From *Nimbus-3* onward, primitive Global Positioning System (GPS) instruments began the evolution in navigation that has led us to the real-time map displays that we now consult while traveling.

The NOAA Series

In the 1970s, the ESSA platform was replaced by the ITOS (Improved TIROS Operational Satellite), a follow-on design that was quickly renamed NOAA for the National Oceanic and Atmospheric Administration, a name that is still in use. *NOAA-1* extended the technological march of previous weather satellites, providing day and night views of the Earth, direct readout to ground stations, and data storage for playback when the satellite was out of range. New uses evolved: measurements of snow and ice and of sea-surface temperatures were added to the mix. Infrared sensors, joined by microwave radiometers, began collecting data over a wide range of wavelengths, providing daily temperature and moisture profiles around the globe. These observations helped to fill the huge information gaps over the oceans and remote areas and were quickly incorporated into numerical models, greatly improving forecast skills and extending the reach of the model to a week or more.

From *NOAA-1* to *NOAA-20,* polar-orbiting spacecraft grew in sophistication while remaining true to the original objectives

FIG. 6-4. *An artist's view of* NOAA-20 *in orbit.*

centered on multi-wavelength observations of the atmosphere. The latest satellites (Figure 6-4) now include multiple-wavelength sensors for imagery, high-resolution infrared and microwave sensors for determining the temperature and moisture profile of the atmosphere, a data-collection platform to receive transmissions from instruments on the ground, radio receivers for search-and-rescue tracking, and a space environment monitor to measure particle flows from the Sun.

In their current configuration, the National Oceanic and Atmospheric Administration (NOAA) maintains several operational NOAA-class satellites, though older spacecraft tend to have one or more instruments in a nonworking condition. A typical NOAA spacecraft travels in an orbit that takes it over the equator at 1:30 P.M. going northward and 1:30 A.M. heading south. In every orbit, the satellite makes a daytime and a nighttime pass over a part of the globe, though overlapping orbits around the North and South Poles give high-latitude regions more frequent coverage than those close to the equator.

Other Polar Weather Satellites

The United States is not alone in launching and operating polar-orbiting satellites and cooperates with the European Organisation for the Exploitation of Meteorological Satellites (EUMETSAT) in Europe to maintain a two-satellite observing system. The European contribution to the pair is called MetOp, and the latest spacecraft in the series is *MetOp-C*. Because of the longevity of earlier MetOp satellites, several are operational at one time and so they are spread around their orbits to give more frequent coverage of the scenes below. *MetOp-C* has an equator-crossing time of 9:30 A.M. and 9:30 P.M., which provides a four-times-per-day view of the Earth in concert with the NOAA satellites.

Low-orbit satellites launched by Russia also have a long history, beginning with the launch of *Meteor-1-1* in 1969. For the most part, operational characteristics of the Meteor-1 series parallels that of European and American satellite programs, though in the earlier days, Russian satellites had higher and very elliptical orbits compared to their United States and European counterparts. Because of the higher altitudes, amateur radio operators who captured the Meteor-1 broadcasts were usually treated to a much larger view of the Earth than was possible with NOAA spacecraft. China also operates its own polar weather satellites under the name Fēngyún, first launched in 1988; this series of spacecraft is similar in capabilities to those of other countries.

In addition to the operational weather satellites run by national meteorological agencies, there are many other low-orbit spacecraft that capture routine images of the Earth's surface. For the most part, these satellites, such as the Landsat series, repeat their coverage at several-day intervals and are not very useful for forecasting. One exception is a pair of NASA satellites called *Aqua* and *Terra* that together provide high-resolution daytime images of the globe at 10:30 A.M. and 1:30 P.M. local time when they pass overhead.

Geostationary Satellites

Place a satellite at an altitude of 22,236 miles (35,786 km) over the equator and it will orbit the Earth every 24 hours. The satellite will hang above the same point on the ground, staring down with its cameras and sensors like an omnipotent forecaster's helper. Such satellites are called geostationary, providing us with not only our weather images but also communications, television, and a host of other services.

The first cloud pictures from a geostationary orbit came with the launch of *ATS-1* (*Applications Technology Satellite 1*) in December 1966. *ATS-1* was primarily a communications satellite, but the addition of a cloud camera allowed meteorologists to observe cloud systems as they moved and developed. Because the satellite was spinning, the images had to be built up in strips, with each strip acquired as the Earth came into view of the camera window. A small mirror tilted with each rotation, directing different parts of the scene into the camera until, after about 20 minutes, an image of the disc of the planet had been acquired. The mirror then returned to its start position at the north edge of the planet and began another scan.

By animating sequences of images, meteorologists were able to study the movement and development of weather systems, an achievement that led to a number of surprising discoveries. The first moving images were assembled by mounting individual hard-copy images on a spinning wheel that was illuminated by a strobe light as each photo passed. Called a Fujita-scope (after Ted Fujita, the developer of the Fujita scale of tornado intensity), it had limited use and was largely scorned, but for a short time brought animation into the operational forecast office. In research environments, where forecast deadlines were not pressing, individual satellite images were photographed using movie film and, after a suitable interval, cut and taped into a

FIG. 6-5. *North and South America are observed from geostationary altitude by a pair of U.S. satellites known as GOES-East and GOES-West. These scenes show the view from each satellite.*

loop that would run continuously in a projector. Today it is all done effortlessly by a computer.

Using these images, especially animated, it was possible to distinguish air motions, measure cloud heights and their development, predict rainfall, and track pollution. The arrival of a steady supply of real-time satellite images into forecast offices in the 1970s gave a huge boost to short-range prediction, particularly for aviation terminal forecasts.

ATS-1 was followed by five others of increasing capability as advances in technology made their way into spacecraft design. *ATS-3* launched with a multicolor camera that captured the first full-Earth images from space, but this function was dropped in later launches and the capability was not reintroduced until *GOES-16* in 2018. Throughout much of their development history, the ATS satellites were used primarily as a communications test bed, but the spacecraft also provided a platform for meteorological imaging that eventually led to geostationary satellites becoming an official, operational program.

The ATS series was replaced by the first of two Synchronous Meteorological Satellites (*SMS-1* in 1974 and *SMS-2* in 1975). The two satellites were placed in separate locations in orbit, at 75°W and 135°W in order to cover the whole of the United States and the surrounding oceans. The satellites came with a new camera that produced images in both infrared and visible light, finally giving forecasters the capability to see cloud evolution at night from high orbit. Over the equator, the camera had a resolution of 0.6 miles (1 km) in visible wavelengths and 4.3 miles (7 km) in the infrared, but for scenes away from the sub-satellite point, resolution decreased steadily around the curvature of the Earth.

COUNTRY	SATELLITE NAME	FIRST LAUNCH
USA	*GOES-E*	1975
USA	*GOES-W*	1977
Europe	*Meteosat*	1977
Russia	*GOMS*	1994
India	*INSAT*	1982
Japan	*Himawari*	1977
China	*Fēngyún*	1988
South Korea	*COMS/Chollian*	2010

TABLE 6-1. *National geostationary weather satellites.*

In 1977, the European Space Agency launched *Meteosat-1* into high orbit, giving geostationary satellite coverage from India westward to New Guinea. Meteosat images had lower resolution in the visible and higher in the infrared, but otherwise were similar to the NOAA satellites. Since those early days, seven countries (Table 6-1) have launched geostationary weather satellites and the whole of the globe is under continuous surveillance.

The SMS satellites were replaced by *GOES-1* (Geostationary Operational Environmental Satellite) in October 1975, followed by two more in the series, one in 1977 and another in 1978. Since those early years, four generations of GOES satellites have been placed into orbit. Typically, one operational satellite is placed at 75°W and one at 135°W so that the United States has coverage across the continent and both the Atlantic and Pacific Oceans (Figure 6-5). When in their nominal positions, they are referred to as *GOES-East* (*GOES-E*) and *GOES-West* (*GOES-W*). Because GOES satellites have long lifetimes, retired satellites are usually given other tasks and revert to their numerical name. In 2021, the operational GOES spacecraft were *GOES-16* and *GOES-17*.

The current, fourth-generation GOES satellites are much more capable than their predecessors. The on-board imager now scans the Earth in 16 wavelength channels, from blue in the visible to 13 microns in the infrared. Ten of the wavelength bands are in the infrared where they are used to view water vapor at various levels in the atmosphere, ozone, heat radiation from clouds and ground, cloud composition, and vegetation. Four are in the near-infrared where they can detect fog, low cloud, snow, and ice. The remaining two are blue and red wavelength channels in the visible where they can be used to produce color images of the Earth and clouds. All of these channels are readily available online and can be used to delve into the fine details of the atmosphere and put your own visual observations into context. Though their main cameras point at Earth, *GOES-16* and *GOES-17* carry solar telescopes with filters at six ultraviolet wavelengths to show the Sun's atmosphere in different temperature bands.

Using Satellite Images

Weather satellites observe the Earth in a variety of wavelength bands or channels, from the shortwave blue light at 0.47 microns to the thermal infrared around 13 or 14 microns. The number of channels in that band of electromagnetic radiation varies according to the satellite, but is usually around 16. All have at least one visible band, usually in the deep red, but more recently launched geostationary satellites have expanded to two or three visible-light channels, which can be used in combination to construct realistic-looking color images.

Out to a wavelength of about 2.5 microns, the scenes captured by the satellite sensors are illuminated by reflected solar radiation and so can only be used in daylight. Between 2.5 and 3.5 microns, the amount of solar radiation gradually fades away and is replaced by infrared radiation emitted by the Earth's surface and atmosphere. Since this glow of infrared light continues day and night, these longer wavelengths can be used to provide a complete 24-hour view of the planet from orbit.

The Earth's atmosphere is transparent to some electromagnetic energy and partially transparent to others. The more opaque the atmosphere, the higher the level from which radiation can escape to space where it can be captured by the satellite. By selecting a particular wavelength, we can produce images that show the atmosphere at different levels—high, middle, or low—or look right down to the surface to view the clouds and ground. Because the opacity is usually dictated by the amount of water vapor, we can "see" the distribution of moisture at a particular level by a clever selection of the wavelength. The various bands are usually described by their major function (Table 6-2).

Images produced from the various sampled wavelengths are usually "enhanced" by applying colors to various intensity levels. Since

WAVELENGTH BAND (MICRONS)	FUNCTION
0.47	blue; used for monitoring aerosols, haze
0.64	red; clouds and ground, volcanic ash
0.86	"veggie"; land-water contrast for flooding, hail swaths, burn scars
1.37	thin cirrus detection; volcanic ash
1.6	snow, ice, and cloud discrimination; cloud water content
2.2	cloud particle size, snow, hot spot detection (fires)
3.9	shortwave window; low cloud and fog detection
6.2	upper troposphere water vapor at about 340 mb
6.9	mid-level tropospheric water vapor around 440 mb; wind flow aloft
7.3	lower-level water vapor around 615 mb
8.4	cloud-top phase (water or ice)
9.6	ozone: high-level wind flow and features
10.3	"clean" longwave window; surface and low-level emission (temperature)
11.2	infrared longwave window; thermal radiation from surface and clouds
12.3	"dirty" longwave window; sensitive to water vapor
13.3	CO_2 longwave infrared; high, cold clouds

TABLE 6-2. *An outline of satellite sensors and their use.*

the infrared radiation emitted by the Earth depends wholly or partly on the temperature of the scene being viewed, the colors in a satellite image are usually assigned by temperature (Figure 6-6).

Individual bands can be combined to derive new products that reveal additional details about the atmosphere. The more common of these is to add the first three bands to produce a color image. Another algorithm combines bands 8, 10, 11, 14, and 15 to produce an estimate

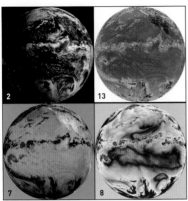

of rainfall. Bands 2, 5, and 14 can be combined to produce a composite image that distinguishes ice and snow from water-containing clouds (Figure 6-7).

Polar and Geostationary

With meteorological satellites costing many billions of dollars each, it seems extravagant to maintain a fleet of both polar and geostationary satellites with very similar specifications.

Because of their orbital characteristics, however, the two are complementary, especially at high latitudes.

Low-altitude satellites give a top-down view of polar regions (Figure 6-8) that improves on the highly distorted view around the curve of the Earth from geostationary heights. On the other hand, the fixed-in-place stationary satellites allow meteorologists to monitor cloud movement and devel-

FIG. 6-6. *This four-panel display shows the view from GOES-West as seen in four wavelength bands.* Top left: *A red-light image (band 2) showing detail in clouds and ground.* Top right: *An infrared view in the 10.2 micron band showing thermal emission from the Earth. Thermal (or temperature) emission allows the forecaster to determine cloud top heights and monitor the development of clouds as they change during the day.* Lower left: *Shortwave infrared image at 3.9 microns. This wavelength band is useful for the detection of fog and low cloud at night.* Lower right: *Mid-wave infrared image at 6.2 microns. This band shows upper-level water vapor distribution and helps trace out the flow of the winds at about the 340 mb level.*

opment. This ability to see movement makes the geostationary orbit more valuable to the forecaster, and that value is so important that polar satellite images are almost never used in the operational weather office unless the forecast region of responsibility is well to the north. The limit of geostationary coverage is surprisingly far to the north—at least as far as the Arctic coast of Alaska at 70°N (Figure 6-9), even though the images are considerably foreshortened.

From a polar orbit at 520 miles (840 km), the field of view from the satellite is limited to a swath that is about 1,900 miles (3,000 km) wide (Figure 6-10). To build up an image of North America (for instance) requires the merging of images from several orbits over a period of six hours or more (the satellite has a period of around 100 minutes). Over

FIG. 6-7. *A multiband image processed to show the composition of the clouds. Dark blue colors represent land surfaces. Greens show snow and cold ice clouds. Aqua shows low clouds composed of water droplets. Yellows and reds are thick and thin ice clouds at high level. The scene shows a mature comma-cloud storm with thunderstorms (thick yellow ice clouds) along the comma tail and thick ice clouds in the comma head.*

tropical regions, adjacent swaths do not meet and so a narrow arc of missing data is visible on each global image. The lower orbits of the polar satellites do not give them an advantage in resolution, as their ability to see fine detail is the same as the geostationary satellites (0.56 km). However, because the low-orbit satellites capture their images as they pass overhead, the resolution is the same at all sub-satellite points in the orbit. For geostationary satellites, image resolution is highest directly beneath the satellite at the equator (½ km in channel 2) but falls off away from the sub-satellite point because of the curvature of the Earth.

Polar satellites are most useful for polar observation and for non-meteorological tasks: monitoring ice movement and formation in the Arctic and Antarctic; observing the development of crops and the health of forests; listening for distress signals; intercepting transmissions from remote, unmanned observing sites; checking up on volcanoes; and so on. In the meteorological realm, sounding instruments that collect infrared data to re-create temperature and humidity profiles at high latitudes provide critical details for numerical models. Nevertheless, for most of the globe, the greatest limitation of low-orbit

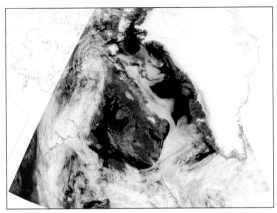

FIG. 6-8. *A high-latitude image of Baffin Island and Greenland from NOAA-20. The straight-down view from the satellite gives a nearly distortion-free view of the polar regions.*

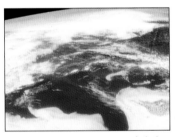

FIG. 6-9. *A geostationary image of Alaska showing the distortion caused by the steep viewing angle from a satellite located over the equator.*

satellites is the 6- to 12-hour interval between successive orbital passes.

For geostationary satellites, capabilities are limited by the curve of the Earth, which stretches out the pixels in the satellite image in the north–south and east–west directions. With the higher resolution of the latest GOES and Japanese satellites, this drawback is not particularly serious in the visible-light images, which have a resolution of 0.5 km at the sub-satellite point and double that at high latitudes. Many of the images you will see online have also been "rectified" to make them appear as if the GOES satellite was overhead. This remapping of the image pixels makes the geostationary images especially useful while disguising the effects of the curvature of our planet.

The very widespread use of satellite images in the daily broadcasts by TV meteorologists relies almost exclusively on the geostationary images, and only the longwave infrared images at that. This is more a matter of convenience than necessity: the geostationary images can be made into an animated display showing cloud movement, and the use

FIG. 6-10. *An image swath from* NOAA-20 *across Florida shows the width of the scene captured by the camera on a polar-orbiting satellite.*

of infrared allows scenes to merge from day to night and back without obvious interruption in the cloud motion as day turns to night. In the infrared, since clouds are usually colder than the ground because of their altitude, they show up white against the surface background. One cannot help but feel sorry for the novice TV meteorologist who becomes confused in the winter when the ground is often colder than the clouds, so that a large mass of white "stuff" appears overnight that mimics the appearance of an approaching weather system.

Meteorology and weather forecasting changed dramatically when weather satellites were launched, and many innovative uses of the technology are yet to come. With the introduction of different wavelength bands and the increasing resolution of the satellite sensors, numerical modeling in particular is expected to reap the greatest benefit. Since the first launches in the 1970s, the accuracy and precision of weather forecasting has taken giant steps and the trend should continue, in no small part thanks to observations from space.

You will find the ready supply of online satellite images a source of endless discovery, particularly if you match the view from orbit with the scenes outside your window. Changes in cloudiness and weather with the approach of fronts and storms will be better understood when matched with the view from above. The explosive growth of thunderstorms, the evolution of a winter storm, the gradual dissipation of a fog bank, or the track of a hurricane all come alive in the view from geostationary altitudes.

CHAPTER 7

WINDS

In Praise of Winds

Winds and ocean currents are the bloodstream of the atmosphere, carrying heat and energy to every nook and cranny of the world. They moderate the temperatures in sunless polar regions, bring sunshine to the tropics and moisture to deserts, storms to the northern and southern oceans; they give us our climates and our human and biological diversity. If you want to understand meteorology, then familiarity with the winds—north, south, and upward—is the place to begin.

The Wind's Engine

Air Pressure

The wind's engine is pressure, or more precisely, pressure differences, for the atmosphere moves in response to variations in pressure, always moving from higher pressures to lower.

Air pressure is the weight of the air. At the surface of the Earth, it is the weight of the entire atmosphere. Above the surface, pressure declines with altitude as the amount of air above the observer declines. In Figure 7-1 we see that air pressure decreases rapidly at first and then more slowly with increasing altitude; at a height of about 3.4 miles or 18,000 feet (5.5 km), pressure (500 mb) is about half of its average value at the surface (1,013 mb). There is no noticeable "top" to the atmosphere—it just fades away gradually into space as the number of molecules and atoms declines. In 1983, a climbing expedition to the 29,029-foot (8,848 m) top of Mount Everest, the highest "surface" on the Earth, measured a pressure one-third of that at sea-level.

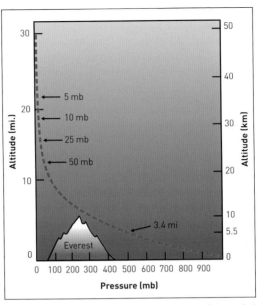

FIG. 7-1. *The decline of pressure with altitude. At about 500 mb (3.4 miles), half the atmosphere lies below the observer, and half above.*

The international unit for pressure is the pascal (Pa)—a rather tiny unit and not very convenient for day-to-day meteorological work. In 1909, the British Meteorological Office began using "bar" to define pressure, a unit derived from the Greek word for weight and set equal to the mean (average) sea-level pressure (MSLP). A bar is too big a unit to be useful in weather maps, so meteorologists adopted the millibar (mb)—1/1000 of a bar—as their working unit of pressure. When international standards were set in 1982, the pascal (Pa) was set as the unit for atmospheric pressure, though millibar still remains in use in many weather offices. For day-to-day use, the hectopascal (hPa) and the kilopascal (kPa) were substituted (*hecto* is the metric prefix for 100, *kilo* is the prefix for 1,000). The hectopascal is rather convenient, as 1 mb is equal to 1 hPa, and so forecasters can go on using the old unit on their charts and just give it a new name. There are many other pressure units in use (Table 7-1), some for scientific purposes and others for day-to-day use; in this book, we will stick with tradition and use millibars.

Air pressure isn't visible to the weather observer, but its impact is

UNIT	SLP VALUE
bar	1.01325
pascal (Pa)	101,325
millibar (mb)	1013.25
hectopascal (hPa)	1013.25
kilopascal (kPa)	101.325
mm Hg (millimeters of mercury)	760
inches Hg (inches of mercury)	29.921
atmosphere (atm)	1

TABLE 7-1. *Units of pressure and their value at sea-level pressure (SLP)*

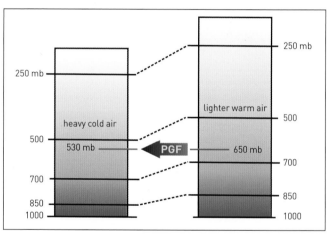

FIG. 7-2. *Vertical air pressure declines more rapidly in a cold air column than in a warm one, leading to the creation of a horizontal pressure gradient (PGF) from warm to cold air. The vertical pressure gradient (the rate of decline of pressure with altitude) is stronger in the left column as a consequence of its colder temperature, a necessary condition in order to maintain hydrostatic balance.*

readily apparent in the wind. However, you will see surface pressure displayed in the daily TV and internet weather reports, which characteristically show "highs" and "lows" scattered across a cartoonlike map of weather symbols with past and future positions used to explain the changes in the forecast.

While wind arises from the response of the atmosphere to pressure differences, a more fundamental question is "What causes pressure variations in the atmosphere?"

One way to lower surface pressure is to remove some of the atmosphere from a higher level so that there is less weight to the air above the observer (and, conversely, to raise pressures by increasing the amount of air aloft). This situation arises in the development and movement of high- and low-pressure weather systems, a subject that we'll discuss a little farther on. Another is to alter temperature and its counterpart, density. Warm air is less dense than cold air, so for a given depth of the atmosphere, there will be lower pressures beneath the warm air than the cold. For two air columns with equal surface pressure, the one containing the warmer air must be deeper than the cold air in order for the two columns to weigh the same. If we send instruments upward through the two columns, the sensors will show that the pressure in the warm air is falling off more slowly than that in the cold air, and so at any given level aloft (but not at the surface), there will be a pressure difference between the two air columns. This pressure difference aloft is fundamental to the creation of upper-level winds (Figure 7-2).

In many cases, we may choose to credit the creation of a wind to temperature or to density variations, but in the end, pressure is the fundamental force that moves the air as both of the other factors result in pressure differences.

Hydrostatic Equilibrium

Open a tire's valve and it will be pretty obvious that gases flow from higher pressures to lower. Why, then, does the atmosphere not blow off into space, since high pressures are found near the surface and lower pressures at the top of the atmosphere?

We can thank gravity for that little convenience, for gravity glues our atmosphere to the surface and gives the air its weight and pressure. The atmosphere isn't squashed against the surface, as pressure forces push back, matching the force of gravity so that the atmosphere doesn't collapse into a layer a few inches thick. This convenient balance between pressure and gravity is known as "hydrostatic equilibrium" and is the more or less normal state of the atmosphere (Figure 7-3). When the balance is upset, the air will rise or sink according to the pressure differences. These vertical motions are usually gentle, but under some circumstances they can become quite intense, such as the updraft winds inside a severe thunderstorm.

Surface and Upper-Air Charts

The measurement of surface pressure is carried out by the thousands of weather stations scattered around the world, and these measurements are routinely plotted on surface-weather maps. From there, it is a simple matter to trace out the pressure pattern by constructing lines of constant pressure (isobars) between stations (Figure 7-4). Because pressure declines with altitude, weather stations in mountains will always record a lower pressure than those closer to sea level, and so measurements must be converted to a common standard—mean sea level (MSL)—by applying a correction factor that depends mostly on temperature (Figure 7-5).

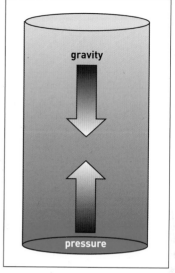

FIG. 7-3. *Hydrostatic equilibrium: upward pressure forces equal downward gravitational pull. The two forces are in near balance throughout the depth of the atmosphere. Pressure declines with height, because there is less mass to balance as we rise upward.*

Structures such as lows and highs appear on surface maps, but other features are also noteworthy. Troughs (often abbreviated on weather maps as "TROF") are elongated regions of low pressure; ridges are the same for high-pressure areas (Figure 7-4). Both are akin to valleys and ridges on a topographic map. Each of these pressure features has meteorological significance, and their motion from one time to another is a fundamental aid in preparing a forecast. Surface lows and troughs are also important in helping to locate fronts (Chapter 8), which tend to string from low to low, bending around the high-pressure regions.

In a working weather office, surface maps are produced at frequent intervals—anywhere from every hour to every six hours. Computer analyses now make this an easy process, but many forecasters prefer to do at least some hand analysis as it is a form of note-taking that reveals small events and features that may signal important changes in the evolving weather pattern. Severe-weather forecasters and storm chasers in particular derive value from frequent high-resolution analyses because of the rapid evolution of convective storms. The ongoing

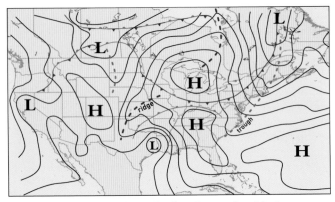

FIG. 7-4. *Surface-pressure analysis with isobars, fronts, and precipitation area. Isobars are traditionally analyzed at 4-mb intervals on small-scale surface charts. Red lines indicate the position of warm fronts; blue, the position of cold fronts. Alternating blue and red are stationary fronts. Trough lines are shown in red dashes, ridges in dashed blue.*

progression of highs, lows, and fronts as they move across the globe is easily tracked in well-done surface charts and gives forecasters a critical tool for short-range prediction.

Some idea of the wealth of information available on a surface map can be ascertained by the data that are measured and plotted on the chart at each station: pressure, temperature, dewpoint, wind speed and direction, pressure change (tendency), visibility, current weather, and precipitation type and intensity. Each of these parameters can be analyzed by hand or by machine. Wind is not only plotted at each station location, but the pressure pattern defines the general nature of the wind flow. Air flows counterclockwise around a low and clockwise around a high. This circulation is encapsulated in a rule first described by Dutch meteorologist Buys Ballot (1817–90): when the wind is at your back, low pressure is on your left and higher pressure on your right. The reverse is true in the Southern Hemisphere.

Mapping upper-level features is a bit of a problem. We could draw maps of the pressure at a given level, say three miles above sea level, or we could make maps of the height at which a certain pressure is found. The solution chosen by tradition is to map the height of a given pressure level. We have already seen in Figure 7-2 how warm and cold air have different altitudes for each pressure value, and so a map of the height of a particular pressure above sea level (Figure 7-6)

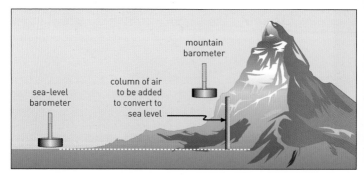

FIG. 7-5. *Because of its higher altitude, the barometer on the right will read a lower station pressure than the one at sea level. To be able to compare pressures at the two stations, they must be converted to a common reference, namely sea level. To do this, the weight of the air in the column between the mountain site and sea level must be added. The weight of this column depends on the temperature assumed for the conversion.*

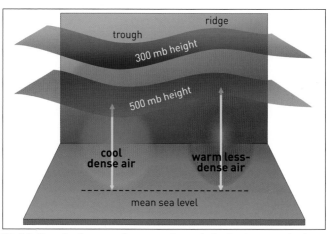

FIG. 7-6. *Upper-level maps are drawn according to the height of a pressure level above sea level. For a given pressure, heights are higher in warm air and lower in cold.*

will also tell us something about the temperature of the air column below. Any pressure level could be selected for mapping, but there are several in common usage: 1,000 mb, 700 mb, 500 mb, 200 mb, and so on (Table 7-2). In just about all weather offices, upper-air features are contoured in tens of meters and degrees Celsius; wind speeds

PRESSURE LEVEL (MB)	TYPICAL HEIGHT IN KM	TYPICAL HEIGHT IN FEET
1,000	0.1	328
850	1.5	4,920
700	3.0	9,840
500	5.5	18,045
400	7.3	23,950
300	9.3	30,510
200	11.7	38,385

TABLE 7-2. *Standard pressure levels and representative heights above sea level. These heights vary according to the weather of the day.*

are plotted in knots, a holdover from early aviation days. While the practice of using height above sea level to map upper-level structures seems complicated, most forecasters regard the features simply as lows and highs without concern for the fact that they are heights and not pressure values.

In standard upper-air charts, low heights are found where cold temperatures are present in the atmosphere, while high heights are associated with warmer temperatures (Figure 7-6). The 700-mb level, for instance, might be found at a height of 2 miles (3.2 km) on a warm day and 1.8 miles (2.9 km) on a cold January morning. In the example of a 300-mb height chart in Figure 7-7, the contours are labeled with three-digit numbers that show their height above sea level in decameters (tens of meters). The lowest height—and the coldest air column—is found in the Canadian Arctic, where a pressure of 300 mb is found at 846 decameters (8.46 km or 5.3 miles) above sea level.

An upper-level chart, such as that in Figure 7-7, maps the rivers of wind that flow above the surface. In some parts of the map, the contour lines are collected into parallel bundles; in others, the contours wander away on their own, curling around highs and lows and joining the main stream somewhere else on the globe. Usually one or more main streams can be easily identified, sometimes joining into one broad flow and at other times maintaining a separate existence. The closeness (packing) of the contours—the contour gradient—is intimately related to the speed of the winds both at the surface and aloft. These charts have other information too: temperature, wind

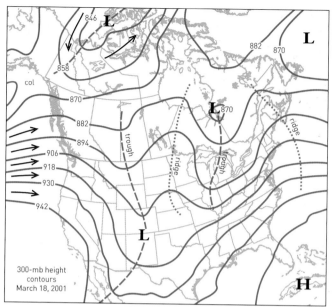

FIG. 7-7. *A chart of the heights of the 300-mb pressure level. Contour labels show that this level is found at 8,580 m (5.3 miles) over the Arctic islands and 9,420 m (5.85 miles) over the south Texas coast. Arrows along the West Coast show the direction of the winds. The troughs and ridges are small-scale ripples (shortwaves) that are associated with low- and high-pressure systems at the surface.*

speed and direction, humidity, and several other more esoteric fields, all of which have their own gradients and their own importance. The high-level flow of the wind and the presence of moisture can also be revealed to the forecaster in infrared satellite images (Figure 7-8).

The relationship between the height contours and temperature hints that the thermal structure of the atmosphere plays a role in determining the depth of the atmosphere and the strength of the upper winds. In fact, this relationship is a fundamental and very important feature of the global atmosphere: temperature gradients in both the horizontal and vertical provide the energy that drives the weather.

The Pressure Gradient Force (PGF)

Inflate your cheeks and blow. Release the valve on a tire. Pop open a soft drink.

Inside your cheeks, the tire, and the can is air that is confined with

FIG. 7-8. *This infrared satellite image shows the distribution of water vapor in the upper atmosphere. The swirling patterns in this image follow the flow of the winds at upper levels in the atmosphere.*

a pressure that is higher than the air outside. When the confinement is broken, air rushes out: a wind is created. The flow is always from high to low pressure, and the wind speed depends on the difference in those pressures, so that the air stream from a tire comes at a much higher velocity than a puff from the cheeks. This force that causes air to move is called the pressure gradient force (PGF) and is ultimately the cause of all winds on the Earth. Visually, the PGF is represented by the concentration or packing of isobars and height contours on the maps that forecasters use.

In the atmosphere, winds also flow out of highs and into lows (Figure 7-9), though there are a few complications along the way that will come up in later discussions. Tight pressure gradients, such as those around intense winter storms, bring strong, damaging winds, while those in the center of a high, where gradients fade away to nothing, may barely stir a flower petal. On a typical surface map, this pressure gradient force encompasses a change in pressure from around 1 mb in 47 miles (75 km) in a high to as much as 1 mb in 4 miles (6 km) in a hurricane. Inside a tornado, the PGF may reach 300 times that of the hurricane.

While the PGF provides the impetus to get winds moving, the actual wind does not flow directly from high pressure to low pressure. Other forces modify the flow, turning its direction and adding or subtracting from its speed. The first and most important of these additional forces is the mysterious Coriolis force.

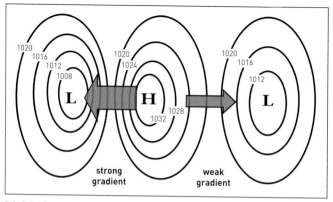

FIG. 7-9. *The pressure gradient force (PGF) causes air to move from regions of higher pressure to lower at a speed that depends (in part) on the rate of change of pressure or pressure gradient. In this diagram, the pressure gradient is much greater on the left side of the high-pressure area where the pressure contour lines (isobars) are more tightly packed. Air moves directly from high to low in this example, but in the atmosphere, there are other forces that modify the wind flow.*

The Coriolis Force

Urban myth tells us that the water goes down the sink in a clockwise direction in the Southern Hemisphere and in a counterclockwise spiral in the Northern. It doesn't—water will disappear down the drain quite comfortably in both directions in either hemisphere. So where did the legend come from? Its origins are lost in time, but examples of the bathtub myth are easy to find: TV episodes of *The Simpsons* and *The X-Files*, the movie *Wedding Crashers*, some physics textbooks, and the touts at the equator in Kenya who "prove" the effect to innocent tourists while manipulating a pan of water. To be honest, carefully controlled experiments have shown that the Coriolis force can be detected in the direction of flow while draining a container, but it requires a very large pan of water, a very small drain, and a temperature-controlled laboratory.

In the lower atmosphere, winds circle around the pressure centers, spiraling slowly outward from a high and inward into a low. In the Northern Hemisphere, the winds flow counterclockwise around lows and clockwise around highs; in the Southern Hemisphere, flows move in the opposite direction. To avoid having to specify the direction whenever we discuss the weather in one hemisphere or the other, meteorologists call the direction of flow around a low *cyclonic* and that around a high *anticyclonic,* recognizing that it will be one direction above the equator and the opposite below.

The pattern of flow around the highs and lows at the surface is at odds with our statement that air flows directly from high to low pressure. Some other force must be acting on the pressure gradient force to cause it to deviate from the expected flow—a force that works at the scale of weather systems but not of bathtubs. That force is called the Coriolis force, named after the French engineer Gaspard-Gustave Coriolis (1792–1843), who first derived it mathematically.

The Coriolis force arises from the rotation of the Earth. Stand just short of the North Pole for a day and you will travel a small circle as the Earth rotates beneath your feet. Stand at the equator for an identical 24 hours and you will make the same circuit, but instead of moving at a few inches per hour, your tangential velocity would be 1,040 mph (1,674 km/h). Fortunately, the atmosphere is also moving with the Earth—a good thing, as the wind speeds against the ground would otherwise wreak havoc.

Now imagine a very powerful baseball pitcher standing near the North Pole who throws a ball to the south. The pitcher is not moving

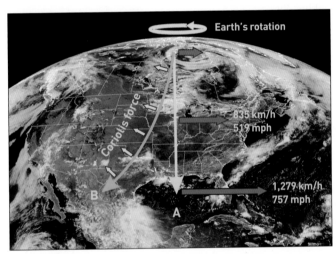

FIG. 7-10. *As air moves southward along the yellow arrow toward A, it travels over regions with an increasing tangential velocity. Unable to keep up, the air follows the trajectory shown by the orange line to B. An Earth-bound observer facing south explains this motion to the right as being due to the Coriolis force, though the force is only an artifact of the planet's solid rotation.*

very fast at all in his northern location, but as the ball flies southward, it passes over ground that is moving to the east much more quickly. In effect, the ground is rotating beneath the ball. A batter standing at a more southerly point will see the pitch coming, but it will pass well to his left, as he is carried away by the Earth's rotation. From the pitcher's point of view, the ball will seem to have curved to the west (to the right) as if some force were acting on it (Figure 7-10). The faster the pitcher throws the ball, the more dramatic the turn to the right.

Replace the baseball with a parcel of air and the same thing will happen. Once an air parcel starts to move, it carries its original Earth velocity with it, but if it heads southward, that initial velocity isn't enough to keep up with the faster moving ground turning under it, and so it falls behind to the west. To explain this mysterious motion to the right (west), we invent the Coriolis force. The Coriolis force is sometimes called fictitious, as it arises only from the observer's rotation and not from any physical basis. To a spectator watching from space, the air parcel and baseball have traveled straight southward, and it is the Earth that has rotated beneath the flow. The Coriolis force works for any direction of travel on our rotating Earth, though east–west motions have more complex explanations. As with the pitcher's fastball, the greater the wind speed, the stronger the influence of the Coriolis force.

A southward-moving air stream moves away from the Earth's rotation axis most quickly as it leaves the poles, so the Coriolis force is highest at high latitudes. At the equator, a southward flow is parallel to the planetary rotation axis and so there is no Coriolis force at all, since the distance from the rotation axis hardly changes as the air stream moves north or south. Those hawkers who pretend to show the unwary tourist that water turns in opposite directions by stepping across the equator are preying on the traveler's inexperience.

The main impact of the Coriolis force is to turn a flow that would normally go from high pressure to low pressure to one in which the winds circulate around the low- and high-pressure centers. Generally speaking, the air has to move about 100 km before the Coriolis force begins to have a measurable effect. On a global scale, the cold atmosphere at the poles and the warmer temperatures at the equator create a pressure pattern in which lower pressures are found at upper levels over the Arctic and Antarctic and higher pressures above the tropics. On a non-rotating Earth, winds would respond to this pressure pattern and flow from the equator to the poles. The Coriolis force turns this flow to the right in the Northern Hemisphere and to the left in the Southern Hemisphere, so that upper-level winds are westerly above 20° latitude. In lower-latitude tropical climates where the Coriolis force fades away, upper winds are light and more variable, and usually from the east.

The Coriolis force is a very important feature of the atmosphere on every rotating planet. At the equator, where the Coriolis force drops to zero, low-pressure weather systems are unknown—the air flows immediately into any low that might form and fills it up. On the other hand, at mid-latitudes the Coriolis force is a critical factor in maintaining the highs and lows that control the daily weather—a force that is particularly noticeable in the spiral structure of big winter storms (Figure 7-11).

To sum up, the Coriolis force:

- is greatest near the poles and zero at the equator.
- changes only wind direction.
- acts perpendicular to the wind direction.
- causes a rightward deflection in the Northern Hemisphere and a leftward in the Southern.
- acts on any moving object on the Earth.
- increases as the speed of the object increases.

FIG. 7-11. *This elegant spiral of cloud shows the circulation around a low-pressure system, a pattern dictated by the influence of the Coriolis force.*

The Role of Friction

Lows would never fill up and highs would never weaken if the Coriolis force were the only influence on the winds—the winds would just go round and round and round. Some other influence is needed to make weather systems decay away, and that role is left to the friction created by the flow over the ground. Friction, which affects only the surface and lowest levels of the atmosphere, usually for a height of a mile and a half (2.4 km) or so, drags on the airflow, causing the wind to slow and weakening the Coriolis force. The pressure gradient force is no longer balanced, so the wind turns across the isobars at a small angle, flowing into a low or out of a high. The angle of the cross-contour flow into lows and out of highs depends on the latitude (through the Coriolis force) and the roughness of the ground, but is typically about 15° over the mid-latitudes, as can be seen in Figure 7-12. Over open water, the frictional force is lower than over land, so winds at the water surface are stronger and steadier (as experienced sailors know) and the cross-contour flow is weaker. Of all of the forces, it is friction that causes the wind to fill lows and empty highs, gradually bringing them to an end.

Some weather systems are so small that the Coriolis force is very

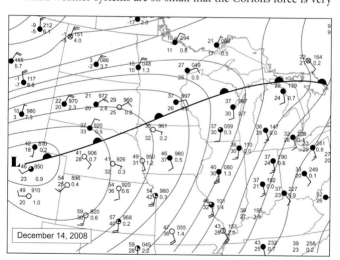

FIG. 7-12. *Surface analysis from December 14, 2008, shows the cross-contour wind flow around a strong winter cyclone (a Colorado low). This flow will gradually fill up the low and cause it to fade away, though it may take a week or more. Winds on the west (left) side of the image cross contours almost perpendicularly because of the constraints imposed by the terrain.*

FIG. 7-13. *A dust devil on the Arizona plains.*

weak and contributes little or nothing to the balance of winds. In these systems, the pressure gradient force is counterbalanced by the centrifugal and friction forces. Such low-pressure systems, called cyclostrophic, include tornadoes, dust devils (Figure 7-13), and waterspouts.

Upper-Level Winds

Figure 7-14 shows a typical 300-mb chart with height contours and wind barbs. The height contours trace out the shape of the high-level flow, and barbs show that wind directions are mostly parallel to the height contours; wind speeds are strongest where the contours are most closely packed. In the figure, there is an upper-level low over the Great Lakes, and a strong northward-bulging ridge over the Great Plains. This wavelike up-and-down shape of the flow is known as a meridional circulation because it undulates along the meridians of longitude. On other occasions, the flow may be nearly straight, flowing with little deviation from west to east; such a flow is called zonal. In a zonal flow, disturbances pass quickly and the weather could be said to be "normal" for the season. Wavy meridional flows, such as in Figures 7-14 and 7-7, bring unseasonably warm and dry conditions to regions beneath the ridge and cool, wet weather in the troughs.

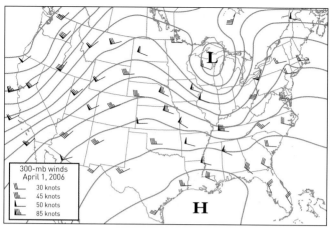

FIG. 7-14. *On this 300-mb chart, observed winds (those measured by balloons) are shown by stylized arrows. Winds flow parallel to the height contours with speeds that generally reflect the strength of the gradient (the packing of the contour lines) in which they are embedded.*

Above about 1½ miles, the airflow feels very little friction from the ground, and the lazy, undulating flow of the contour charts seems to imply an environment in which changes happen slowly and infrequently. In fact, just the opposite is true, as each twist and turn, each change in speed, introduces unbalanced forces into the flow, disturbing the equilibrium and forcing the atmosphere below to respond. The upper air stream is always changing: troughs and ridges move along from west to east, new waves form and grow and dissipate, and zonal flows alternate with meridional flows. A cluster of thunderstorms may block the flow and force a new set of troughs and ridges to develop downstream. Mountains will impose their own distortions on the wind, and large storms may completely reset the original flow and force a dramatic change in the weather.

Wind Streams Aloft

Jet Streams

Embedded in the strongest part of the upper-atmospheric flow, usually tucked just under the tropopause, lie two belts of high-speed wind known as jet streams. Jet streams are located within the tightest packing of the height contours on the 250- or 300-mb charts in a region of

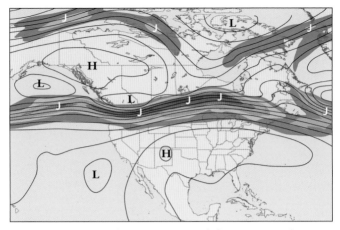

FIG. 7-15. *A 250-mb chart showing jet-stream winds flowing across North America. Red colors indicate the zone of strongest winds, which lies where the contour gradient is greatest. This is an example of a zonal flow.*

strong temperature contrasts between north and south (Figure 7-15). These strong gradients of temperature form at the interfaces where Arctic air pushes against mid-continent polar air and where polar air butts up against tropical air. The associated jet streams are known respectively as the polar jet and the subtropical jet.

On an upper-air chart, the jet stream is a ribbon of stronger winds that stretches around the globe at mid-latitudes. Along this flow, there are localized regions of higher wind speeds (Figure 7-15), with maximum velocities that rise and fall with the seasons. These jet maxima or jet cores are slow moving, and so upper-level winds flow through them rather than push them along. In the winter, when the contrast between Arctic and polar airmasses is particularly strong, winds in the jet cores may reach speeds of more than 275 mph (440 km/h). Summertime wind speeds are much lighter, usually less than 150 mph (240 km/h).

The jet stream is a vagabond, sometimes flowing in a nearly straight line from west to east, sometimes meandering far to the north and then back to the south. The core of maximum winds is not fixed to a single altitude, but has a significant depth and wanders up and down a bit at higher levels of the atmosphere (Figure 7-16). The polar jet stream tends to have a semi-continuous structure; the higher, subtropical jet is more fragmented and is typically found over a limited range of longitudes. The northerly polar jet can be found over Canada

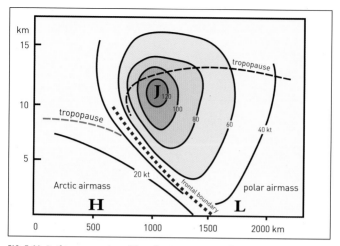

FIG. 7-16. *In this cross section of the polar jet, we can see the location of the jet with respect to the tropopause and the Arctic frontal zone. The jet is located on the warm side of the break between the two tropopauses.*

in the summer months and over the northern Plains states in the winter, though it has a considerable migration north and south. The subtropical jet forms across northern Mexico and the Gulf States in winter and moves into mid-continent for the summer. Infrared satellite images are able to show the flow of upper-level winds as it is traced out by water vapor into globe-spanning curves (Figure 7-17).

The discovery of the jet stream was one of a gradual unveiling rather than a sudden *Eureka!* moment. In 1919, Robert Millikan, chief of the Science and Research Division of the United States Signal Corps (and winner of the Nobel Prize in Physics in 1923 for his measurement of the charge of the electron), summarized the results of over 5,000 balloon flights by noting that "observations show air currents increasing in intensity with increasing altitude and approaching the huge speed of 100 miles per hour. Such speeds are perhaps exceptional but not at all uncommon" (Millikan 1919). In the 1920s, Japanese meteorologist Wasaburo Oishi (1874–1950) collected the results of 1,300 balloon observations to construct a seasonal wind chart over Japan. His summary showed that winds were markedly stronger in winter, with an average speed of 157 mph (250 km/h) at the 10-km level.

In 1943, an Allied bomber squadron over Europe found itself in headwinds of 235 mph (380 km/h) and unable to make substantial

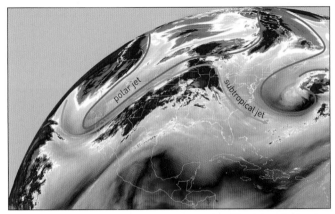

FIG. 7-17. *Satellite images taken in the 6.2-micron infrared band show the distribution of water vapor in the upper atmosphere. The patterns at this level show the flow of the high-level winds. The positions of the jet streams are shown by red and orange arrows.*

headway against the wind. Running low on fuel, the crews were forced to parachute into occupied Europe and were captured by the German army. Throughout the later stages of the war, aircrews reported winds of similar strength in both the European and Pacific theaters.

The position and movement of the jet stream is usually displayed in television broadcasts to show the character of the current weather pattern, a role for which they are admirably suited. Because the jets reflect the strongest part of the upper-level flow, they are the winds that drive the movement of lower-level weather systems; the strength of the jet stream dictates the intensity of those systems. Winter storms that bring cold outbreaks across the Midwest or along the Atlantic Seaboard are often blamed on a jet-stream flow that has meandered unusually far to the south.

From the ground, the presence of the jet stream is sometimes apparent in cirrus clouds, visible as a sharp edge along an elongated band of clouds. Striations in the cloud lie parallel to the upper winds, and there may be small wave clouds lying across the flow signaling a turbulent atmosphere aloft (see page 142). Jet streams, especially near the higher winds in the core, are frequently associated with aircraft turbulence and are usually avoided by pilots. If you suspect that the clouds you are watching are a part of the jet stream, a quick look at an upper-level chart on an internet weather site should confirm or reject the diagnosis.

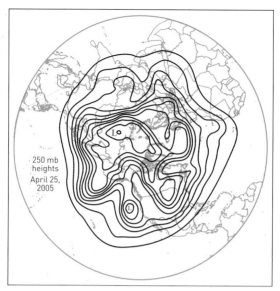

FIG. 7-18. *A view from the North Pole of the circulation at 250 mb on April 25, 2005. Five irregular Rossby waves are visible on this day. Smaller ripples in the main flow are shortwaves.*

Rossby Waves

Cast a casual glance at a global chart of the mid-latitude westerly air stream at any level between about 700 mb and the tropopause (Figure 7-18), and you cannot help but notice the sinusoidal character of the flow with undulations in the jet stream that meander between the 30th and 60th parallels of latitude. The wavelike nature of this flow was first identified by the Swedish-American meteorologist Carl-Gustaf Rossby in the 1940s, and so the longest of them are often called Rossby waves, though you will also find them referred to as longwaves or planetary waves. On any given day, there are usually three to seven of these irregular Rossby waves circling the globe in the latitude band between the 30th and 65th parallels. Planetary waves move slowly from west to east at an average speed that depends on their size, with shorter wavelengths moving more quickly than longer. An average speed for a major wave is about 3 to 5° of longitude eastward per day, but every now and then, one or more of the waves may slow and become stationary or even back up to the west.

Rossby waves are one of the mechanisms by which the atmosphere

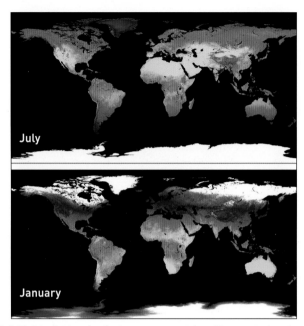

FIG. 7-19. *Distribution of surface temperatures in July and January. In the winter, a strong gradient of temperature is present across middle latitudes. This temperature gradient supplies the energy that feeds low-pressure systems in middle latitudes.*

mixes the heat of tropical and equatorial regions with the colder air of the Arctic in a never-ending attempt to even out temperatures around the globe. The process is driven by solar energy, which warms low latitudes of the Earth much more than those to the north. At the start of a cycle, the temperature gradient between north and south is relatively small, and the upper flow is close to zonal, with only a gentle undulation from west to east. Wind speeds tend to be high, especially in winter, and surface weather systems move quickly, though they may be intense. In summer, when the temperature difference between pole and equator is smallest, the ripples in a zonal flow are likely to bring thunderstorms rather than large cyclonic storms.

As the tropics warm under the relentless energy of the Sun, the temperature gradient increases across the mid-latitudes. Disturbances aloft, which may start as a small wave in the flow, extract energy from the temperature gradient and begin to grow larger, often aided by the flow over a mountain chain such as the Rockies, which amplifies the growing wave in the upper wind. Cold air begins to move southward in the wave trough, while warm air pushes to the north in the ridging part of the flow in front. Depending on the season and on the magnitude of the temperature contrast between cold and warm air (Figure 7-19), a surface low forms, extending the influence of the growing meridional circulation down to the ground. Once the meridional pattern is established, warm tropical air is carried northward and mixed with colder Arctic air until the temperature gradient is weakened, dissipating the atmosphere's energy, returning the atmosphere to a quiescent state, and re-establishing the zonal flow. Then, as the cold and warm reservoirs rebuild, the zonal flow gradually regains its mojo, leading to the start of another cycle. The cycling between meridional and zonal patterns (called the index cycle) is quasi-periodic, but does not have much predictive value for the forecaster, since its period, typically three to eight weeks, is highly variable and not very useful in forecasting relief from hot or cold weather.

The swing between zonal and meridional flows has an important bearing on the week-to-week weather and beyond. Outbreaks of cold winter weather across the eastern United States are often attributed to a "polar vortex" that has escaped its Arctic home, but a more precise attribution would be that a meridional flow has developed and the trough in that flow has settled along the Appalachian Mountains or over the Atlantic states. A downstream ridge may lie over the mid-Atlantic, which, if strong enough, brings pleasant winter weather to Iceland or even the British Isles. The amplitude of the meridional pattern will dictate the intensity of the unusual weather, with warm and cold spells varying in severity, duration, and location.

In recent years, obstinate meridional patterns in the jet stream that bring extended spells of unusual weather to the Northern Hemisphere have been attributed to changes in the Rossby circulation brought on by the effects of global warming. According to this hypothesis, the reduction in the temperature gradient between north and south (because of the widespread warming of the Arctic) has "unleashed" the Rossby waves, which are normally held in check by strong zonal flows. Record-setting warm winter temperatures along the Pacific Coast, unusual summer dry spells in the Midwest, persistent winter cold over eastern North America, and melting temperatures at the North Pole have all been ascribed to more-frequent and persistent meridional circulations. More time and research are needed to sort out the changes and their cause.

Blocking Patterns

Occasionally the upper-level circulation adopts a particular configuration that stagnates and blocks the regular flow of weather systems in their movement from west to east. The jet stream is forced to divert around these blocks, giving the region under the barrier a spell of persistent weather. Most blocks usually involve high-pressure systems and can remain in place for days and even a week or more. Blocking highs that settle in over the Southeast states in summer bring major heat waves with extended dry spells (Figure 7-20). An omega block, named for its similarity to the Greek letter omega (Ω), is a combination of a high-pressure system with lows anchoring its east and west sides (Figure 7-21). Cool and wet conditions form under the lows, while dry sunny weather lingers under the high.

Another common block is one in which upper lows are left stranded outside the main flow and meander on their own as independent weather systems. These cut-off lows may have very little forward movement for days at a time. A cut-off low over Texas and Oklahoma in June 2007 brought over 19 inches (480 mm) of rain to central Texas overnight. In winter months, California is no stranger to cut-off lows, which bring thunderstorms on their approach and heavy, continuous rain and snow in their wake.

The Connection Between the Surface and Upper Atmosphere

From a forecaster's perspective, it is most often events in the upper atmosphere that control the movement and development of weather systems at the surface in mid-latitude temperate zones. Upper features are connected to the lower levels by up and down vertical motions in the atmosphere, called ascent and descent. We've already alluded to this process: when a mass of air is removed at an upper level, a compensating flow is set up that causes air to ascend from lower levels to replace the missing mass. When air accumulates aloft, the column of air beneath sinks and the excess mass is removed. The accumulation of mass is known as convergence; removal is called divergence. These up and down movements in response to the convergence and divergence are responsible for much of our day-to-day weather.

The twists and turns of the winds in the higher atmosphere seem to have a simple structure when viewed in an upper-atmosphere chart, but that seemingly bland flow harbors several important physical features that control the convergence and divergence of mass aloft. When the height contours come together, it is a sign that mass is piling up;

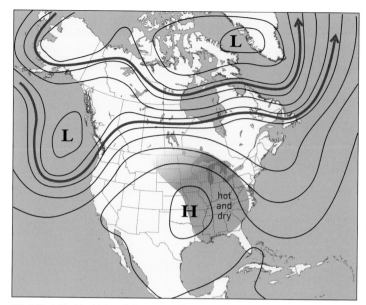

FIG. 7-20. *A blocking high and the associated temperature impact.*

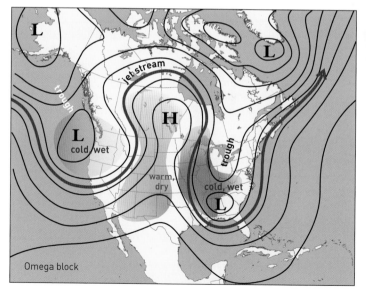

FIG. 7-21. *An omega block, showing regions of warmer and colder temperatures.*

when contours separate, mass is removed. When the wind accelerates at some location, such as a jet core, mass is removed behind and piles up in front. When the flow turns in a counterclockwise direction, mass is removed in front of the turn and added behind; the reverse is true if the turn is in the opposite direction. Horizontal wind shear—the change in wind speed from place to place at the same level in the flow—also introduces turning motions in the atmosphere that draw the air upward or push it downward. Each of these additions and subtractions of mass aloft triggers a response in the layers below. That response does not necessarily correct the imbalance in the atmosphere, for the upper flow typically generates divergence and convergence that go on for the many-day lifetime of a storm, ending only when friction and the movement of frontal systems rob the system of its energy.

The upper disturbances come in all scales and sizes: sometimes barely evident and able only to manufacture a thin layer of cirrus clouds; sometimes triggering the start of an outbreak of severe thunderstorms; at other times, creating large and long-lasting winter storms. Influences aloft may be assisted by other factors that cause an air column to rise: flow over a mountain barrier, the advection of warm air (which causes the atmosphere to expand upward), convection in an unstable airmass, or lifting along warm and cold fronts.

A very good analogy for the convergence and divergence processes can be found in the flow of traffic along a highway. When the number of lanes changes from three to two, traffic piles up at the constriction. When lanes increase from two to three, the traffic flow speeds up and diverges. When speed limits fall, traffic becomes congested as faster vehicles catch up with slower, and when signs permit an increase in the speed limit, the cars separate as they draw apart. More complicated patterns arise when, for instance, the number of lanes falls from three to two, but the speed limit increases. Whether or not the traffic diverges or converges in this situation will depend on the relative amount of the speed increase versus the reduction of the number of lanes. The upper atmosphere behaves in a similar way.

Mass cannot be created or destroyed in the atmosphere, and so the movement of air upward must be compensated by downward motions somewhere else. In a convective sky, the updrafts of a thunderstorm are compensated by balancing downward flows somewhere nearby—thunderstorms are usually accompanied by neighboring clear skies. Large storms generated by a trough aloft are typically preceded or

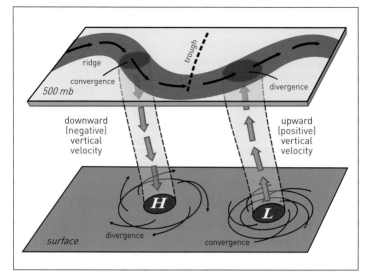

FIG. 7-22. *Air converging into a low is compelled to rise upward, supported by a region of divergence (outward flow) in the higher atmosphere. In a surface high, outflowing air is replaced by a downward flow supported by a region of convergence aloft. The alternating pattern of highs and lows in mid-latitudes is supported by this pattern of divergence and convergence in the upper atmosphere.*

followed by a ridge: in the trough, the air rises; in the ridge, it sinks back. This leads to a cycle of ascent and descent in which air flows into a surface low, rises upward to balance the divergence created by the wind at some higher level, flows horizontally to a trailing or leading region of convergence, and sinks back to the surface into a high-pressure cell. Outward-flowing air from the high then closes the cycle by moving into the low that began the circuit (Figure 7-22).

This cycle that sees air rising in lows, spreading outward, and sinking back in highs is a characteristic of all cyclonic storm systems in the mid-latitudes. A winter storm is followed by cold air and clear skies as air converging into the center of the low is replaced by a descending circulation with the approach of a high. The ascending air in the low carries air to saturation, forming clouds and precipitation. The descending air in the high brings clearing skies and dry weather, though it may not be pleasant because of the cold and wind. For this reason, it is generally thought that highs bring good weather systems and lows bring bad, but the reality is much more variable.

Atmospheric Dynamics

More than anything else, upper-level global-scale winds resemble the flow of a stream. In a stream, water flows slowest along the banks and fastest in the center. There are twists and turns in the stream's course. Rocks at the bottom cause the flow to rise over them, and obstructions create whirls that then flow downstream until they gradually dissipate. A stick floating on the surface rotates as it gets caught between the slower flow along the bank and the quicker flow in the middle of the stream, but where the stream widens and slows, the stick may drift along without changing its orientation. In some places there are back eddies and in others a whirlpool that persists for a considerable time.

All of these features and more can be identified in the atmosphere, but there is one feature that is distinct from the stream: all those twists and turns, whirlpools, meanders, and variations in flow speed upset some balance and cause the air to move upward and downward. The wind is a large part of the planet's atmospheric dynamics—the physical processes that influence the motions in the troposphere and above. Each one disturbs a balance, and that balance is often regained by up and down movements in the air column. As we'll see later, those vertical motions, continuously searching for a balance, are the cause of our weather and our climates.

Global Circulations

The Structure of the Earth's Weather Systems

The Earth has a problem—too much heat accumulates at the equator, while the poles are cold. Left alone, low pressure would form at lower latitudes and high pressure would build over the north and south, eventually leading to a surface flow toward the equator and an upper flow that moves to the poles. Alas, as soon as this flow would begin to move, the Coriolis force would get in the way, turning the winds to the right in the Northern Hemisphere and the left in the Southern.

When we construct a map of the multiyear seasonal averages of global pressure, a very distinctive pattern is revealed (Figure 7-23). Around the Earth's middle, an extended low-pressure zone meanders north and south across the equator, following the Sun as it brings summer first to one hemisphere and then the other. In tropical mid-latitudes, high-pressure anticyclones hold sway, strengthening and weakening with the seasons but never disappearing. Farther from the equator, temperate zones have no dominating pressure pattern, but

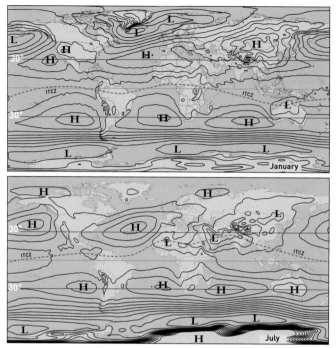

FIG. 7-23. *Thirty-year average of global January and July sea level pressure. The ITCZ is indicated by the heavy dashed line. Note the movement of the ITCZ northward during the Northern Hemisphere summer.*

instead are subject to passing highs and lows that bring changeable weather that swings from warm to cold and back. Over Arctic latitudes, pressure patterns are weak, though there are some stubborn lows near Greenland and Iceland in winter months. How do these structures accommodate the need to move heat from the equator to the poles?

The high, equatorial Sun bathes the midriff of the globe with a generous year-round flow of energy, creating a climate of warm, sultry temperatures that hardly changes with the seasons. This solar heating forms a zone of low-density, tropospheric air that is marked by an equatorial low-pressure trough that draws in the winds from both hemispheres. Those colliding winds create a region of convergence known as the Intertropical Convergence Zone (ICZ or ITCZ), which is often described as the Earth's "weather equator." The merging

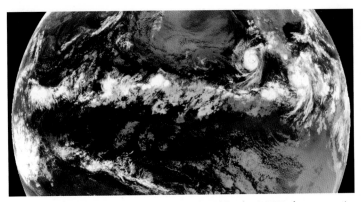

FIG. 7-24. *An infrared weather-satellite image acquired October 9, 2008, shows convective and mid-level clouds associated with the ITCZ stretching across the Pacific Ocean. The line of cloud in the lower left is the South Pacific convergence zone (SPCZ).*

winds have no option but to rise upward, creating a discontinuous band of showers and thundershowers that are prominent features in satellite images, tracing out the day-to-day position of the ITCZ (Figure 7-24).

Within the ITCZ, rising air ascends to the tropopause at an altitude of about 11 miles (17 km) and then spreads out horizontally, flowing away from the equator to the north and south. As this upper-level flow moves to higher latitudes, it encounters a strengthening Coriolis force that gradually deflects the stream to the right in the Northern Hemisphere and to the left in the Southern until they become a zone of westerly winds on each side of the ITCZ, at about 30° latitude. Because of this westerly turn, the air that has risen from the ITCZ can no longer move northward, and so it sinks back to the surface to become a part of the subtropical anticyclones that are so prominent in Figure 7-23. The descending air is warmed and dried by adiabatic compression, making the tropics a region of clear skies and pleasant winter temperatures that serves as a destination for the global tourist industry.

At the surface, the pressure difference between the subtropical anticyclones and the ITCZ draws some of the subsiding air back toward the equator. Now, the Coriolis force deflects the low-level winds to the northeast in the Northern Hemisphere and to the southeast on the other side of the equator, creating a steady and persistent air current that is unique to the tropics. Because these easterly flows provided sailing ships with a steady supply of wind on their voyages (Figure 7-25),

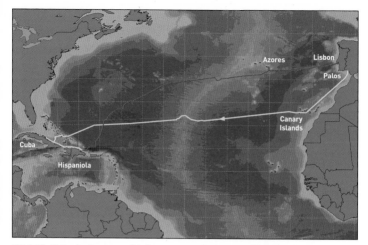

FIG. 7-25. *Columbus's route on his first voyage to the New World. In the 15th century, Portuguese navigators discovered the wind systems that surround the ocean anticyclones. Expeditions to the Canary Islands (on the south side of the Azores high) found that an alternative to the way home along the African coast was to sail northward to the Azores and catch westerly winds back to Portugal. In 1492, Columbus took advantage of the discovery of the trade-wind system, heading southwest to the Canaries to pick up and ride the trades to the Caribbean. He didn't go far enough south to find reliable winds on his first voyage, but corrected his navigation in three later trips. On his return voyages, he headed to the northeast, finding and riding the westerlies to the Azores and back to Spain.*

they are known as the trade winds, or simply "the trades." Eventually, the two hemispheric trade wind systems converge on the ITCZ (Figure 7-26) and we come back to the start of the cycle.

This giant circulation—rising at the ITCZ, flowing away from the equator, sinking into the anticyclones, and finally flowing back to the ITCZ—is known as a Hadley cell (Figure 7-27), first proposed in 1735 by George Hadley (1685–1768), a British lawyer and amateur meteorologist. Hadley circulations are a characteristic of all planets with atmospheres, even slow-turning Venus. In spite of its ubiquitous nature, it must be noted that the Hadley circulation is a long-term average over the tropical regions and is not readily observed in the daily weather patterns.

The Hadley cell only explained the transfer of heat from the equator to a latitude of 30° or so, and it was only after 130 years had elapsed that other components of the global circulation were proposed by the

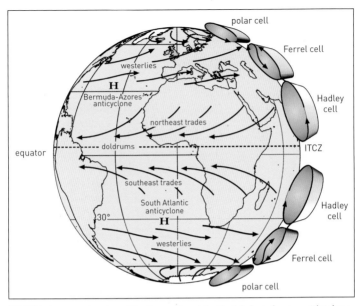

FIG. 7-26. *A perspective view of the three-cell model with global wind systems. This drawing shows the northern summer situation in which the ITCZ lies north of the equator.*

American meteorologist William Ferrel (1817–1891). Ferrel added two more cells to the one proposed by Hadley: one that explained wind and energy flows in polar regions, and a second that operated in temperate regions between 30° and 60° of latitude (Figures 7-26 and 7-27). These circulation cells extended our understanding of the role that the atmosphere plays in distributing the excessive heat of the equator to cooler regions.

The long winter nights at polar latitudes create a dense, cold atmosphere that flows aggressively southward, pushed by a strong high-pressure cell located over the poles—the so-called Arctic vortex. The Coriolis force turns the south-flowing winds to the right in the Northern Hemisphere and left in the Southern to create polar easterly winds. At about 60° latitude, the cold air encounters temperatures warm enough to generate upward motion and the air rises. Once aloft, the pressure gradient created by the temperature contrasts between the center and edges of the polar cell drives a high-altitude flow back toward the pole—a flow that eventually cools and descends to the surface in the midst of the polar anticyclone (Figure 7-27).

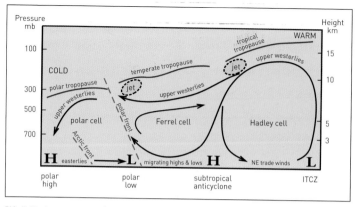

FIG. 7-27. *A cross section from the equator to the North Pole of the main latitudinal circulation cells in the atmosphere. Warm moist air rising at the equator flows northward (and southward) to descend into the semipermanent subtropical anticyclones. At the surface, the flow splits, with one branch returning southward back to the equator, while the other carries warm air northward under the Ferrel cell. Migrating highs and lows within the dynamic temperate latitudes mix the warm air with cold outflows from the Arctic regions. The complex weather systems of the Ferrel cell feed warm air into the polar cell at higher levels, which then sinks to the surface to become a source of cold outflowing air.*

The polar-cell model is not a good explanation of the winds in the Arctic and Antarctic since easterlies are not the dominant surface wind direction, though they can be teased out by taking long-term averages. Instead, high-latitude flows are probably better explained by the extreme cold and the strong temperature gradients that dictate an average southward flow at the surface and a compensating northward flow aloft, both turned by the Coriolis force.

Between the polar cell and the Hadley cell lies the Ferrel cell, the middle gear in the three global circulations. The Ferrel cell is probably best visualized as a region of turbulence in which eddies—high- and low-pressure systems—mix the air from the tropics with that of the poles, transferring the heat extracted from solar energy to higher latitudes. Over an extended period of time, the complex winds within the Ferrel cell average out to a westerly flow, particularly at mid- and upper levels of the atmosphere. These westerlies are driven by the gradients in temperature and pressure heights between the tropics and the poles, turned to the east by the Coriolis force.

Because the Ferrel cell circulation is relatively disorganized, there is usually considerable deviation from a steady westerly wind in the day-to-day circulation. As we've seen, upper-atmosphere flows alternate between meandering loops that bring cold air southward and warm air north, and strong west-to-east flows that hold temperature exchanges at bay. These changeable patterns are what gives the temperate zone its changeable weather and its interesting meteorology.

The Earth's Climatic Zones

The Anticyclones

Much of the world's climatology can be explained by the effects of the Hadley, Ferrel, and polar cells and the influence they have on precipitation, wind, and cloud. In the map of January precipitation (Figure 7-28), the ITCZ is marked by the band of heavy rainfall along the equator. Light or no precipitation falls under the anticyclones, while regions of heavier precipitation in temperate zones delineate the main storm tracks.

The most striking features on a map of the Earth's pressure systems (Figure 7-23, marked "H") are the tropical high-pressure anticyclones that stretch in two chains along the 30th parallels of latitude, north and south. The anticyclones have a dynamic personality, moving north and south with the Sun, waxing or waning with the seasons. When the Hawaiian high is at its summer position, California experiences its trademark dry weather, light winds, and mostly sunny skies. In winter, the West Coast climate falls under the influence of the westerlies as the high sinks southward and summer sunshine turns to cool, wet, and occasionally stormy weather. When a ridge of high pressure builds

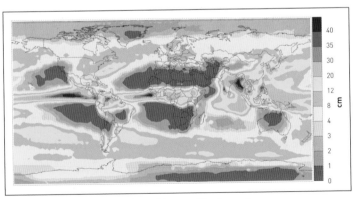

FIG. 7-28. *January precipitation derived from satellite observations.*

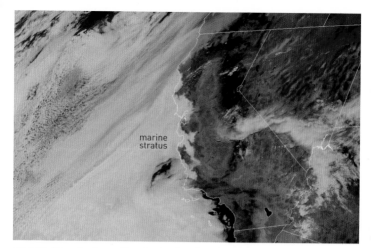

marine
stratus

FIG. 7-29. *Extensive sheets of low cloud gather along the Pacific Coast in this satellite image looking toward California. The cloud is trapped below the inversion created by subsiding air in the Hadley circulation. The brown streak is a plume of forest-fire smoke.*

northward over England or France from the Atlantic anticyclone in summer, dry spells and droughts result, though vacationers usually find the weather to their liking.

A glance at Figure 7-23 shows that the subtropical highs tend to be located on the eastern side of the ocean basins, pressing their strongest pressure gradients against the west coasts of the continents. This places the strongest subsidence and divergent winds along those coasts, drying and stabilizing the air and bringing an exceptionally dry climatology to those locations, at least seasonally. The descending currents do not sink all the way to the surface and so trap a shallow cool layer under an inversion against the ocean and nearby land.

Along the Pacific coasts of North and South America, moisture beneath the inversion condenses to form a shallow layer of fog or low stratus, a feature that is well known to residents of San Francisco (Figure 7-29). Rainfall is almost unknown beneath the subsiding air, since the cloud layer is very shallow. Along the Peruvian coast (and, to a lesser extent, along the Namibian coast of Africa), morning fog beneath the subsidence inversion provides sufficient moisture to support sparse vegetation, while inland regions are among the driest in the world. It is no coincidence that the world's great deserts lie beneath the influence of the anticyclones.

The Intertropical Convergence Zone

The annual back-and-forth migration of the Intertropical Convergence Zone creates a climate marked by a seesaw between rainy and dry seasons for many countries in the tropics. For most subtropical regions, there are two rainy seasons, one when the ITCZ passes on its way northward, the other when it returns on its way south (Figure 7-30, Libreville and Nairobi). Usually one of these wet spells is more active than the other, and they are often given names such as "big wet" and "little wet." At the end points of the north and south migration, where the ITCZ pauses and then retreats, there is only one rainy season (Figure 7-30, Cairns, Mopti). Over the centers of the continents and along the equator itself, where the atmosphere is unstable and moisture in good supply, rainfall is a year-round event and the impact of the ITCZ is barely noticed.

The rainfall that comes with the ITCZ is most critical to regions of Africa bordering the south side of the Sahara Desert, an area known as the Sahel. At the northern extremity of the Sahel, rainfall amounts to less than 4 inches (100 mm) per year, and because the rainy season

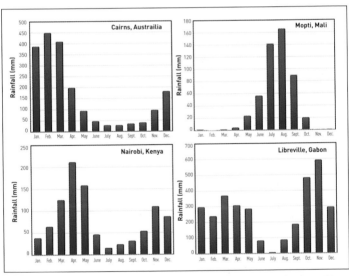

FIG. 7-30. *Graphs of monthly precipitation for selected regions influenced by the ITCZ. Note that Mopti, at the limit of the northward movement of the ITCZ, and Cairns at the south, have only one wet season. The other stations have a wet season when the ITCZ passes while going north and another on its return to the south.*

can last as little as a few weeks, the area is prone to droughts when the ITCZ weakens or fails to arrive. Long-term records show that droughts can persist for extended periods of time—sometimes as long as two decades. In contrast, the intersection of the ITCZ with the steep slopes of the Andes gives the town of Buenaventura, along the Pacific coast of Colombia, a drenching annual rainfall of 265 inches (6.73 m).

The Atmospheric Design

Our dissection of the global wind and pressure system has taken us into a much wider-ranging exploration of the Earth's circulation system than you might have expected at the start. The forces that control the movement of air are limited in number: temperature gradients in the horizontal and vertical, the Coriolis force, the upper-level flow, and friction. These are moderated by land-ocean differences, terrain, and seasonality. Their integration within the thin skin of air surrounding our planet produces complex weather systems and a good part of the large-scale global climate. We hope that the subjects in this section have surprised you a bit, and left you with an appreciation of the grand scheme of things in the atmosphere.

Regional Circulations

Previously, we discussed the global circulations that drive the transfer of heat and energy from the Earth's warm midriff to the poles. The accumulation of heat is not a uniform process—while tropical latitudes are certainly warmer than polar, the accumulation of heat also varies along the longitudes, with some meridians packing on the heat more efficiently than others. One of the most important factors in this uneven heating is the difference in the way heat accumulates over land and water, although other features of the Earth's geography, particularly terrain, are also significant.

In this section, we discuss regional wind systems such as monsoons and the El Niño circulations, leaving local wind systems such as sea breezes for later in the chapter. Regional winds follow seasonal to multiyear cycles. One of the largest and most important of the regional circulations is the monsoon, which brings seasonal weather to several locations around the globe. After monsoons, we will go on to the famous El Niño and La Niña circulations with their global impacts. Finally, we'll end our exploration of regional winds with a peek at some other hemispherical climate oscillations and their confounding but important impact on large-scale and long-term weather.

Monsoons

The word "monsoon" comes from the Arabic "*mausim*" meaning "season" or, sometimes, "seasonal wind." For most readers, "monsoon weather" will bring thoughts of heavy rainfalls in midsummer India. Climatologists, however, generally accept a more global application of the original Arabic meaning, and recognize individual monsoons in India, East Asia, Australia, Africa, and even in both North and South America.

In some cases, what is called a monsoon is a reflection of the movement of the Intertropical Convergence Zone (ITCZ) in its annual back-and-forth oscillation between Northern and Southern Hemispheres. The ITCZ is often "captured" by the monsoon circulations and carried northward over land to latitudes beyond those characteristic of its unperturbed (oceanic) state, a feature of the monsoons in India and China.

We owe the first description of monsoon weather in the western world to Edmond Halley, of Halley's Comet fame. Halley first described the Indian monsoon in 1686, attributing it to the seasonal warming of the land as the Sun travels northward in the spring and summer. This heating causes a low-pressure cell (a thermal low) to form over the land, drawing in cooler, high-moisture-content air from the surrounding oceans. This humid marine air fuels the frequent and heavy convective storms that distinguish the monsoon season's weather. For the most part, this definition is still accurate, though it describes only the wet monsoon's personality.

We now recognize that monsoon circulations extend through the depth of the atmosphere, incorporating upper- and low-level jet streams, topographic forcing, fronts, cold and warm ocean currents, the Intertropical Convergence Zone, and mid-latitude highs and lows. Halley wasn't wrong; the story just had many more chapters than he was able to read.

Monsoons are not just rainy seasons. The definition borrowed from the original Arabic requires a contrasting dry season with a noticeable change in wind direction, and so all true monsoon climates have a dry and usually cool season to go with the wet. In India, Southeast Asia, and China, the wet monsoon is often labeled the southwest or southeast monsoon for the prevailing wind direction. The winter season brings the cool and dry northwest and northeast monsoons.

The Indian Wet Monsoon

The India Meteorological Department designates four seasons: winter (January to February), the pre-monsoon (March to May), the southwest monsoon (June to early September), and the northeast monsoon or post monsoon (October to December). In large part, it could be said that India has wet (southwest monsoon) and dry (northeast monsoon) seasons with two intervening transition periods. In some regions, largely because of the influence of the terrain, the southwest monsoon is actually the driest time of year, while the northeast flow brings wet weather (Figure 7-31). The hottest weather comes just before the onset of the wet season, as the arrival of humid monsoon air brings an increase in cloudiness and cooling rains. In the west and south, April is the hottest month, while in the north, May has that distinction.

In the Indian subcontinent (and elsewhere), the wet monsoon is caused by the heating of the land as the northward-moving Sun brings increasing levels of solar insolation in April and May. Air temperatures rise and surface pressures begin to fall across Somalia, Saudi Arabia, Pakistan, and northwest India. By the end of May, when the heat low becomes well established across the Indian landmass, lower pressures (Figure 7-32) draw a southwesterly wind from across the surrounding ocean waters, and humid oceanic air is pulled onto the land. The onset

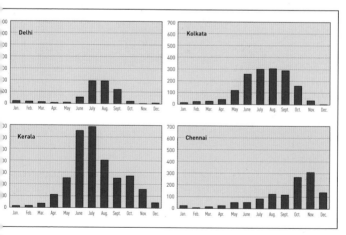

▶ 7-31. *Selected monthly precipitation graphs for Indian stations. Note the early and heavy onset of monsoon rainfall at Kerala, the northeast monsoon rainfall late in the year at Chennai, the short monsoon season at Delhi, and the longer and heavier one at Kolkata (formerly Calcutta).*

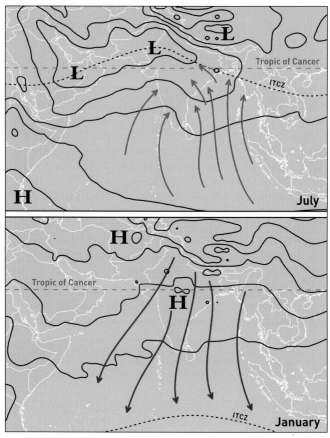

FIG. 7-32. *Wind flows associated with the wet monsoon (top) and dry monsoon (bottom) over the Indian subcontinent.*

of these moist winds along the west coast of India in late May marks the end of the dry season and the start of the monsoon; the onset is often sudden and is called the "burst" of the monsoon.

The first monsoon winds invade the southeast coast near Sri Lanka, immersing the continental borders with moist and unstable air (Figure 7-33). As June advances, this layer of humid air spreads north and westward, eventually crossing the Pakistan border in mid-July. As the humidity arrives at each successive location, blue skies give way to thunderstorms and rain, bringing much-needed and welcome pre-

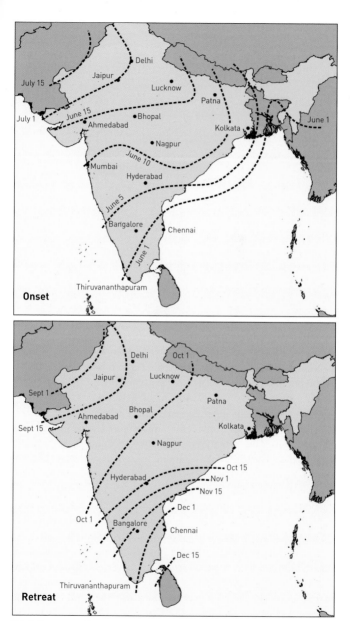

FIG. 7-33. *Average dates of onset (top) and retreat (bottom) of the Indian monsoons.*

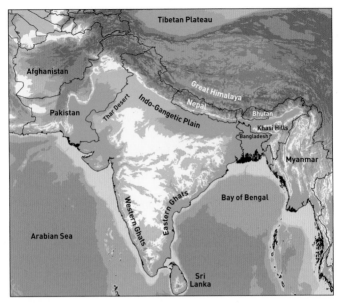

FIG. 7-34. *Topography of the Indian subcontinent.*

cipitation that eases the oppressive heat of midsummer. The start of the monsoon is so regular that newspaper accounts of the start of the season typically mention the number of days by which it is early or late.

India has a highly variable topography (Figure 7-34) and monsoon rainfall accumulations respond dramatically to the rise and fall of the terrain. Heavy accumulations are found along windward-facing mountain slopes—the Western Ghats, the Khasi Hills, the coast ranges of Bangladesh, and the southern slopes of the Himalayas. Much smaller amounts fall in protected interior valleys (Figure 7-35), particularly over the Indo-Gangetic Plain and on the lee side of the Western Ghats. World-record rainfalls have been recorded in the region along the India–Bangladesh border where monsoon winds encounter the Khasi Hills, and the air is squeezed into narrow valleys or lifted over 4,500-foot (1,400-m) peaks. Mawsynram, near the Bangladesh border, has an average annual rainfall of 39 feet (11.9 meters), making it one of the wettest places on the globe. In 1861, nearby Cherrapunji recorded a world-record, single-year rainfall of nearly 87 feet (26.5 meters)! These two communities have an ongoing joust as to who has the world's largest rainfall and rainfall rate.

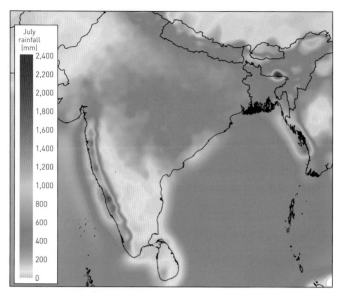

FIG. 7-35. *Average July rainfall (1999–2013) across the Indian subcontinent from satellite and ground measurements. Note the very high precipitation on mountain and hill slopes that face into the monsoon winds.*

Over the Indo-Gangetic Plain, just south of the Himalaya Mountains, the mid-June arrival of the monsoon circulation and the flat topography give the region a relatively low precipitation in a short season that lasts only two and a half months at Delhi. Farther to the northwest, dry Pakistan barely feels the monsoon, which arrives in mid-July and departs before September; the short season makes the duration and intensity of the rainfall even more critical than over India. Across both countries, the rains are essential for agriculture and reservoir recharge. Rice, the region's major food source, is especially dependent upon the timely arrival of copious amounts of precipitation. For farmers, it is a tense time: will the rains ensure prosperity or even survival, or will Mother Nature prove perverse, with delays and too-small amounts?

Monsoon weather is not one of continuous rainfall, but of frequent afternoon and overnight convection in showers and thundershowers. The weather undergoes larger-scale variations as well, with both active and inactive periods (called "breaks") that lend uncertainty to the summer season. During a monsoon break, the Indo-Gangetic

Plain experiences a period of dry weather, while heavy precipitation becomes focused instead along the Himalayan foothills and northeast India, often bringing floods to Nepal, Assam, and Bangladesh. Typically, a break will last for three to five days, but can go on for much longer and contribute to midsummer droughts in mid-northern parts of the country. In drier southern India, the breaks have the opposite effect, tending to bring heavy rainfall that offsets the lee-side drying of the coastal mountains.

Because they supply nearly 80 percent of the annual precipitation in north-central regions, the seasonal rains are critical for agriculture, a sector that generates nearly 18 percent of India's gross domestic product. The cooling rains bring relief from the 104°F (40°C) and higher temperatures that build during the pre-monsoon season, fill reservoirs for irrigation and power production, and water the forests that cover 20 percent of India. However, the daily downpours also bring flooding, landslides, an increase in certain diseases, and the destruction of vulnerable infrastructure.

The Indian Dry Monsoon

The inexorable movement of the Sun to the south side of the equator in September deprives the wet monsoon of its major energy source. The ground and overlying troposphere cools, and dry northeast winds push onto the plains from the Himalayas (Figure 7-32). The transition to the post-monsoon season begins in Pakistan and Rajasthan and pushes steadily southwestward (Figure 7-33), eventually bringing an end to the rainy season. In the winter season, when the Sun is farthest south, the land-based thermal low disappears. Air flows outward from the land, driven in part by the massive winter anticyclone that forms over the interior of Asia. In its travel from the high plateaus of Tibet into India, the already-dry continental air is further warmed as it descends the slopes of the Himalayas and so brings a mostly rainless and pleasantly cool season to much of the country. Intervening months between the two monsoons are transitional periods, often with showery weather, but little significant accumulation of rainfall.

The winter months are not the dry season for all of India, however. When the dry and cool air of the northeast monsoon reaches the Bay of Bengal, it is quick to absorb moisture from the warm waters, which it then carries over the southern reaches of India and over Sri Lanka. The precipitation associated with this flow exceeds that of the southwest monsoon, so the wetter season in these regions comes in the winter months (Figure 7-31, Chennai).

The Monsoon of Southeast Asia

The monsoon climatology of continental Southeast Asia (Vietnam, Laos, Cambodia, Thailand, Myanmar [Burma], and the Malay Peninsula) is very similar to that of India, with a gradual influx of marine air in response to the formation of temperature-induced lows over the land surfaces. In the southern parts of the region, the warm waters of the Bay of Bengal and the South China Sea are never far away, but in the rugged northerly reaches of Thailand and Myanmar (Burma), the nearest ocean may be 600 miles (1,000 km) distant. As in India, terrain and exposure to winds flowing from the ocean play a major role in the local distribution of precipitation, sometimes reversing the rainy season.

The wet monsoon season begins with weak and variable flows that converge into a low located in the interior of Thailand, drawing in humid airmasses from the Bay of Bengal, the Andaman Sea, and the Gulf of Thailand. Precipitation is heaviest on the eastward-facing slopes of Vietnam and Laos, and on westward-facing slopes of Myanmar (Burma) and Malaysia, with relatively light amounts in the terrain-protected interior.

As May turns to June, the southwest flow from the Bay of Bengal comes to dominate the region. Falling pressures over the Gobi Desert draw the humid ocean air northward into China. The weather is mostly convective, and afternoon thunderstorms are a common feature of the climate, especially near the coasts, where sea breezes push onto the land each afternoon. Rainfall peaks in July and August with amounts strongly tied to the exposure of the terrain and the direction of the wind. The southwest flow makes the west-facing slopes of the coastal mountains of Myanmar (Burma) and the mountains along the Vietnam–Laos border especially wet, and monthly rainfall accumulations can easily exceed 20 inches (500 mm). Rainfall tends to come in spells that usually last for several days, followed by a period of drier weather.

The Asian continent begins to cool in late September, and the pressure forces that drive the Southeast Asian monsoon wane and retreat to the south. Weather in October mimics that of the spring, with variable flows and ephemeral lines of thunderstorms, but the transition to the dry season is much more rapid than the onset of the wet monsoon.

Precipitation falls abruptly in November when cool and dry northwest winds from China, driven by a growing anticyclone over Siberia, move southward across the region.

The China Monsoon

The flow of marine air into China is largely blocked to the south and southwest by the Himalaya Mountains, so the main low-level air currents must approach from the southeast, following the lower terrain from Indochina or coming across the waters of the South China Sea. The northward-flowing air stream finds little topographic resistance from the flat plains of central China, so high-humidity air is able to envelop the eastern half of the country, reaching as far north as the 35th parallel. This high-latitude reach brings the ocean air into contact with mid-latitude frontal systems and low-pressure disturbances, greatly complicating the personality of the daily weather during the monsoon season.

Eventually the south and southwest flow reaches toward Japan and Korea, where northward movement is blocked by the mid-latitude westerlies that dominate above the 35th parallel. A frontal boundary forms between the monsoon air and the dry and cool airmasses from

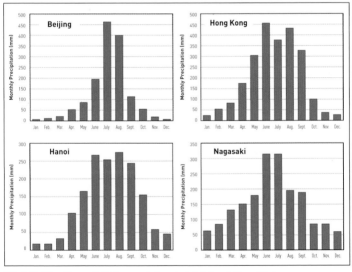

FIG. 7-36. *Monthly precipitation graph for selected Asian stations. Their monsoon season is not related to the position of the ITCZ, so all have a similar precipitation profile.*

the north. Over China, this boundary is known as the Meiyu front, a term that means "Plum Rain." Over Japan, the front is called the Baiu; over Korea, it is the Changma. The Meiyu moves slowly northward during the summer months, bringing a season of rainfall as it arrives and drier weather when it departs. It is a moot point whether the movement of a frontal system into a region should be regarded as the start of a monsoon, but the position of the front is certainly influenced by the influx of monsoon air to its south. The graphs of monthly precipitation in Figure 7-36 show the delayed arrival and quick departure of a short monsoon season in Beijing and Nagasaki, but a much longer monsoon season in Hanoi and Hong Kong where the tropical climate makes all months wet. To the tourist, the overriding characteristic of the monsoon season is usually a stifling humidity that robs the unaccustomed body of energy and ambition.

The China monsoon season reaches its most northerly extent in August and begins to retreat shortly thereafter as the cool-weather season begins to develop over Siberia and Mongolia (Figure 7-36, Beijing). As winter settles, an immense high-pressure anticyclone forms over Mongolia and central Siberia, driving cold and dry air southward across China and into Southeast Asia. The transition is rather abrupt, for the dry-season weather in China is more akin to a North American winter than to the dry and temperate climatology over India.

The Australian Monsoon

Christmas in Northern Australia brings rain. It's the monsoon season—known colloquially as "the wet"—that stretches from November to April over Western Australia, Northern Territory, and Queensland. As the Sun moves south of the equator, the deserts of central Australia are heated, dropping pressures over the land and forming a thermal low (the Pilbara low) that draws the ITCZ and tropical moisture southward across the continent. Tropical maritime air then invades Queensland (Figure 7-37) and the "Top End" of the northern parts of Northern Territory and Western Australia. On rare occasions, the humid air can penetrate deep into the outback deserts, bringing monsoon weather to the interior of the continent.

In the early monsoon season, wet weather comes from afternoon thunderstorms that bring occasional flooding rains and damaging winds (Figure 7-38). As the season advances, precipitation tends to come more from passing cyclonic storms that can turn into tropical cyclones and dump prodigious amounts of rain. As in other monsoon

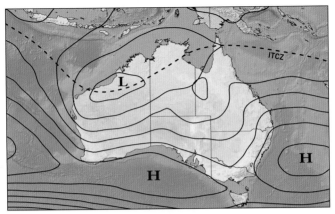

FIG. 7-37. *This composite pressure pattern for January over Australia shows the summer position of the ITCZ, embedded in the equatorial trough. The ITCZ separates the very humid air over the Indonesian archipelago from the dry inland atmosphere over the Australian continent.*

FIG. 7-38. *This image of the Pacific regions acquired by the Earth Polychromatic Imaging Camera aboard the* Deep Space Climate Observatory *satellite shows the monsoon cloudiness over Northern Australia.*

climates, the weather alternates between active and inactive phases; the inactive phase or "break" comes when the trough weakens or retreats northward to the Arafura Sea, replacing the heavy weather of the active period with random showers and thundershowers.

Seasonal rains associated with the wets are highly variable, and

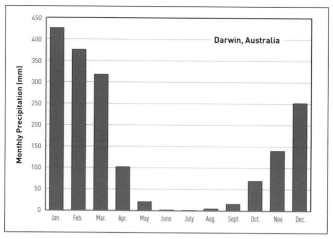

FIG. 7-39. *Annual precipitation graph for Darwin, Australia.*

when they fail it has serious consequences for agriculture and nature. Of particular concern is the state of ENSO—the El Niño Southern Oscillation. This mid-Pacific phenomenon (discussed on page 265) has two personalities. During La Niña episodes, the monsoon typically begins early and brings a high probability of heavier-than-normal precipitation. With El Niño, the monsoon is late and there is an increased risk of dry weather and droughts.

As March turns into April, the Sun moves back to the north side of the equator, the Southern Hemisphere cools, and the ITCZ and monsoon retreat from Australia. The southeasterly trade winds return to the north of the continent, and the rainless dry season (Figure 7-39) sets in for the next half-year.

The North America Monsoon

The North American monsoon is not as well defined as those of Asia and Australia, but it is a familiar summer visitor to residents of the southwestern United States. The basic causes are the same as in other monsoon climates—seasonal heating of the land, formation of a temperature-driven heat low, and a flow of humid air from a nearby ocean. This monsoon provides as much as 70 percent of the annual precipitation to western Mexico and 40 to 60 percent of the yearly total to the southwestern states—a critical moisture supply for a desert region with a burgeoning population.

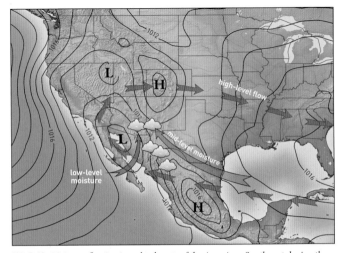

FIG. 7-40. *Moisture flowing into the deserts of the American Southwest during the monsoon season comes from the Gulf of California and the eastern Pacific, with a mid-level contribution from the Gulf of Mexico. A clockwise circulation (red arrows) around the upper-level Bermuda high carries humid air from the subtropics across the Baja Peninsula and into the American Southwest. Sea-level-pressure contours are a seven-year average for July and August.*

The transition to the monsoon flow begins in May and June when intense solar heating over the Mexican Plateau and the American desert builds a broad thermal low over the Colorado River Valley (Figure 7-40) with lowest pressures centered at the top of the Gulf of California near Yuma and Mexicali. This thermal low steers low-level moisture from the Gulf of California, the western Pacific, and the mountains of northern Mexico into southern Arizona and New Mexico.

Heavy thunderstorm rainfall begins in late May in southern Mexico, and spreads slowly northward along the slopes of the Sierra Madre Occidental, crossing the United States border in early July. The monsoon typically begins around July 3 in Tucson and July 7 in Phoenix, with a variation of about a week at both locations. The start of this wet and cooler weather is both abrupt and welcome, relieving the intense heat of early summer. Arizona and New Mexico are at the northern limit of the monsoon circulation, so rainfall is highly variable from day to day and year to year. Thunderstorm activity is tied to the availability of moisture and to mid-level instability, both of which are sensitive to small changes in the circulation.

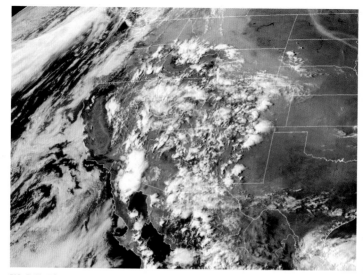

FIG. 7-41. *This GOES-14 satellite image from September 8, 2017, shows afternoon thundershowers developing over the American Southwest and northern Mexico during the 2017 monsoon season.*

When the circulation is active, solar heating and moist airflows that rise up on the terrain (Chapter 9) initiate the development of thunderstorms, which then leave the higher ground and head westward to spread out across the lower desert floor as the afternoon wanes. A major focus of convective activity is the Mogollon Rim, a steep escarpment that stretches along a northwest–southeast line across central Arizona, marking the edge of the Colorado Plateau. The intensely white thunderstorm buildups along the Rim and over other mountains in the state (Figure 7-41) are a powerful sight in the evening Sun. These same thunderstorms can have an evil side, however, bringing spectacular and dangerous lightning displays, damaging winds, large hail, and flash flooding.

As summer tapers off in late September and October, monsoon rainfall retreats southward into the tropics. Cold fronts and mid-latitude lows begin to intrude into the Southwest, perhaps triggering a few late-season storms. Dry weather returns, though by now it is the peak of the Pacific hurricane season, and the moisture from some of these storms can be caught up in the decaying monsoon flow to bring heavy rains and disastrous flooding to Mexican and American deserts.

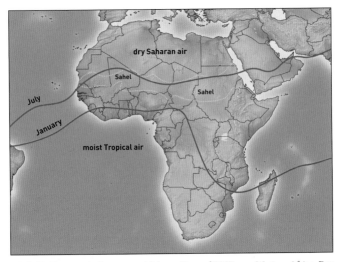

FIG. 7-42. *The average January and July positions of ITCZ over Western Africa. Dry desert conditions to the north of the ITCZ are replaced by humid Atlantic air as the convergence zone moves northward, bringing critical rainfall to the Sahel region.*

Monsoon Circulations in Africa

The monsoon of Western Africa is tied tightly to the seasonal movement of the Intertropical Convergence Zone (ITCZ). The ITCZ is created by the convergence of winds from the north and south, which in sub-Saharan Africa is the convergence of dry northerly winds from the Sahara Desert with the humid southerly winds from the tropical Atlantic. On the Atlantic side of the ITCZ, humid ocean air brings life-sustaining rainfalls, while on the north, bone-dry desert air shrivels the landscape.

During the Northern Hemisphere winter, the ITCZ moves to its most southerly position (Figure 7-42), exposing inland Western African countries to low Saharan humidities. When the ITCZ returns northward in the spring, Atlantic moisture and the rains return to the southern fringes of the Sahara (the Sahel), initiating a rainy season that irrigates the summer months (Figure 7-43, Mopti). It is a critical transition, as famine hangs in the balance if the monsoon is weak or remains farther south than normal.

In Eastern Africa, south of the equator, rainy and wet seasons are reversed. In Northern winter, the ITCZ sinks well to the south, allowing Indian Ocean air to spill onto the African coast. The monsoon season, linked to the passage of the Sun, typically has two components: the long rains from March to May and the short rains from October to December, though locations close to the Tropic of Capricorn, the limit of the Sun's southerly journey, experience only one rainy season (Figure 7-43, Blantyre).

ENSO: El Niño and La Niña

Along the Pacific coast of South America, winds blow steadily out of the south, driving a northward-flowing surface ocean current—the Humboldt Current—that carries cold water past the shores of Chile and Peru. North of the Peruvian border, the current turns out into the ocean, pulling away from the coast and drawing cold subsurface water upward from the depths in replacement. This coastal upwelling is rich in nutrients that foster the growth of plankton that supports rich pelagic ecosystems.

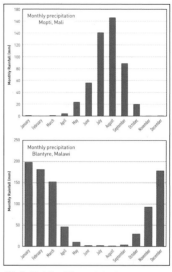

FIG. 7-43. *Monthly precipitation patterns for Mopti, Mali, and Blantyre, Malawi. Precipitation amounts are in mm.*

In the late 1800s, Luis Carranza, a Peruvian geographer, drew attention to a smaller, north-to-south-flowing, warm ocean counter-current that appeared annually off of the coast of northern Peru just after Christmas. The fishers in Paita had nicknamed the warm current *"Corriente del Niño"* or "Current of the Christ Child" in recognition of the time of year in which it usually appeared. Modern research has shown that this flow is part of a very complex mixing of surface and subsurface ocean currents along the South American coast.

The warm countercurrent noted by the Paita fishers puts in a minor and barely noticeable two- or three-week appearance nearly every year along the coast of Peru, but every three to seven years, the flow from the north is unusually warm and persistent, lasting for up to 18 months. With the passage of time, the name *Corriente del Niño* was co-opted by geographers, shortened to "El Niño," and applied only to this longer-lasting event. It was soon realized that the local El Niño (pronounced *neen*-yo) was in fact a Pacific-wide phenomenon linked to other meteorological changes: a weakening in the easterly trade winds; a periodic shifting of pressure patterns in mid-ocean; and a seesaw of rainfall and drought in Asia and South America. These events are now part of what is called the El Niño Southern Oscillation, or ENSO.

The earliest inklings of a relationship between Pacific pressure patterns and local weather events were gathered by the first director of the India Meteorological Department (IMD), Henry Blanford (1834–1893), who noticed that atmospheric pressures were unusually high during the failure of the monsoon in 1877. Gathering data from observatories around the Indian Ocean and Australia, Blanford found that the region of abnormally high pressures extended across the western Pacific and Asia, from Siberia to Australia. Blanford and Sir John Eliot (the second director of the IMD) combined the pressure relationship with other climate parameters, such as variations in the trade winds and Himalayan snowfall, in an attempt to predict the character of the Indian monsoon, but were largely unsuccessful.

Following up on this work, the third director, Sir Gilbert Thomas Walker, took on the task of collecting and analyzing a more extensive set of meteorological measurements. In the course of his investigations, Walker (1923) identified three important pressure oscillations that seemed to influence global weather patterns, including "a swaying of pressure on a big scale backwards and forwards between the Pacific Ocean and the Indian Ocean." He went on to note that "the influence of the Pacific Ocean–Indian Ocean swayings upon world weather seems to be much greater than that of either of the other two." In a 1924 paper, Walker named his three swayings the Southern Oscillation, the North Atlantic Oscillation, and the North Pacific Oscillation; they are still studied to this day. Because his methods were based strictly on observation and experience, Walker's critics found it easy to dismiss his statistical results, but today he is generally regarded as the discoverer of the global nature of El Niño.

As a part of this research, Walker formulated the Southern Oscillation Index (SOI), calculated from the monthly or seasonal difference in the air pressure between Darwin on the north Australian coast and Tahiti in the mid-Pacific. His work showed that a positive SOI (lower pressures at Darwin) is associated with cold Pacific Ocean waters, now nicknamed "La Niña" (*neen*-ya), while large negative values of the SOI were characterized by warm Pacific waters and the El Niño phenomenon.

The connection between El Niño and the Southern Oscillation Index was placed within a theoretical framework through the work of the Norwegian meteorologist Jacob Bjerknes (1897–1975). In 1969, Bjerknes proposed that El Niño and the Southern Index were related through a coupling between the atmosphere and the ocean, a hypothesis made possible by the intensive collection of meteorological data during the International Geophysical Year of 1951–52, during which a major El Niño occurred. Bjerknes demonstrated that a weakening of the equatorial trade winds brought an increase in Pacific Ocean temperatures, which in turn weakened the winds even further.

El Niño, La Niña, and the ENSO Cycle

Statistical techniques that disentangle the components of the climate record and reveal underlying cycles show that the ENSO phenomenon is the second most important process in the ups and downs of global weather; only the regular march of seasons between summer and winter is more significant. The ENSO reaches all parts of the globe, though not equally, affecting, among other events, seasonal precipitation and temperature in North America, the severity of Arctic winters, droughts and floods in Southeast Asia, the fate of the Indian monsoon, and food shortages in Africa. These relationships between ocean temperatures and distant events are known as *teleconnections*.

In its simplest form, El Niño is characterized by warmer-than-normal sea-surface temperatures over the equatorial Pacific; its counterpart, La Niña, is marked by cold-temperature anomalies. The two are part of a semiregular oscillation in the ocean-atmosphere system of the tropical Pacific that cycles from El Niño to neutral to La Niña and back at intervals that range from three to seven years (Table 7-3). ENSO is more than a change in ocean temperatures—it comes with significant transformations in the southeasterly trade winds, the temperature structure of the upper layers of the Pacific Ocean, precipitation, and locations of the subtropical and polar jet streams.

In neutral ENSO conditions, trade winds blow steadily from the east and southeast across the tropical Pacific, driven by the flow around the semipermanent anticyclone that lies along the 30th parallel of latitude in the Southern Hemisphere. The force of the wind against the ocean surface (surface stress) pushes equatorial waters to the west side of the Pacific where, heated by the high equatorial Sun along the way, they accumulate to create a half-meter-high mound of warm water northeast of Australia and east of Indonesia.

STRONG EL NIÑO YEARS	STRONG LA NIÑA YEARS
2015–2016	2010–2011
1997–1998	2007–2008
1991–1992	1999–2000
1987–1988	1998–1999
1982–1983	1988–1989
1972–1973	1974–1976

TABLE 7-3. *El Niño and La Niña years*

In turn, this Sun-warmed equatorial water raises the temperature of the overlying atmosphere in the western Pacific, creating rising air currents that promote the formation of rain-producing towering cumulus and cumulonimbus clouds (Chapter 9). As a result, the north coast of Australia and the islands of Indonesia, Borneo, and New Guinea are carpeted in tropical forests that reflect the abundant rainfall in the area. At higher levels in the atmosphere, the rising convective currents spread out, with some of the air returning to the South American side of the Pacific Ocean in the upper-level westerlies. This return flow completes an enormous circulation loop that spans most of the width of the Pacific. This immense loop is known as the Walker circulation (Figure 7-44, top panel), named by Bjerknes in honor of the man who first recognized the global significance of the swings in pressure and wind over the Pacific Ocean.

As the upper-level return branch of the Walker circulation descends into the high-pressure cell west of the Peruvian coast, it dries the atmospheric column and suppresses every form of rain-bearing cloud. This part of the world is home to the Atacama Desert of northern Chile, one of the driest places on Earth. Lima, Peru, also beneath the descending branch of the Walker circulation, has an annual precipitation of one-quarter of an inch (6 mm).

The Walker circulation is not the only such cell embedded within the tropical latitudes. Ascending branches of other circulations can be found over Africa and South America with corresponding descending branches over the Atlantic and Indian Oceans (Figure 7-44). As with the Walker circulation, rainfall is increased under the ascending branches and reduced beneath the descending flow. The Walker cell that straddles the Pacific makes Peru dry and Indonesia wet, and when

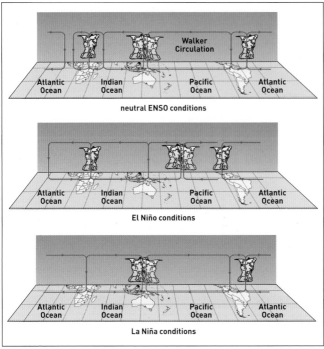

FIG. 7-44. *The Walker circulation and its evolution during El Niño and La Niña events. The top diagram shows a cross section of the average east–west circulation for neutral years over the equatorial Pacific. The middle diagram shows the same during an El Niño year; the lower diagram, for a La Niña year. Note the change in position and intensity of the convection (cloud symbols) during the various stages of the cycle. Other similar circulations can be seen over Africa and South America.*

the balance is intensified or reversed during El Niño or La Niña, both human and natural ecosystems are put into stress.

El Niño

In some years, for reasons that are largely unknown, the normal trade winds weaken, sometimes even reversing direction to blow from west to east. At the same time, the Southern Oscillation Index (SOI) begins to decline, and the elevated pool of warm water near Indonesia begins to spread into the central Pacific. Without strong trade winds for support, the small mound of warm water begins to flow back toward Peru, and the upwelling of cold water along the South American coast declines. At first there is only a hint of these changes, usually in March or April, but if the trend persists and strengthens, about six months later, in the fall of the year, an "official" El Niño begins. The moderate El Niño of 2018–19 became established in September and ended the following June.

The signs of an impending El Niño are diagnostic:

- a rise in surface pressure over Darwin and a fall over Tahiti, making the SOI negative,
- easterly trade winds in the mid-Pacific weaken or even reverse direction to westerlies,
- a steady rise in surface water temperatures along the equator and the coast of Peru, eventually exceeding 0.9°F (0.5°C) above normal, and
- the coastal upwelling of cold water along the coast of Peru weakens or disappears.

The oceanic impact of strong El Niño conditions is evident in the upper panel in Figure 7-45, which shows an anomalous band of warm ocean temperatures stretching along the equator in the eastern Pacific off of South America. In this anomaly chart, which shows the sea-surface temperature changes averaged over five El Niño episodes, we see a dramatic 3.5 to 4.5° Fahrenheit (2 to 2.5°C) warming in the eastern equatorial Pacific and a 0.9 to 1.8° Fahrenheit cooling (0.5 to 1°C) over the tropical South Pacific.

Tropical and equatorial weather responds quickly to the developing warm episode, particularly if the El Niño is a strong one. The normally reliable convective rainfall over Indonesia begins to slacken and then re-forms in the central Pacific as the Walker circulation weakens (Figure 7-44, center panel). In concert, Australian rainfall eases. Stormy weather increases over Tahiti and the surrounding islands of Polynesia, bringing heavy rainfall and local flooding. On the eastern side of the Pacific, Peru and Ecuador begin to see the first thunderstorms, promising heavier rains in the months to come.

Sea-surface temperature anomalies usually reach a peak in December before gradually returning to normal, unperturbed values in late April or in May. Occasionally, an El Niño will last for two years; in rare cases, much longer, such as the years 1911–15 and 1939–41. Eventually, however, the warm waters gradually cool, trade wind circulations return to normal, precipitation reverts to its unperturbed pattern, and ecosystems recover. And then, sooner or later, comes La Niña.

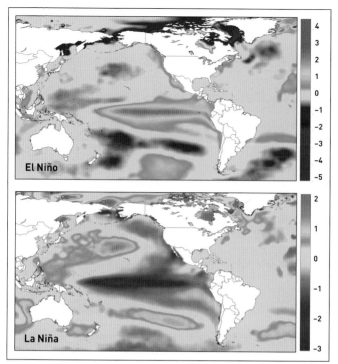

FIG. 7-45. *Sea-surface temperature (SST) anomalies during strong El Niño and La Niña events. An anomaly is the difference between average temperatures and temperatures during an ENSO event.*

La Niña

The name La Niña is not derived from historical stories but was invented in recent times to designate the opposite personality of the cold phase of the ENSO cycle (*niña* is a girl child, *niño* is a boy). During La Niña, the core of 82 to 86°F (28 to 30°C) temperatures retreats to the west side of the Pacific (Figure 7-44, lower panel), and a tongue of cooler water, with temperatures around 73°F (23°C), reaches westward along the equator from the cold pool along the coast of Peru. In effect, La Niña is nearly a mirror image of El Niño.

During the La Niña episodes, the SOI becomes more positive; mid-Pacific trade winds become stronger; upwelling intensifies along the western coast of South America; ocean temperatures climb in the western Pacific between New Guinea and the Philippines; and precipitation patterns become more extreme, with wet areas getting wetter and dry areas drier.

The La Niña of 2010–11 brought one of Australia's worst natural disasters, with widespread flooding over south and central Queensland. Over 200,000 people in 70 towns were affected; thousands of houses in Brisbane were damaged by flooding when the Brisbane River overflowed its banks. At the same time, landslides and heavy rains in Luzon in the Philippines affected 1.6 million people, killing over 50.

Monitoring the ENSO Cycle

Though the first signs of the birth of an El Niño or La Niña episode are detectable in March or April, they are usually only confirmed when the event is conclusively underway in midsummer or early fall. In the normal ups and downs of the meteorological record, there are many false starts in the SOI and the sea-surface temperature (SST) records. Computer models are largely unsuccessful at predicting a start to an El Niño or La Niña until the event is underway, and even then with limited success. Once the start has been confirmed, however, the state of the ENSO is a powerful long-range prediction tool.

For monitoring purposes, a number of regions have been designed that stretch along the tropical Pacific from east to west—Niño 1, 2, 3, 4, and 3.4 (Figure 7-46). Of these, Niño 3.4 (a region that combines parts of 3 and 4) is most often used to designate ENSO status, though

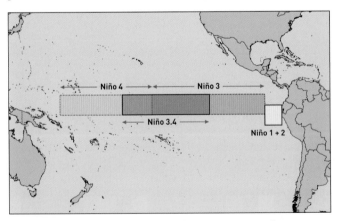

FIG. 7-46. *The locations of ENSO regions used to monitor ocean-surface temperatures. The most commonly used measure in North America comes from the Niño 3.4 region.*

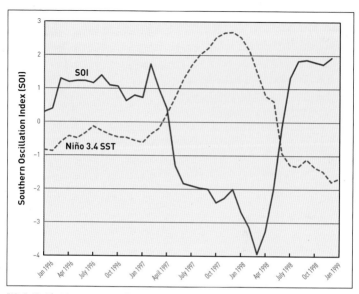

FIG. 7-47. *The Niño 3.4 sea surface temperature (SST) index and the Southern Oscillation Index (SOI) are anti-correlated in this graph of the evolution of indices for the record El Niño of 1997. Either one can be used to monitor the status of the ENSO cycle.*

each region and index has application for different ENSO impacts. The sea-surface temperature (SST) in Niño 3.4 best reflects the changes in rainfall across the Pacific and has the widest global application; Niño 1+2 (the combined measurement) is usually the first to respond to an impending event; and Niño 3 has the largest changes in SST. The SOI, which is highly correlated with the SST indices, is also a popular measure of the state of the ENSO.

One of the more widely accepted definitions of an ENSO episode (there are several) is a five-month or longer warming or cooling of at least 0.9°F (0.5°C) averaged over the Niño 3.4 region. Three-month averages of sea-surface temperatures for very strong El Niños (such as the 2015–16 episode) will reach values of nearly 5°F (3°C) above normal, while the strongest La Niñas (1973–74) see temperatures decline to about 3.6°F (2°C) below average.

In Figure 7-47, we see the evolution of the record El Niño of 1997–98. The Niño 3.4 SST index first crossed the 0.5° threshold in May 1997, but did not satisfy the five-month duration condition until September. At that point, monitoring agencies declared that an El Niño cycle was underway. The index peaked in December and then began a sharp decline, crossing the lower threshold for El Niño status in June of 1998. Sea-surface temperatures then made a fast transition into a strong La Niña that lasted until February 2001. In its eight-month lifetime, the 1997 El Niño brought unprecedented floods to Peru, forest fires to Borneo and Sumatra, record flooding to Europe, 108°F (42°C) temperatures to Ulaanbaatar in Mongolia, and mudslides and flooding from California to the Mississippi Valley. By the time this El Niño had run its course, over 2,100 people had died, and damage amounted to more than US$30 billion. There were many benefits too, particularly in Peru, where crops thrived in the coastal deserts, cattle grew fat on lush grasslands, and fishers were able to take advantage of the migration of warm-water species instead of the cold-loving anchovy that normally provided their income.

Teleconnections

It is not surprising that the enormous changes in the heat content of the tropical Pacific Ocean in the warm and cold phases of the El Niño Southern Oscillation should have impacts around the globe. Because the Earth's climate is a closed system in which moisture, heat, and momentum are largely conserved, a perturbation in one part of the system must be compensated by adjustments in some other part. Such linkages between upstream and downstream events are known as "teleconnections." For the most part, teleconnections occur through changes in the large-scale, upper-level flow that go on to influence meteorological processes at some faraway location.

The three teleconnection patterns noted by Sir Gilbert Walker have now grown into a family of ten or more, with both regional and hemispherical applications. The majority of these patterns tend to be recurring, persistent, regional-scale events that last for weeks to months, though a few types can linger for several consecutive years or even a decade. Delineation of teleconnection patterns in the scientific literature is a bit of a cottage industry, but they provide few insights for the operational meteorologist, since they operate at longer time scales than the valid period of a typical weather forecast. They are, however, critical to climatological studies and long-range predictions.

In Figures 7-48 and 7-49, we show some of the more important changes that accompany the most intense warm and cold ENSO events in the December-to-February time period—the Northern Hemisphere winter following the start of an episode. The main impact

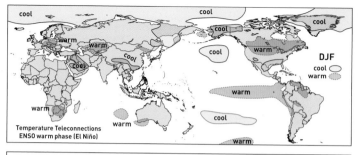

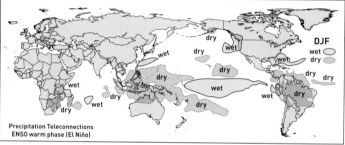

FIG. 7-48. *Major temperature and precipitation teleconnection patterns associated with strong El Niño events for the months December through February. These teleconnections can be quite different for moderate and weaker El Niños.*

is felt in the winter months, fading away in May as spring turns into summer, though in the Arctic and over Siberia, a cold anomaly goes on to intensify during those later seasons.

In North America, a strong El Niño has a Jekyll-and-Hyde personality. Colder-than-normal temperatures are more probable over parts of Alaska (Figure 7-48, upper panel), northern Mexico, and the southwestern states, stretching along the Gulf Coast into Florida. These cool temperatures are counterbalanced by warmer-than-normal temperatures over the heart of the continent, extending along the Canada–United States border from Washington to Maine—warm weather sandwiched between two cold slices. Impacts in Europe, Russia, and Africa are muted, but there are pockets of warming and cooling that may be better delineated once more data are available.

Changes in precipitation brought on by El Niño are most dramatic in the central Pacific, where rainfall amounts are much higher than normal—it is, after all, one of the defining characteristics of the warm phase of ENSO (Figure 7-48, lower panel). There is a strong tendency

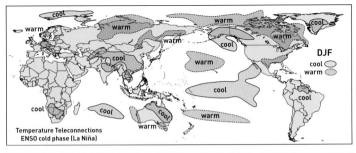

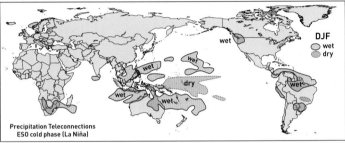

FIG. 7-49. *Major temperature and precipitation teleconnection patterns associated with a strong La Niña pattern for December, January, and February.*

to drier weather over Brazil and nearby regions. Along the equator and tropics, from the mid-Indian Ocean to the central Atlantic, anomalies are negative, with less rainfall than normal. In North America, El Niños—at least the strong ones—subject the Gulf Coast and the nearby Caribbean islands to heavier-than-normal rainfall in the winter months. Along the coast from Vancouver to San Francisco, winters tend to be a little wetter, a response that greatly favors the skiing industry but also leads to a heavy accumulation of snow that blocks mountain passes through Washington and Oregon.

For the most part, the teleconnections associated with La Niña are opposite those of El Niño (Figure 7-49), though the impact of La Niña tends to be more intense. With a strong La Niña, southern Alaska is cold. In the rest of the world, a brawny La Niña moderates the normally cold temperatures of central Russia and Canada's eastern Arctic. Some of Europe is a shade warmer, Southeast Asia cools, and Australia has both warm and cold anomalies. The largest impact on temperature is over the oceans with cooler temperatures over the central and eastern Pacific.

La Niña's effect on precipitation is largely confined to the tropics and subtropics, especially over Southeast Asia and Australia, where much of the land is drier than normal but the western Pacific is wetter.

Over North America, changes in winter precipitation are modest and limited, though media and social commentary often suggests a much larger impact. It is much the same for the rest of the world: precipitation anomalies are reflected in small, local deviations from average. These modest and variable effects lead to considerable ambiguity in predicting the impact of ENSO in regions that are far from the Pacific's equator.

The ENSO cycle also has a modest impact on the frequency and intensity of tropical cyclones in the Atlantic and Pacific Oceans. In the Atlantic basin, the stronger subtropical jet during an El Niño year increases the strength of the jet stream in the prime hurricane-forming region that lies over the warm Atlantic waters (Figure 7-50, top panel). The effect of stronger winds aloft is to carry off some of a storm's energy, reducing or even preventing its development. Both the number and intensity of Atlantic hurricanes tend to fall during El Niño years, and the storms that do form are disposed to take a track that avoids the United States mainland.

For the most part, La Niña is the reverse of El Niño at upper levels, bringing a weaker subtropical jet and a stronger polar jet (Figure 7-50). The weaker flow in the low latitudes gives the Gulf Coast a warmer winter than is the case with El Niño. The polar jet adopts a west-to-east flow with ridging over the western mountains. This subjects Western Canada to a stronger temperature gradient, promoting the intrusion of cold Arctic air and bringing a much-less-welcome winter climatology, while the predilection for cold weather is diminished over the rest of the Great Plains. The upper-level flow is more variable in a La Niña winter than in one with an El Niño, and so the interior of the continent is not necessarily cast into a three-month deep freeze, but instead gets a more erratic winter weather pattern.

Limits in our ability to forecast the onset and intensity of the phases of ENSO and the probabilistic nature of an El Niño or La Niña condemns long-range forecasts of warm or cold, wet or dry seasonal weather to have a large, built-in uncertainty. The magnitude of ENSO teleconnections is strongly dependent on the intensity of an El Niño or La Niña. For weak El Niños, some teleconnections patterns may disappear or even be reversed. During strong ENSO events, the regional teleconnection pattern often expands to spread an impact

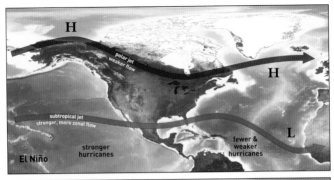

FIG. 7-50. *Changes in the upper flow during strong ENSO episodes. L and H show the location of the anomalous low- and high-pressure (or heights) centers that form in response to the ENSO cycle. Also shown is the impact of the stronger (El Niño) and weaker (La Niña) flow in the subtropical jet on hurricane development in the tropical Atlantic and eastern Pacific.*

across regions that would normally be unaffected. Some future day, numerical models will be able to make an accurate prediction of a coming ENSO episode, but until then, seasonal forecasts must incorporate a high degree of uncertainty.

The whole subject of ENSO teleconnections is a convoluted tangle of relationships that obscure precise characterization: a meteorological soap opera without a written plot. Patches of warm and cold, wet and dry, lie scattered across the globe, shifting back and forth, disappearing entirely, or morphing into opposite personalities as sea-surface temperature anomalies change, evolve, and fade away. The ENSO puzzle is one of the great meteorological challenges for climatologists and modelers: What drives the cycle? How are the teleconnections "connected"? What is the role of topography and surface characteristics? And how do other events in the global arena moderate its influence?

Other Teleconnection Patterns

Over the decades, meteorologists have identified several other configurations in the atmosphere and ocean that cause detectable changes in seasonal and longer-term weather patterns through their teleconnections with other parts of the globe. Ordinarily, these cycles (usually called oscillations) would be confined to the scientific literature and be used as input into statistical models for seasonal weather forecasts (warm or cold winters, or high or low precipitation, more or fewer storms)—for instance, the Pacific Decadal Oscillation and the Arctic Oscillation. While these cycles are not as well known as El Niño and La Niña, you may occasionally hear your TV meteorologist mention them in an effort to explain an unusual pattern of seasonal temperature or precipitation.

The Pacific Decadal Oscillation (PDO)

The Pacific Decadal Oscillation, or PDO, is a very long-term fluctuation in the pattern of North Pacific sea-surface temperatures (SST). Because it is a rearrangement of warm and cold water and not a change in the ocean temperatures themselves, the numerical value of the PDO is represented by an index that must be calculated from a collection of different variables. During a positive phase (also called the warm phase), above-normal SSTs can be found along the Alaska and British Columbia coasts, while colder-than-normal temperatures stretch across the rest of the North Pacific, as far west as the Russian coast (Figure 7-51). In the negative or cold phase, the pattern reverses.

The PDO cycles between its phases over a period of 20 to 40 years, though the phenomenon is so variable that its characterization as a "cycle" is probably overstating the case. Long periods of relatively stable positive and negative values of the PDO can be identified in the early part of the twentieth century but the pattern seems to have reverted to a more variable cycle of five to ten years in recent decades.

Over North America, the positive phase of the PDO brings warm winter temperatures to Alaska, western Canada, and the northwest United States (Figure 7-52). Cool temperatures are found across a broad band from Texas to Maine and over northern Quebec. The influence on precipitation is spottier, bringing drier conditions to the

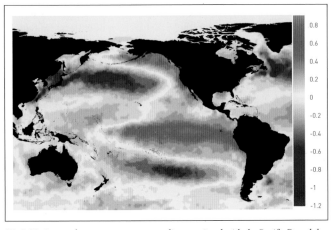

FIG. 7-51. *Sea-surface temperature anomalies associated with the Pacific Decadal Oscillation (PDO) in its positive (warm) phase. This phase is characterized by cool SSTs in the central Pacific with warm temperatures along the North American coast. The negative phase of the PDO reverses the pattern of warm and cold SSTs.*

West Coast from British Columbia to Oregon, and wetter weather to Florida and the nearby Caribbean. During the cold phase, the pattern is more complex and variable: the entire West Coast is drier in winter; inland British Columbia and Washington are wetter and snowier than usual; and the Mountain states are slightly drier. These teleconnections are very "fuzzy," as the PDO is variable on a month-to-month basis and it is only through long-term averaging, or selection of the years with the most extreme values of the PDO index, that the teleconnection between North Pacific temperatures and continental weather is revealed. It is not very useful in predicting seasonal weather, but it may reinforce or moderate an El Niño or La Niña.

The Arctic Oscillation (AO)

The Arctic Oscillation (AO) is a complex index that gives a measure of the strength and variability of the upper-level flow and the polar jet stream. This flow and its jet stream control the track of cyclonic storms and the spread of cold air to more southerly latitudes.

In the positive configuration of the Arctic Oscillation, the jet stream assumes a strong zonal (west-to-east) flow. This flow holds cold polar air at bay over higher latitudes, and causes winter storms to adopt a more northerly track, along the edge of the cold air (Figure 7-53).

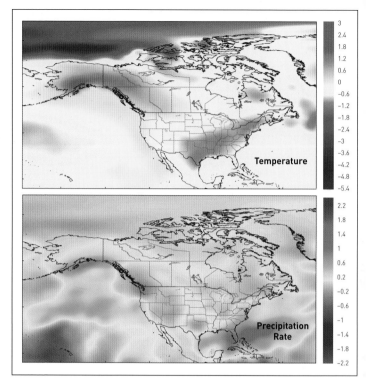

FIG. 7-52. *The influence of the positive phase of the PDO on North American temperatures and precipitation. The negative phase has the opposite impact.*

This brings heavier-than-normal precipitation to Alaska, Iceland, and Scandinavia, but drier and warmer weather to the eastern United States and Mediterranean countries. In contrast, the negative configuration of the AO is characterized by a tendency to form meandering north-south patterns that allow cold Arctic air to surge southward in winter. This usually generates deep, low-pressure disturbances that reach far into southern latitudes to bring fierce winter storms. The severity of this kind of winter weather is often enhanced by blocking patterns in which upper-level ridges and surface highs stall in place, bringing persistent cold spells and frequent stormy weather to the continents.

Because of its influence on the location and intensity of winter storms, the Arctic Oscillation is the leading mode of climate variability in the Northern Hemisphere. Nevertheless, it is not a useful parameter for forecasting long-term weather because it varies on a scale from weeks to months, despite its inclination to favor one phase for intervals lasting for several years. In recent years—since the 1960s—the AO has shown a tendency to more positive values, which has contributed to a part of the warming that has been recorded at high northern latitudes and to the loss of Arctic sea ice.

The Final Word on Indices

Meteorologists love indices. They are a form of shorthand, replacing complex relationships with simple numbers that can be served up in PhD theses, research papers, newspaper accounts, and climate predictions. Some are extremely useful, such as the Niño 3.4 index used to monitor the state of the ENSO cycle, and provide very good warning about the possibility of floods and droughts in the tropical Pacific. Others are vague compilations of observed events without a well-determined utility. Indices are used most often as input into seasonal and longer-term forecasts, but even here, their usefulness is limited by their unpredictability. Reliable forecasting is made even more difficult because the many cycles interact: we might have an El Niño modified by a warm Pacific Decadal Oscillation superimposed on a cold-phase Arctic Oscillation. The whole nest of related, competing cycles is rich fodder for internet blogs but leads to little enlightenment about next season's temperatures.

Local Wind Systems

Winds have various names. There are mistrals in France, boras in Eastern Europe, the williwaw in Alaska and the Straits of Magellan, the Squamish on Vancouver Island, the diablo in San Francisco, the nor'easter in New England, and the Elephanta in India—and many, many more. Winds are like distant relatives, sometimes welcome and sometimes regretted, usually enveloped in a long, historical tradition. Many of these winds are unique to a small region so that only a few residents know their name. Other wind names are known more widely—the chinook or the harmattan—and over time have spread across continents to regions far beyond their home. In contrast to hurricanes, whose names are given once and are then gone, wind names seem to have settled in to live with humans—a meteorological cat or dog on the atmospheric hearth.

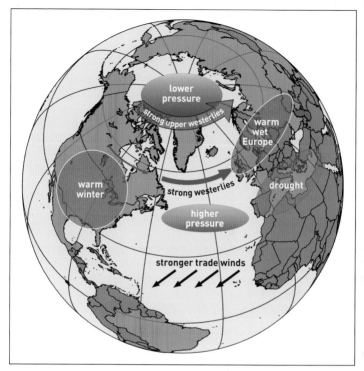

FIG. 7-53. *When the Arctic Oscillation (AO) is in its positive phase, mid-temperate zones tend to have warm winters. In Europe, strong westerlies bring Atlantic weather systems onshore, giving a season of heavier precipitation. The stronger upper-level westerlies in the high Arctic help to keep cold polar air from breaking out to lower latitudes. When the AO is in its negative phase, winter weather tends to adopt the opposite personality.*

Local Winds

Land and Sea Breezes

Every respectable sailor is familiar with the regular cycle of coastal winds, blowing onshore during the day and offshore at night. It's a historic familiarity, extending back in time to ancient Greece and Phoenicia, as these daily reversing winds are a common feature of the Mediterranean coast. In the days of sail power, offshore evening breezes were used to depart port, while the morning onshore winds proved useful in returning.

Aristotle and Theophrastus both struggled to describe the cause of these winds, believing the nighttime breeze to be a "dry exhalation" from the land. This presented some difficulties in explaining the daytime winds from the sea, as a dry exhalation could not be expected to form over a moist ocean; in the end, they were compelled to explain it as the rebounding of the land breeze from various obstacles. Today we call the daytime onshore wind a lake or sea breeze, and its nighttime offshore counterpart a land breeze. In a sense, land breathes in during the day and out at night.

Perhaps the best practical description of a sea breeze comes from the English privateer and explorer William Dampier (1651–1715) in the supplement to an account of his travels, *A New Voyage Round the World*. According to Dampier (1697):

> *These sea breezes do commonly rise in the Morning about nine a Clock, sometimes sooner, sometimes later; they first approach the shore so gently, as if they were afraid to come near it, and oftimes, they make some faint breathings, and as if not willing to offend, they make a halt, and seem ready to retire. I have waited many a time both ashore to receive the pleasure, and at Sea to take the benefit of it.*
>
> *It comes in a fine small black Curle upon the water, whenas all the Sea between it, and the Shore, not yet reach'd by it, is as smooth and even as Glass in Comparison; in half an Hour's time after it has reached the shore, it fans pretty briskly, and so increaseth gradually until 12 a Clock, then it is commonly strongest, and lasts until 2 or 3 a very brisk gale; about 12 at Noon it also veres off to Sea 2 or 3 Points, or more in very fair weather. After 3 a Clock, it begins to dye away again, and gradually withdraws its force till all is spent, and about 5 a Clock, sooner or later, according as the Weather is, it is lull'd asleep, and comes no more till the next Morning.*
>
> *Land-Breezes are as remarkable as any Winds that I have yet treated of; they are quite contrary to the Sea-Breezes; for those blow right from the shore, but the Sea-Breeze right in upon the shore; and as the Sea-Breezes do blow in the Day and rest in the Night; so on the contrary, these do blow in the Night and rest in the Day, and so they do alternately succeed each other. For when Sea-Breezes*

have performed their Offices of the Day, by breathing on their respective Coasts, they in the evening do withdraw from the coast or lye down to rest; Then the Land-Winds whose Office it is to breathe in the Night moved by the same order of Divine Impulse, do rouze out of their private recesses and gently fan the Air until the next Morning, and then their task ends and they leave the Stage.

Today we know that the alternating daily winds described by Dampier are provoked by the difference in the heating and cooling rates of land and water. Under sunny skies and light winds, the rising Sun will warm the land more quickly than the water, because the land has a darker albedo and a lower heat capacity. In turn, the ground heats the lower atmosphere, and the warm air begins to rise; this causes surface pressures to fall by 1 or 2 millibars. The drop in pressure on the land draws cooler air from the ocean surface onto the shore (Figure 7-54) to begin the sea-breeze circulation.

Pressures fall more slowly with altitude in warm air than in cold air, and so a weak high-pressure cell forms above the land at an elevation of around 1 mile (1–2 km), reversing the pressure gradient between land and water (Figure 7-54). This reverse gradient sends the air that

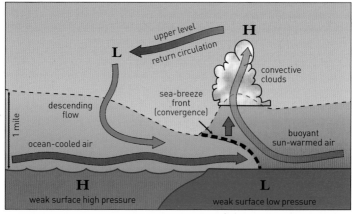

FIG. 7-54. *Schematic diagram of a sea-breeze circulation. The morning Sun warms the land and the lower atmosphere, causing pressures to fall as the heated air expands and rises. Cooler ocean air flows onshore, displacing the warmer air over land and creating a sea-breeze front. Aloft, the pressure gradient is reversed, leading to a return flow that completes the circulation.*

is rising from below back out toward the sea, where it descends to replenish the landward-moving air that first began the sea-breeze circulation. In effect, the sea breeze is a small-scale circulation powered by the daytime temperature differences between land and water.

As long as skies remain sunny through the afternoon, the land continues to warm, drawing an ever-stronger flow of cool marine air onto the shore. Late in the day, as the Sun sinks toward the horizon, the ground and air temperatures begin to fall, and the pressure gradient weakens, so that by sunset, the sea breeze has faded away. Nighttime reverses the process, since, with darkness, the land cools more rapidly than the water, pressures rise onshore, and a gentle land breeze begins, continuing until the dawn, when it reverses once again. Aloft, a return flow forms that carries the circulating air back toward the land.

Sea-breeze winds may travel inland for as little as a few tens of miles (kilometers) or for more than 200 miles (300 km), depending on the shape of the coastline, the roughness of the terrain, the strength and direction of large-scale winds, and the amount of heating on the land. The interface between the invading, cool marine air and the warm air over the land is known as a sea-breeze front. It is a region where sea-breeze and terrestrial winds converge, and the atmosphere, with no place to go, is given an extra upward push, which strengthens the warm convective currents that are already rising over the land.

Sea and lake breezes play a major role in the local temperature and precipitation along the margins of water bodies, particularly in tropical regions, where large-scale wind circulation tends to be light. Florida is the sea-breeze capital of North America—a very welcome reputation, as the energy-sapping heat of summer is moderated by the daily winds from the ocean. Average annual high temperatures at the coastal Miami Beach weather station are 2°F (1.3°C) cooler than those at Miami International Airport, 8 miles (13 km) inland, because of the influence of sea-breeze winds. In Australia and occasionally South Africa, the stronger sea breezes are known as "Doctors," a term with an obscure origin, but which presumably comes from the respite they bring from the heat of the day. The best-known of these is the southwesterly "Fremantle Doctor" of Perth, Australia (so named because its southwesterly flow appears to come from the nearby city of Fremantle). This breeze typically begins around noon, cutting off the normal daytime heating and dropping temperatures to more tolerable values (Figure 7-55).

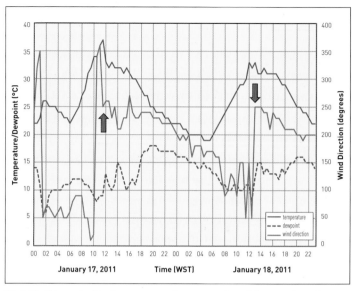

FIG. 7-55. *This graph of Perth temperature, dewpoint, and wind direction shows the arrival of the Fremantle Doctor (large arrows) on two successive mornings. The time of arrival, around noon, abruptly ends the rise in temperature but has only a small impact, if any, on the dewpoint.*

Sea breezes do much more than bring cool marine air onto land to relieve the day's heat—they also have a considerable impact on precipitation and cloudiness. The little upward push given by the moving sea-breeze front is frequently the location where the first convective clouds form on an unstable day. At the same time, the cool air behind the front suppresses the buildup of cloud, so in satellite photos (Figure 7-56) the early afternoon front is marked by a line of cumulus clouds a little inland from the coast with clear skies behind. Later in the day, the small buildups of convective clouds along the front may grow into thunderstorms if the day is particularly unstable.

The interaction of a sea breeze with all types of boundaries—gust fronts, lines of wind convergence, cold fronts, and even other sea breezes—magnifies the strength of the wind convergence and the upward forcing. These collisions are important to the severe-weather meteorologist, as they are frequently sites of the strongest thunderstorm convection (Figure 7-56). Florida's sea-breeze climatology, with all of these forces at work, gives it the highest thunderstorm frequency

FIG. 7-56. *This satellite image of the Gulf Coast and Florida from 1:30 P.M. October 2, 2014, shows an almost continuous line of small convective clouds (yellow arrows) that outline the sea-breeze front on the west side of the peninsula. A second sea-breeze front on the Atlantic side of the Florida peninsula has pushed well inland, helped by the prevailing easterly winds, and has begun to develop thunderstorms between "A" and "A."*

in the United States and one of the highest rates of lightning strikes in the world.

The nighttime land breezes have their own suite of convective clouds, forming offshore in the convergence of the seaward-moving air (Figure 7-57) with the environment air over the water. Satellite images often reveal the development of thunderstorms a few dozen miles offshore from the Gulf coasts of Texas, Louisiana, Mississippi, and Alabama on summer nights, triggered by winds flowing from the shore.

Valley Winds and Slope Winds

Winds in mountains can be exceptionally complicated. When strong highs and lows are passing, mountain winds refuse to play by the rules; they flow across, instead of along, the pressure gradient, ignoring Coriolis and curvature forces. Instead, they twist and turn to follow the contours of the terrain, speeding up when compressed by the embrace of a narrow passage and slowing for open meadows. Like water in a lake, colder air collects in mountain valleys until deep enough to flow over passes and through gaps in the topographic barrier. Along the west coast of the Alaska Panhandle and British Columbia, fjord winds, blowing from deep indentations in the coastal mountains, can bring dangerous winter winds and above-deck icing on fishing boats when deep, cold air races down the inlets to the ocean.

When synoptic-scale winds are weak, however, daytime heating and nighttime cooling become the architects of the wind, especially on cloud-free summer days and nights, when the diurnal temperature range is greatest. Air movement in complex terrain then becomes even more sensitive to topography and variations in heating, with flows sometimes changing over distances of only a few feet. In spite of the complexity, however, there are common features of mountain winds around the globe that can be used as a framework for forecasting. In particular, two types of wind are commonly identified: slope winds, which result from buoyancy forces; and valley winds, which are driven by temperature-induced pressure differences. Both are diurnal events, flowing uphill or up-valley during the heat of the day and downslope or down-valley during the cooler nights. When warm air drifts upslope, it is said to be anabatic; downslope flows of cool air are katabatic.

FIG. 7-57. *This* Terra *satellite image shows a land breeze front along the coast of West Africa. This image was captured about 10:30 A.M. local time, when heating of the land should have eroded the land breeze, but later satellite images showed that the front persisted into the afternoon.*

Slope Winds

The complexity of anabatic and katabatic winds is derived, in large part, from the intricacies of the rugged terrain in which they arise. Variations in albedo play a large part in the generation of upslope winds: vegetation is usually darker than rock; sunlit steep slopes heat more quickly than shallow slopes; and gullies concentrate heat, while ridges dissipate it. The terrain "aspect" or angle toward the Sun is particularly important. In north-south trending valleys, the east-facing slope (on the western side of the valley) is heated first by the rising Sun, while the west-facing slope awaits the afternoon and evening. Valleys aligned east-to-west may see little or no direct energy from the Sun on north-facing slopes, while south-facing terrain bathes in bright light through the day. Daytime winds, responding to this pattern of differential heating, become concentrated on one side or the other of the valley, sometimes leading to a distinctly asymmetrical flow that migrates from one side of the valley to the other from sunrise to sunset. Mountain heating is an efficient process—the anabatic flow forms very quickly once the Sun makes its appearance, often beginning only a few minutes after the first rays touch the ground.

Katabatic winds at night are less complex, as they respond mostly to the cooling brought on by the emission of longwave radiation to space. Even so, there are small-scale variations in the flow that derive from local differences in topography and ground cover: forest slopes cool more slowly than bare rocks; gullies concentrate the colder air, while ridges hold the warmer; elevated depressions store cold air until the increasing depth of a pool of cold air allows it to spill over the high spots and continue flowing downhill.

In the daytime, solar heating of the ground produces a shallow, warm, low-density layer of air next to the surface. This buoyant layer rises up the sides of the valley (Figure 7-58), feeding on a continuing supply of heat from the sun-warmed slopes. This initially shallow anabatic current increases in both depth and velocity as it flows upward along the slopes. The buoyant updrafts are sensitive to the fine details of the topography, favoring ravines that face into the Sun and dark, sparsely vegetated surfaces, where the heating is more concentrated.

Once an upslope flow reaches the ridge line, the heat borrowed from the ground comes to an end. The rising plume often forms cumulus clouds along the ridge line (Figure 7-59), and if the atmospheric column is unstable through a large depth, these small build-ups may grow into taller showers and thundershowers later in the

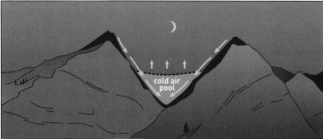

FIG. 7-58. *In the upper figure, daytime heating of the valley slopes generate convective plumes and upslope winds that increase in intensity and depth as they flow upward. The slower compensating subsidence in the center of the valley warms and stabilizes the air column by adiabatic heating. At night, cooling slopes generate a downward flow that fills the valley bottom with a pool of cold air. The dashed line in the nighttime image represents the inversion at the top of the cold pool.*

day. If, however, conditions are stable aloft and synoptic winds above the terrain are relatively light, then adiabatic cooling of the updrafts will bring them to a halt at a short distance above the ridge line. The airflow will then turn inward toward the valley axis, where it will descend as a sinking flow (Figure 7-58, top panel) that partly replaces the air removed by the slope winds. The descending flow, warming and drying by compression, will evaporate any cloud that may linger in the center of the valley—a circulation that gives valleys a reputation for sunny skies at their midriff, while cloudier weather lines the slopes.

In the evening and overnight, the mountain slopes lose their heat by emitting longwave radiation to space. Cold air forms against the surface and then courses downslope, following the steepest path to the bottom. These katabatic winds are a shallow, stable, and slow-moving current that is easily blocked by obstructions such as trees and small

FIG. 7-59. *Lines of cumulus clouds form above the ridge line on this early morning in northern India. Solar heating of the dark-toned terrain has generated rising columns of air along the Sun-facing slopes that turn into small convective clouds above the hilltops.*

rises until the pooling of cold air reaches a depth that allows them to flow around or above the obstacle. An evening walk along a path on the side of a valley will reveal the sinking flow as a slightly chilly downhill breeze in the gullies, interspersed with noticeably warmer air where higher ground diverts the drainage.

As colder air accumulates in the valley bottom overnight, it lifts the warm, residual air upward, creating an inversion that increases in depth as the night continues. The lifted air above the inversion will cool adiabatically and, if it reaches its saturation point, will turn into a layer of stratus, effectively putting a lid on the longwave radiation. If, however, skies remain clear, then the ground and overlying air will keep cooling until sunrise. Fog or frost may form if the ground-layer air reaches its dewpoint, an event that is most common in deep mountain valleys during the long nights of fall and winter. Satellite photos of the Rocky Mountains often show persistent cloud in the valleys during the winter season (Figure 7-60). This valley-bottom cloud and fog and the inversion that lies above them severely limit the amount of ground-level solar heating on the following sunrise. It is not uncommon for gray skies to linger for days or even weeks in the winter months, waiting for synoptic winds that can stir the atmosphere and dissipate the cloud.

FIG. 7-60. *Fog collects in the mountain valleys of central British Columbia in February 2009. The strong inversions that form during the long nights of winter are frequently very persistent because slope and valley flows are not strong enough to dislodge them in the few daylight hours.*

Valley Winds

Valley winds are winds that flow along the valley axis, up-valley in the day and down-valley at night. While slope winds are quick-acting responses to solar heating, valley winds are more leisurely in their formation. They are the product of local pressure gradients caused by temperature differences between air in the valley and air at the same level over an adjacent plain or a wider section of the valley. Valleys are often warmer than nearby plains: they have a smaller volume of air to heat, are protected from synoptic winds by the terrain, and are heated by subsiding air along the valley axis in the descending branch of the slope-wind flow.

Up-valley winds usually begin in the late morning or early afternoon, when the whole of the mass of air within the valley is heated. The warming of the air column creates a low-pressure region near the surface within the valley, generating a pressure gradient between the valley interior and the open atmosphere over the plains beyond the valley mouth. This gradient draws air into the valley, typically within the lowest few hundred feet (Figure 7-61). At some point above the valley floor—a mile or two—pressures are higher than at an equivalent

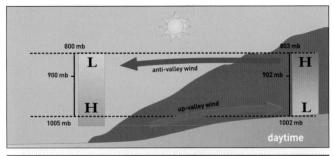

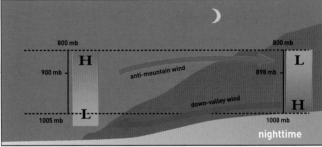

FIG. 7-61. *Up-valley and down-valley winds develop in response to the temperature differences between open plains and the confining topography of a mountain valley. Warm air in the valley during the day creates an anti-cyclonic circulation (in this diagram) between low and elevated levels. At night, cool valley temperatures reverse the flow.*

level on the plains, and the pressure gradient reverses. The upper-level current then flows back out onto the plains as an anti-valley wind. In most cases, the flow is relatively gentle, with maximum up-valley wind speeds in the early afternoon reaching only 10 to 15 mph (15 to 25 km/h).

The upslope and up-valley winds are not independent events. Part of the heating of the air column that drives the valley wind comes from the adiabatic warming of the air along the valley axis by the descending branch of the upslope winds (Figure 7-62). And while valley and slope winds are common events around the world, each valley has its own unique personality, modified by many of the same factors that regulate the slope winds: the steepness of the slope, the orientation of the valley with respect to the Sun, the albedo within and without the valley (which is sensitive to vegetation), the width of the valley, and any narrowing and widening within. These, in turn, are

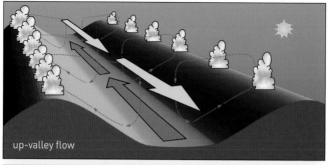

up-valley flow

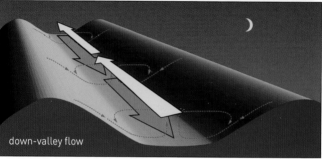

down-valley flow

FIG. 7-62. *The interaction between slope and valley wind systems during day and night.*

modified on a daily basis by synoptic winds and clouds, particularly convective clouds.

After sunset, a gradual changeover from up-valley to down-valley winds begins. The katabatic downslope flow forms a pool of cold air on the valley floor. The pool deepens until it begins to drain along the valley, following the slope of the land. Boundary-layer pressures rise in response to the accumulation of cold air, forming a high-pressure region that creates the gradient that will keep the air moving through the night. Down-valley currents are usually lighter than the up-valley flow, but there are occasions when the pressure gradient becomes particularly strong. Such gradients are found most often near the mouth of valleys that make an abrupt transition to the plains or where the slopes are very steep; the ensuing wind is called an "exit jet." Exit jets have been measured through depths of 130 to 650 feet (40–200 m) above-ground with speeds ranging up to 45 mph (70 km/h), extending 6 to 13 miles (10 to 20 km) out onto the plains beyond the valley mouth.

For the most part, mountain breezes are not particularly strong, but they have a singular importance in regulating pollution and air quality within the mountains. The daily in-and-out breathing of the valley carries airborne pollutants both up and down the mountain terrain. This ventilation is important in the design and placement of industry, as conflicts arise quickly when favorite scenic vistas are hidden in a haze of pollutants.

Chinooks and Foehn Winds

Communities that lie along the front range of the Rockies in Alberta, Montana, Wyoming, and Colorado put out the welcome mat many times during the winter months to greet the chinook, a warm, dry, and blustery wind from the mountain peaks that stops winter in its tracks (Figure 7-63). Legendary temperature changes come with the arrival of a chinook, frequently as much as 36°F (20°C) in an hour or two and sometimes much more. On January 22, 1943, a chinook made a dramatic appearance at Spearfish, in the Black Hills of South Dakota, causing a temperature rise of 49°F (31°C) in two minutes. Two hours later, the temperature was back where it had started. This event is claimed as a world record, though a few anecdotal com-

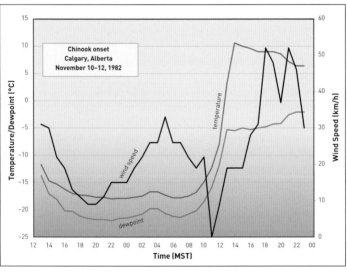

FIG. 7-63. *On November 11, 1982, a dramatic chinook reached Calgary, Alberta, abruptly raising temperatures by more than 40 degrees Fahrenheit (24 degrees Celsius).*

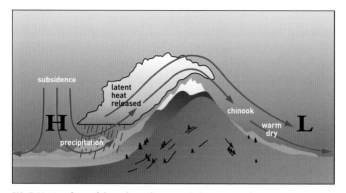

FIG. 7-64. *One form of chinook wind is created when a moist flow crosses a mountain barrier, leaving cloud and precipitation on the upwind side. Latent heat is released into the air column as water vapor condenses and the heated air is then further warmed adiabatically during descent above the leeward slopes. The combination of the two processes brings a warm and dry flow to the downwind side of the mountain barrier.*

ments suggest that there are other contenders around the world for that honor.

"Chinook" is a North American name given to a foehn (or föhn)—a warm, dry, and blustery wind that crosses over a mountain range and descends on the lee side. The name chinook refers to the Chinook Indians of the West Coast from where the downslope winds originate, though it is frequently and incorrectly said to be the Native word for "snow eater." Foehn winds are associated with mountain ranges around the world, and there are a large variety of local names for the phenomenon besides chinook: *zonda* in Argentina; *puelche* in the Andes; *Canterbury northwester* in New Zealand; *aspre* in southern France, and *schneefresser* in Switzerland.

A foehn begins when prevailing winds rise over the terrain on the upwind slopes, cooling at the adiabatic rates (Chapter 2) until water vapor condenses and releases latent heat to warm the surrounding air column. After crossing to the leeward slopes, the airmass descends, warming by compression until it arrives at lower elevations, warmer and drier than it was on the windward side (Figure 7-64). An essential feature of this type of foehn wind is that condensation occurs, perhaps with precipitation, on the upwind side of the terrain, so that latent heat is released and a warmer airmass descends on the lee side. If condensation does not occur, adiabatic warming during descent will match the cooling during ascent and temperatures on each side of the mountain range will be similar.

During the winter in North America, the descending Pacific air in a chinook often displaces a much colder Arctic airmass entrenched over the Great Plains. The change from Arctic to Pacific air by itself would turn a cold day to a warm one even without a contribution from adiabatic warming. The next day's newspapers would probably herald the arrival of a chinook, when it could more accurately be described as the arrival of a warm front. This complication makes the classification of a chinook on a particular day somewhat fuzzy in the scientific literature, but from a popular point of view, the mechanisms are not important. The chinook has always been a welcome visitor to freezing Albertans, as this 1900 comment from the *Calgary Weekly Herald* testifies:

> *Those who have not the warm, invigorating Chinook winds of this country, cannot well comprehend what a blessing they are. The icy clutch of winter is lessened, the earth throws off its winding sheet of snow. Humanity ventures forth to inhale the balmy spring-like air.*

At times, frigid ground-level air on the east side of the Rockies resists being displaced by the descending mountain air, so that the warmer air of the chinook comes to rest on top of the Arctic layer. A strong inversion is created that suppresses vertical mixing, and air quality can deteriorate rapidly as pollutants are trapped in the surface layer. The trapped Arctic air may be so shallow that shirt-sleeve weather can be enjoyed by upper-floor residents of high-rise apartments, while those at the ground are freezing at −4°F (−20°C).

A second type of foehn occurs when an inversion at or below a mountaintop dams the air on the upwind side of the mountain chain. Higher-level air will take its place, dropping down on the leeward side to deliver a drier and warmer flow fueled by compression warming alone (Figure 7-65). If winds are strong and the stability limited, the flow will cross the mountains in an orderly fashion, bringing a modest chinook flow to the opposite side. However, at a critical combination of terrain elevation, wind speed, and stability—a Goldilocks event, with winds neither too fast nor too slow—the flow across the mountain barrier will produce a series of high-amplitude mountain waves that will accelerate the wind stream downslope onto the foothill plains

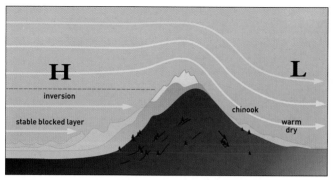

FIG. 7-65. *When an inversion blocks the up-and-over flow across a mountain barrier, mid- and upper-level winds will descend the leeward slopes, bringing a chinook that is fueled by adiabatic warming alone.*

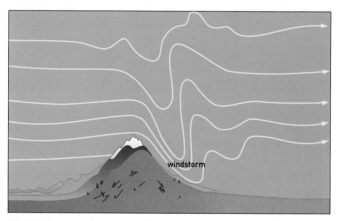

FIG. 7-66. *Severe windstorms caused by mountain waves occur when the combination of terrain height, wind speed, and atmospheric stability allow the energy in the flow to be concentrated on the downwind slopes of the mountains.*

(Figure 7-66). The most intense waves then hug the side of the terrain, bringing severe windstorms along the slopes and for a short distance over the foothills.

Nowhere in the United States are severe chinook winds more evident than in Boulder, Colorado, which has a widespread reputation as one of the windiest cities in America. On the night of January 16, 1982, chinook winds gusted to 137 mph (220 km/h) at Table Mesa on the outskirts of Boulder. In the city itself, 40 percent of buildings

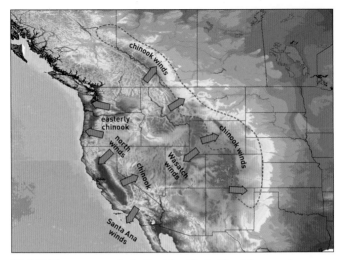

FIG. 7-67. *The many ranges in the Coastal and Rocky Mountains generate a number of recognized foehn wind systems.*

were damaged and 20 people were injured. In Canada, the foothills between Calgary and Pincher Creek in southern Alberta compete for the windiest place in the country. In late November 2011, chinook-generated, hurricane-force winds reaching 90 mph (144 km/h) tore through this part of Alberta, bringing down power lines and even flipping cars on the street.

Along the east side of the Rocky Mountains, chinooks are most common over southern Alberta and less so farther south along the Front Range in the United States, as far as northeastern New Mexico; they are particularly common in the stretch from Great Falls, Montana, to Calgary, Alberta. Chinooks are also found on the east side of the Cascade Range in Washington and Oregon, and east of the Sierra Nevada in Nevada (Figure 7-67). Globally, foehn winds are found wherever a mountain barrier is presented to the winds: in central Europe, in southern Argentina, in Australia, and in southern Africa.

At Calgary, Alberta, one of the more striking effects of a foehn wind is the presence of the "chinook arch" that appears in overcast skies when the chinook approaches. The subsiding air in the lee of the mountains forms a slot of clear sky against the western horizon, bordered by an arch of mid- and high-level cloud (Figure 7-68). This vault of clear sky, eagerly awaited when warming is predicted, pres-

FIG. 7-68. *A chinook arch (in this case, a straight line) hangs where the western skies have cleared in the downslope flow from the distant mountains.*

ages the arrival of the foehn winds by a few hours. The chinook arch is often prominent in satellite images, showing as a narrow cloud-free slot (known as a foehn gap) to the east of the Rockies (Figure 7-69).

Clouds that form in the upslope flow on the windward side of a mountain chain are often visible as a white wall looming above the distant terrain, peering out onto the plains (Figure 7-70). The clouds don't move from their lofty position, but time-lapse photography will show that they are continually forming on the upwind side and dissipating as winds carry the moist air across and down from the mountain peaks. On occasion, they

FIG. 7-69. *This MODIS satellite image shows a narrow slot of clear skies (a foehn gap) along the foothills of Alberta and Montana, just downwind from the mountain peaks. From the ground, this gap would appear as a chinook arch.*

cascade partway down the side of the mountain, an ephemeral "cloud fall" that is as entertaining as it is promising.

FIG. 7-70. *Chinooks are both creators and destroyers of clouds. In this scene, near Flagstaff, Arizona, heavy convective clouds have formed in the upslope flow on the ridge line in the distance, only to dissipate as the winds cross the peaks and descend onto the flat plateau. A few wispy tendrils of gray* fractus *clouds in the left foreground mark the last cloud traces within the descending air.*

Santa Ana Winds

Santa Anas are dry, blustery, northeasterly katabatic winds that originate over the high plateau of Nevada's Great Basin and flow out to the ocean through California. During the winter months, cold air piles up over the Great Basin, where it is trapped between the Sierra Nevadas in the west and the Rocky Mountains in the east. Airflow from the high pressure beneath this cold-air dome is drawn out to the coast when a low-pressure system moves along the California coast. This combination of high and low creates a strong pressure gradient that starts the air moving downslope from Nevada toward the ocean. The flow is slowed when it encounters the coastal Transverse Ranges, but quickly finds its way through gaps in the terrain, exiting onto the coastal plain as surges of damaging winds.

The Santa Ana's extreme winds are further accelerated by the downhill drainage of the cold air and the constriction as the current passes through the narrow canyons of the Transverse Mountains. Already parched, the desert air is dried further as it warms adiabatically in its descent to the coast, arriving at sea level with a relative humidity of 25 percent and sometimes as low as 10 percent. The combination of low humidity, strong gusty winds that sometimes exceed 100 mph (160 km/h), and high temperatures desiccates coastal vegetation and sets up the conditions for explosive brush fires. In the strongest Santa Anas, upper-level, mountaintop winds that are aligned with the gaps in the mountains also contribute to the wind speed at the ground.

Boras

A bora is a gusty north to northeast katabatic wind native to countries surrounding the Adriatic Sea, but the circumstances of its creation are applicable throughout the world wherever cold air flows downhill. The name is thought to have been derived from the Greek figure representing the north wind, *Boreas*. As with the Santa Ana winds, the bora is formed when cold air associated with a high-pressure cell is enticed to begin flowing toward the sea, drawn by a passing low-pressure system. In this, it is very similar to the Santa Ana, except that boras are typically so cold in their source region that they arrive at sea level as a cold wind.

Some of the strongest boras in the world are found in Antarctica and Greenland, driven by the high-density, frigid air that collects on the ice caps before gravity pulls it down the steep coastal slopes to the ocean. This katabatic flow is enhanced by temperature and pressure differences aloft between the plateau and the coast and by pressure gradients set up by passing low-pressure systems. When funneled by valleys, Antarctic winds can reach over 190 mph (300 km/h) and blow for several days. The winds ease only when the supply of cold air runs out.

In Praise of Wind

The Earth's weather is driven by the energy that the planet receives from the Sun, but in this chapter, we have seen that it is more accurate to say that weather comes from the redistribution of that energy, at all scales, from global to regional to local. Understand the wind, and you will be more at ease with the features in the atmospheric landscape around you.

CHAPTER 8

AIRMASSES, FRONTS, AND WEATHER SYSTEMS

Formation and Movement

It's nine o'clock on a hazy summer morning, the sky a depressing mix of gray and brown. Temperatures are already a sultry 75°F (24°C), the humidity a muggy 78 percent. Paper wilts; ties are loosened and collars opened, watchbands are pushed back and forth. No adjustment provides more than temporary relief. Pedestrians plod along the sidewalk, moving from shade to shade, braving the muggy heat to seek passing refuge in air-conditioned shops.

At two in the afternoon, desultory cumulus clouds pass overhead, moving from the west; the sky turns from grayish brown to sparkling blue. The thermometer pauses in its afternoon climb and then settles back a few degrees, just short of the 86°F (30°C) mark. The dewpoint collapses, falling from the low 70s into the mid-50s, and the relative humidity drops by 30 percent. Streets spring to life, and iced coffees are eschewed in favor of hotter stuff.

A cold front has passed.

It is obvious from the change that new air has replaced the old, heralded by a weak cold front, and distinguished by a lower temperature, a comfortable humidity, a change in wind, and a cleaner-looking sky. The atmosphere has undergone a dramatic change as a fresh airmass was exchanged for the old. Where did the new airmass come from and how long will it last? Will the now-departed steamy air come back? Where has it gone?

Airmasses form when air overlying a ground or water surface for a long enough period—days or weeks—reaches a temperature and moisture equilibrium with the underlying surface, especially if that surface itself has relatively uniform characteristics. The nature of the surface is passed to the air above by exchanges of longwave radiation, by turbulent and convective transport of heat, and by evaporation and condensation. In the Northern Hemisphere, the best airmass-forming regions are found under the warm, subtropical high-pressure centers; during the long, cold winter nights of the Arctic and Siberia; and over the slow-varying surfaces of the Atlantic and Pacific Oceans.

Airmasses, then, are large regions of the atmosphere where temperatures and dewpoints exhibit only small differences over a wide area. That area may extend over several million square miles horizontally and through the depth of the atmosphere in the vertical, though there are some circumstances when the size and depth are much smaller. Understanding the characteristics of airmasses, their movement across the globe, and the transition from one airmass to another are fundamental challenges for the forecaster working on the operational desk.

Meteorologists have defined a half-dozen types of airmasses, each with particular characteristics that make for easy reference. Complications set in when an airmass moves away from the area where it forms, as, like any other traveler, it begins to take on the character of the region it visits. In short order, the airmass begins to blend in with its new surroundings and after a week or two its origin and identity have been obscured. Meanwhile, back at "home," a new airmass is forming to replace the one that departed.

Airmasses also have a seasonal character. Arctic air can build up and persist only in the Northern Hemisphere winter. In the summer it disappears completely, replaced by polar air that migrates southward. In turn, tropical air pushes northward to fuel the thunderstorm climates of summer.

The boundaries where airmasses butt against each other are called fronts. If the boundaries are moving, we will have an active warm or cold front. If the two airmasses are content to remain in peaceful coexistence without much movement, the frontal boundary is deemed to be quasi-stationary. The location of frontal zones is important for the daily forecasts, as the border between warm and cold air is a source of considerable potential energy and a region where storms can form quickly if triggered by upper-level impulses.

Types of Airmasses

Airmass names are composed of two parts: one part that reflects the moisture content (maritime or continental); another that reflects the region of origin and, by implication, the temperature. Over North America, airmasses are given names and symbols according to the following scheme:

Origin: Arctic (cold): A
           Polar (cold or cool): P
           Tropical (hot): T
Moisture: Maritime (moist): m
           Continental (dry): c

With this system, we can construct names such as "continental Arctic" to describe the cold and dry air of midwinter (Figure 8-1) or "maritime polar" to portray an airmass with moderate temperatures and a modest humidity (Figure 8-2). Higher-humidity air might be described as maritime tropical, though usually "tropical" is sufficient by itself, as continental tropical is limited to a small region of the American Southwest. For simplicity, the airmasses are designated by abbreviations: cA for continental Arctic, mP for maritime polar, and so on. The identity of airmasses is fairly casual, even in weather offices, so a cold outbreak from Canada into the northern United States might be called Arctic, when in fact it may be a cold polar airmass that is heading southward. In practical terms—that is, for forecasting—the nomenclature is not usually important.

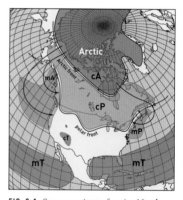

FIG. 8-1. *Source regions of major North American airmasses in winter. Arctic air forms only in the darkness of the far north. Continental polar air is formed over the boreal forests of Canada and the upper Great Plains when the air stagnates under winter highs. Maritime polar and maritime Arctic air masses form in the overwater trajectory of Arctic air in the North Pacific and Western Atlantic and are confined to coastal regions.*

Once airmasses leave their source regions, they undergo a

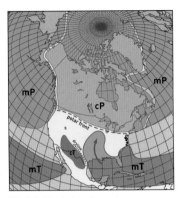

FIG. 8-2. *North American airmass source regions in summer. Over land, the two types of polar airmass are modified to the extent that they are virtually indistinguishable. In the zone colored yellow, the atmosphere typically does not remain stagnant for a long enough period for airmasses to form.*

continuous modification process that begins in the surface layers where the energy and moisture exchanges with the surface are most active. After several days, it becomes difficult to find the low-level boundary between the new airmass and the older one that it displaced, but the distinction between the two can persist for a week or more at higher levels in the atmosphere.

Arctic Airmasses

Arctic air (and in the Southern Hemisphere, Antarctic air) is born under the semipermanent high-pressure area that surrounds the pole, an environment that has been

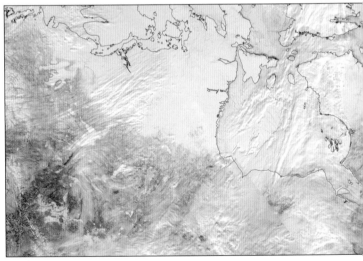

FIG. 8-3. *Frozen lakes, snow-white surfaces, days without sunlight, and snow-dusted trees set the stage for Arctic latitudes to form the cold, dry airmasses of winter. This polar satellite image shows the landscape over northern Canada in early March 2017, when sunlight is just returning to the higher latitudes.*

FIG. 8-4. *Arctic airmasses, with their low moisture content and bitter temperatures, usually reward the sufferer with cloudless skies and enduring transparency.*

dubbed the "polar vortex" by many broadcast meteorologists (Figure 8-1). It is a winter airmass, formed under the darkness of the polar night in a region where moisture is locked away in ice and snow (Figure 8-3).

Arctic air is very dry, allowing longwave infrared radiation to escape to space with little impediment—a cooling process made even more efficient because snow and ice surfaces are particularly effective infrared radiators. Even where sunlight is present during the short winter days, the bright snow surface reflects most of the solar energy back to space. This cold underlying surface is passed to the overlying atmosphere, giving the Arctic airmass one of its defining characteristics—a strong temperature inversion that may extend a considerable distance aloft.

Continental Arctic air (cA) is very dense and heavy and, once it settles, forms a high-pressure dome that is difficult to dislodge by intruding low-pressure storms. Instead, the storms go around the edges of the cold airmass, so the arrival of Arctic air often brings a prolonged spell of below-normal temperatures with plenty of sunshine (Figure 8-4). High, thin clouds are frequent in the cold air, but thicker cloud is uncommon provided the ground has frozen solid. Because of its strong surface inversion, Arctic air is very stable and forms only stratiform cloud when moisture becomes available, frequently during melting weather in spring. Where moisture is available, usually in the

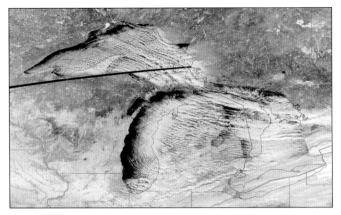

FIG. 8-5. *Cold air and strong northwest winds streaming over the open water of the Great Lakes gives birth to long lines of convective clouds. These clouds can drop prodigious amounts of snow when they reach the opposite shore.*

flow off an unfrozen body of water, the cold air is very quick to saturate and form cloud (Figure 8-5).

Periodic outbreaks of Arctic air (Figure 8-6) are the bane of the winter season over the United States. Not only do they bring freezing temperatures, but the temperature contrast that forms along the boundary of the invading cold airmass and the retreating warm air provides a supply of energy for the development of winter storms. These storms are especially prevalent along the Gulf Coast and the Atlantic Seaboard, where they have names such as Hatteras low, nor'easter, and Gulf low, though they are often given popular names such as the "Presidents' Day Storm."

Maritime Arctic (mA) air is uncommon, found mainly along the north coast of British Columbia, where it forms from Alaskan continental Arctic air after a short passage across the Gulf of Alaska. On reaching the coast, it is then blocked by the Rocky Mountains, which prevents it from moving farther inland. This is also the fate of Antarctic airmasses, which are also quickly modified once they leave the continent and move over the ocean.

Winter Movement of Continental Arctic Airmasses

In the depths of winter, continental Arctic air can take many pathways southward from Canada: sometimes it hugs the Front Range of the Rockies before turning eastward across the Great Plains; at other times, it curls across the Great Lakes into New England; yet another trajectory takes it directly southward until it curls around the bottom of the Appalachians and invades the Eastern Seaboard. If the cold air is particularly deep over the Plains, it will pile up on the foothills from Alberta to Colorado before spilling across the Rocky Mountains to descend onto the coasts of British Columbia, Washington, and Oregon. The cold air warms adiabatically as it descends to the coast but often not enough to raise temperatures above the freezing point. Whenever the evening news has a story about heavy snow in Seattle or Vancouver, a cross-mountain invasion of cold Arctic air, overtopped by oceanic mP air, is usually a part of the narrative.

The typical path followed by Arctic air is southward across the Great Plains, most often in the northerly winds behind a strong low-pressure system such as a Colorado low. This type of outflow brings wintry weather into Arkansas, Mississippi, and even Louisiana (Figure 8-6), though much of the sting of the cold has been tempered by warming of the airmass as it heads toward the Gulf. When Arctic air crosses the warm, open water of the Great Lakes, the lower levels of the atmosphere are quickly saturated with water vapor from turbulent mixing by strong winds and cumulus clouds (Figure 8-5). On reaching the downwind shore, the convective clouds can drop huge amounts of snow, a phenomenon known as "lake-effect" snowfall. Many local snowfall legends along the south shores of the Great Lakes can be traced to the overwater trajectory of cold continental polar and Arctic air. Buffalo, New York, on the northeast side of Lake Erie, has a particularly intimate relationship with lake-effect snowfalls.

When eastward-heading continental polar or Arctic air encounters the Appalachian Mountains, especially after being moistened by passage across the Great Lakes, it is

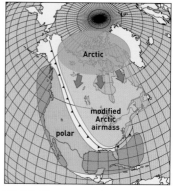

FIG. 8-6. *Winters in North America are made even more challenging when Arctic air breaks out of its traditional winter home and spreads southward across the eastern states, as shown in this figure. The eastern boundary of the cold air is a region of strong temperature contrasts, providing energy to intensify winter storms that travel up the Atlantic Seaboard. Such outbreaks are usually blamed on a "polar vortex."*

cooled to saturation as it rises over the west-facing slopes. Saturation brings convective buildups and sometimes very heavy snowfalls from Pennsylvania southward into Tennessee and even Alabama. Once the cold air is across the Appalachians, the air dries as it descends to the coast, bringing cool but sunny and pleasant weather. For shallow outbreaks of cold air, the Appalachians act as a dam, forcing the Arctic air to flow southward into Georgia to make an end run around the bottom of the mountain chain and then circle northward into Virginia and other seaboard states.

Polar Airmasses

Polar airmasses build up over land and water across middle northern latitudes, generally between 40° and 65° north latitude. It's an unfortunate name, as "polar" implies a rather cold airmass rather than the normal airmass of winter and summer that covers much of the United States and Canada. In North America, continental polar (cP) air is primarily a Canadian airmass (Figures 8-1 and 8-2), especially in summer when Arctic air disappears. Distinctive for its cool temperatures and modest dewpoints, continental polar air is usually regarded as the most comfortable of the airmasses, greeted with considerable relief when it pushes southward to replace humid, subtropical air in summer. Continental polar air is easily modified; when it moves southward, it is warmed by the higher Sun and, in summer, humidified by evapotranspiration from the underlying vegetation.

Maritime polar (mP) air is born over the northeast Pacific where it forms a cool, humid, and unstable airmass (Figure 8-1) that abuts the coast of Alaska, British Columbia, and the northwestern states. In autumn, maritime polar air can also form from drier continental polar air that lingers over the unfrozen waters of the Arctic Ocean or over the open lakes, swamps, and muskeg of northern Canada. On the Pacific Coast of North America, maritime polar air brings generous precipitation when it rises along the windward slopes of the coastal mountains. On the lee side of the Rockies, however, it is warmed and dried as it descends to lower altitude and becomes more like continental polar air.

The two polar airmasses are stirred by migrating lows and highs as they cross North America, leading, in the end, to a sort of mongrel airmass that has lost the distinction between maritime and continental. Forecasters often tag the prevailing airmass simply as "polar" without discriminating between cP and mP. Nevertheless, and in spite of their similarity, frontal boundaries still exist between them. Such fronts are weaker than those between polar and tropical air but still capable of providing a focus on which to generate thunderstorms and synoptic-scale lows.

Summertime polar airmasses are temperamental residents. If adequate moisture is available and the airmass is provoked by any one of a number of irritants, it is prone to erupt into thunderstorms and occasional severe weather. One of those irritants is often provided by colliding wind flows that converge along the weak frontal boundaries between mP and cP air. Since moisture is typically readily available from evapotranspiration and other sources, summer thunderstorms are a daily feature of polar airmasses. Polar airmasses nurture a more threatening storm environment after they have passed over the Rockies and settled in over the Great Plains atop a layer of low-level maritime tropical air. This atmospheric layer cake puts a cool, dry airmass above warm, moist air—classical conditions for the development of severe thunderstorms.

With no mountains to block the flow of air from the Atlantic, central Europe is usually covered by maritime polar air that originates in the vicinity of Iceland or to the west of England. This air has had a long traverse over relatively warm water and so is laden with moisture, though at a moderate temperature. European continental polar air is of Scandinavian origin, arriving after a brief crossing of the North Sea over which it experiences only a little warming and humidification. The lack of a coastal mountain range to wring moisture from polar air gives Europe a much cloudier climate than similar latitudes in North America.

Tropical Airmasses

Once you've met a maritime tropical airmass (mT), you will never need another introduction. These airmasses are hot and laden with moisture; they feel sticky and discourage outdoor activities. Think of July in New Orleans or Houston or Shanghai. Summer weather over the eastern half of the United States is dominated by moist tropical air, occasionally relieved by a welcome influx of polar air from the northwest. On the Eastern Seaboard, tropical air arrives from the Atlantic, while on the Great Plains, mT air comes northward from the Gulf of Mexico, occasionally reaching into Canada when the southerly, low-level flow persists for several days in a row.

From December through February, maritime tropical air is held at

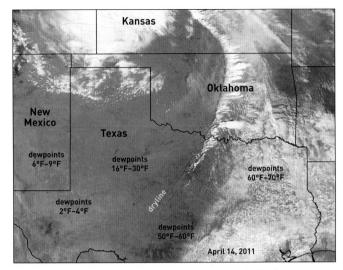

FIG. 8-7. *A sharp moisture boundary (dashed line) is created when the maritime tropical air from the Gulf of Mexico meets the drier continental tropical air that forms over the high deserts of Arizona and New Mexico—a boundary known as the West Texas dryline. There is little or no temperature contrast across the dryline, but the moisture difference can be very large. In this map, from April 14, 2011, dewpoints in the dry air are as low as 2°F, while those in the moist air range between 50° and 70°F.*

bay by the large amount of polar and Arctic air across the continental United States and makes only short incursions into the Gulf States and Florida when southerly winds push wintry air back to the north. Once March arrives, however, tropical air begins to nudge northward, following the summer sun to higher latitudes. Gulf of Mexico air seldom penetrates deep into the mountains, but surges of maritime tropical air from the Gulf of California occasionally move into Arizona, Nevada, and parts of Southern California to fuel the summer monsoon season in those states.

Continental tropical air (cT) is hot and dry—the sort of air that envelopes Phoenix and Tucson in the summer months. The only source region in North America is found in the summer in northern Mexico and the adjacent desert areas of the American Southwest (Figures 8-1, 8-2), primarily Arizona and New Mexico. It is an airmass of low relative humidity, little cloudiness, and no rainfall. The meeting point between cT and mT air over Texas and Oklahoma is not treated as a frontal boundary, but is instead referred to as the West Texas dryline (Figure 8-7). The dryline plays a major role in initiating thunderstorms that later move northeastward into Oklahoma and Kansas.

Globally, tropical airmasses are found over the warm ocean waters and dry deserts at low latitudes. Favorite areas for the formation of maritime tropical air straddle the equator over the Atlantic, Pacific, and Indian Oceans at about 20° north and south latitude. The Earth's largest source of continental tropical air is the Sahara Desert and surrounding regions, with smaller source regions over Australia and over Brazil in the dry season.

Airmass Modification

When an airmass moves out of its source region, it begins a process of modification that changes its properties in response to the new underlying surfaces. The most important influences are temperature, moisture availability, and terrain, with modification proceeding from the surface upward. The greater the difference between the recently arrived airmass and the underlying surface, the faster the modification will proceed.

Temperature is the most important of the factors that regulate airmass transformation, especially when cold air flows over warmer ground. If that ground is warm enough, the stability of the cold air will be overcome and heat and moisture will be able to spread very quickly through a large depth of the atmosphere. In general, movement over water surfaces will have the greatest impact in the transition of one airmass to another, as water vapor itself carries a considerable amount of latent heat that can be deposited into the newly arrived airmass. In the reverse situation, where, say, a tropical airmass moves over cold water, a low-level inversion will be created, and the modification will be slow to move upward from the surface layers.

Fronts

Fronts are transition zones between two airmasses. On the daily weather map (Figure 8-8) that you might find online or in a newspaper, the forecaster delineates the frontal position with long, arcing lines, but in reality, the borders are seldom so clear-cut. The change from one airmass to another is rarely abrupt, but instead takes place over a distance that ranges from tens to hundreds of miles. Frontal

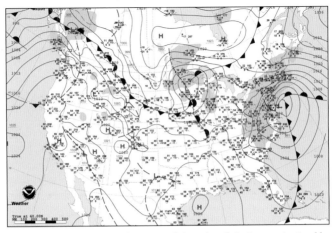

FIG. 8-8. *A typical surface weather map with frontal analysis. A strong Arctic cold front is surging southward over South Dakota and Iowa, while a winter storm is moving northward along the Eastern Seaboard. Traditionally, cold fronts are delineated by sharp barbs along the frontal line; warm fronts by half-circles. Stationary fronts have a mix of symbols.*

analysis is as much an art as a science, and different forecasters often arrive at very different positions for the airmass boundaries. Warm fronts are especially tough to demarcate as their transition zones are usually very large and diffuse. Some of the most active weather that we encounter comes along a frontal boundary, so airmass movement not only brings new kinds of weather, but often does so with considerable drama.

Fronts take the name of the airmass on their cold side, so we have Arctic and polar fronts but no tropical front. The Arctic front lies between Arctic and polar airmasses; the polar front divides polar and tropical air. A warm front brings warm air; a cold front brings cold. If the front between two airmasses is not moving, it is said to be quasi-stationary. An occluded front is one in which the advancing cold air has caught up with the retreating warm air; the cold air may ride up on top of the warm front or slide beneath it, depending on the relative temperatures of the two airmasses at that location.

Frontal strength is measured not only by the temperature difference between the two types of air, but also by the temperature gradient—how rapidly the temperature changes from one airmass to the other (Figure 8-9). Two airmasses may have very different temperatures, but

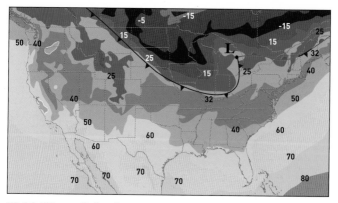

FIG. 8-9. *This map displays the temperature pattern across the continental United States on a day in February 2014. Frigid Arctic air is advancing southward behind a cold front over the Upper Midwest and the Central Plains while warm air is pushing northward over the northeastern states and Quebec ahead of a low. The strong contrast in temperatures supplies energy for the development of the low.*

if the transition from one to the other is gradual, the frontal zone will be weak and the associated cloud and weather correspondingly muted. Frontal boundaries are important places in the atmosphere, as strong temperature gradients are regions of considerable energy. Active fronts—those that are moving and creating weather—are always tied to low-pressure systems that feed off of the energy contained in the temperature gradient between two airmasses, creating the winds that cause the fronts and airmasses to move.

When airmasses collide along a frontal boundary, the heavier, cold air acts like a wedge and slides beneath the warmer, so that fronts always consist of warm air above cold. Fronts are not straight up-and-down features, but typically slope upward toward the cold air side. The magnitude of the slope is an important factor in determining the type of weather that accompanies the front. For the most part, cold fronts are steeper, with a typical incline of about 50:1 (1 mile vertically for every 50 miles horizontally). Warm fronts have more gentle slopes, characteristically, about 300:1.

Cold Fronts

Cold fronts mark the leading edge of advancing cold air. These fronts are usually easy to find on a weather map (Figure 8-8), as they come with abrupt changes of surface temperature and dewpoint across the frontal zone. A balloon released after the cold air has arrived will show a layer of warm air above the surface, with a temperature inversion in the zone where the two airmasses meet. Because of their steep slope, fast-moving cold fronts tend to have well-defined bands of cloud

FIG. 8-10. *A strong polar cold front stretches from the Great Lakes to western Texas in this satellite image from September 24, 2010. A low-pressure center is located over Lake Superior with a warm front extending eastward, just within the southern boundary of the cloud in the upper right of the scene.*

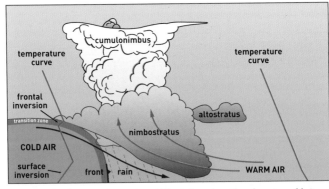

FIG. 8-11. *This diagram of an active cold front shows how the advancing cold air undercuts the warmer air in front, lifting it to saturation, where it forms convective and layered clouds. Precipitation is usually found ahead of the surface frontal position, though the heaviest rain or snow is typically found at the front. This example represents a summer cold front; in winter, the cumulonimbus cloud would probably not be present.*

and precipitation that sharply outline the position of the front when viewed using radar, satellite imagery (Figure 8-10), or a weather map. Slower-moving fronts have broader cloud bands and a more varied mix of cloud types.

Cloud along cold fronts is often convective (Figure 8-11), particularly in the summer season, and the fronts often bring extended lines of severe weather, especially when they push into maritime tropical air. The nose of a cold front tends to be rather blunt, and so the greatest upward push comes right at the frontal position. On a steadily moving front, this leading edge is likely to be the position of heaviest precipitation or deepest convection. In winter, convection is usually limited by the stability of the atmosphere and cold fronts then have a mix of low- and mid-level stratiform cloudiness, though still confined to relatively narrow bands.

Cold fronts are typically accompanied by winds that shift from south to north or northwest, pressures that rise sharply after passage, and a noticeable drop in humidity and temperature. They are a meteorologist's friend, because cold fronts are easy to find on a weather map and they move at steady speeds that permit accurate forecasting. Over the oceans, cold fronts sometimes appear as a very narrow cloud line (called a rope cloud) when the cold air is pushed out ahead of the main frontal cloud mass (Figure 8-13).

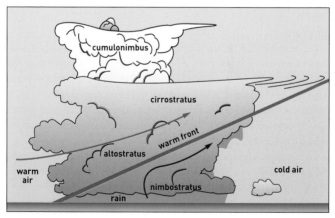

FIG. 8-12. *Warm fronts tend to form thick layered clouds, occasionally with embedded thunderstorms if sufficient instability is present. Though the front is moving slowly to the right in this example, the warm air tends to ride up and over the cold air rather than pushing it along.*

FIG. 8-13. *A narrow rope cloud marks the position of the cold front as it moves across the warm waters of the Gulf Stream. Note that the front does not move as a straight line, but in a more scalloped pattern.*

Warm Fronts

While cold fronts are sharp and well delineated, warm fronts are diffuse and spread out over a large distance. "Front" is not a good descriptive term—a better one might be "warm advection zone" or something similar. In spite of their timid character, warm fronts do have a personality: a gentler slope than cold fronts, winds that shift from easterly to southerly as the front passes over a station, pressures that fall as the warm air approaches and then become steady in its wake, and a gradual rise in temperature and dewpoint across the front.

Because of the gentler lift that they impart to the moving air, warm fronts tend to have stratiform cloudiness, though convective clouds, including heavy thunderstorms, are often embedded in the larger cloud shield in summer. An approaching warm front will herald itself first with thin cirrus, then an increasingly dense cirrostratus, a gradually thickening altostratus, and finally a mixture of convective and stratiform low cloudiness, as shown in Figure 8-12. Warm fronts tend to bring steady and sometimes heavy continuous precipitation, and in winter, a complex transition from snow to freezing rain to rain as the front approaches and temperatures climb.

Occluded Fronts

In a large low-pressure system that contains both cold and warm fronts, the faster-moving cold front typically overtakes the warm as they circulate around a low-pressure storm. When the two come into contact, the warmer air gets squeezed upward, leaving only the coldest air against the ground. The warm air is still very active and able to produce heavy cloudiness and precipitation, but its elevated frontal position becomes much more difficult to recognize on a surface weather map. Such fronts are referred to as "occluded" fronts, as they are closed off or occluded from the surface.

Drylines

One of the more important nonfrontal boundaries in North America is the West Texas dryline, which, as we have seen on page 314, is the place where dry continental tropical air meets humid maritime tropical air. When unstable air settles in over Texas, storm chasers often head west to the dryline to await the first severe thunderstorms of the day. Dryline boundaries of a weaker sort can be found all along the western Great Plains in summer, from Kansas and Nebraska northward to Alberta and Saskatchewan, though they usually form between dry and moist polar airmasses.

The West Texas dryline can be an extremely sharp boundary, with dewpoints changing by 36°F (20°C) in as little as a few miles. Afternoon temperatures in the dry air are usually higher than those in the moist air, since solar heating is more efficient in the absence of humidity. A typical maritime tropical airmass might have an afternoon temperature of 90°F (32°C) and a dewpoint of 60°F (15°C). The adjacent continental tropical air may have a temperature of 97°F (36°C) or more, but have a dewpoint of only 32°F (0°C) or lower, as shown in Figure 8-7. The contrast between the dry and moist airmasses, though not a classical front, can act as a triggering mechanism (Figure 8-14) that initiates the development of thunderstorms in the maritime tropical air. Drylines also have an atypical frontal behavior, as they advance eastward from the foothills in the afternoon and retreat at night, oscillating back and forth over the High Plains each day.

Frontolysis and Frontogenesis

Fronts are not static structures; rather, they form, intensify, weaken, and dissipate. The creation of a new front or the regeneration of an older one is known as "frontogenesis." Its opposite, "frontolysis,"

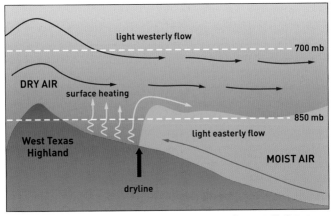

FIG. 8-14. *The West Texas dryline marks the convergence of moist Gulf of Mexico air with the dry desert air of the American Southwest. The boundary moves forward and back during the course of the day as dry air mixes downward to replace the tongue of Gulf moisture. At night, the dryline retreats to its original position. The dryline is a favored location for the development of thunderstorms and is popular with storm chasers.*

describes the weakening or dissipation of a front. Since the strength of a front is determined by the difference in temperature between the cold and warm air sides, frontolysis occurs when the temperature contrast is reduced, and frontogenesis when the contrast is enhanced. Usually, modification is caused by surface warming or cooling, from either the nature of the ground (for instance, ice-covered or bare), solar heating, or the release of latent heat when precipitation begins to fall. In the vertical, frontolysis and frontogenesis are controlled by stability, which governs how heat and moisture are spread upward and downward. Ultimately, all fronts become victim to frontolysis as airmasses move away from the region where they formed and become modified in their new environment.

Trends in frontal strength are important and are sometimes overlooked in the construction of a forecast. The intensity of a frontal zone can change in just a few hours. During frontogenesis, the sudden strengthening of a front may cause the weather to turn ugly and bring on a sudden dump of heavy snow or rain where it was not expected. Frontolysis is not as threatening, as it produces more benign weather—the forecast may be wrong, but the consequences are less hostile and the public is more willing to forgive.

The Norwegian Cyclone Model

Cyclogenesis

In both the Northern and Southern Hemispheres, the meteorology between 30° and 60° of latitude is ruled by moving (migrating) high- and low-pressure weather systems—the heroes and villains of every daily weather forecast on television and radio. In meteorological parlance, the lows are known as mid-latitude, or extratropical, cyclones. (It's an unfortunate moniker, as the word "cyclone" is also used for hurricane-like lows that form over the Indian Ocean and over waters near Australia, and sometimes even for tornadoes.) Mid-latitude lows are the organs by which energy and heat accumulated over the tropics are passed to polar latitudes. Along the way, the atmosphere is stirred so that neither excessive cold nor excessive heat accumulates in one place or another for any length of time.

We owe our current insights of how cyclones form (cyclogenesis), mature, decay, and disappear to Norwegian meteorologist Vilhelm Bjerknes of the Bergen School of Meteorology. Using the abundant surface data available in Europe in the early 1900s, Bjerknes and his colleagues were able to assemble a conceptual model of the evolution of a mid-latitude cyclone—a concept now known as the Norwegian Cyclone (or wave cyclone) model. It is a surprisingly simple and immensely valuable description. That model is still valid, in spite of the monumental advances in observation and computer modeling in the ensuing years.

Conceptual models of atmospheric structures are a critical component of operational meteorology (forecasting), as they provide a framework on which forecasters can evaluate the current state of the weather and predict its future evolution. Such mental models are constructed from the average characteristics of many weather systems and represent the "typical" behavior of a low and its associated fronts. Such models are fundamental to meteorology, not just for understanding the evolution of a low-pressure storm. You will find them useful in understanding phenomena such as thunderstorms, wind flow over mountains, precipitation types, clouds, and the global climate, as we've used mental constructs many times in this book. The Norwegian Cyclone model is one of the most useful in the history of meteorology, but research, observation, and modeling over the past half-century have exposed other processes important in cyclone evolution.

In the Norwegian model, the development of a mid-latitude

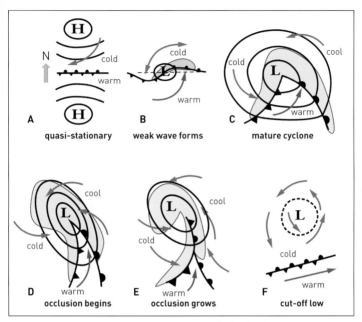

FIG. 8-15. *Schematic diagram of the wave cyclone model developed by the Bergen (Norway) School of Meteorology.*

cyclone begins along a quasi-stationary (QS) front (Figure 8-15, A). In order for development to progress, the front should divide airmasses of relatively different temperature—a few degrees are not enough. The front is not active—it is not moving—but is probably outlined by a broken band of cloudiness and perhaps a bit of light precipitation here and there along its length. The contrast of temperatures across the frontal zone represents a considerable amount of potential energy— energy that can go toward turning a quiescent weather system into an intense storm. The trigger for such development is usually a weak upper-level disturbance that crosses the frontal boundary and disturbs the uneasy balance between the contrasting airmasses.

The upper-level disturbance causes the air column above the front to rise and spread out aloft, a process known as divergence. In response to this divergence, pressures begin to fall at the surface and in the lower layers of the atmosphere, and a weak low is born (Figure 8-15, B). Surface winds respond quickly and begin to flow cyclonically (counterclockwise in the Northern Hemisphere) around the developing low in response to the newly formed pressure. Warm air begins to move northward on the east (front) side of the low, and cold air heads southward on the west side, forming a small wavelike perturbation on the frontal surface with the peak of the wave in the center of the low. Whether this low continues to deepen and go on to form a bigger storm now depends on the strength of the upper disturbance and the temperature and moisture contrast between the airmasses through the depth of the atmosphere, a feature known as "baroclinicity." A baroclinic atmosphere is one with a significant temperature gradient and lots of energy; one with a small or no gradient is called "barotropic."

Given sufficient baroclinicity and a strong enough upper-level perturbation, pressure in the developing low continues to fall, and the winds intensify around the low center. Cold air surges southward on the back side of the cyclone, while warm air plods northward in front (Figure 8-15, C). Thickening cloud layers and the onset of precipitation mark the advance of warm air, while convective clouds, showers, and a sharp transition to colder and drier air follow the cold (Table 8-1). In autumn, when the deeper lows and stronger fronts first appear during the transition to winter, nearly every type of weather may be found within the wave cyclone: wind and snow to the north of the system; freezing rain and rain along the warm front; thundershowers—perhaps severe—along the southerly parts of the cold front; pleasant temperatures in the warm sector. Everything is in a hurry to move along and get the warm and cold airmasses mixed together and the temperatures evened out. At maturity, the low may contain a pronounced frontal system that extends from central Canada to the Gulf Coast.

In nearly all mid-latitude cyclones, the cold front moves more quickly than the warm in the circulation around the low. Eventually the cold air, led by the cold front, catches up to and undercuts the warm front and the warm sector is lifted upward by the denser cold air. With no warm air at the surface, the surface position of the frontal wave drops southward out of the center of the low (Figure 8-15, D, E) as the warm sector is "zipped up" by the incoming cold air. The new boundary between the warm and cold airmasses is called an occluded front or simply an "occlusion." Thermal contrasts and active weather will continue in the air aloft, but the temperature contrast between warm and cold air that formerly existed at the surface is significantly weakened. As the occlusion process continues over the next day or two, the warm-sector air is raised ever higher in the atmosphere until the baroclinicity surrounding the center of the low nearly disappears.

COLD FRONT

	BEFORE PASSAGE	DURING PASSAGE	AFTER PASSAGE
Wind	south–southwest	west–northwest, gusty	northwest–north, brisk
Temperature	warm, steady	sudden drop	cooling steadily
Pressure	falling slowly	abrupt rise	rising, then steady
Clouds	increasing high cloud, possible thundershowers	convective clouds: showers, thundershowers	clearing, cumulus in summer
Precipitation	none except in thundershowers	heavy showers, heavy thunder-showers, snow in winter	none
Visibility	fair to poor in haze	low in precipitation	good
Dew point	steady, moderate to high	falling abruptly	decreasing slowly

WARM FRONT

	BEFORE PASSAGE	DURING PASSAGE	AFTER PASSAGE
Wind	southeast–east	variable	south–southwest
Temperature	cool, slow warming	warming	warmer
Pressure	falling	slow falling	small rise
Clouds	lowering, cirrus to stratus	stratus	clearing, occasional thunderstorm
Precipitation	light to moderate rain, snow, icy in winter	tapering off	dry, possible thundershower in summer
Visibility	poor in precipitation, fog	improving	hazy in summer
Dewpoint	increasing slowly	steady	rising, then steady

TABLE 8-1. *Characteristics of warm and cold fronts*

Bereft of energy, the low weakens, slowing its eastward motion and eventually coming to rest as a "cut-off low"—a low that is no longer embedded in the normal west-to-east flow, but spins forlornly off to the side in the cold air and gradually fades away as surface pressures rise (Figure 8-15, F). In winter, these cut-off systems are often captured by pre-existing upper lows, becoming trapped in "cyclone graveyards" that are typically found over Hudson Bay and northern Quebec, or in the waters near Iceland. Farther south, where the warm sector has not been pinched off and the thermal gradients are still significant, a second (usually weaker) low may form at the peak of the frontal wave and continue the occlusion process.

As pressure gradients weaken, winds decline and the southward-moving cold air eventually slows and comes to a stop. The frontal boundary now takes up the characteristics of a quasi-stationary front, even though the baroclinic zone may have considerable energy, at least until the cold air has modified in its new environment. This baroclinicity is available to support the development of another low along the quasi-stationary front, awaiting only another upper-atmosphere perturbation to set it off. In concert with the weakening of the surface and upper low, clouds and precipitation gradually dissipate along the occlusion and winds decline as the surface pressure gradients fade away.

A Satellite View of Cyclogenesis

In the 1970s, routine images of the Earth and its weather systems became available after a series of United States polar-orbiting and geostationary satellites were launched and put into operational use. At first, attention was focused on thunderstorms and their evolution, but right from the start, it was obvious that there was considerable structure in the synoptic (large-scale) cloud systems. Analysis of those patterns was taken on by Roger Weldon, a legendary figure within the operational meteorology community at that time. Weldon never published his insights in the professional literature, but instead compiled them in a series of training notes that were widely distributed across forecast offices in Canada and the United States. *Weldon's Notes,* as they came to be called, are still available on the internet with a careful search.

Weldon related the evolution of storm systems as seen in the high-level cloud to patterns in the upper wind fields. He was able to see the various flow patterns in time-lapse animations of the half-hourly

FIG. 8-16. *Three comma cloud systems are visible in this* GOES *satellite image of the central Pacific Ocean. The most prominent is in the center of the scene, stretching from a curled-up low above center to a long tail past Hawaii to the bottom left. A second comma cloud lies near the west limb, and the third is offshore from the Washington coast.*

satellite images, constructed from loops of movie film that were run through a projector to repeat over and over again. He noted that most storm systems took on a comma-shaped form that was structured by the upper winds. Such comma systems are ubiquitous in satellite images, particularly in the winter season (Figure 8-16).

There are many variations in the formation of a comma system, and the one we will describe is that shown in Figure 8-17. Our developing weather system begins with a small area of cirrus-level cloud with a smooth back (western) edge, embedded within the temperature gradient of a baroclinic zone—most likely an old frontal zone. The jet stream lies along and just outside the smooth cloud edge. The beginning of the eventual comma development becomes noticeable when the cirrus cloud band adopts an S-shaped back edge (Figure 8-17, A), a sign that winds along the jet stream are beginning to distort the shape of the cloud.

Over the next 12 to 24 hours, the S-shape becomes more and more pronounced until the cloud has an unmistakable comma shape, mostly formed by the intrusion of dry air that carves a "slot" into the middle of the system (Figure 8-17, B). This "dry slot" is caused by the jet stream as it arcs through the cloud mass, bringing air from

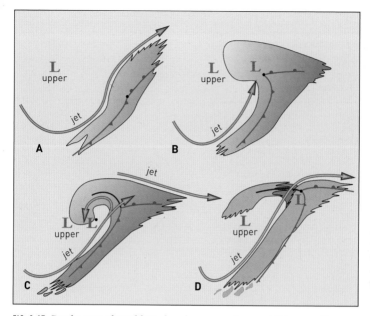

FIG. 8-17. *Development of a mid-latitude cyclone as seen from a satellite perspective. This set of images shows one type of evolution, in which the cloud mass first develops an S-shaped back edge and then goes on to gradually wrap up around the atmospheric low, forming a comma-shaped cloud in the process. The jet stream is an intimate part of the growth and decay process and is responsible for the indentation carved into the cloud mass that gives it the comma shape.*

lower levels up and over the middle of the formation. The jet stream broadens out as it enters the head of the comma, with one part turning around the upper low and the other turning eastward into the main cloud mass (Figure 8-17, C).

The release of latent heat within the comma system and the advection of warm air by the low-level winds changes the thermal structure within the developing cyclone. A new jet stream forms on the north edge of the comma head in response to the building temperatures within the cloud mass. With time, the jet passing through the dry slot connects with that on the northern edge of the comma cloud shield to form a continuous band of high winds through the system. At this stage, the comma cloud is past its prime, the head is beginning to fragment, and the baroclinicity weakens as the warm air moves out of the system. In the end, the inactive baroclinic zone is re-established

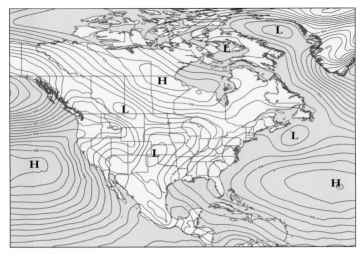

FIG. 8-18. *This map shows the average sea-level pressure for February and March, 2003–2013. The low pressure centered over the Alberta-Saskatchewan-Montana border is the formation region for Alberta lows. The center over Colorado-Kansas is the site of Colorado low cyclogenesis. The track of Hatteras lows does not show up well on a long-term average such as this, as these lows do not have as distinct a region of cyclogenesis. The low offshore from Nova Scotia is formed because all three types of lows tend to pass through this region on their travels eastward.*

to await another jet-stream disturbance to begin the process again (Figure 8-17, D).

Today, comma clouds are a staple of TV weather. If you watch the animations carefully, you will recognize the flows that structure a storm as it winds up into a comma shape (Figure 8-17). If you wonder why, in March, it snows in Minnesota while Mississippi has tornadoes, the comma cloud system with its large snowy head and unstable, dangling tail is usually responsible.

Regions of Cyclogenesis

Cyclogenesis—the formation of new lows—can occur wherever large amounts of baroclinicity accumulate, but there are certain areas of the globe where cyclogenesis is favored more than others. These favored regions are places where some feature of the underlying surface promotes the development of atmospheric disturbances.

One of these cyclonic nurseries is along the Front Range of the Rocky Mountains, from Alberta south through Montana and Wyoming to Colorado (Figure 8-18). When air flows over the Rockies and drops down onto the Great Plains, the atmospheric column in the lee of the mountains is stretched in the vertical to adapt to the new surface elevation. This stretching causes pressures to decline along the eastern foothills and the resulting low-pressure "lee trough" then becomes a nursery for the formation of new lows. Cyclogenesis is triggered when a strong upper disturbance crosses the mountains and couples with the surface trough, promoting a further decline in pressure. If enough energy is present in the form of contrasting cold and warm airmasses over the Great Plains, then the initial modest pressure drop will accelerate and go on to grow into a major storm.

Another region of cyclogenesis is found off of the East Coast of North America where cold air flowing off the continent passes over the warm Gulf Stream current. Energy in the form of sensible and latent heat is injected into the atmosphere, providing a critical energy supply to rapidly deepen the central pressure of an otherwise modest low-pressure disturbance. This form of energy injection and rapid cyclogenesis can also be found over Lake Superior in midwinter, though the effect is much smaller over the lake than over the Atlantic Coast with its warm Gulf Stream current. Low-pressure centers that deepen very rapidly—more than 24 millibars in 24 hours—are known by various names, such as "bomb cyclone," "weather bomb," or simply "bomb." Such storms most often form over the oceans in winter, though they are not unknown in continental environments. (Don't talk about them in an airport!)

In North America, winter storms originating in the favored cyclogenesis regions have characteristic and familiar names. Alberta Clippers, Colorado lows (Figure 8-19), and Panhandle lows are well known to residents of the Great Plains and the northeastern states, while Gulf lows and Hatteras lows (Nor'easters) taunt the Appalachians and the Eastern Seaboard. The Alberta low (and close cousin, the Montana low) forms in strong west-to-east zonal flows, while the others form where the upper flow has large north-to-south (meridional) excursions.

The 3-D Structure of Cyclones

In satellite imagery, mature cyclones have a distinct comma shape (Figure 8-16). The tail of the comma is associated with the cold front, while the head is made up of the cloud along the warm front and the occlusion. Animated satellite images show a complex flow of air through these systems—flows that are not apparent in the two-

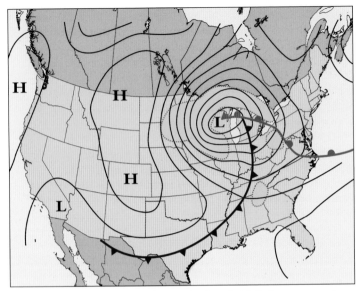

FIG. 8-19. *Colorado lows are a class of storms that form ahead of a deep upper trough; they typically move northeastward toward the Great Lakes and then eastward. This example is of a low that took a more northerly track than usual, ending up in northwest Ontario (and later, northern Quebec) instead of the Gulf of St. Lawrence.*

dimensional surface and upper-air diagrams that meteorologists traditionally use. To understand them properly, we have to examine the three-dimensional flows through a mature cyclone by way of another conceptual model.

This conceptual model describes the mid-latitude low in terms of three flows or "conveyors" (Figure 8-20). One, the "warm conveyor belt," originates far to the south of the system and carries warm, humid air northward through the warm sector and up over the sloping warm front. The flow rises slowly along its path across the warm sector, from about 900 mb in the most southerly parts to above 300 mb north of the warm front. Adiabatic cooling during this ascent causes the formation of warm-frontal cloud and precipitation, which in turn provides an injection of thermal energy by the release of latent heat.

The "cold conveyor belt" is a west-flowing circulation that begins at low levels to the east of the cyclone and flows beneath the warm front toward the low center. When it reaches a position northeast of the low,

FIG. 8-20. *Conveyor belts in a Colorado low. In an animation of this system, low-level clouds would be seen moving into the warm conveyor belt at its start north of Bermuda. The flow in the dry conveyor belt could be traced by the movement of low cloud near the comma tail. The cold conveyor belt would not be easily seen, however, as it lies below the cloud of the warm conveyor.*

a part of it turns anticyclonically (clockwise) away from the low and joins the higher-level westerly flow in which the storm is embedded. Though it's relatively dry, the cold conveyor belt is moistened by precipitation falling from the clouds along the warm front above. Rather than being a distinct wind flow on its own, the cold conveyor belt is a "storm-relative flow"—it is formed from air that is overrun by the moving cyclone and incorporated into its structure. This belt forms the western part of the comma head.

The "dry conveyor belt" is what gives the cloud shield of a mature cyclone its comma shape by forming the dry slot. The conveyor belt follows the jet stream (Chapter 7) that originates in the upper troposphere to the west, and then descends into the storm before rising again to pass over the cold conveyor belt. This flow helps to maintain the thermal structure of the cyclone by injecting cold air into the system. From a forecasting perspective, the dry conveyor belt brings the clearing skies that characterize the airmass behind the cold front. To the operational forecaster, the dry slot is also often the cause of a surprising few hours of sunshine or a dry spell in the midst of a winter storm when it proves more effective at dissipating clouds than expected.

FIG. 8-21. *A large comma-cloud system stretches from Iceland to the tropical Atlantic. The parent low-pressure system lies under the wound-up cloud spiral south of Iceland. The bulge in the comma tail is a new disturbance moving northward where it will intensify the system.*

Fronts and Cyclones in Perspective

The frontal and mid-latitude cyclone structures we have described above provide a useful abstract framework for the meteorologist, but the real atmosphere is much more complex. The model of three conveyor belts is a highly simplified description of the airflow through a large extratropical storm; a detailed case study would show that the airflow twists and turns much more than we have shown. The flows into the cyclone would change as the storm evolved, precipitation and convection would blend the layers together, jet-stream flows would wax and wane, and topography might limit or control some of the flows in and out of the storm. Nevertheless, you will find it easy to recognize most of these structures and their effects in the satellite animation on the display behind the TV weather forecaster. If you keep a close eye on the satellite imagery available on the internet, you will be able to identify the structures as they pass overhead and perhaps even surprise your neighbors with a forecast of a temporary clearing when you spot a dry slot headed your way.

For the observer on the ground, knowledge of the commalike structure of storms will allow you to relate the clouds above to their place in the storm system. An end to precipitation or a partial clearing of the clouds may indicate the arrival of the dry slot; a wind shift, falling temperatures, and a start of precipitation will signal a cold front as the comma tail swings past. You may anticipate a change to freezing rain and to snow as winds turn counterclockwise as a storm approaches. A winter storm in Minnesota may signal that a day of severe thunderstorms is in the offing as far away as the Gulf Coast.

We have shown how the movement of airmasses and their frontal boundaries, and the associated cyclogenesis that builds temperature gradients into storms, are more than just two-dimensional surface-based processes. Events higher in the atmosphere play a critical role in initiating and supporting development—especially cyclogenesis—along the frontal boundaries. Winter storms now have a larger meaning for you: born in the energy of temperature gradients, fed by a complex mixture of upper and lower winds, intensified by the injection of latent heat, and shaped by jet streams into continent-sized commas. As the lows and fronts arrive and leave, we leave you with a set of conceptual models to interpret the shifting patterns in the weather. In the next chapter, we'll introduce some other conceptual models.

CHAPTER 9

EXTREME WEATHER

Convective Monsters

Few sights in meteorology are the equal of a majestic cumulonimbus cloud glowing in bright sunlight across a flat prairie horizon. Artists and storm chasers alike are captivated by these imposing 10-mile-high (16-km-high) convective clouds, enchanted by both their impressive appearance and their implied threat. It is somewhat incongruous that clouds bred by nothing more than the buoyancy of warm air and the conversion of latent heat could turn into the monstrous Great Plains storms of Tornado Alley.

Severe weather from convective storms comes in five forms: heavy rain, damaging winds, hail, lightning, and tornadoes. The largest and toughest thunderstorms—supercells—can produce all five, often from the same storm (Figure 9-1). Their lesser cousins, multicell and single-cell storms, are not so fearsome, though no forecaster would ignore their potential for danger and damage.

Winds

The cool air that flows from beneath a thunderstorm is often a welcome respite from the hot, muggy conditions that breed cumulonimbus clouds. The winds originate in the mid-levels of the atmosphere and are collectively known as downdrafts or downbursts when they descend and spread out along the ground. All precipitating convective clouds have them, though they are usually subdued and difficult to recognize in weaker, towering cumulus cells. The spreading pool of cool air has a Jekyll-and-Hyde personality, sometimes arriving as a welcome, gentle breeze and at other times as a violent windstorm.

FIG. 9-1. *A massive supercell thunderstorm hovers over the prairie landscape. The storm is viewed from its south side.*

The leading edge of the outflow is known as a "gust front" if it's a weak one, and a "squall line" if it comes from a line of storms.

Precipitation that forms early in the development of convective clouds is held suspended by the updrafts in the storm until the raindrops or ice crystals grow large and heavy enough to descend. The falling rain or snow drags some of the cold upper-level air downward, creating a downdraft that eventually reaches the surface. Though the descending air is warmed and dried by adiabatic compression, that rise in temperature is offset by cooling as raindrops evaporate into the descending air. Small raindrops are particularly prone to evaporation, and so the cooling of the descending air column tends to be greatest in the lower and warmer parts of the storm, where falling drops have already lost some of their mass.

Though sinking, cold air is the main source of outflow winds, larger thunderstorms may also divert winds from jet-stream levels toward the surface to intensify the downdraft flow. Water loading—the weight of water in the mid-layers of a storm—also contributes to the downward acceleration of air parcels, a factor especially important in heavy-precipitation storms that contain the largest water drops. And finally, in the strongest thunderstorms, called supercell storms, additional dynamic forces may also be at work—high-pressure regions in

FIG. 9-2. *A gust front begins to spread outward from its parent supercell thunderstorm. The dark cloud arcing beneath the storm is the outrushing shelf cloud.*

the middle of the storm that help to push the air downward—though these seem to make only a minor contribution to the outflow winds. Whatever the forcing, the net result of all of the processes is a surge of heavy, cool air that contacts the surface and spreads out across the landscape, often marked by a dramatic cloud formation known as a shelf cloud (Figures 9-2 and 9-3).

Downbursts come in two flavors: dry and wet. On the western plains, dry downbursts arise from low-precipitation thundershowers where the only sign of the descending wind might be a tail of evaporating raindrops (virga) hanging from an otherwise innocent-looking cumulonimbus cloud. Dry microbursts tend to be relatively short-lived and their winds often arrive without much sign other than an approaching swirl of dust. Those windstorms less than 1½ miles (2½ km) in size are known as "microbursts"; larger windstorms may be called "macrobursts," though this term is not in common usage. Small or large, both types are capable of causing significant damage.

Wet microbursts (Figure 9-4) are the most common form of convective windstorm east of the High Plains, where the climate is more humid. Thunderstorms that form or move east of the Missouri River typically carry a large volume of water that evaporates readily, especially when dry air is entrained or mixed into the cloud from the

FIG. 9-3. *A dramatic and somewhat ominous shelf cloud marks the leading edge of a thunderstorm's cold outflow. The shelf cloud is moving rapidly toward the left, bringing promise of a sudden onset of damaging winds.*

FIG. 9-4. *Heavy precipitation beneath a thunderstorm spreads outward to the left along the ground—a sign of strong, outflowing winds. This formation is known as a "rain foot" to storm chasers.*

FIG. 9-5. *A line of multicell storms. The oldest storm is on the left; storms are progressively younger to the right. This line dropped golf-ball-sized hail and brought damaging winds as it passed.*

surrounding environment. The combination of water loading and evaporative cooling can give wet microbursts wind velocities in excess of 85 mph (135 km/h) and sometimes over 100 mph (160 km/h); they are often heralded by dramatic outflow shelf clouds (Figure 9-3). Fortunately, high-precipitation storms are easily detected by radar, allowing warnings to be issued in advance.

Multicell storms (Figure 9-5) are formed from a collection of thunderstorms that work cooperatively (Figure 9-6) to produce lines or clusters of regenerating storms. These systems can generate windstorms that continue for hours or even days, traveling across hundreds of miles before finally dying out. Particularly long-lasting storms are known as "derechos" (Spanish for "straight ahead"), defined by the National Weather Service as "straight-line windstorms that include periodic winds in excess of 58 mph (93 km/h) over a total distance of at least 240 miles (400 km)." When the leading edge of a downburst has a linear appearance, it is commonly known as a squall line.

Visually, the approach of a shelf cloud is a sign that winds are coming, though most shelf clouds are not as distinct as that in Figure 9-3. Shelf clouds often run a mile or more in front of the storms that generated them and so give you an early warning of the potential for trouble.

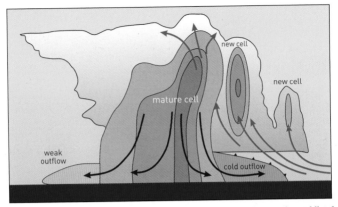

FIG. 9-6. *A crosssection through a multicell line of storms. At center, in the middle of the thunderstorm, heavy precipitation has reached the ground and a pool of rain-cooled air is spreading out around the storm. To the right, the cool air flows along the ground, lifting the warm, moist air in the environment ahead of the storm, creating new convective cells that later grow to maturity and add to the outflowing cold air. Because the initiating mechanism for multicell storm complexes is contained within the storm cluster and not caused by daytime heating, the storms can continue through the night.*

Nighttime derechos are more difficult to anticipate, but a dark, ominous horizon or a distant line of continuous lightning will be a clue to keep a watch for severe winds. If you are fortunate, lightning may illuminate an approaching shelf cloud and give more timely warning.

Because wind is capable of blowing down large trees, lifting roofs from buildings, and destroying sheds and barns, damage is often misidentified as being caused by a tornado, particularly when events occur at night when no one is watching. On radar, windstorms tend to form rapidly moving, curved or bow-shaped lines ("bow echoes") of high-intensity thunderstorms (Figure 9-7). Within and ahead of these lines, individual downdrafts with dimensions of 4 to 6 miles (8 to 10 km) and a lifetime of several minutes often merge together to form a semi-continuous line of destructive winds with tornadic force.

Derechos and similar severe convective winds occur most frequently in areas east of the Rocky Mountain foothills (Figure 9-8) in both the United States and Canada in the summer months. On the evening of May 30, 1998, a derecho developed along the Minnesota-Iowa border and sped across Wisconsin, Michigan, and southern Ontario before fading away near noon the next day in western New

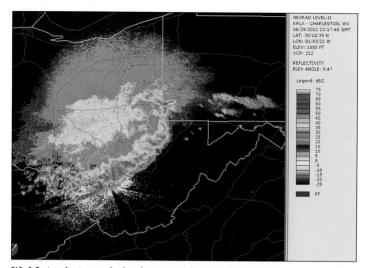

FIG. 9-7. *A radar image of a derecho in Pennsylvania and West Virginia acquired on June 29, 2012, at 7:18 P.M. EDT. The leading edge of the derecho winds is located along the green and blue rim of echoes ahead of the intense red-colored thunderstorms that make up the squall line.*

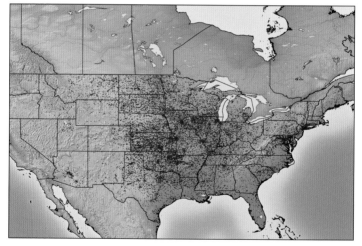

FIG. 9-8. *A map of damaging wind reports (blue dots) collected by the Storm Prediction Center for the warm season, April–October, 2010–2019. Each marker indicates a report of winds of 60 knots and over (69 mph; 111 km/h), almost all of which were thunderstorm outflow winds.*

York. The storm caused six deaths and $300 million in damage during a 9-hour, 970-mile (1,560-km) rampage.

Hail

Hail is born several miles high in the updrafts of strong thunderstorms. Though temperatures are well below freezing at this altitude, the water droplets carried aloft remain in a supercooled, liquid state until they encounter an ice nucleus on which to freeze. Once formed, the novice hailstone may remain suspended in the updraft of the thunderstorm, growing rapidly by scavenging passing water droplets. When too large and heavy to be supported by the updraft, the hailstone will fall, passing through several different temperature and liquid water environments as it grows from pea to golf ball and even to baseball size. Eventually the stone will fall to the ground, causing all-too-familiar damage to roofs, crops, and automobiles.

In North America, large hail (larger than 1.25 inches; 30 mm) is most frequent over the Great Plains and along the foothills from central Texas to the Canada border (Figure 9-9) and beyond; it is rare west of the Rockies and less common east of the Mississippi. Globally, the greatest frequency of hail is found in mountainous northern India and Bangladesh, where moisture-laden monsoon winds encounter abrupt mountain slopes. In Canada and the continental United States hail is

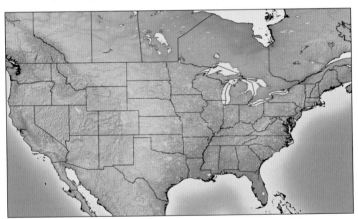

FIG. 9-9. *Distribution of reports of 1.25-inch (30 mm) hail or larger across the United States from 2010 to 2019 (yellow dots). Note the concentration of reports over the central Great Plains and the sharp onset of hail reports along the Front Range of the Rockies. The pattern of hail reports in Canada is very similar, though of lower count.*

FIG. 9-10. *Alternating layers of opaque and cloudy ice in these hailstones speak of their up-and-down travels during their formation and development within the parent thunderstorm.*

most common in the early summer months, when a combination of warm surface temperatures and cold air at relatively low levels creates the best conditions for ice growth.

Hailstones, especially the larger ones, often show alternating layers of clear and cloudy ice that reflect the conditions of their growth (Figure 9-10). Opaque white layers are formed where the impacting water droplets freeze most quickly, either because the droplets are small, or because the stone is high in the storm where temperatures are coldest. The quick freeze traps bubbles of air within the ice, making it opaque. Clear layers of ice in a hailstone are formed in an environment with warmer temperatures or a supply of larger water droplets where freezing is prolonged, and air bubbles have time to escape the droplet before it hardens. Latent heat released during the freezing process, especially from the larger water drops, contributes to this delay. The individual layers also reflect periodic variations in the supply of moisture and droplets in the updraft. The largest hailstones are frequently an aggregate of smaller stones, giving them an irregular spiky shape when they reach the ground (Figure 9-11).

Pea- and dime-sized hail tends to fall in the core of a storm, while larger hailstones are apt to be flung to the edges. A large swath of hail may be up to 10 miles (16 km) across and more than 100 miles (160 km) long. Falls of pea- and nickel-sized hail can cover the ground to a depth of several inches, bringing winterlike scenery to a summer

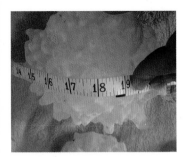

FIG. 9-11. *The largest hailstone found in the United States, collected on July 23, 2010, near Vivian, South Dakota, measured 18.75 inches (47 cm) in circumference and weighed 2 pounds.*

day. And while large hail may be most damaging to automobiles and roofs, small hail that is driven by the wind can wreak havoc with vulnerable crops. In 2020, the National Oceanic and Atmospheric Administration (NOAA) gathered more than 4,500 reports of hail one inch (2.5 cm) or greater in diameter that caused over $3.5 billion in damage.

Tornadoes

No place on Earth has more tornadoes than the United States. The combination of geographical and climatological factors makes the American and Canadian Great Plains a breeding ground for the intense, rotating thunderstorms that spawn "twisters" every spring and summer (Figure 9-12). On average, the United States produces nearly 1,300 tornadoes each year; Canada, with the world's second-largest tornado frequency, produces about 100.

Tornadoes come from thunderstorms, but very few thunderstorms

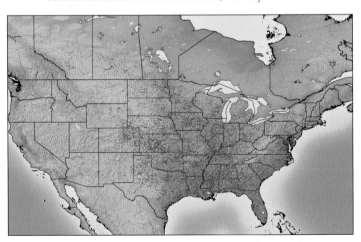

FIG. 9-12. *Distribution of tornadoes across the contiguous United States and western Canada from 2000 to 2019 (red dots). U.S. data are for F1/EF1 or stronger tornadoes; Canadian data are for all tornadoes. There is a total of 26,000 tornadoes in this map, but even so, many tornadoes are unreported in low-population-density areas.*

form tornadoes. What, then, is the critical factor that turns an otherwise benign thunderstorm into a tornado producer? Somehow, concentrated rotation must be added into the mix of factors that go into the construction of large convective clouds.

Localized regions in the atmosphere that contain rotation in the wind are measured by a quantity known as vorticity. Vorticity is common—so common that an atmosphere without vorticity of some sort would be impossible. To build a tornado, however, requires just the right amount and type of vorticity in just the right place at just the right time.

There are three flavors of tornado, each one formed from a different source of vorticity. The weakest type is the gust tornado, or gustnado (a name generally disparaged for being rather ugly), that forms along outflow boundaries generated by a thunderstorm. The turbulence at the edges of such gust fronts frequently forms small transitory vortices that lift dust and light debris as they swirl across the ground (Figure 9-13). Gust tornadoes cause only minor damage, if any, as their lifetime is very short—a few seconds up to a minute or two. Generally, they are not connected to the parent thunderstorm, and storm researchers tend to regard them as a non-tornadic phenomenon. They're just interesting.

FIG. 9-13. *A gust tornado, formed in the outflow from a thunderstorm located beyond the left side of this image, angles across a dusty field. This rotation had a lifetime of two minutes.*

FIG. 9-14. *Landspouts are not predictable, so it is the lucky storm chaser who finds one waiting. This slender tornado touched down near Goodland, Kansas, on June 8, 2019.*

Landspout Tornadoes

The second flavor of tornado is colloquially known as a landspout, a term that links it with waterspouts, which form in a similar way. Landspouts tend to be tall, stately tornadic columns that move slowly across the ground (Figure 9-14), though the stronger ones can look a little ugly from the debris they assemble. Because they form most commonly in dry airmasses, they tend to be semitransparent, displaying a hollow core surrounded by a dusky outer shell. Landspouts cause weak to moderate damage (EF0 or EF1 in Table 9-1), and they typically last less than 15 minutes. Their visible column is often discontinuous and appears only as a spinning whorl of dust on the ground below a funnel-cloud-like extension from the convective cloud above. While we tend to associate tornadoes with strong thunderstorms, landspouts can form beneath much weaker convective clouds, including towering cumulus.

Landspouts develop where low-level winds converge, such as along a lake-breeze front, a cold front, or even the outflows from other convective cells. As the winds in these systems meet, small, upright, rotating columns or vortices are created, spinning unseen until captured by the updraft in a passing convective cloud. The updraft concentrates and stretches the vortex, which becomes visible as it picks up dirt and dust. A good analogy of this process is the rotation induced in a pencil,

FIG. 9-15. *The formation of tornadoes depends on the pattern of winds in the atmosphere. For landspout tornadoes, horizontal wind shear—a difference in wind at the same level in the atmosphere—creates an up-and-down rotation in the air that can be drawn up into a thunderstorm. This type of rotation is mimicked by the sliding hands in the left image. For supercell tornadoes, vertical wind shear—the change in wind between levels—creates a horizontal rotation, mimicked by the right-hand photo. This rotation must be turned upright before it can create a rotating thunderstorm, a process that is accomplished by the updraft into a storm.*

held vertically, that you rub between your palms (Figure 9-15, left image). The palm-to-palm differential motion generates a shear that causes the pencil to turn—a demonstration that has an exact counterpart in atmospheric winds.

Because the rotation in a landspout comes from invisible vortices in the air, tornado chasers usually encounter them serendipitously, as the local wind circulations that cause their formation are not yet predictable. Most weather radars are unable to detect the parent vortices unless operated in a particularly sensitive fashion known as clear-air mode.

Supercell Tornadoes

Supercell thunderstorms create the strongest and most damaging tornadoes. In contrast to the ready-made vortices presented to the landspout, supercell tornadoes must manufacture their own rotation from the vertical winds present in the atmosphere. The early stages of the tornado-creation process are reasonably well understood, but the final chapter—the growth of the tornado itself—is still a work in progress.

A supercell storm is a thunderstorm that has a rotating updraft. As a consequence of that rotation, a supercell has a distinct structure, appearing as a vertical convective tower with heavy rain falling to its front (usually northeast) side, a rain-free base to the rear, and an

FIG. 9-16. *A supercell storm approaching maturity.*

updraft core in the middle of the rain-free area (Figure 9-16). It may be accompanied by a prominent cirrus and mid-level anvil stretching far downstream to the front and a short distance upstream, to the rear. A small percentage of supercells may spawn a tornado (Figure 9-17). The most important characteristic to the operational forecaster is that the thunderstorm's rotation, known as a "mesocyclone," is detectable with Doppler radar and so can be used to issue an early warning, even though a mesocyclone is weak evidence that a tornado is present. Instead, the mesocyclone associated with the supercell thunderstorm provides an environment that is rich in rotation beneath which the additional factors necessary to form a tornado can be assembled.

The rotation needed for the formation of a mesocyclone comes from the horizontal winds flowing beneath the base of the thunderstorm. These below-cloud winds change direction and speed as they go upward, a characteristic that is often visible in the movement of clouds at various layers. This changeable nature of the winds as we ascend in the atmosphere is called vertical wind shear. Shear creates horizontal rotation or vorticity in the air beneath the thunderstorm, similar to the rotation created in the right-side image of Figure 9-15, where the hands represent winds at two different levels and the "shear" is the difference in motion between them. The rotation is then lifted from a horizontal to a vertical position by the supercell's updraft (Figures 9-18 and 9-19), making the whole storm spin slowly around an upright axis.

Supercells are most frequently found in environments that have

FIG. 9-17. *A supercell tornado. Note the heavy precipitation to the distant right and the absence of rain in the vicinity of the tornado.*

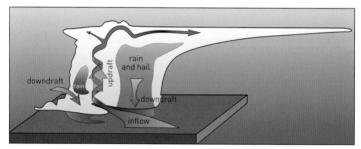

FIG. 9-18. *Supercell thunderstorms are simply those with a rotating updraft, but the rotation gives them a unique structure and the ability to capture wind shear and produce tornadoes. In this schematic, the storm is shown at its mature stage, with a warm, humid inflow, rising and twisting updraft, and front downdraft. The rotating updraft is the site of the mesocyclone, and if a tornado were to form, it would likely lie beneath the updraft, between the rain areas. The most distinguishing visual characteristic is the absence of rainfall in the updraft region, a feature that allows supercell storms to have a very long lifetime.*

high values of instability and that are rich in rotation-inducing wind shear—a parameter known as "helicity." For most supercell storms, the highest values of helicity would occur with modest southerly winds at the surface that turn clockwise to stronger southwest winds a mile (2 km) or so aloft, and then continue as strong westerlies at and above

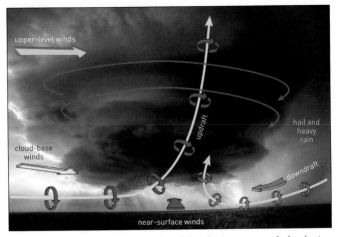

FIG. 9-19. *Mesocyclone rotation in a supercell thunderstorm is created when horizontal vorticity is tilted upright and ingested into the thunderstorm updraft, as shown by the yellow arrow in this diagram. That vorticity is itself created by a particular pattern of surface, low-, and upper-level winds, similar to that depicted by the large wind arrows. Once the rotating mesocyclone is created, horizontal vorticity formed in the outflow downdraft is then ingested into the storm and turned upright, where it may turn into a tornado.*

the two-mile (3-km) level. The presence of a jet stream high above the rising thunderstorm cell will also add substantially to the severe weather potential.

The mesocyclone is a critical feature of a supercell because it organizes the inflows and outflows of the storm. One of the most significant aspects of this organization is that rain doesn't fall into the updraft but instead falls to the front of the storm (that is, in the direction of motion) and, later in the life cycle, to the rear flank. Just behind the front-side precipitation is a rain-free area in which warm and humid inflow winds feed into the updraft, giving the supercell a much longer lifetime than ordinary thunderstorms. Rain-cooled air from the front flank of the storm is caught up in this inflow and pulled into the updraft, where it quickly reaches saturation and adds to the latent heat available for storm development. In effect, the supercell storm recycles part of its own rainfall. In the rear of the supercell, smaller convective clouds merge with the main updraft to provide another ready-made supply of moisture and heat.

While the mesocyclone causes the supercell to organize into a twister-friendly environment, it isn't enough by itself to make a tornado. To do that requires another source of rotation that can be concentrated and drawn up into the thunderstorm.

Current research suggests that one source of rotation may be the outflow from the heavy rain area in the front flank of the storm that brings this second ground-level rotation into the storm. The cold outflow runs beneath the flanks of the warm inflow, creating a vertical zone of high temperature contrast and wind shear that generates a second source of horizontal vorticity (Figure 9-19). This rotation-rich cold air is then lifted into the already-rotating storm updraft, even though it is colder and heavier than the surrounding air and resists the upward suction. This new vorticity-laden air is stretched out in the updraft, concentrating the rotation by as much as 100 times. The whole process is very sensitive to initial conditions: Is the downdraft too cold? Is the updraft in the storm enough to overcome the lack of buoyancy? Does the outflow reach or overrun the most intense updraft location and cut off the tornadic potential? There is some evidence that ground-level rotation is relatively common beneath supercells but present at a strength that fails to form a visible and damaging funnel. Consequently, less than 10 percent of supercells with mesocyclones go on to generate visible tornadoes.

The creation of the supercell thunderstorm is an intimate balance between rotation and instability. Weak vorticity (or helicity) coupled with strong instability is often just as effective a tornado producer as the combination of very favorable vorticity with weak instability, though the character of the tornado—particularly its strength and duration—will depend on other details that affect the combination. When instability and helicity are strong, the result can be the legendary EF5 tornado (Table 9-1) that destroys everything in its path (Figure 9-20).

Waterspouts

Waterspouts form by the same mechanism as landspouts: upright circulations created by wind shear are ingested into growing showers and thundershowers, stretched in the vertical, and then spun up into a visible or semitransparent funnel that meanders slowly across the water. While most waterspouts are relatively tame, with wind speeds in the 60 mph (100 km/h) range, the strongest measured have winds that reach 190 mph (300 km/h). In September 1974, Joseph Golden, the father of waterspout research, flew through 16 Florida

FIG. 9-20. *A supercell tornado near Ralph, South Dakota.*

FIG. 9-21. *A waterspout over the Celebes Sea north of Borneo.*

waterspouts in a specially modified airplane to study their internal structure. Because the friction of moving air over a water surface is less than that over land, waterspouts have an easier time developing than their land-based counterparts, and it is not uncommon to see several waterspouts at one time. Because of that same frictional drag, most waterspouts dissipate shortly after reaching land.

Waterspouts are typically creatures of tropical waters (Figure 9-21), though they can also be found throughout temperate regions, both inland and over the oceans, in the heat of summer and fall. At lower latitudes, waterspouts can be found year-round over all of the world's oceans, though the Mediterranean, Gulf of Mexico, and the tropical oceans of Southeast Asia seem to be especially favored. The waters surrounding Key West, Florida, probably have the highest frequency of waterspouts in the world, with up to 500 reported in a single year. Over the Great Lakes and Lake Winnipeg, they are spotted most often from August to October when cool airmasses move southward to overrun lakes that are at their warmest at that time of year.

Chasing Storms

Since the advent of accurate computer models, and with the availability of forecasts from NOAA's Storm Prediction Center, widespread radar coverage, and numerous online resources, tornado chasing has become a popular summer pastime, particularly across the Great Plains. It is not a pastime to be taken lightly, as supercell storms come in so many flavors and combinations that every storm must be evaluated according to the conditions of the day. On the High Plains, storms are usually isolated and precipitation is light, so that storm structures—forward flank precipitation, wall cloud, shelf clouds, and the like—are readily identified and safe viewing sites are easier to find. In more easterly sections of the Plains states and across the rest of the eastern United States, higher humidities foster more concentrated storm clusters such as multicell storms or families of tornado-producing supercells in which a safe location may be difficult to find.

If you want to take up storm chasing, this book gives you only a taste of what's in store. Make use of the resources online to study up on techniques and forecasting, and join with someone who knows the ropes to conduct your expeditions. You won't be ready to solo until you've done a number of storm intercepts and are comfortable with radar interpretation, model characteristics, and storm structure.

Measuring Tornado Damage

In 1971, Dr. Theodore Fujita at the University of Chicago developed a scheme for characterizing the intensity of a tornado based on the damage caused during its passage. Fujita gave tornadoes a numerical rating from F0 to F5: F0 and F1 were "weak"; F2 and F3 were "strong"; F4 and F5 were "violent." The scale was not entirely satisfactory, as it was based on the damage done to buildings, so tornadoes that did not strike a building could not be rated. Print and broadcast media tend to focus on the typical wind speeds associated with each category in the Fujita scale, so the public sees it more as a measure of the wind velocity in a tornado rather than an indication of the damage caused.

The shortcomings of the Fujita scale and its unintended use as a wind-speed indicator led to the development of a new scale in 2007 that greatly expands the circumstances in which tornado strength can be evaluated. The new Enhanced Fujita Scale (EF Scale) retains the six levels, from EF0 to EF5, but now incorporates descriptions of impacts on more types of structures, including damage caused to trees and telephone poles. The EF scale expands the degree of damage and accounts for variability in construction quality.

The strongest and largest tornadoes often have a hollow core marked by several—perhaps six or eight—circulating vortices, much like horses on a circus carousel; these are known individually as suction vortices. Suction vortices have a short lifetime—of the order of a quarter-rotation or thereabouts—but are continually forming and dissipating. The wind velocity within a suction vortex can add as much as 100 mph (160 km/h) to the rotation of the parent tornado, causing narrow arcs of extreme destruction, in the EF4 and EF5 range, within the larger damage path.

The Climatology of Tornadoes

There is no better place in the world to go looking for tornadoes than the central plains of the United States. Reports collected by the Storm Prediction Center in Norman, Oklahoma, document an average of 1,308 events per year (Table 9-2) from 2000 to 2019. Canada holds down a very distant second place in tornado statistics, with approximately 100 per year. Though tornadoes are found in temperate zones all around the globe, there are no places that can challenge the huge number of twisters found in North America.

Tornadoes are distributed widely across the United States east of the Mountain states with no particular center of activity. Over the years, the high frequency of tornadoes on the Central Plains has given the region the moniker of "Tornado Alley," but a quick look at Figure 9-12 will show that the so-called alley has wide and diffuse borders.

EF VALUE	WIND SPEED		PERCENT FREQUENCY (USA)	DAMAGE DESCRIPTION
	mph	km/h		
EF0	65–85	105–137	53.5	minor: removes roof tiles; damage to gutters; branches broken; shallow trees pushed over
EF1	86–110	138–178	31.6	moderate: roof stripped; mobile homes overturned or badly damaged; windows and glass broken
EF2	111–135	179–218	10.7	considerable: roofs torn off well-constructed homes; foundations shifted; mobile homes destroyed; large trees snapped; cars lifted
EF3	136–165	219–266	3.4	severe: entire stories destroyed; severe damage to large buildings; trains overturned; trees debarked; heavy cars lifted; weak structures blown away
EF4	166–200	267–322	0.7	devastating: well-constructed and frame houses completely leveled; cars lifted and thrown; small missiles generated
EF5	>200	>322	<0.1	extreme: frame houses leveled and swept away; car-sized missiles thrown 100 m or more; steel-reinforced concrete buildings damaged; high-rise buildings substantially damaged

TABLE 9-1. *The Enhanced Fujita damage scale for tornadoes.*

Texas has the greatest number of tornadoes each year (155) with Kansas (96) and Florida (66) far behind in second and third place. In Canada, tornadoes are most frequent in regions near the United States border, but the low population density across much of the country means that many tornadoes go unseen and unreported. In Manitoba, tornadoes have been spotted as far north as Churchill, on the shores of Hudson Bay, including one over the ice pack in spring!

The annual tornado season begins in mid-March in the southeast states, moving westward through Arkansas in late April and northward into Oklahoma and Kansas through May. South Dakota sees the peak activity in the third week of June, and southern Manitoba and

Saskatchewan in the first days of July. By mid-July, North American activity is on the wane, declining sharply through July and August. Tornadoes are uncommon in the depths of the winter months, and most often found in the Gulf States and Texas when they do occur.

A compilation of observations from 25 countries in Europe shows an average of 169 tornadoes and 160 waterspouts per year. Current thinking is that only about half of the actual number of rotating storms is reported, so when the frequency is adjusted for the undercount, the sum reaches about 700 tornadoes and waterspouts annually. The largest counts come from England and the Netherlands, where high population densities promote the detection and reporting of severe storms. Though European numbers challenge those of the United States, the brawny supercell tornado is relatively rare. Only 13 EF4 and EF5 tornadoes were reported between 1950 and 2015 in Europe. Elsewhere, Australia estimates about 25 tornadoes per year, Japan 20, and New Zealand 25, though the numbers are not well known, and there are probably many undercounts.

Why Does the United States Have So Many Tornadoes?

A supercell thunderstorm that forms a tornado requires four elements, three to form a thunderstorm and the fourth to get it rotating. These elements are moisture, instability, a triggering mechanism, and rotation-generating wind shear. All of these are found in abundance on the Great Plains and, to a lesser extent, across the eastern half of the United States, thanks to a very favorable geography.

Moisture on the Great Plains originates over the Gulf of Mexico and is pushed northward across the flat topography of the prairies in the summer months by low-level jet-stream winds (Figure 9-22). These fast-moving air streams develop within the lowest half-mile of the atmosphere and can carry Gulf moisture northward at speeds ranging from 30 to as much as 75 mph (50 to 120 km/h). Found mostly in the warm season between April and October, they are important predictors of severe weather, so most forecasters and storm chasers pay close attention to their location and strength.

Of particular importance is the nocturnal low-level jet (LLJ in Figure 9-22), which can be found on about half of summer nights on the plains. These jets form from a complex interaction involving temperature and pressure differences between the Rocky Mountains and the plains, the cooling of surface layers in the evening, the influence of upper-level jets, and the physical turning of the wind stream by the mountain barrier. While the low-level jet is most common on the southern plains, it may reach as far as the Canada border at the height of the summer severe-weather season. Low-level jets are also found on the east side of the Appalachians, where they feed moisture from the warm subtropical waters offshore into storms along the Eastern Seaboard.

Instability is promoted by high-altitude westerly and southwesterly winds that bring in a cool flow from the Pacific that is lifted over the Rocky Mountains and then dried as it descends the Front Range onto the Great Plains. The combination of cool and dry Pacific air above Gulf of Mexico moisture is a recipe for instability, allowing thunderstorms, once they get started, to explode upward with enormous energy. Because high summer humidity is entrenched across the lower Plains states in summer, the presence of a southwesterly flow aloft is a virtual guarantee of severe weather somewhere on the prairie from the Gulf to the Canadian border and beyond.

To complete our storm-forming triad, we usually require some sort of trigger to push the moist low-level air upward and start convective development. It can happen spontaneously if heat and moisture accumulate to sufficient levels, but usually there is some sort of converging wind flow that will get one location started ahead of the others. Convergence occurs whenever wind streams flow into each other or where a faster wind catches up with a slower-moving flow. At the junction

YEAR	NUMBER OF TORNADOES
2000	1,072
2001	1,219
2002	938
2003	1,394
2004	1,820
2005	1,262
2006	1,117
2007	1,102
2008	1,685
2009	1,305
2010	1,543
2011	1,894
2012	1,119
2013	943
2014	1,057
2015	1,259
2016	1,059
2017	1,522
2018	1,169
2019	1,676
Average	1,308

TABLE 9-2. *Tornado frequency, 2000–2019, in the United States.*

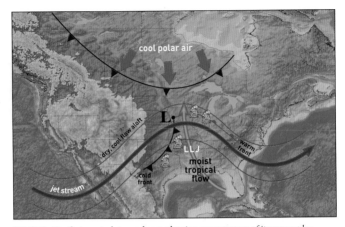

FIG. 9-22. *North America's tornado weather is a consequence of its geography. Moist tropical air can flow freely northward from the Gulf of Mexico, often carried by a low-level jet stream (LLJ). Aloft, westerly and southwesterly flows of dry Pacific air contribute to the instability in the upper atmosphere and the containment of low-level moisture until triggered by a lifting mechanism, often a frontal system crossing the Plains. Finally, the combination of southerly winds below and southwesterlies aloft generates the wind shear needed for storm rotation.*

of these colliding flows, the air is lifted upward (it can go nowhere else) to kick-start the beginning of convection. Commonly, there is a low-level inversion (known as a lid or cap) in the lowest mile or two of the atmosphere that must be overcome before the warm surface air can begin rising freely. The role of the various convergences is to shove the air through the cap and allow the storm buildups to begin. Triggers may be structures such as frontal systems, outflows from earlier storms, sea-breeze fronts, terrain-induced flows, or low-pressure troughs—common features that are usually readily available. Cold fronts are particularly good storm generators, and the flat prairie landscape is wide open to cool Canadian airmasses pushing toward the south.

To move from the creation of an ordinary thunderstorm to the formation of a rotating supercell storm, we have to add rotation to the mix, as we've noted above. Rotation arises from a particular pattern of lower-atmosphere wind shear, both in direction and strength. This is most often a pattern consisting of a southerly wind at the ground that turns to become a strong southwesterly or westerly jet-stream wind aloft—the pattern shown in Figure 9-22. Such a pattern, when caught in the updraft of a strongly ascending convective plume, can turn a thunderstorm into a supercell and bring a greatly increased risk of severe weather.

In the end, the thunderstorm personality of the North American spring and summer is a result of geography: warm ocean waters to the south and southeast, an open prairie terrain that allows moisture to flow northward, a bordering mountain barrier that dries cool Pacific air as it flows in aloft, and an open pathway for cold fronts to flow southward from Canada. Few other locations on the Earth put the topography, moisture source, frontal triggers, and wind shear together quite so well as on the United States prairies, and so the Great Plains are the home where the supercells roam.

Forecasting Severe Thunderstorms

Severe thunderstorm forecasting is not for the faint of heart.

Summer storms grow late in the day and are usually small in areal extent, leaving a forecaster with the task of predicting an event that has few early visible clues. When they start, they begin suddenly and blow up quickly. Observing stations, especially those that monitor conditions aloft, are too widely separated to resolve all of the elements of the atmospheric flow. Computer models can fill in many of the details, but models smooth out patterns in the atmosphere, losing the fine details that may prove critical to the forecast. On many severe-weather days, a successful forecast may turn on the prediction of a single convective cloud. Yet, in spite of this complexity and ambiguity, convective forecasting has improved markedly over the past 40 years.

The forecaster on the severe-weather desk assembles all of the important meteorological parameters that we have discussed in previous sections into a comprehensive picture of the convective potential of the atmosphere. This picture includes the position of jet streams and their cores, the presence of upper-level disturbances, measures of instability and helicity, patterns of moisture and temperature, warm and cold areas aloft, upper troughs and ridges—all assembled into a grand conceptual model to elicit where convective potential is greatest. With so many tools to work with, the forecaster must focus on areas with the most favorable moisture, instability, triggers, and wind pattern aloft.

To make a forecast, meteorologists can turn to a technique developed by two U.S. Air Force forecasters, Captain Robert C. Miller and

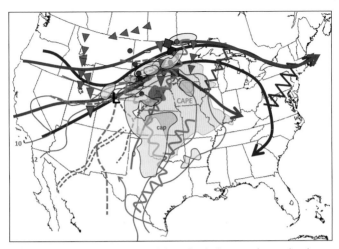

FIG. 9-23. *A "Miller diagram" used to help predict the location of severe thunderstorms. This chart combines and summarizes the factors that are important in storm forecasting. On this day, tornadoes formed in North and South Dakota.*

Major Ernest J. Fawbush, after they successfully predicted a tornado in 1948. In their technique, the various elements important to storm development are combined on a composite map in a form of graphical note-taking. This allows the evaluation of the many atmospheric patterns and parameters in one place so that their relationship to each other can be assessed. These so-called Miller diagrams can be a critical tool in appraising the location and type of severe convective weather. One forecaster's version of a Miller diagram is shown in Figure 9-23. Arrows denote winds at various levels; green "snakes" show where low-level moisture is available; various colored outlines show the presence of instability (an index called CAPE for Convective Available Potential Energy) and of a low-level inversion or cap that might suppress storm development. Also present are several triggers that might initiate the first storms of the day.

This type of diagram or its computer equivalent is used to make an initial forecast of severe weather potential and perhaps issue the early storm watches. As the day advances, data are reassessed at hourly intervals. Radar and satellite are used to watch for the first sign of development, and reports from storm chasers and weather watchers are evaluated for clues. When the signs coalesce, watches will become warnings, issued and then updated as new information continues to arrive. Storm forecasting is a high-stress job, as every forecast comes with life-threatening consequences.

At the end of the day, the assessment begins: Where did the forecast work out, and where did it fail? What clues were missed and what observations might have helped? Did the warnings go out in time? Did everyone who needed them get them? Summer storm forecasting is at one moment the most stressful of a forecaster's duties and at another, the most rewarding when lives are saved.

Winter Storms and Other Plagues

Blizzards and Cyclones

Work only a short time as a forecaster, and it will become apparent that much of North America is a land of two seasons: a summer of convective weather and a winter of synoptic-scale storms. Spring and fall are transitional months. We say that with tongue in cheek, but the change from one storm regime to another is quite distinctive in climates above about 35° latitude.

The strong temperature gradients of the cold season provide the energy needed to create burly low-pressure systems that bring heavy snows, freezing rain, bitter winds, extreme wind-chills, and sharp temperature changes (Chapter 8). Over North America, there are two major classes of winter storm, based on the shape of the upper-level flow: fast-moving zonal storms and slower, more powerful meridional lows.

When we look at a map showing the upper-level flow, we see that the height contours form a pattern of rising and falling "waves" of various wavelengths and amplitudes. Sometimes the flow is zonal and stays more or less along the same latitude (Figure 9-24, top). At other times it is "meridional," forming a large-amplitude, undulating pattern that may crest in a ridge over northern Canada before sinking into an angled trough over the Midwest (Figure 9-24, bottom). These upper flows control the movement of surface highs and lows, so that the path of a winter cyclone under a zonal flow pretty much follows a slightly concave west-to-east track. A surface low moving within a meridional flow has a pronounced south-to-north track. With both types of low, but particularly for the meridional-flow pattern, there is considerable variation in the amplitude and wavelength of the upper flow and the speed of the winds, leading to storms with many different strengths and tracks.

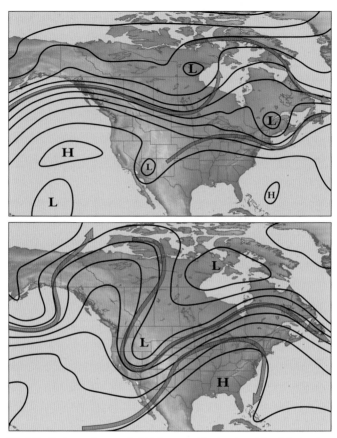

FIG. 9-24. *Contours of pressure height show zonal (top) and meridional (bottom) flow patterns at 250 mb. Associated jet streams are shown in red. Zonal flows have a flat west-to-east alignment with only small "waves" in the flow. Meridional flows have a high-amplitude wave with ridge-to-trough distances that span most of a continent. These upper flow patterns and their jet streams control the movement of storms at the surface.*

The storms that form beneath these different flows have names that will be familiar to every casual weather watcher. Those that speed along under a zonal flow are nicknamed Alberta Clippers or Alberta lows. Slower-moving meridional-flow storms have names such as Colorado low, Hatteras low (called nor'easters in New England for their stormy northeast winds), Texas hooker, and Panhandle low (Figure

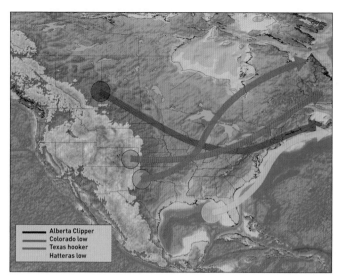

FIG. 9-25. *Winter storms have a nomenclature of their own, with descriptive names based on their origin or their tracks. Texas hookers are also known as Panhandle lows; Hatteras lows are nor'easters in New England.*

9-25). In general, meridional-flow storms are more dangerous than zonal speedsters, as they have more energy and more variety to their dangerous weather, and they last longer because of their lower speed.

Alberta Clippers

The Alberta Clipper typically develops east of Calgary, Alberta, near the Saskatchewan border. Driven by a fast upper-level flow, it adopts a shallow, curving track that takes it into Montana, across North Dakota and Minnesota, and over the Great Lakes, before turning northeastward to head for the Atlantic Ocean. If the upper-level trough has a little more amplitude, the Clipper may dip farther south, passing under the Great Lakes and across Ontario and the upper New England states. Because the Clipper forms in relatively cold air, a strong thermal contrast is missing, and the low tends to undergo only modest development, though it can still bring vicious weather with its bitter winds.

Snow production is light in a Clipper—perhaps an inch or two (2–5 cm)—but winds are not, and short-lived blizzard conditions usually accompany these systems. As it moves past the Great Lakes, snowfall amounts usually increase because the storm has time to ingest moisture drawn up from the south and from the lakes themselves if they are not frozen over. The strong northerly winds behind a Clipper can drive Arctic air far southward, bringing a sharp change to colder weather across the Upper Midwest that may last for several days. Freshly fallen snow or loose snow from previous storms can be caught up by the bitter northerlies to generate long-lasting blizzards in regions well away from the storm track. Wind-chill values in the −40°F (−40°C) range are not uncommon. Once the low has passed the Great Lakes, the same frigid northerlies will bring lake-effect snowfalls, sometimes burying communities such as Buffalo, New York, with wind-blown accumulations of 9 to 12 feet (3 to 4 meters) of snow.

Meridional-Low Storms

Meridional lows—Colorado lows, Hatteras lows, and Panhandle lows—are storms that develop ahead of deep upper-level troughs, giving them a pronounced southwest-to-northeast (and sometimes south-to-north) track. That path and the relatively slow motion of these winter lows allow them to dredge warm and moist polar air from the Gulf of Mexico or the Atlantic on their front side, pushing it northward. In their rear, cold Arctic air surges southward carried by bitter north winds. The thermal contrast between polar air and Arctic air endows meridional storms with plenty of energy and gives them a nasty reputation for wind and heavy snow or rainfall, often punctuated by a band of freezing rain.

On the plains, the most common of the meridional storms is the Colorado low, named for the state of origin. These storms most often move in a gentle northeastward direction across the Great Plains and pass south of Chicago. When upper troughs have a more north-to-south orientation, Colorado lows will move sharply northward, passing through North Dakota into Manitoba before turning to the northeast (Figure 9-25). In a satellite image, they are large comma-shaped cloud systems that can straddle the continent from northern Canada to the Gulf Coast. Colorado lows bring an expansive menu of bad weather—not only heavy snow and freezing rain in the north, but also heavy thunderstorms and tornado outbreaks far to the south in the Gulf States.

The first evidence of an impending Colorado low appears on the Pacific side of the Rockies, typically as an innocent-looking low with modest amounts of precipitation. The low virtually disappears as it struggles across the Continental Divide, only to reappear as a

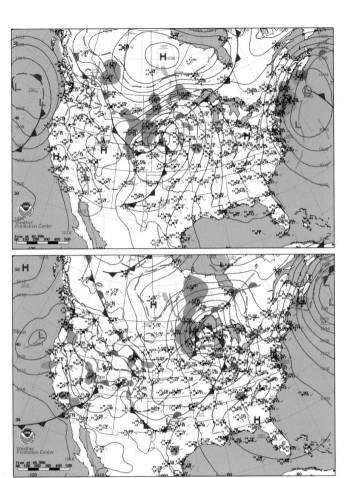

FIG. 9-26. *Surface pressure maps show a Colorado low making its way across the western plains, March 31–April 1, 2014. The northeastward track of the system is typical of meridional lows, though this one has a little more northerly track than usual. Under very deep upper troughs, the lows can move straight north into Manitoba.*

vague area of reduced pressure on the east side of the Rockies, usually in Colorado. After a few days to organize, waiting for the upper trough and jet stream to get into place, the vague low-pressure system is reborn as a Colorado low and heads out toward the Great Lakes (Figure 9-26), growing rapidly in strength and determination. Even though it's still in early development, a steady accumulation of snow over the foothills of Colorado and Wyoming marks the start of the storm's disabling weather.

As the low moves out of Colorado, cold air from Canada or from the heights of the Rocky Mountains rushes into the gap that opens between the mountains and the storm center. This "cold air injection" causes the low to intensify very rapidly, increasing the winds circulating around the system. On the front side of the low, warm, moist air flows northward from the Gulf, forming a sharp temperature contrast with the cold air surging behind. Rain begins across Iowa and southern Minnesota, with snow farther north, up to the Canada border. A warm front stretching eastward from the low divides rain from snow, usually with a band of freezing rain and sleet to highlight the boundary.

As the center of the low passes, temperatures plummet, rain changes to snow, and northerly winds begin to blow, bringing blizzard weather that shuts down travel, sometimes for several days. Huge drifts build up behind fences, trees, and buildings, and whiteout conditions can persist for the better part of a day. Highways close, schools have a holiday, and danger threatens any traveler who is tempted to brave the elements. After a day or two, the Colorado low finally crosses the Great Lakes into northern Ontario and eventually Quebec, where it may get captured by a persistent low over Hudson Bay or go farther eastward to become a part of the Icelandic low near Greenland.

The Hatteras low, a more easterly cousin of the Colorado low, typically undergoes cyclogenesis in the northern Gulf of Mexico and then crosses the Florida peninsula and turns northward to run parallel to the Atlantic coastline (Figure 9-27). Development begins in earnest as the system passes the Carolinas, after which the low deepens steadily until reaching a minimum pressure opposite the Canadian Atlantic provinces. Typically, the Hatteras low will travel a little offshore, but if the track is over land, storm development will be somewhat subdued. On- or offshore, the low will direct Atlantic moisture inland against the slopes of the Appalachians, where waiting cold air will turn precipitation to an icy mix of freezing rain and snow. Hatteras weather typically brings a very large snowfall followed by an equally unwelcome cold snap when the system has passed. A nor'easter is similar to a Hatteras low but forms farther north before it turns up the Eastern Seaboard.

One of the most noteworthy East Coast storms was the 1993 "Storm of the Century." The track of that low took it across northern Florida, after which it hooked northward to cross coastal regions of Georgia and the Carolinas before moving offshore beyond Cape Hatteras. The storm was unique for its size and intensity, with a record-low central pressure (960 mb), hurricane-force winds, and, in Florida, 11 tornadoes that resulted in five deaths. The Great Smoky Mountains in Tennessee were buried in 56 inches (142 cm) of snow; many other communities from North Carolina to New York reported accumulations in excess of 40 inches (100 cm). Power outages affected 10 million people, damage

FIG. 9-27. *An intense Hatteras low or nor'easter moves past the New England coast on March 26, 2014, raking the coast of Massachusetts with hurricane-force winds and snowfall amounts up to 10 inches (25 cm). The storm tracked far enough offshore that its impact was limited mostly to coastal areas.*

amounted to more than $3 billion, and 300 deaths were attributed to the storm and the subsequent blizzard conditions. Record-low temperatures were set in many southeast communities in the wake of the cyclone, halting the onset of spring for a week.

Coastal meridional storms are not unique to North America, but the topography along the eastern side of the continent, a source of cold air in the interior, and the presence of a warm Gulf Stream offshore contribute to a production rate that exceeds most other regions of the globe.

Blizzards

The National Weather Service in the United States defines a blizzard as a sustained wind or frequent gusts greater than or equal to 35 mph (56 km/h) accompanied by falling and/or blowing snow that frequently reduces visibility to less than ¼ mile for three or more hours. The Meteorological Service of Canada has a similar definition. However, blizzards are ephemeral beasts, so that news stories often tag a storm as a blizzard when it doesn't quite make the official list.

Because blizzards are defined according to wind and visibility, they need not be associated with storms or recent snowfalls. Snow left behind by a long-departed weather system and moderate-to-strong winds are often sufficient to reduce ground-level visibilities, so blizzards can and do occur under clear, blue skies. Blizzards require open terrain for the snow to blow, and so are largely confined to the unforested parts of the Great Plains. Southern Saskatchewan and the Front Range of Montana have experienced rare weeklong whiteouts caused by the strong winds around a cold Arctic high after the passage of a low that left only a light snowfall. Such storms are legendary, in part because they build huge, ice-hard drifts that can be used for tobogganing from rooftops or for building impressive snow forts. In February of 1947, a week of successive blizzards buried a kilometer-long train in Saskatchewan under 25 feet (8 meters) of snow.

Fresh snow is usually loose and easy to blow around, but as the winds continue beyond about a day, the snow becomes hard packed and visibility usually begins to improve. Once winds have declined enough that the snow crystals suspended in the air drop below eye level, blizzard warnings are ended and the forecast changed to "blowing snow." In open areas, packed snow is aligned into narrow, hard ridges known as "sastrugi" that vary in size from inches to feet. They resemble linear sand dunes but are instead compacted, rippled, icy snow ridges—the bane of polar travelers.

Freezing Rain

Freezing rain (Figure 9-28) occurs when raindrops in an elevated layer of warm air fall into a layer of cold air hugging the ground and freeze on contact with the surface (Chapter 2). The resulting coating of glaze is one of the most dangerous forms of precipitation. Broken trees, downed power lines, and impossible or hazardous travel are its hallmarks; if heavy enough, the ice will bring normal activities to an abrupt halt for a considerable time. A massive series of ice storms in January 1998 coated Ontario, Quebec, New Brunswick, New York, and central Maine with up to 4 inches (100 mm) of ice during an 80-hour period. Over 1,000 power pylons and 35,000 power poles collapsed, leaving 4 million people, mostly in Canada, without power, some for as long as a month. More than half of Maine's population went without power; many were in the dark for two weeks before electricity was restored. Millions of trees were broken, farm animals died in collapsed barns or unheated buildings, and 30 people died from hypothermia or from carbon monoxide poisoning caused by the use of unventilated generators and heating appliances in confined spaces.

Freezing rain is commonly found in the vicinity of a warm front, where warm air overrides colder air to create the necessary temperature stratification. The low-level freezing layer cannot be too deep or too cold, otherwise the falling raindrops will turn to ice before they reach the ground, and the resulting precipitation will become ice pellets or sleet. In most cases, the air temperatures at the surface will be only a few degrees below freezing, but the ground itself may be much colder because of a recent cold spell. Colorado lows are notorious for the production of freezing rain, but just about any winter-season low will do, if the appropriate temperature structure is in place.

FIG. 9-28. *After a night of freezing rain, branches and leaves are coated with ice.*

When raindrops freeze quickly on a cold surface, air is trapped inside the ice, and it takes on an opaque white color with a crumbly texture, known as "rime." Rime is usually made up of smaller raindrops that are supercooled but remain liquid because of the absence of a condensation nucleus on which to freeze. As soon as they contact a surface, they abruptly turn to ice. Rime icing is not as hazardous as freezing rain, because the ice is fragile and easily breaks off trees and power lines.

Rain that freezes more slowly, either because drops are larger, accumulation is more rapid, or temperatures are closer to the melting point, forms a transparent and much harder and denser ice called "glaze." The release of latent heat as the liquid droplet turns to ice prolongs the freezing process, and the large size of the raindrop slows the dissipation of this heat. Glaze ice is much more damaging than rime because of its heavier weight and its ability to coat surfaces to a considerable depth.

Freezing rain can fall just about anywhere in North America, although it is uncommon or almost unknown in the southwest states and the Front Range of Wyoming and Colorado. The greatest frequency of freezing rain is found over the northeastern states and the adjoining Canadian provinces of Ontario and Quebec. A second maximum is found over British Columbia, Washington, Oregon, and Idaho, where cold air is often left behind in mountain valleys after the passage of a higher-level warm front. In this case, raindrops fall into the residual colder air where they freeze.

Hurricanes, Typhoons, and Cyclones

Hurricanes, typhoons, cyclones—all of these names refer to the same type of subtropical storm. In the Atlantic and in the Pacific east of the date line, the name "hurricane" is used. "Typhoon" is reserved for storms located on the west side of the date line in the northwest Pacific, and "cyclone" is a term used for storms in the southwest Pacific Ocean and the Indian Ocean. Collectively, the name "tropical cyclone" covers all of them; the name "cyclone" by itself can refer to any low-pressure storm or even to a tornado. All of the tropical storms possess a clear circular area or "eye" in their middle at maturity, and this feature alone is usually sufficient for classification. To have official status as a hurricane, however, one-minute sustained surface winds somewhere within the cloud mass must reach at least 74 mph (120 km/h).

In the lexicon of the National Hurricane Center in Miami, a tropical cyclone is a "warm-core non-frontal synoptic-scale cyclone, originating over tropical or subtropical waters, with organized deep convection and a closed surface wind circulation about a well-defined center." They are creatures of the lower latitudes, where temperatures are high, the air humid, the ocean warm, and the atmosphere ready to blossom into convective clouds at the slightest opportunity. Because the Sun is always high in the sky, the seasons in the tropics are muted and generally oscillate between wet and dry rather than hot and cold. All in all, it seems a benign environment in which to spawn the Earth's fiercest storms.

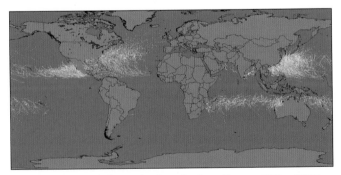

FIG. 9-29. *The tracks of all tropical cyclones that formed between 1950 and 2014. Colors represent the maximum wind speed at stages along each storm track: yellow shades are weaker storms, orange and red represent stronger storms.*

The map of the world's tropical-storm tracks (Figure 9-29) reveals many climatological secrets:

- Tropical storms don't occur in all ocean basins—they are curiously absent in the South Atlantic and southeast Pacific.
- The largest number of storms is found in the northwest Pacific, off the coasts of the Philippines, Taiwan, China, and Japan.
- Northern Hemisphere storms tend to persist into high latitudes, sometimes reaching into the cold waters south of Greenland.
- Storms tend to follow a straight-line path from east to west in the early part of their life cycle and curve northward in the latter stages.
- Storm tracks are shorter at lower latitudes in the Southern Hemisphere.
- There are no storms in a 10-degree-wide band of latitude along the equator.
- Storms weaken quickly after they leave the oceans and move over land.

Though warm ocean temperatures that supply heat and moisture are widely available at lower latitudes, there is a notable shortage of storms along the equator where environmental conditions should be nearly perfect. The explanation for the gap lies with the Coriolis force (Chapter 7), which is absent at low latitudes. Without the Coriolis force, lows fill quickly and are unable to develop into strong circulating systems.

Hurricanes form in the warm waters of the Caribbean Sea, the Gulf of Mexico, and the central Atlantic west of the Cape Verde Islands. Young storms first move toward the west, gradually intensifying as they are pushed into the Caribbean or onto the U.S. East Coast by the easterly trade winds that dominate subtropical latitudes. They continue on that westerly heading until they encounter upper-level winds that turn or "recurve" the storm to the northeast. For Atlantic hurricanes, this curving track often places them on a collision course with the United States Gulf Coast or the Eastern Seaboard. Once on land, the hurricane loses its underlying moisture and decays rapidly, though its flooding rains may go on for several more days as it moves northward across farmlands and cities. Those that recurve early remain out at sea, following the warm waters of the Gulf Stream into Canadian waters and beyond.

Cyclone seasons follow the warming of the ocean basins in which they form. The subtropical Atlantic reaches its peak temperatures in August and early September, spawning a hurricane season that starts at midyear and continues to late November; a few rare hurricanes form in December and January. The largest number of Atlantic hurricanes occurs in September, with a sharp drop-off in October. In the Southern Hemisphere, cyclone season peaks between January and March. In the northwest Pacific, typhoons have no distinct season, though there is a minimum in activity in February and March and a peak in August and September.

Anatomy of a Mature Hurricane

From a satellite (Figure 9-30), a midlife hurricane is unmistakable: a 375-mile (600-km) diameter circular cloud mass with a hole in the middle surrounded by counterclockwise-spiraling bands of thunderstorms. The most distinguishing characteristic of a hurricane is the "eye"—a region in the center of the storm with light winds; benign, fair-weather cumulus clouds; and the lowest pressures. An observer inside the eye would see patchy blue skies overhead. Inside this opening (Figure 9-31), air is descending and drying adiabatically, dissipating the clouds and suppressing the instability.

Cyclone eyes are usually circular or slightly oval in shape, and range

FIG. 9-30. *Hurricane Earl developed over the eastern Atlantic in late August 2010, and curled up the United States East Coast in early September. In this image, from September 2, 2010, Earl is near its maximum strength—a Category 4 hurricane—as it makes the turn northward toward Cape Hatteras. Visible and infrared images from the GOES-East satellite have been combined to make this false-color composite picture.*

in size from 2 to 230 miles (3 to 350 km); rapidly developing storms have the smaller eyes. In contrast to a mid-latitude low, a hurricane has warm air in its center, though the temperature in the eye is only slightly higher than the surrounding environment. The low pressure at the center of a hurricane draws moist oceanic air into the storm, where it is caught in the thunderstorm updrafts and deposited high in the atmosphere as a blanket of cirrus cloud (Figure 9-32). This high cirrus cloud spirals outward from the center of the storm in a clockwise direction, a process that is readily observed in animated images from weather satellites.

In the outer parts of the hurricane, organized rain bands spiral into the low-pressure core, growing more intense as they approach the center of the storm (Figure 9-32). The rain bands converge around the eye to form the eyewall, a zone of very intense convective activity with the strongest winds, largest thunderstorms, and heaviest precipitation. Thunderstorms in the eyewall may grow to reach an altitude of 60,000 feet (18 km) and produce rainfall rates that can exceed 4 inches per hour (100 mm/h). These storms are the main energy source for the cyclone.

Eyewalls and rain bands undergo cycles of intensification and weakening, and surface winds respond with changes in speed that match the level of convective activity. In strong hurricanes with small eyes, a second eyewall can form outside the first. This second band of thunderstorms will contract toward the storm center, choking off the first wall and weakening the storm. Thereafter, the storm may regain its strength as the newer eyewall continues to contract. A cyclone's winds also have a diurnal cycle, slowing down at night and speeding up during the day.

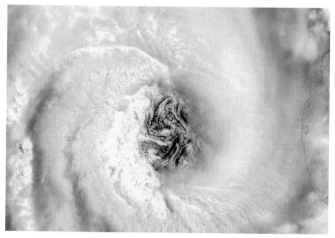

FIG. 9-31. *A detailed view of the eye of Cyclone Haruna while the storm was centered over the Madagascar Strait (February 22, 2013). The chaotic cloud patterns in this image testify to the turbulent wind flow within the eye of the cyclone and the rapid changes in wind direction as the eye passes. Equally impressive is the dramatic eyewall on the right side of the eye. Even though descending air in the center of the storm has eroded the high-level cloud, considerable low-level convection continues near the surface.*

Life Cycle

Most Atlantic cyclones are initiated by convective disturbances that form over sub-Saharan Africa and drift eastward, eventually crossing the coast and emerging into the tropical Atlantic. The disturbances are composed of clusters of thunderstorms within a weak low-pressure region and are known as easterly waves for their wavelike form on a surface-pressure chart. When they encounter water temperatures of 80°F (26°C) or warmer west of the Cape Verde Islands, the easterly waves receive an injection of heat and moisture that is critical to their future development. Some of those waves intensify and adopt a slow, rotating circulation as the thunderstorms within them grow. At this stage, they are classified as "tropical disturbances."

As central pressures continue to fall, thunderstorms begin to organize themselves into the spiral bands that define the structure of a hurricane. The Coriolis force, though weak at low latitudes, dictates the initial shape of the storm by causing winds to adopt a counterclockwise flow around the center of the low (in the Northern Hemisphere). Without a spiraling cyclonic flow, winds would fill the low-pressure core rapidly, and the incipient storm would dissipate.

Intensification of the developing cyclone requires enormous amounts of energy, and so tropical cyclones build up their initial resources over warm ocean waters that lie under low-level inversions that trap and concentrate the moisture in the air. The ingested humidity is cooled to its condensation point in storm updrafts, releasing the energy that was stored as latent heat. Temperatures rise in the core of the storm and pressures fall at the surface as the spiral pattern becomes more obvious; at this stage an eye begins to develop at the center of the storm.

A critical factor in the growth of hurricanes is the absence of strong wind shear—the difference in speed between low- and high-level winds—in the overlying atmosphere. A difference in wind speed between upper and surface levels in the atmosphere of only 22 mph (35 km/h) is usually the limit for hurricane development, as stronger winds remove the heat and moisture at the top of the cyclone, limiting its energy supply and future development.

Tropical storms must have a balancing flow that brings air back to the surface to compensate for the immense mass that is being transported upward by the thunderstorms in the eyewall and spiral bands. Part of this compensating flow occurs in the eye of the storm, where air descends from the upper troposphere to the surface. This descend-

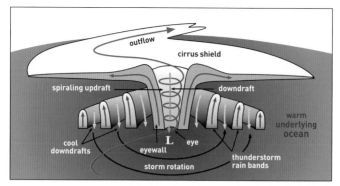

FIG. 9-32. *Hurricanes form around a deep low-pressure center surrounded by spiraling rain bands and an intense thunderstorm eyewall. Air rises in the rain bands and eyewall and sinks in the intervening spaces. The core is formed by descending cool air that dries the air in the center of the storm. Moisture carried aloft forms the outflow.*

ing flow dries adiabatically to form the eye at the hurricane's center.

When surface winds increase to at least 23 mph (36 km/h) and at least one closed pressure contour can be drawn on a weather map, the tropical disturbance becomes a "tropical depression." A further increase in wind speeds, to 40 mph (63 km/h), turns the tropical depression into a "tropical storm," and it is given a name by one of the meteorological agencies (the National Hurricane Center for storms surrounding the United States). At 74 mph (120 km/h), the tropical storm becomes a hurricane, typhoon, or cyclone, depending on its location.

Dissipation

Over warm ocean water, the lifetime of a tropical cyclone is a week or ten days, though Hurricane Tina made it to the ripe old age of 24 days over the North Pacific in 1992. In spite of their intensity, the imposition of even one unfavorable environmental factor can bring them to an end. The most obvious of these is the movement onto land.

Landfall brings an abrupt end to the supply of warm, moist air, and the intensity of the eyewall engine drops rapidly. Hurricanes typically lose half their wind speed at landfall in the first 12 hours, though heavy rains and moderate winds can go on in the decaying storms for several more days. If landfall is made over an island or across a peninsula, the cyclone can intensify again once it returns to suitably warm water; this is a common occurrence on Taiwan and in the Dominican Republic. Low-lying landscapes, such as the Florida peninsula and the Gulf Coast, impose a lesser burden on the storm, and cyclones can retain their identity for a few extra hours after coming ashore along those coasts.

Cold ocean waters will also take the energy out of a cyclone. A drop of 5°F (2.5°C) in the water temperature under the eyewall is enough to dissipate a tropical storm. Hurricanes stir up the surface waters as they pass, dredging up colder waters from below and leaving an unfavorable environment for any trailing storm that might happen along in the days following.

Another cyclone killer is a strengthening upper-level wind pattern that brings an increase in shear to rob the storm of its high-level support. The subtropical jet stream that blows over the Caribbean and the Gulf of Mexico is a leading actor in this role. In the prime hurricane season in September, storm-ending wind shear usually arrives in the form of an upper-level trough that drops down into tropical latitudes from the north.

Northern Hemisphere tropical storms that remain offshore will recurve northward, eventually moving onto colder waters and dissipating. In the Atlantic, recurving storms may strike the coast of the United States north of Cape Hatteras, the Canadian Atlantic provinces, or even Ireland and England. As they move northward, they may encounter eastward-moving upper troughs that "capture" the storms, so that tropical characteristics are lost. This process is known as "extratropical transition"; the cyclone acquires characteristics of a mid-latitude low with warm and cold fronts and distinct temperature contrasts. In spite of the name change, it may retain a hurricane-like intensity for several more days.

Hazards

Hurricanes, typhoons, and cyclones bring wind—lots of wind. Peak wind speeds reached as high as 254 mph (408 km/h) in Cyclone Olivia (Australia) in October 1979. The strength of a hurricane is characterized by the Saffir-Simpson Scale, which assigns a category from 1 to 5 according to the maximum wind speed at the time (Table 9-3). A Category 1 storm will cause light damage to vegetation and mobile homes; Category 3 will cause structural damage to small buildings; Category 5 will completely demolish small buildings and cause extensive damage to doors and windows.

Maximum winds in a tropical storm are typically found on the right-hand side when looking along the direction of travel, where the speed of the storm along the track is added to the wind velocity around the eye. The relationship is reversed in the Southern Hemisphere. Damage caused by wind increases as the square of the wind speed, so even small changes in intensity can bring about substantial inflation of damage and costs. Insurance statistics show that a Category 5 storm typically causes 500 times more damage than a Category 1.

While winds are the focus of most attention around tropical storms, by far the larger part of the destruction along affected coasts is caused by a rush of water that comes onshore and the subsequent flooding. This "storm surge" is caused by the piling up of wind-driven water in front of the cyclone and is exacerbated by the low pressure in the storm center, which raises the sea level by a small amount like a giant atmospheric straw. A rise of 3 to 6 feet (1–2 meters) is typical for most hurricanes, but if the flood comes at high tide and is magnified by terrain and a shallow coastline, the storm can send a wall of water ashore up to 23 feet (7 meters) high.

The greatest hurricane disaster in United States history came with

CATEGORY	CENTRAL PRESSURE (MB)	MAXIMUM WIND SPEED MPH (KM/H)	DAMAGE
1	≥ 980	95 (153)	large branches broken from trees, mobile homes damaged, damage to power lines
2	965–979	110 (177)	shallow-rooted trees snapped, mobile homes heavily damaged, roofs removed on some frame houses
3	945–964	129 (208)	trees snapped or uprooted, mobile homes destroyed, roof and wall damage to frame homes
4	920–944	156 (251)	signs blown away, roofs and exterior walls heavily damaged or destroyed, most trees down, power grid heavily damaged with extended outages, high risk of injury
5	≤ 920	>157 (>252)	many frame homes destroyed, considerable wind-borne debris, high-rise windows blown out, power outages for weeks, high risk of injury

TABLE 9-3. *The Saffir-Simpson Hurricane Wind Scale*

FIG. 9-33. *New Orleans, Louisiana, after 2005's Hurricane Katrina, looking along Interstate 10 toward Lake Pontchartrain.*

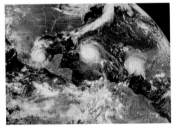

FIG. 9-34. *Three hurricanes, Irma, Katia, and Jose, line up across the tropical Atlantic and the Caribbean in this image from September 8, 2017. These three hurricanes were followed by Hurricane Maria two weeks later.*

the Galveston Hurricane of 1900, a Category 4 hurricane that drove a devastating storm surge ashore and killed between 6,000 and 12,000 people. In 2005, Hurricane Katrina created one of the largest surges to affect the United States mainland—23 feet (7.6 meters)—and was a major factor in the swamping of New Orleans (Figure 9-33). In 2017, Hurricanes Irma, Jose, and then Maria (Figure 9-34) caused extensive and widespread devastation across the eastern Caribbean. Each of the storms then went on to bring heavy rain and occasional damage to the United States mainland: Maria to North Carolina, Irma to Florida (and especially the Florida Keys) and Georgia, and Jose to New England.

A Global Perspective

Storms result from imbalances in the atmosphere—usually an excess of temperature or humidity that must be relieved in a relatively short time. With thunderstorms, it is the accumulation of moisture and heat at the surface; with hurricanes, an excess of energy within the tropical atmosphere and ocean; with winter storms, an imbalance in the temperature distribution between the tropics and the poles. The manifestations of the rebalancing—wind, tornadoes, hail, heavy precipitation, and so on—are the most exciting parts of meteorology and the most rewarding and challenging for an operational forecaster.

The sunward-facing slopes of this coastal mountain have warmed more quickly than the surrounding plains in the morning Sun. Plumes of warm, moist air rising from the slopes have condensed into this unusual arrangement of tall cumulus clouds. The soft edges and tops of these clouds are a consequence of the mixing of drier surrounding air with the rising column.

"Watch out for rain" is the message in this image, in which convective clouds have built into towering cumuli and formed ominous gray bottoms. The hard, round top of the cloud in the middle distance suggests a turret that is still growing strongly upward. Cumulus clouds whose vertical rise is greater than their horizontal extent may be called swelling cumulus or cumulus congestus, but the code used for these clouds by aviation forecasters is TCU, an acronym for towering cumulus.

This jumble of towering cumulus clouds is growing in a marginally unstable environment that dictates a short lifetime and modest development. In the background, rain is just beginning from one cell, and mistiness along the horizon suggests it will soon spread laterally. The precipitating cell is one that has managed to reach temperatures cold enough for supercooled cloud droplets to freeze and assemble into larger particles. As the larger ice crystals fall, they will melt and turn into raindrops. In temperate regions, convective clouds, with few exceptions, must reach subfreezing temperatures (usually around 5°F/–15°C) before ice particles can grow large enough to fall.

At the end of the day, as the ground cools and the sunlight disappears, the last buildup from a multicell line attempts to reach thunderstorm size—unsuccessfully. Evening light makes thunderstorms and other convective types some of the most attractive of all the clouds. This system will fade away without precipitating, the final convective cell in a day of severe weather.

Nighttime skies are great for lightning photography, especially if you can find an isolated storm that is flashing rapidly. The illumination in this thunderstorm reveals some of the internal structure and the flanking convection. The green glows on the horizon come from distant communities.

Growing cumulus clouds—soon to reach towering cumulus size—are on the threshold of precipitating, as indicated by their gray bottoms. In spite of the cloudy nature of the day, these cells are unlikely to climb much deeper, as the day is late and their fuzzy tops are a sign there is not much more energy left within them.

This line of multicell thunderstorms glows softly in the evening light, outlining a convective genealogy. The oldest buildup lies to the right, the youngest on the left, and new cells are growing in the lower left, above the structure on the horizon. Heavy precipitation—perhaps hail—falls from the right tower, but it is only getting started from the one on the left. In less than half an hour, the new cells will have grown as tall as those in the background. Each new storm forms on the outflow of those that came before, hoisted into the air with the help of the pool of rain-cooled air that flows out from the older precipitating cells. On the right of this image, small sunset-illuminated mammatus clouds can be seen hanging under the anvil of the oldest cell.

An unusual shelf cloud rotates slowly under a supercell thunderstorm. In spite of its appearance, no tornado touched down, despite the wishes of watching storm chasers.

Evening thunderstorms bring cloud-to-ground lightning to Tucson, Arizona, in this image taken from the 8,500-foot summit of Mount Hopkins on August 31, 2015.

Glowing fields of canola tint the low-level clouds that linger in the wake of a line of distant heavy thundershowers. Heavy convective rainstorms are frequently replaced by a canopy of lower clouds that continue the precipitation after the major buildups have moved on.

Strong thunderstorms are usually flanked by a "feeder line" of smaller convective clouds that flow toward and are incorporated into the larger storm. This short feeder line, tapering from small convective buildups on the right to larger cells on the left, provides an integral part of the energy and moisture required by the mature precipitating storm on the left.

A tornado funnel reaches down to touch the ground on an extremely unstable day in North Dakota. A half-dozen tornadoes were reported in the state that day.

This lonely anvil cloud shows a symmetrical shape that identifies its parent as a tropical thunderstorm, for only in the tropics is the wind aloft so light that a storm top can spread out evenly in all directions. The anvil stands alone, as its lower portions have dissipated and all that remains is the top, gradually evaporating in the upper atmosphere.

A powerful thunderstorm grows over the highlands of Ethiopia, dominating the smaller surrounding convective clouds on the lower hills. The prevailing winds, blowing from the photographer's location, rise upward on the mountain slope, triggering the early initiation and stronger development of convective clouds above the higher terrain.

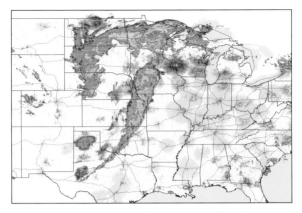

A radar view of a comma-cloud system with an intense squall line along the tail of the comma. A squall line is a line of continuous or semi-continuous thunderstorms (red in this image) that move, for a time, as a cohesive unit. In most cases, a squall line is associated with a cold front. This particular image was acquired in the evening of June 5, 2008, and illustrates the convective character of the comma tail compared to the more sedate continuous precipitation of the comma head. While many tornado and hail reports were received early in the day at the start of the line's formation, by the time it reached the stage of development seen in this image, damage was almost entirely from straight-line winds, which reached 80 mph (128 km/h).

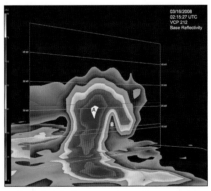

A radar cross section from the Charleston, South Carolina, radar acquired at 10:15 P.M. on March 15, 2008, shows the very high reflectivity values (A) suspended at 20,000 feet (6 km) in a severe thunderstorm. The indentation in the reflectivity at B is the location of a strong storm updraft, where large precipitation particles have not had time to grow to radar-detectable size, forming a hollowed-out region of weak echoes surrounded by much stronger echoes. The structure is known as a bounded weak-echo region (BWER) or a vault. This storm left 2- to 3-inch (5- to 7.6-cm) hail in its wake.

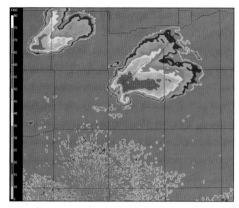

A radar display from the National Weather Service radar at Hastings, Nebraska, shows a well-defined hook echo associated with a tornado-producing thunderstorm on June 18, 2009. The hook echo signifies the presence of a mesocyclone circulation and is produced by rain or hail caught in the circulation and wrapped around the inflow region. While only a small percentage of storms with hook echoes produce tornadoes, they are considered to be a significant indicator of tornado potential and evidence to justify a tornado warning. This storm produced a half-mile-wide, 18-minute tornado near the town of Aurora, Nebraska.

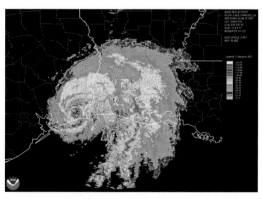

A view of Hurricane Humberto from the Lake Charles, Louisiana, radar as it made landfall in southeast Texas as a Category 1 hurricane on September 13, 2007. This view shows the small eye of Humberto and the asymmetrical nature of the thunderstorms around the eye. The heaviest activity in the eyewall was concentrated on the north side of the eye, as seen in the deep red colors in this image. The hurricane has a shape reminiscent of the comma shape of a mid-latitude storm, with a band of strong convection, separate from the eyewall, forming the backbone of a tail region. This tail region is known as the "principal band."

CHAPTER 10

ATMOSPHERIC OPTICS

Physical Processes

The sky is an ongoing movie, playing an endless drama of clouds and weather. When the plot demands, the starring actors enter the scene: halos, rainbows, rings, aurorae, and other optical treasures that bring unanticipated turns in the plot. Our atmosphere is loaded with substances that play with light waves, creating magical images in the air. Ice crystals in high, cold clouds provide the most spectacular backdrops, but water droplets, pollen, volcanic dust, and other aerosols have their own canvas to paint and do so with a surprising frequency.

Light and atmosphere interact with each other in many fascinating ways. Sometimes the interplay is straightforward and almost obvious: the red of a sunset, the color of a cloud, the view through a fog bank, a shadow on the ground. At other times, the interaction is more complex—halos, rainbows, or the magical green flash, for instance. Most of these optical phenomena can be traced back to the wavelike nature of light and the response of different wave frequencies to an interaction with matter—atoms and particles—in the atmosphere.

Light is composed of an extended spectrum of electromagnetic waves—an electrical wave and a magnetic wave oscillating together—of various frequencies or wavelengths (Figure 10-1). In the visible part of the spectrum, long wavelengths are seen as red colors by our eyes, while the shortest wavelengths are seen as deep purple. All of the other colors fit in the spectrum between these two extremes according to the classroom mnemonic (whom we think of as a friendly fellow) "ROY G BIV": Red Orange Yellow Green Blue Indigo Violet. The eye sees these colors as white when they are mixed together. When the

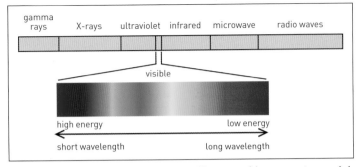

FIG. 10-1. *The electromagnetic spectrum. The visible portion of the spectrum is expanded below the chart. Short-wavelength radiation (gamma, X-ray, and most ultraviolet) is absorbed by the atmosphere before it reaches the surface. Infrared and microwave radiation may be blocked or may pass through the atmosphere, depending on wavelength.*

atmosphere distorts the color spectrum of sunlight (which contains all of the colors, most powerfully the green and yellow), then strange and wonderful phenomena may become visible.

Electromagnetic radiation is affected by six processes in the atmosphere: interference, refraction, dispersion, diffraction, reflection, and scattering. Individually or in combination, these processes are responsible for all the optical displays that our atmosphere has to offer. Because they are a characteristic of waves in general, you will find these six present in water and sound waves as well.

Interference

Waves are oscillations that conduct energy; they can be sound waves, water waves, light waves, or any other type of wave. When two similar waves meet, they interact to form a wave with an amplitude (intensity) that is a combination of the two original oscillations (Figure 10-2). Where two peaks or troughs coincide, the intensity of the wave will reach a maximum. Where a peak coincides with a trough, the combined wave will have a weaker intensity and may be canceled altogether. Wave interactions in which the intensity increases are exhibiting constructive interference; when the intensity decreases, it is known as destructive interference.

Interference becomes a much more interesting phenomenon when physical circumstances allow light waves to constructively and destructively interact to strengthen some wavelengths and weaken others. This has the effect of splitting light into its colors, concentrating

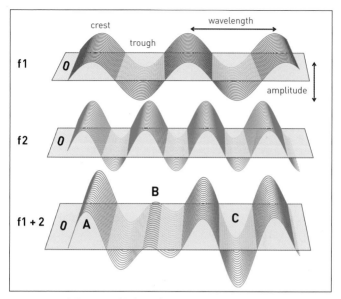

FIG. 10-2. *Two light waves of different frequency and the result of their constructive and destructive interference. The largest peaks and valleys (A and C) show where the two waves have combined constructively and intensity will be highest. Small waves (B) that barely leave the flat midline are positions of destructive interference where the two light waves cancel each other; the intensity here would be close to zero.*

red wavelengths in one position, blue in another, and all the intervening colors spread out between them in the form of a spectrum.

Refraction

Light moves at 186,000 miles per second (300,000 km/s) in the vacuum of space. Its speed through transparent matter—ice, air, glass, water—is slower, adopting a pace that depends on the material's density and composition. In water, the speed of light is three-quarters that of its speed in a vacuum. These differences in the speed of light from substance to substance cause light to bend (refract) as it moves into and out of the separate transparent materials, except when it passes perpendicularly from one medium to the other. We can see how this happens in Figure 10-3, which shows a beam of light passing from a material of low density into one of higher density—in this case, from air to water. The side of the beam that first makes contact with the

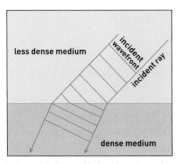

FIG. 10-3. *A beam of light is bent toward the perpendicular when it moves from a less dense medium to a denser one. Density fluctuations in the atmosphere distort light waves in a similar fashion, leading to the creation of mirages and other related phenomena.*

FIG. 10-4. *The refraction of light in passing from water to air causes this plywood stick to appear to have a bend at the air-water interface.*

water surface is slowed, followed by the rest of the beam, which undergoes the same fate. The effect is to turn the light beam toward a more perpendicular orientation, a process known as refraction. On leaving the water at an angle, the light will bend away from the perpendicular. The consequences of the refraction of light as it passes from water to air can be seen in the apparent bending of a stick immersed in a glass of water (Figure 10-4). Without refraction, lenses would not work and eyeglasses, binoculars, cameras, and most telescopes would be impossible.

Air density increases steadily from space to the ground, so unless the light comes from directly overhead, rays will follow a slightly curved path as they make their way through the atmosphere. A consequence of this refraction is that objects appear to be higher in the sky than their true position. The amount of this deviation depends on the altitude of the object, but at the horizon, the Sun and Moon appear lifted by about their own diameters (Figure 10-5).

The atmosphere is peppered with pockets of air at lower and higher density, usually caused by "bubbles" of slightly warmer and colder temperature and by turbulence. These temperature variations are the reason why stars twinkle and why telescopes are placed into orbit for the best quality images. Density fluctuations are most conspicuous near the ground, where strong temperature gradients can be created by such factors as solar heating, advection of warm or cold air, and the type of surface (snow, water, ground) over which the air flows. We see the effects on light waves everywhere: the apparent "water" on the

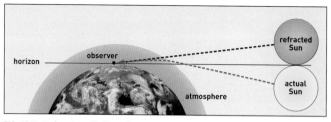

FIG. 10-5. *Refraction of light in the atmosphere will make the Sun or Moon appear to be higher in the sky, delaying the visible moment of setting or advancing the time of rising by about two minutes. The observer sees the Sun or Moon along the direction of the blue light path.*

highway ahead of us on a hot day (Figure 10-34), the football shape of a setting Sun, mirages over a lake, the "heat" rising from a barbeque, or the shimmering of a distant scene.

Dispersion

Short-wavelength blue light is refracted more than long, red waves, so refraction will separate light into its various colors. The process is known as dispersion, but refraction and dispersion are so closely allied that the name "refraction" is usually used to describe the combination of the two. Dispersion is the source of the colors in rainbows, halos, the green flash, and the splash of colored spectra that dance across a floor from prisms hung in sunny windows (Figure 10-6).

Diffraction

We tend to think of a light beam as following a straight line from its source (ignoring any refraction along the way), but when the beam comes to a small obstacle or a narrow aperture in a barrier, it re-forms itself as a spreading circular ripple on the downstream direction in a process called diffraction (Figure 10-7). The diffracted light beam seems to bend around the obstruction or spread out from the opening. The type of wave doesn't matter—a water wave and a light wave will do pretty much the same thing. If there is more than one opening or obstacle, adjacent newly generated waves will undergo constructive and destructive interference as they encounter each other in the space beyond the obstacle.

This downstream interference becomes a more interesting phenomenon if the particle or apertures causing the diffraction are approximately the same size as the wavelength of the passing light.

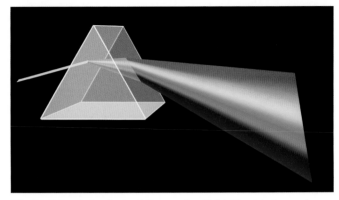

FIG. 10-6. *Prisms both refract and disperse colored light at two interfaces and can be used to separate light into its constituent colors or wavelengths. In the atmosphere, ice crystals with prismatic shapes can do the same, giving rise to halos of many different forms.*

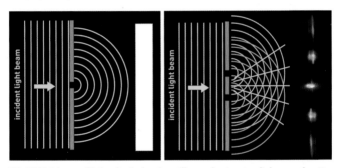

FIG. 10-7. *A beam of light of a single color will spread out as a radial wave when it passes through a small opening in a barrier, forming a spot of light on a screen on the other side. If the same monochrome beam passes through two or more apertures, the light waves passing through each gap will interfere constructively or destructively with those from other openings, forming a series of bright spots on a viewing screen. If a white-light source is used to illuminate the apertures, spots of spectral colors will form on the screen, as seen on the right.*

When white light—which is a mixture of all colors—diffracts around an obstacle or through two or more openings, each color in the beam will take a slightly different path onward. The multiple interferences between the light from different openings will cause the light to be spread out into its various wavelengths. Place a screen to intercept the diffracted light and it will show several bands of color, with red on the outer edges of each band and blue in the inner.

Diffraction is often illustrated with a diffraction grating—a device consisting of a series of extremely narrow lines ruled on a transparent glass or film or on a reflecting surface such as a mirror. Such gratings have a huge number of lines, on the order of 15,000 per inch (625 per mm) and higher, equal to about two wavelengths of red light; the spaces between the lines are equivalent to an opening in a barrier. An excellent example of diffraction from grating can be

FIG. 10-8. *The very fine recording tracks on a compact disk can act as a grating, diffracting light into its component colors when they are reflected from the surface.*

seen in the spectrum of colors reflected by the thousands of grooves on the shiny back surface of a compact disk (CD), as shown in Figure 10-8. In the atmosphere, diffraction occurs where light interacts with single water droplets or ice crystals in a cloud, but volcanic dust, pollen, and other aerosols will also do the trick.

Reflection

Reflection is a pretty familiar process—who hasn't looked in the mirror or admired a mountain scene in a smooth lake? Both of these are examples of "specular reflection" or mirrorlike reflection from a microscopically smooth surface (Figure 10-9). On the other hand, if a surface is rough at the microscopic level, light will be reflected in many directions and no image will be formed—a process known as "diffuse reflection." In an ordinary scene, most reflection is diffuse. Both processes are important in the atmosphere and in daily life. At night, dry pavement reflects headlights diffusively, so a driver is able to see the road and the lane marks clearly by the light scattered back from the asphalt and paint. When the road is wet, the water smooths out the roughness in the road, and the light scattering becomes mirrorlike, reflecting off the road in a forward direction and not back to the driver, so that distinguishing the lane markings ahead becomes considerably more difficult. In the atmosphere, flat, smooth-sided ice crystals can become specular reflectors, giving rise to a number of attractive optical phenomena.

Scattering

When light passes through the atmosphere or any transparent medium, it is scattered by particulates such as dust, microscopic water droplets and ice crystals, meteoric particles, pollen, and even the molecules of air itself (Figure 10-10). The process can be separated into three types: Rayleigh scattering, Mie scattering, and nonselective scattering.

Rayleigh scattering (named after Lord Rayleigh, a nineteenth-century British scientist) is caused by scattering from molecules and extremely small particles in the atmosphere and is strongly wavelength dependent. The result of this dependence is that short-wavelength blue light is scattered about five times more efficiently than red. When you look at a blue sky, you are seeing the highly scattered blue photons from the Sun. Red and green light are still there but in much smaller proportions, because those wavelengths haven't been scattered as effectively and there are fewer reaching your eyes. Toward the horizon on a clear day, the blue color of the sky turns to a slightly whiter shade, because the light's path through the atmosphere is long enough that even the reds and greens are scattered strongly, blending all of the colors together. At sunset and sunrise, blue light is scattered away by atmospheric molecules, leaving behind the oranges and reds to color the Sun and clouds.

Mie scattering (named for Gustav Mie, a German physicist) applies

FIG. 10-9. *On a calm morning, the still water beneath this heron acts as a specular reflector and produces a mirror image of the bird.*

FIG. 10-10. *A green laser beam shining from the right is nearly invisible in the glass of water but shows up dramatically in diluted milk. Particles in the milk scatter the light beam to the sides and throughout the volume of the glass, making it visible to the observer and coloring the contents.*

to larger atmospheric particles—typically about the size of the light's wavelength—and redirects all colors more or less equally, but in a forward direction. Mie scattering from atmospheric particulates is primarily responsible for the white glare around the Sun in all but the cleanest atmospheres. Our third type, non-selective scattering, is used to describe situations in which light undergoes multiple redirections, either by Mie or Rayleigh scattering or both. This diffusive scattering gives clouds their white appearance and causes the semi-transparency of hazes and fogs.

The Play of Light in the Atmosphere

Ice-Crystal Halos

Ice crystals are like tiny prisms, reflecting and bending light rays and sending them off in new directions, usually separated into the colors of the spectrum. While there are only two basic forms of crystal—pencil-like and plate-like—their orientation, the extent of their clumping, and the path of the ray through these minuscule prisms give rise to the many forms of the sky's halos. Some halo forms are seen frequently; others are much rarer, perhaps coming only once a year or even once in a lifetime. Some linger for hours, while others pass in a few minutes. Some are subtle and largely unnoticed, while others fill the sky and command attention.

The 22° Halo

The 22° halo is a circle around the Sun (Figure 10-11) that is caused by light refraction through poorly aligned or randomly oriented hexagonal ice crystals in cirrostratus clouds. The inner edge typically has a reddish color, but the rest of the ring is white because of multiple overlapping refractions from the multitude of scattering ice crystals. It is one of the most common halos and has a special meaning to many cultures. To Inuit observers, the rings were regarded as harbingers of storms. At Bathurst Inlet, Nunavut, the circle suggested something pleasant, as it resembled the rim of a drum. To some native communities of the Canadian Arctic islands, the rings were omens of sudden death: if it was incomplete, someone had died. Among the Hopi, a circle around the Sun was a sign to people to live in harmony with nature. In American folklore, a ring around the Sun or Moon means rain or snow is coming soon—a dependable prediction, as the ring is produced in thin cirrus that often heralds an approaching weather disturbance.

FIG. 10-11. *Sundogs and a 22° halo around a North Dakota sun. The horizontal extensions to the left and right of the Sun, through the sundogs, form a section of the parhelic arc. A modest upper tangent arc appears at the top of the halo, and a vertical sun pillar stretches above and below the Sun.*

Sundogs (Parhelia)

Sundogs, or parhelia, are bright glints in the sky on either side of the Sun, separated by an angle of 22° or more (one hand span) and often superimposed on the 22° halo when near the horizon (Figure 10-11). The origin of the term "sundog" is uncertain, but dates to the 1600s; starting in Aristotle's time and continuing to today, they were called "mock suns." The Greeks of Aristotle's time regarded mock suns as a sign of an approaching storm, an association that has some basis in fact, since the high-pressure system that brings the ice-laden clouds is likely to be replaced by a stormier low in the following days. To the Inuit around Point Barrow, Alaska, sundogs are the walking sticks that the Sun holds out to support itself in an impending gale.

Sundogs are formed by small, hexagonal, plate-shaped ice crystals that float with their flat side facing down. When the plates are approximately level with the Sun, light can enter the narrow edge of the six-sided crystal, where it is refracted into its spectral colors before it exits on the opposite side (Figure 10-12). For this reason, sundogs are found at the same level in the sky as the Sun, tinged with red on the inner edge against a yellow or whitish middle (Figure 10-13). Because light entering the crystals is bent through an angle of 22° or more, only rays from crystals that are at least that degree of separation from the

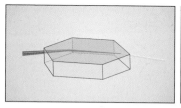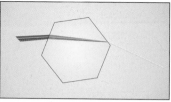

FIG. 10-12. *To create sundogs, sunlight must enter the narrow side of flat ice crystals, a limitation that restricts the parhelia-forming crystals to those that are at the same altitude as the Sun in the sky. Because the larger part of the light is bent through an angle of 22°, the parhelia are found to the sides of the Sun at that angle. Refraction of the light in the crystal also separates it into colors, giving the sundog a red inner edge and a blue outer.*

FIG. 10-13. *A short exposure of a brilliant sundog shows its red sunward edge, the yellowish middle, and the white tail of the parhelic arc.*

Sun can reach our eyes. Parhelia are frequently tethered together by a narrow arc of light passing through the Sun, which, on very rare occasions, can be further traced around the horizon (the parhelic circle).

Winter is the best season for sundogs, but they can be spotted at any time of year, as the crystals responsible for their construction typically lie at the cirrus level (Chapter 3), where all clouds are made of ice. Sometimes, when the Sun is low, the parhelia are nearly as bright as the Sun itself and impossible to watch without sunglasses. On rare winter mornings when the sky is filled with diamondlike motes of tiny ice crystals, sundogs can be seen superimposed on nearby buildings and other foreground objects.

FIG. 10-14. *The circumzenithal arc is centered on the overhead point and is often found when sundogs are present.*

Circumzenithal Arc

Whenever sundogs are present, it is worthwhile looking straight overhead toward the zenith for a circumzenithal arc. This short arc is one of the more colorful of the halo phenomena and is a common apparition, with or without parhelia (Figure 10-14). It is formed by the refraction of light rays that enter a plate crystal from the top side and leave through a side face. Because these faces are at 90° angles, the colors formed are well defined and bright. The circumzenithal arc forms only when the Sun is less than 32° high and is brightest and longest at a solar elevation around 22°.

Circumhorizontal Arc

The circumhorizontal arc is an exceptionally colorful ice halo that can be seen only when the Sun is high in the sky—at least 58° elevation—when hexagonal plate crystals in cold cirrus clouds are present (Figure 10-15). Sunlight enters the crystals from the side facet and exits through the bottom. This unforgettable halo has been dubbed "fire rainbow" in the popular press thanks to an exuberant journalist who wrote about it during a spectacular display in Seattle in 2006.

The Sun's rays are strongly refracted in passing through the crystal and so the circumhorizontal arc appears as a brilliantly colored band about two hand spans beneath the Sun, superimposed on the cirrus clouds that provide the oriented crystals. When the ice-crystal cirrus

FIG. 10-15. *The circumhorizontal arc is one of the most brilliant of the halos. In this image, the arc is shining in an old contrail.*

cloud is small or patchy, only fragments of the arc may be seen. It can be mistaken for iridescence in a cloud, but its size and location below the Sun, parallel to the horizon, and its extreme brilliance will give it away.

Because the Sun must be at least 58° high for the circumhorizontal arc to form, its appearance is limited to the months between May and August in Seattle and from mid-March to October in Houston. Visibility is further restricted by the daily rising and setting of the Sun, so that an altitude of 58° might be obtained for only a few hours on a summer day in northern latitudes. Because the Sun doesn't ascend high enough in the sky, the circumhorizontal arc is never visible above 55½° latitude in the Northern or Southern Hemispheres.

Upper and Lower Tangent Arc

Upper tangent arcs lie along the top of the 22° halo, forming a gull-wing shape that flattens as the Sun rises higher in the sky (Figure 10-16). Some color—especially red—is usually noticeable above the Sun where the arc touches the 22° ring. The upper tangent arc is formed from columnar (pencil-shaped) ice crystals whose long axes are oriented horizontally. Light enters the crystal through one of the long facets and exits through the opposite side.

A lower tangent arc is formed by the same process as the upper, except that the light rays are bent upward on exiting the crystal instead of downward. The lower arc becomes visible as a hyperbolic-shaped halo as the Sun climbs above an altitude of 22°. As the solar altitude increases, the hyperbola opens and the wings begin to spread outward. Above 30° elevation, the upper and lower arcs join in a large oval-shaped "circumscribed halo" that surrounds the Sun. At even higher elevations, the circumscribed halo gradually merges with the 22° halo until the two are coincident with an overhead Sun.

Other Forms of Halos

Halo phenomena are enormously complex, occasionally once-in-a-lifetime events, and not completely understood, so it is a lucky person indeed who is treated to some of the more complicated patterns that can be seen in the sky (Figure 10-17). The more obscure types go by names such as the heliac arc, the Parry arc, the Wegener arc, and the anthelion. Just about any distinct light path refracted through or reflected off of ice crystals and water droplets will produce a unique halo pattern, sometimes in spectral colors and sometimes as white arcs and curls.

Water Droplets and the Play of Light

Rainbows

Who has not been captivated by a sparkling rainbow, arcing across the landscape in the remnants of a departing shower? While halos are introverts, usually haunting cold winter skies, rainbows are gregarious, glowing in brilliant colors that arc over the landscape. Over the history of human development, the storm-ending rainbow has often been associated with omens and mystic events, usually favorable.

To the Greeks and Romans, Iris, the Goddess of the Rainbow, was represented as a maiden with bright-colored wings and robes who traveled across the sky on a rainbow highway as she carried messages for the gods and recharged the clouds with water. In Polynesian mythology, the rainbow is the path taken by the gods. In Hindu legend, the rainbow is called the bow of Indra or *Indrahanush* after the God of lightning, thunder, and rain. The first scientific attempt to explain the rainbow may have been made by Aristotle, who proposed that it was the reflection of light at a fixed angle from very small droplets in the clouds. Aristotle's rainbow had only three colors—red, green, and violet—created, in his opinion, by a weakening of the light as it was reflected.

FIG. 10-16. *A highly enhanced photo of an upper tangent arc at the top of a 22° halo. Note the darkness in the interior of the halo, resulting from the deflection of light into the surrounding halo.*

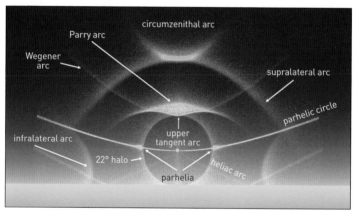

FIG. 10-17. *A schematic diagram of a series of common and uncommon halos produced using the program HaloSim.*

Primary and Secondary Bows

Rainbows are formed by the refraction, dispersion, and reflection of light in water droplets when the Sun is behind the observer. Refraction, which occurs when the light beam both enters and leaves the drop, disperses the light beam into its constituent colors. Reflection

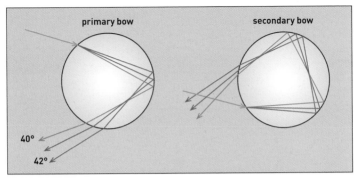

FIG. 10-18. *Geometry of the primary and secondary bows. The extra reflection that forms the secondary bow also inverts the arrangement of the colors.*

FIG. 10-19. *Primary and secondary rainbows after a heavy shower. The secondary bow is the fainter rainbow above the bright primary. Note the reversal of colors in the two bows and the bright interior of the primary bow.*

within the drop returns the colored light beam toward the observer, forming different types of bows according to the number of reflections (Figure 10-18). A single inner bow (the primary bow) is formed from one internal reflection; a second bow (secondary rainbow) may appear when light makes two reflections (Figure 10-19). In the primary bow, the outer edge of the arc is always red; the inner, blue or purplish; with oranges, yellows, and greens filling the intervening space. Colors are reversed in the secondary bow.

Primary bows are centered opposite the Sun and subtend an angle of 40° to 42° on the sky. This limits the appearance of a bow to the morning and evening hours when the Sun is no higher than that angle, for otherwise the rainbow would be seen against the ground and largely invisible unless the raindrops were very close to the observer (such as looking into the spray from a garden hose). The bow is highest in the sky when the Sun is lowest, becoming more and more prominent as the solar disk sinks toward the horizon.

The secondary bow, formed from two internal reflections, lies at an angle of about 51° from the antisolar point in the sky. Its arc is nearly twice the width of the primary bow and fainter, partly because of the second reflection and partly because of its larger size, which spreads and dilutes its light. When raindrops are small—around 1/25 of an inch (1 mm) or less—you may notice fainter pink and purple arcs just inside the primary bow (Figure 10-20). These are supernumerary bows and are caused by the constructive and destructive interference of light waves within each raindrop.

The fundamental characteristics of the rainbow—size, intensity, and color—depend on the size of the raindrops in the shower. Large drops (⅛ inch or several mm across) in heavy showers produce intense, narrow rainbows. As drops decrease in size, the colors become muted, but the rainbow itself grows broader. If droplet sizes are very small—drizzle drops or cloud droplets for instance—the arcs

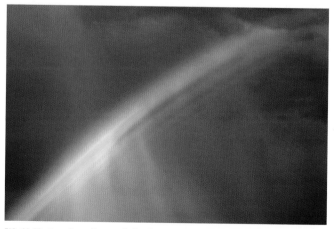

FIG. 10-20. *An enlarged view of a bright rainbow showing the supernumerary bows beneath the primary bow.*

are colorless and usually called fog bows or cloudbows. Color also changes as sunset approaches. When the rising or setting Sun is at low elevations, the rainbow takes on a reddish hue as the blue and violet colors fade away.

Raindrops do more than turn ordinary sunlight into a band of spectral colors; they also redistribute the light inside and outside the bows. Single reflections that form the primary bow redirect light to the interior of the arc, causing it to brighten. The double reflections that form the secondary bow redirect light to the outside of the pair of arcs. This leaves a deficiency of light in the space between the two arcs and so the space appears darker than the surrounding sky. This dark region is called Alexander's dark band, after Alexander of Aphrodisias, who first described it around 200 CE.

Moonbows

Just as the Sun can form rainbows in the daytime, so the bright Moon can do the job at night. The Moon should be close to full, lower than 42° in the sky, and it must be raining in the direction opposite the Moon. These are more restrictive conditions than those for seeing a rainbow, and so a moonbow is spotted only rarely. To the naked eye, moonbows are grayish or have a very subdued color, since the eye does not respond to color at low light levels.

Coronae

When a thin veil of cloud covers the sky and the cloud droplets or ice crystals are all approximately the same size, the Sun or Moon may be surrounded by a circular halo of colored light called a corona (Figure 10-21). The corona will have a bright bluish-white center, called an aureole, usually set within a series of one or more colored rings, bluish on the inside grading to a pale brick red on the outside. The very best coronae (or coronas) will have more than one ring, perhaps extending outward for 15° from the center if the clouds are just right.

Coronae are produced by the diffraction of light by individual water droplets or ice crystals, though any small particle, including pollen and volcanic dust, will suffice. Because diffraction spreads red wavelengths farthest from the optical axis and blues much less, the coronal rings show red tints toward the outside and yellows through blue toward the interior. The size of the corona is related to the size of the particles causing the diffraction, with the largest particles producing the biggest rings. The most distinctive colors are formed when droplets are small and of uniform size; if the cloud has a variety of droplet sizes, the corona's colors will be washed out. You will probably see a lunar corona more often than one around the Sun, as they are more prominent when superimposed against a dark sky background.

Iridescent Clouds

Iridescent clouds are a form of corona, also formed by diffraction of light in an environment of water droplets and ice crystals. The main distinction between coronas and iridescent clouds is mostly location;

FIG. 10-21. *A double-ringed lunar corona formed in high altostratus with dark tendrils of stratus in the foreground.*

the corona surrounds the Sun or Moon, while iridescence is often found at some distance to one side or other, visible as random patches of color within mid- and high-level clouds (Figure 10-22). Iridescence can appear in a wide range of clouds: small cumulus, lenticulars, altocumulus, cirrus, and nacreous clouds.

FIG. 10-22. *Iridescence in patchy altocumulus clouds.*

Iridescent colors tend to favor pastel shades though at times they can be quite concentrated. Here again, color intensity depends on the droplet size spectrum, so freshly formed clouds that contain a uniform distribution of droplets produce the richest colors. Iridescence is possible only in thin clouds where the concentration of droplets is small, so the color display will be confined to the edges of thicker clouds.

Glories

Whenever you book a flight, try to be on the shadowed side of the aircraft. Not only is the ground more visible and contrasty in the down-sun direction, but you will often be treated to the sight of a glory on the clouds below, surrounding the aircraft shadow and centered at your location on the plane (Figure 10-23).

A glory is a series of nested colored rings seen against a cloud background in the antisolar direction. Its center is a muted white, while each ring is delicately colored, blue on the inside fading to red on the outside. Clouds with a narrow range of droplet sizes give the most distinct glories, with the largest and brightest colors coming from the smallest droplets. Most glories will sport two or three rings, and four are possible.

Though the glory is caused by diffraction and reflection in a cloud drop, it is still a bit of a scientific mystery in spite of its very common occurrence. Diffraction is commonly observed in the direction of the Sun or Moon, but a glory forms in the opposite direction, looking away from the light source. How does the light beam get turned

FIG. 10-23. *A glory, seen projected against altocumulus clouds. Glories seen from aircraft are very common.*

back toward the observer from the cloud droplets, much like a mirror reflection?

As we saw in the description of a rainbow, light entering a cloud droplet can undergo a single internal reflection and be returned approximately to the direction from which it came. The problem is that it cannot be reflected exactly back to its origin, and comes up short of the necessary 180° by about 14°. One idea suggests that the returning light beam travels along the back surface of the water droplet for a short distance before reflecting back toward its direction of origin and to the observer. The colors of a glory are then caused by diffraction and interference between light waves traveling within the drop. It's not the only explanation, but it does predict the glory's position and colors.

Because glories are found at the antisolar point, they are always seen below the observer except when the Sun is on the horizon. Morning fog banks may display a glory around the shadow of an observer's head at sunrise and shortly afterward. From mountain vantage points, glories may be seen at any time of day as long as the observer's shadow falls on a cloud or fog bank at a lower level. The observer's shadow usually adopts a spooky, elongated shape as it is projected into the depths of the mist. This ethereal shadow has the name Brocken Spectre (*Brockengespenst*), after Brocken, the highest peak in the Harz Mountains of Germany, where the frequency of fog and cloud made the specter a regular occurrence.

Heiligenschein

When the grass is wet with dew, and the Sun casts long shadows upon the ground, a bright glow might be seen surrounding the shadow of your head. This is the *"heiligenschein"* or "holy light," named for its obvious resemblance to a halo (Figure 10-24). The glow is formed by dewdrops suspended on the leaf surface that crudely focus the Sun's light onto an underlying leaf. The focused light scatters from the grass, but a disproportionate amount of the scattered light is captured again by the dewdrop and returned in the direction of the Sun, surrounding the shadow of the observer's head with a field of brightly illuminated white droplets. As with the glory, each observer will see a unique *heiligenschein*.

A similar glow can be found superimposed on the shadow of an airplane while flying over grassy fields or a forest, in the same position that a glory might form if there were clouds below. This manifesta-

FIG. 10-24. *A brighter greenish glow surrounds the shadow of an observer cast on a dew-covered plot of grass at the bottom of a hill. The phenomenon, known as* heiligenschein, *is caused by backscattered light focused by dewdrops on the blades of grass. The glow in this image is spread out by the large distance between the observer and the grassy field.*

tion is known as a dry *heiligenschein* and is caused by differences in the shadowing by small irregularities at the antisolar point and those slightly off to the side. Directly opposite the Sun, objects at the ground cover their own shadows from the observer's vantage, while those to the side reveal at least a part of the shadow. This gives the impression that the aircraft shadow is surrounded by a subtle bright spot that fades to a darker tone off to the side. It is easily spotted from a moving car when the rising or setting Sun casts a long shadow into roadside fields. If the crop stands tall, the *heiligenschein* will form a streak of light instead of a round orb.

Shadows in the Sky

Crepuscular and Anti-crepuscular Rays

Combine broken clouds on the horizon with a dusty or hazy atmosphere and a low Sun, and chances are you will be treated to crepuscular rays spreading outward across the sky from the sunrise or sunset point as in Figure 10-25. These divergent sunbeams are the shadows of clouds cast upon the atmosphere, adding spectacle to an otherwise ordinary sunset. The rays are parallel, but appear to converge toward the Sun in the same way that highways or railway tracks converge

FIG. 10-25. *Crepuscular rays mark the location of the setting Sun.*

toward a horizon. Convective clouds form the best crepuscular rays, because they build upward instead of horizontally and tend to form dark shadows because of their density.

When crepuscular rays are erupting from the sunset horizon, turn your back to the Sun and look toward the opposite skyline. On occasion, you will see the rays converging again toward the east. These are anti-crepuscular rays and though they aren't quite the spectacle of those in the direction of the Sun, they deserve attention because of their uniqueness. Put anti-crepuscular rays together with a rainbow and you will have a "rainbow wheel" in which the crepuscular rays form spokes that converge at the antisolar point. While neither crepuscular rays nor rainbows are rare, the combination is a unique occasion.

Mountain Shadows

The observatories on the top of Maunakea in Hawaii are famous for their scientific achievements, but the 13,800-foot (4,000-m) altitude of the volcanic peak is also well known for its spectacular sunsets. Visitors who arrive and stay the evening can capture a view of the shadow of the volcano on the lower clouds and the ground, growing longer with each passing minute (Figure 10-26). Similar views can be had from any mountain, though isolated peaks produce the most dramatic shadows.

From a mountain vantage point, an observer looks along the shadow to its convergence point in the distance. In contrast, a watcher

FIG. 10-26. *The shadow of Maunakea points toward the rising (nearly) full Moon. The reddish band along the horizon is the Belt of Venus; the darker region below is the Earth's shadow.*

looking toward the mountain from distant lower ground will see a shadow that appears like a crepuscular ray, also converging in the distance, but now in the opposite direction to that viewed from the peak. Irrespective of the shape of the terrain, long mountain shadows have a triangular appearance from the top because of perspective effects. When the Sun is just above the horizon, the shadow may stretch 200 to 300 miles (300 to 500 km) toward the horizon.

The Belt of Venus and the Shadow of the Earth

The ultimate shadow cast by the setting Sun is that of the Earth itself. That shadow is over a million miles in length but is visible in our atmosphere over a low eastern horizon on every clear evening. It appears as a dark purple-gray band, topped in pink or somber red, that rises higher in the sky as the Sun sinks in the west. In Victorian times, the pink glow was called Venus's girdle, or the Belt of Venus; the color comes from the heavily reddened light from the Sun, still illuminating the upper atmosphere after the Sun has set.

The Belt of Venus first becomes visible as pink shading along the eastern horizon shortly after sunset. Over the next few minutes, the pink band rises higher and the atmosphere next to the horizon is replaced by a darker shadow (Figure 10-26). The two rise together over the next 15 minutes or so as the setting Sun moves farther below the western horizon. Eventually the pink shading fades away, but the descent into darkness is evident for much longer, especially in northern latitudes during summer.

Colors in the Sky

Red Sunsets and Blue Skies

> *Red sky at night, sailors' delight.*
> *Red sky at morning, sailors take warning.*

Light travels in a straight line from the Sun but when it encounters a molecule in the Earth's atmosphere, it is briefly captured and then re-radiated in a random direction. This process is called scattering, and the likelihood that a light ray will be scattered depends on the wavelength. Short-wavelength blue light is about nine times more likely to be absorbed and scattered than longwave red light.

During the daytime, the light toward the Sun is a yellowish color because the atmosphere is thinnest in the overhead direction and the amount of scattering is relatively small. Off to the sides, away from the Sun, we see the light that has been captured by molecules and re-radiated in our direction. Since it is blue light that is most readily captured and scattered, the sky around us has a blue color; without that scattering, the sky would be black in directions away from the Sun. That blue color is washed out toward the horizon where the sky becomes whiter because the thicker atmosphere in that direction scatters all of the wavelengths, not just the blue ones.

When the Sun is low on the horizon and light has a very long path through the densest part of the atmosphere, the molecules in the air scatter blue, green, and yellow light in all directions, leaving the longer orange and red wavelengths to reach our eyes and give sunrise and sunset their marvelous warm colors (Figure 10-27). The best sunsets come with a clear, pollution-free atmosphere that allows the light scattered by oxygen and nitrogen molecules to be seen at its best. Pollutants tend to dilute the red shades of the setting sun and wash out the colors.

Large volcanic eruptions, such as that by Mount Pinatubo in 1991, greatly enhance the worldwide colors of sunsets for months at a time by depositing huge amounts of sulfate aerosols and ash particles into the stratosphere. Smoke particles and other pollutants injected into

FIG. 10-27. *Rayleigh scattering colors this South Dakota sunset, lending a red tone to horizon, clouds, and landscape.*

the atmosphere by forest fires give the Sun a distinctive pink color, even when it is relatively high in the sky.

Polarization of the Sky

A light wave consists of matched, perpendicular, electric and magnetic fields (Figure 10-28) oscillating with a frequency that determines its position or color within the electromagnetic spectrum. The direction of oscillation is perpendicular to the direction of motion, but may be at any orientation when seen head on; left to right, up and down, or any angle in between, and may even rotate through all angles in a regular pattern. The orientation of that wave is referred to as the wave's polarization.

Normally, the sunlight that surrounds us is a mixture of light waves with all possible polarizations. However, when a light beam interacts with an atmospheric molecule, waves that have a vertical polarization will be scattered to the sides; light with a horizontal polarization will be scattered up or down. When we look around the sky, we see blue light waves that have been scattered and are no longer unpolarized. When the Sun is high, the sky near the horizon will have the strongest polarization; when it is low, the sky to the sides will be polarized.

The degree of polarization is governed by the amount of scattering, with the largest polarization at right angles to the direction to the Sun. In a very clear atmosphere, light perpendicular to the Sun may be as much as 90 percent polarized—that is, the light waves will almost all be oscillating with the same orientation. If you own polarizing sunglasses, the sky will appear noticeably darker in that direction when viewed through the glasses (Figure 10-29). If you rotate those sunglasses, the blue sky will lighten and darken as the glasses alternately pass and absorb the polarized blue

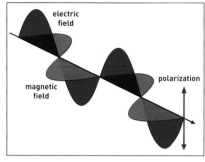

FIG. 10-28. *A light wave, with alternating electrical and magnetic waves. The angle of polarization is defined by the orientation of the electrical wave.*

light. Photographers use polarizing filters to increase the contrast between clouds and sky, making the sky appear darker and bluer, but the contrast enhancement works only in directions away from the Sun. Reflected light is also often polarized, which you can test by rotating your sunglasses while viewing a water surface or a flat, shiny object.

There is some evidence that songbirds make use of the polarization of the morning and evening skylight to calibrate internal compasses during migration. At those early and late times of day, the polarization

FIG. 10-29. *In this wide-angle view of the sky through a polarizing filter, the brightness of the blue sky drops dramatically to the upper right, where sunlight is most strongly polarized.*

of the sky is most intense along an overhead north-to-south band. Birds seem to cue on the polarization along the horizon to set the north-south direction, a reference that doesn't depend on the time of year.

The Green Flash and the Green Rim

The green flash is an atmospheric phenomenon seen at sunrise and sunset in which, for a few seconds, a small piece of the Sun's disk turns green. Not just any green, but a surprisingly intense apple green, occasionally accompanied by a greatly distorted disk of the Sun that provides a fascinating backdrop during the evolution of the spectacle. The green flash and its close cousin, the green rim, are legendary meteorological events that are enormously more complicated than they first appear, and subject to a large amount of storytelling and speculative explanation.

The green flash had its coming-out in Jules Verne's *Le Rayon vert* (*The Green Ray*), a rather awful love story published in 1882 (and yet, still made into a film in 1986) based on a fictitious Scottish legend about the green flash. In Verne's description, the green flash was

> . . . a green which no artist could ever obtain on his palette, a green of which neither the varied tints of vegetation nor the shades of the most limpid sea could ever produce the like! If there is a green in Paradise, it cannot be but of this shade, which most surely is the true green of Hope.

Scientific literature about the green flash developed fairly slowly after Verne, with the first serious analyses not appearing until the 1920s. The physical underpinnings are still evolving, for the structure of the atmosphere at the very lowest altitudes—even below the geographical horizon—can be remarkably complex. Green flashes are entangled with the phenomena of mirages, and so to understand the first is to have a good knowledge of the latter.

On especially clear evenings and mornings when the Sun is less than 4° above the horizon, an exceedingly narrow green rim can be seen lying across the top of the solar disk. The rim is too small to be seen with the naked eye, so some sort of magnification is required—a hazardous pastime without proper filters such as those used by amateur and professional astronomers to view the Sun. However, if the Sun is attenuated sufficiently by aerosols in the atmosphere, a camera with a telephoto lens should be able to capture the green rim (Figure 10-30), as long as the scene is not overexposed.

When you see the Sun at the horizon, it has actually already set. Its lingering visibility is due to the refraction of light rays in the atmosphere that lifts the Sun above its geometrical position. For an average atmospheric temperature profile, the Sun is raised by more than its own diameter (0.53°) when at the horizon (Figure 10-31). The amount of refraction depends on wavelength, with red rays being bent less than blue, and so, if our eyes were capable of resolving them, a blue image of the Sun should appear a tiny amount above a green one that in turn is a little above a red one and similarly through all of the colors.

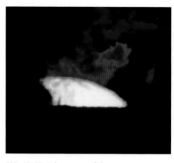

FIG. 10-30. *This view of the setting Sun during a partial eclipse reveals a thin green edge along the top limb in this highly magnified image. The clouds and foreground are very dark because of the need to use very short exposures to avoid overexposing the solar surface. No green flash occurred with this sunset.*

The superposition of the displaced images of a blue, a green, and a red Sun should be visible in a telescope except that aerosols in our atmosphere scatter blue light so strongly that there is usually none there to see. Water vapor preferentially absorbs the yellow and orange light, leaving mostly green and red to survive the passage to the observer. A green rim then is the visible consequence of the near-superposition of green and red images of the Sun. As the Sun sinks

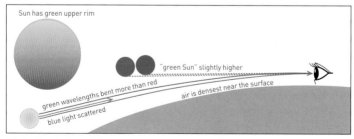

FIG. 10-31. *The Sun will have a green rim on its upper edge as a consequence of the wavelength-dependent refraction of light in the atmosphere. In this diagram, the Sun has already set for the observer, but bending of light in the atmosphere ensures that it is still visible.*

lower in the sky, however, the ever-thickening atmosphere absorbs even the green rays, and so that color often fades away to invisibility, leaving only a red orb to sink below the horizon.

It is very **important to take proper precautions** when observing the Sun in order to prevent serious damage to your eyesight! Even when near the horizon and attenuated from the atmospheric opacity, the Sun is still very bright, and concentrated observation with the naked eye or with optical instruments can be harmful. Observations should be kept short and made through proper filters that absorb dangerous ultraviolet and infrared wavelengths. Better yet, use a camera and telephoto lens to capture the moment. Exposures must be very short.

The green flash is caused by the magnification and enhancement of the green rim by a mirage as the Sun sinks below the horizon. There are two types of green flash, each with its own characteristic mirage. In its most common form, the flash appears as a small green segment of the solar rim just as the last piece of the Sun's disk sinks below the horizon—a so-called "last-glimpse" green flash (Figure 10-32). In contrast, the second form begins to evolve while the Sun is still about one solar diameter above the horizon. In this type, the Sun's disk breaks into several linear segments, the topmost of which acquires a green color as it settles toward the horizon (Figure 10-33).

The "last-glimpse" flash is associated with an inferior mirage, an apparition that is familiar to most of us when it causes the "wet" spot on an asphalt road that appears in the middle distance while we are driving on a hot day (Figure 10-34). This wet spot is actually a portion of the light from the sky, turned toward the eye and inverted as it is refracted by heated, low-density air that lies above the hot roadway. Inferior-mirage green flashes arise from the same thermal stratification: a layer of warm air next to the surface with a cooler layer above.

The first sign that conditions for an inferior mirage are present is the development of a "foot" under the Sun as the lower limb touches the visual horizon (Figure 10-32, A). This foot spreads out along the horizon and gives the Sun a shape much like a candy apple sitting in its puddle of toffee, or of the Greek capital letter omega (Ω). As the solar disk sinks lower, it loses the foot and acquires a noticeable green top and sides (Figure 10-32, B). Shortly afterward, the inverted mirage appears beneath the Sun, and the original and mirage images then blend together to form a football-shaped, green-rimmed, yellow Sun just above the horizon (Figure 10-32, C and D). At the last

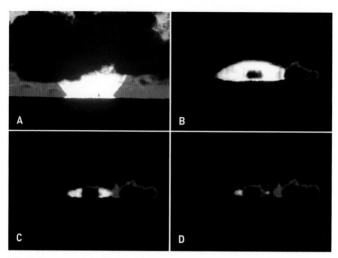

FIG. 10-32. *A sequence of images of the setting Sun shows the gradual formation of a green flash. The foot on the setting Sun in photo A is the sign of a temperature stratification that may form a green flash. In photos B, C, and D, the Sun sinks progressively lower behind a small cloud, while the yellow disk gradually acquires a strong apple green tinge. In C and D, the inverted mirage of the Sun joins the real image to form a green-rimmed, yellow-centered, football-shaped Sun that will eventually shrink to leave only the green rim visible. This last stage occurred a few seconds after D, but was hidden by the cloud.*

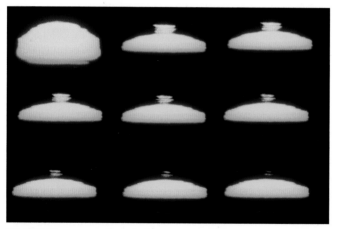

FIG. 10-33. *This sequence shows the formation and evolution of a mock-mirage green flash.*

FIG. 10-34. *A highway mirage created by the bending of light above a warm road surface.*

moment, the yellow center of the mirage is squeezed out and the conjoined rims then present a pure green flash to the observer. On rare occasions, when the atmosphere is exceptionally transparent, the blue wavelengths are not entirely removed by scattering aerosols in the atmosphere and the green flash turns into a blue flash in the final instants of sunset.

The second type of green flash is produced by a different mirage, called a "mock mirage," that forms under an inversion when cold air lies next to the ground and warm air settles above. These conditions can be found over a cold lake during a warm summer evening, across a cool ocean surface in the subtropics, or over a cold Arctic landscape in winter. The mock-mirage green flash must be viewed from an elevation above the temperature inversion, a location that may be as low as a few meters above the ground or as high as a mountaintop or aircraft.

In a mock-mirage green flash, the Sun appears distorted and oval shaped with small indentations on its sides as it approaches the horizon (Figure 10-33). As it settles lower, the indentations become more pronounced, until the disk may appear to be composed of a half dozen or more layers stacked one atop the other like a plate of pancakes. The indentations appear to float upward across the disk of the Sun from bottom to top, as the solar disk sinks through the layers of the atmosphere. This type of green flash typically forms in the topmost of the layers while the Sun is still above the horizon. After a few seconds, the green layer will pinch off and disappear, usually before the Sun has fully set.

One of the complications of watching for the green flash is that the color response of the human eye changes while looking at the bright surface of the Sun. The warm light of the low Sun causes a photobleaching of the red-sensitive pigments in the cones of the eye, resulting in a marked reduction in sensitivity to long-wavelength light. This causes yellow shades to appear green, so the visual observer may see a green rim or green flash on the Sun when photographs reveal none. However, the green flash is a real physical phenomenon, not a physiological adaptation of the eye, as proved by every photograph or by the sighting of a green flash at sunrise, when the eye has not had a chance to be dazzled by the solar surface.

Auroral Antics

Aurorae in History and Folklore

As they ventured into ice-laden waters, European explorers became captivated by the spectacle of the aurora, a phenomenon long cherished by northern peoples (Figure 10-35). During his second Arctic expedition, the American explorer Charles Francis Hall (1821–1871) served up this description of the lights (Hall 1879):

> At 10 P.M. I went out, and the aurora was spanning the azure vault. A smart breeze from the north was blowing nearly the whole night. This seemed to add to the briskness of the merry dancers as they crossed the heavens to and fro. An hour before, the sky was clear, not a cloud or an aurora ray to be seen; now, a belt extended across the heavens, arch-like, some 25° above the horizon, its direction being from southeast to northwest. I watched the rising arch. Every few moments gave varied and magnificent changes. At length patches of aurora burst forth here and there. Gradually the main arch reached the zenith, and then was the grand part of the scene. Much of what was before in perpendicular rays shot athwart and across the heavens swiftly like a river of molten gold, here and there forming vast whirlpools, here and there an eddy, here and there a cataract of stupendous fall. When above my head, it seemed less than a pistol-shot distant . . .

FIG. 10-35. *The aurora arc takes on a more dramatic form when seen from below, as in this image taken in northern Norway.*

In more southerly latitudes—across the Canadian Prairies, for instance—a display frequently starts out as a faint green arc, low against the northern horizon, and barely visible alongside the stars. Over the next half hour or so, the arc will increase in brightness and spread upward in the sky. A few shafts of light may shoot toward the zenith, feebly at first, fading away, and then starting up again. This may be the end of it, but if the night is right, the northern half of the sky may explode again in twisting green sheets and ribbons that mark the onset of an "auroral substorm." Within minutes, the entire sky lights up, the zenith-pointing rays become more intense, dissolve into curtained feet, and the sky begins to dance with green flowing ribbons that wander from one horizon to another, pulsing with a two-second frequency. Ephemeral shades of purple, red, orange, and yellow anchor the bottom of each green curtain or sway at the top, occasionally fading away before returning with renewed intensity (Figure 10-36). If the energy in the aurora is particularly high, the sky will fill with swirling green light of sufficient intensity to read a book.

In more southerly locations—over Montana and North and South Dakota, for instance—an active display might fill the sky with red drapery, glowing above greenish veils that lie along the horizon. But the best viewing of all comes farther north, in communities that lie directly beneath the auroral display where the observer looks upward into the aurora and the light swirls and twists in green hanging curtains caught in some gigantic electrical breeze. Aurorae (or auroras) are creatures of middle and polar latitudes, as evinced by their popular names: "northern lights" for the aurora borealis and "southern lights" for aurora australis.

In the eastern Arctic, aurorae are known as "*aqsarniit*," or "football players" to the Inuit. Inuit legend characterizes the Northern Lights as a game of football played by the spirits of the dead using a walrus skull for a ball. The back-and-forth motion of the lights mimics the to-and-fro of the game. Tradition holds that whistling would bring the aurora closer, but also that it was a dangerous practice, for the whistler could be caught up and carried into the sky if the curtains dropped too low.

An aurora is created when electrons and protons flowing from the Sun are collected by the Earth's magnetic field and then injected into the atmosphere near the poles, colliding with atoms and molecules of oxygen and nitrogen in the thermosphere. The collisions ionize some molecules and lift electrons in others to a higher-energy, excited state. The glow of the aurora comes from the emission of light when electrons return to the low-energy position or when ionized molecules recapture their lost electrons.

Aurorae are concentrated in higher latitudes in a ring that circumscribes the North and South Geomagnetic Poles. This region of concentrated activity is known as the auroral oval or the auroral zone. In 2020, the North Geomagnetic Pole was located over Canada's Ellesmere Island. In quiet conditions, the auroral oval lies over northern Canada, Alaska, Iceland, northern Scandinavia, and along the Russian north coast in the Northern Hemisphere (Figure 10-37). In the Southern Hemisphere, the oval lies over remote parts of Antarctica and the South Indian Ocean near Australia. During nights of intense activity, the northern auroral zone expands equatorward, bringing displays to the northern United States, the British Isles, and Europe. Subtropical latitudes see aurorae very infrequently, at intervals of years

FIG. 10-36. *Purple shafts of light dance along the northern horizon with heads in the stars and feet embedded in a green auroral landscape in this image from the Canadian Prairies.*

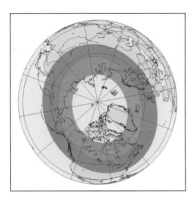

FIG. 10-37. *This figure shows the average position of the auroral oval during low (orange) and high (purple) levels of geomagnetic activity. The red dot over Ellesmere Island shows the 2014 position of the geomagnetic pole. The blue dot is the position of the magnetic pole. The auroral oval is associated with the geomagnetic pole.*

and decades, but the historical record shows appearances as far south as Cuba and into North Africa. Auroral displays are best seen in the hour or two around local midnight and when the Sun is near a maximum in its 11-year cycle, flinging electrons and charged atoms toward the Earth with increased frequency.

The Solar Wind

Space above the Earth's atmosphere is not empty. It is an environment filled with a tenuous gas of positive and negative particles—a plasma—that flows outward from the Sun in a steady "solar wind." About 900,000 tons of material boil off of the Sun every second, flowing away in all directions at supersonic velocities ranging from 120 to 500 miles per second (200 to 800 km/s). Half of the plasma particles are negatively charged electrons; the other half are made of positively charged hydrogen (95 percent) and helium (4 percent) ions with a smattering of heavier atoms.

The electrons and ions in the solar wind capture a part of the Sun's magnetic field as they boil off into space and fill the void between the planets with the interplanetary magnetic field. As this interplanetary magnetic field encounters our own planet's magnetic field, the two engage in a pushing match that compresses our planet's field in the direction of the Sun and stretches a magnetic tail (called the magnetotail) that extends for over 800,000 miles (1 million kilometers) in the anti-sun direction. On the sunward side, the boundary between the two magnetic fields (the magnetopause) lies about 45,000 miles (70,000 km) above the surface. The Earth lies within its magnetic cocoon (the magnetosphere), largely protected from the solar ion bombardment.

Our Sun is an inconstant star with an 11-year cycle in activity that is marked by a similar cycle in the number of sunspots and in the intensity and frequency of magnetic outbursts. More dramatically, the Sun will occasionally erupt with an abrupt and intense release of plasma into space—outbursts related to two mechanisms: solar flares and coronal mass ejections (CME). If either of these is directed toward the Earth, a dramatic increase in auroral activity can be expected in the next day or two when the particles arrive at the magnetopause. A third and more gentle type of particle injection comes from openings in the Sun's magnetic field called "coronal holes."

FIG. 10-38. *A large coronal mass ejection expels a plasma of electrons and protons and an embedded magnetic field into space. This eruption will not affect the Earth, as it is directed to the side and not in the direction of our planet. The spacecraft is equipped with an occulting disk that covers the Sun to a distance of about two solar radii outside its limb (edge) to prevent the bright solar surface from overwhelming the spacecraft sensors.*

Flares are short-lived explosions on the solar surface that release enormous amounts of energy, heating the surrounding atmosphere to tens of millions of degrees and accelerating ions and electrons into space with velocities near the speed of light. Flares tend to be associated with sunspots and are believed to be caused by an abrupt release of magnetic energy that has accumulated on the Sun's surface. Because of their association with sunspots, flares are much more numerous during the peak of the 11-year sunspot cycle.

Coronal mass ejections are much larger but less abrupt and somewhat cooler explosions than flares. A coronal ejection affects a large part of the solar surface and expands outward over a much broader area (Figure 10-38), so it is much more likely to cause an increase in auroral activity. From satellites, CMEs resemble huge bubbles of gas expanding upward and outward at velocities that allow them to reach the Earth one to five days later.

Coronal holes are quiet areas on the Sun over which the magnetic field is open to space. This open magnetic field allows charged particles to readily escape the Sun's surface, making the holes the main source of one component of the solar wind. Storms resulting from a coronal hole tend to begin gradually and bring less intense aurorae; they are most frequent during sunspot minimum.

The Earth's Magnetic Field

When seen from a distance, the Earth's magnetic field (the geomagnetic field) is often compared to that of a bar magnet with a north and south pole and lines of magnetic force that curl between the two of them, forming a pattern much like that produced by a tabletop magnet and some iron filings. This magnetic field is greatly distorted by the solar wind, which compresses the field in the sunward direction and stretches it into the magnetotail in the down-sun direction (Figure 10-39). The geomagnetic poles do not align with the geographical pole, but lie a little more than 11° to the side. A third pole, the magnetic pole, is the location on the surface of the Earth where a modified compass needle would point straight down, following the local magnetic field into the Earth.

The shape of the Earth's magnetic field brings the field lines closest to the planet in the region of the geomagnetic poles. Solar particles trapped in the magnetic field dip deepest into the atmosphere at this point, bringing the high frequency of auroral activity associated with

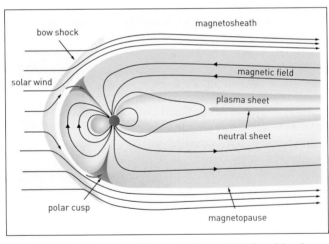

FIG. 10-39. *The Earth's magnetic field is greatly distorted by the flow of the solar wind, compressing the field in the direction of the Sun and stretching it downwind for millions of miles in the anti-sun direction. Arrows show the flow of the solar wind and the direction of the Earth's magnetic field. The red arrows show the flow into the polar cusps, which allows electrons and ionized atoms from the solar wind to reach the upper levels of the atmosphere during stormy conditions. The bow shock is where the solar particles first encounter the planetary magnetic field and begin to decelerate.*

the auroral oval. Regions of the globe that lie near or beneath this oval have the highest frequency of northern and southern lights—in some lucky places, nearly every night.

The solar wind with its embedded magnetic field encounters our planet's magnetic field about 45,000 miles (70,000 km) from the Earth. The two magnetic fields with their associated plasmas are reluctant to mix, so a boundary—the magnetopause—forms between them. All along the magnetopause, the magnetic fields of the Earth and Sun lie in close proximity, but because solar-wind ions and electrons are glued to the interplanetary magnetic field, solar particles are unable to easily pass to the magnetosphere.

Every now and then, through a process known as magnetic reconnection, the two magnetic fields can splice together, allowing particles from the Sun to enter the magnetosphere. The Earth's magnetic field also contains two "cusps" (Figure 10-39), where the magnetic fields emerge from the geomagnetic poles and turn to the north and south. The cusps are weak spots in the Earth's magnetic defenses and allow the interplanetary magnetic field to make an easy connection with the Earth's field, permitting solar electrons and ions to flow readily into the magnetosphere.

Much of the solar plasma that enters the magnetosphere goes into temporary storage in the magnetotail, where it forms a vast sheet of plasma lying between the two lobes of the magnetotail. The plasma sheet is a huge reservoir of charged particles, around one to three Earth diameters in size, lying above the midnight equator at a distance of about 28,000 miles (45,000 km). When the Sun is quiet, the accumulation of charged particles into the plasma sheet is slow and steady. When the Sun is active, the flux increases dramatically as solar storms inject a flood of particles and strong magnetic pressures into the near-Earth environment.

Auroral Storms

Auroral activity comes in bursts, sometimes quite unexpectedly, and at other times, when the Sun has undergone an outburst, very predictably and long-lasting. Short-lived and more localized storms are known as substorms, while their long-lived predictable cousins are called magnetic storms (Figure 10-40). To the observer, a substorm brings a sudden and largely unpredictable increase in the intensity and size of the aurora, turning an otherwise unremarkable night sky into a swirling ballet of greens, reds, and purples.

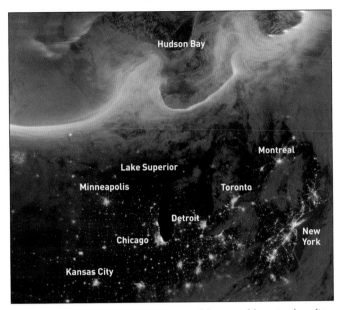

FIG. 10-40. *NASA's* Suomi *polar satellite acquired this view of the aurora borealis on the morning of October 8, 2012. The northern lights visible across northern Canada were caused by a geomagnetic storm that night.*

The release of energetic ions in a substorm occurs when the magnetic containment in the plasma sheet breaks down, allowing a sea of electrons and ions to be injected into the Earth's atmosphere. The sudden release of energy forces ions deep into the atmosphere—a process that has been compared to the snapping of an elastic band or the release of a slingshot.

Long-lasting magnetic storms result from solar flares and coronal mass ejections, which provide both the supply of ions and the necessary magnetic pressures. In the late summer of 1859, the largest solar storm ever recorded (the "Carrington event") sent solar plasma speeding toward the Earth, reaching the planet after a journey of only 18 hours. Auroras were reported as far south as Cuba, Italy, and Hawaii. In 1989, a similar storm caused the collapse of the Quebec power grid in only a few seconds, leaving six million people without power for nine hours. Extreme magnetic storms such as these can degrade spacecraft operations, affect satellite navigation, send large electrical currents down pipelines, and interrupt communications. For these reasons, "space weather" forecasting has become an essential military and public service.

Auroral Colors

When the high-speed solar particles first encounter the molecules in the Earth's atmosphere, typically at an altitude of around 300 miles (500 km), they initiate a torrent of collisions that eventually reach deep into the atmosphere. The collisions may knock an electron completely free of an atom (called ionization) or, if the collision is less energetic, boost its electron into a higher-energy, but still bound, excited state. The initial collisions usually release a large supply of electrons, which then go on to engage in further collisions, ionizing and exciting atoms deeper and deeper into the atmosphere, until their energy is expended. Collisions come to an end at about 40 miles (70 km) altitude, beyond which the energy of the incoming particles is largely exhausted.

An atom in an excited state is unstable. Its high-energy electrons quickly fall back to a lower state, jettisoning the excess energy by emitting a photon of light with a very specific wavelength (color). The transition to a lower energy level (and eventually to the lowest level, called the ground state) may be in one step or in a series of steps, so the excited atom may emit one photon of light or several, each with different colors. When we examine the spectrum of the light that comes from an aurora, we find these emission lines, spread out in lines of varying intensity and color, each one the signature of a particular atomic transition (Figure 10-41).

Oxygen is responsible for two primary auroral colors: the common green color at a wavelength of 558 nanometers (nm) and a less-often-seen deep red at 630 nm. Neutral nitrogen molecules emit at red and blue wavelengths that combine to create purplish red colors along the rippled lower edges of the aurora. Rare, all-red aurorae are caused by solar ions and electrons with relatively low energies that cannot penetrate deeply into the atmosphere. All-green aurorae are created by moderately energetic electrons and ions that penetrate to the 100- to 60-mile (150–100 km) level. Emission from nitrogen atoms also occurs at this level, but the light is emitted in deep blue wavelengths, where the eye is not very sensitive. The most energetic electrons can reach down to 50 miles (80 km), where oxygen and nitrogen molecules are abundant. These molecules emit photons over a large range of wavelengths in the red region of the spectrum.

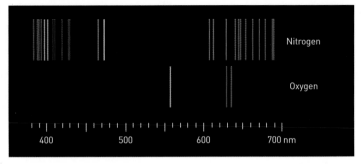

FIG. 10-41. *This schematic diagram of an auroral spectrum shows emission lines of nitrogen and oxygen in the atmosphere.*

How to Find an Aurora

To see the aurora, you have to go to where aurorae are, which usually means as far north or south as 50° to 65°. In the Northern Hemisphere, only eight countries can claim a position beneath the auroral oval. A considerable travel industry has been built up around aurora-watching, with popular northern observing locations in Norway, Finland, Sweden, Canada, Alaska, and Iceland. Because most of these lie north of 60°, summer observing is likely to be unrewarding, as the nights are short and often not completely dark.

Figure 10-37 shows that the auroral oval comes farthest to the south over the middle of North America, reaching as far south as 55° in central Manitoba. The northern road network in Manitoba is very limited, but the oval can be reached by road with a day's travel north of Winnipeg. More popular destinations are at Churchill, Yellowknife, and Whitehorse in Canada and in Fairbanks, Alaska. Churchill cannot be reached by road. In Europe, a large aurora-viewing industry has grown around a half-dozen or more communities in northern Norway, Sweden, and Finland and even Russia. Even if your destination doesn't take you to the oval itself, reliable aurora-viewing can be found in Canadian cities such as Edmonton, Saskatoon, and Winnipeg, especially when the sunspot cycle is close to maximum.

Because the frequency of an aurora display depends on solar activity, expeditions should be selected to fit with the peak of the sunspot cycle, or at least within three years either side of the maximum (expected around 2025). Under the oval, quiet auroral activity is not affected greatly by the state of the sunspot cycle, but the frequency of the most intense auroral displays is reduced during solar minimum.

Weather is also a big factor in making an expedition to the auroral oval, and different locations have favored seasons. Generally speaking, the coldest months have the least nighttime cloud except in coastal locations that are exposed to open water.

Auroral activity tends to peak around local midnight (which means you have to adjust for daylight saving time), but on a very active night, the auroral displays may become visible as the sky darkens and disappear with sunrise. If the night is quiet, don't give up watching until an hour or two after midnight; a substorm can fill an empty sky in less than a minute. NASA maintains a website that predicts the probability of auroral activity and its location—information that is captured and displayed on many other websites. While the space agency's measures of magnetic activity and prediction of auroral activity do not guarantee a good show, they reduce the chances of a wasted night when the sky is quiet. In particular, look for nights when a coronal mass ejection is forecast to reach the Earth or when favorable magnetic alignments make the magnetosphere particularly leaky.

Photographing the Aurora

Without a camera, your first auroral experience is likely to be underwhelming. Quiet auroral nights will usually present you with a faint greenish glow along the northern horizon, or a few wispy tendrils overhead. Cameras, however, can capture the light and will enhance the colors, presenting you with a much improved view of the sky's activity.

Digital cameras make auroral photography downright easy—in fact, it's just about impossible to fail. All that is required is a tripod, a camera, and a dark sky. When an aurora is forecast, go to your favorite dark-sky site, set up the tripod and camera, and take a series of 5- to 15-second exposures with a moderately high ISO setting. It's that simple. The longer exposure will smear out the details of the moving display, while short exposures will capture fine details and colors if the display is bright. Experiment with a number of camera settings, including the ISO and focal ratio, until the view in the camera matches or betters the view to the eye. For more of a treat, take pictures at short intervals—15 seconds will do—and string them together into a movie to display the flow and drama of the auroral display.

Auroras are usually best around the midnight hour when the Sun is on the opposite side of the Earth; sometimes it comes to life for only a few minutes or a part of an hour. If you live well south of the auroral oval, travel northward to greatly improve your odds, and go in the fall or spring when nights are still relatively long and temperatures are pleasant. While our notion of the northern lights is usually associated with snow and ice, they are visible to some extent nearly every night across the northern plains and the Canadian Prairies when the Sun is near its sunspot maximum. On the uncommonly spectacular nights when the skies come alive with light, you might experience the same sense of awe that enchanted Charles Hall (Hall 1879):

> . . . The rays of the aurora were vertical; it appeared all alive, as if in high glee, dancing to and fro with almost the rapidity of lightning. The three belts extending from southeast to northwest were the most interesting, as they often flashed into the brilliant colors of the rainbow. Each belt occasionally resolved itself into two lines or tiers of rays; as one line would dance rapidly to windward, the other would dance as quickly in the opposite direction.

This extraordinary display lasted five minutes—an unusual time. Hall was so impressed with it that he wrote, "If at home it could be witnessed for one moment, one would say, 'I never saw northern lights before.'"

Look Up and Carry a Camera

If you've made it to the end of this chapter by beginning at its start, then you are ready to take the next step: to watch the sky, the clouds, the Sun, and the Moon for the treats that nature provides. Your efforts will probably be casual at first—perhaps a momentary decision to look around and up, searching the sky for signs of color and shadow. After a few successful encounters, perhaps with a halo, a bit of iridescence, evening crepuscular rays, or an unexpected aurora, you may feel a growing compulsion to take a deliberate survey of the sky's vault whenever opportunity presents. You will probably be surprised at the frequency at which you will be rewarded.

There is a private pleasure in finding and interpreting the sky's signs. Where ancient magicians may have invoked gods and demons, you will be able to appreciate the play of light through clouds, water droplets, and ice crystals in nature's great laboratory. You will have your own Merlin moment.

Beams of sunlight radiating from behind a tropical cumulus cloud lend a sense of finality to the late afternoon. The beams, known as crepuscular rays, are shadows cast by clouds or other obstructions between the Sun and the observer and made visible because of dust, humidity, aerosols, or water droplets in the atmosphere. The beams are parallel to each other, but appear to radiate from the Sun because of perspective effects. Under favorable conditions, the crepuscular rays can be followed across the sky, where they converge on the opposite horizon as anti-crepuscular rays.

When the Sun is high, the rainbow lies lower in the sky. If the sun were much higher in this scene, the bow would not be visible to the observer, as it would disappear into the ground level. A low Sun causes the rainbow to adopt a reddish color for the same reason that sunsets are red.

Just about any flight above the clouds will reward down-sun, window-seat passengers with a view of a glory—a circular bull's-eye of colors surrounding the shadow of the plane, though in this image, the shadow is too distant to see. The glory's dimension depends on the size of the water droplets in the clouds.

A sun pillar is very similar to a subsun (see caption page 438), except that the ice crystals forming the reflection are oriented in a quasi-random fashion so that the image of the sun is stretched out vertically. In this image, the sun pillar is formed by crystals floating in the air after a day of blowing snow and near-blizzard conditions.

This is a star that lies just above the horizon, photographed through a telescope. Refraction in the atmosphere has spread the light from the star into a spectral band, from short green wavelengths at the upper left to long red wavelengths on the lower right. The refractive effect of the atmosphere is one of the factors that contribute to the green flash.

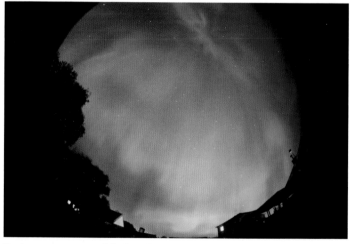

During very active auroral displays, the entire sky may be filled with red and green rays and dancing curtains. Both colors are emitted by atomic oxygen, but the red color comes from higher in the atmosphere—up to 375 miles (600 km)—than the green. This display "turned on" in less than one minute and persisted for 40 minutes before fading away.

Temperature gradients across the surface of a lake are often very good at distorting distant features as the light from a distant shore is refracted by changes in air density above the water surface. This view of distant cumulus clouds is taken across Kenya's Lake Turkana.

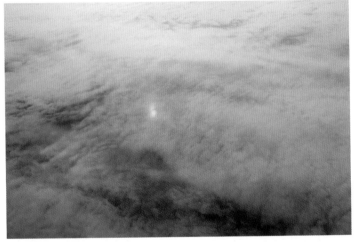

A subsun is a reflection of the Sun produced by flat ice crystals and seen when the observer is above the clouds. The bright reflection is round when most of the ice crystals are aligned in a horizontal plane but becomes elongated as the crystals lose their orientation. When the crystals are completely randomly aligned, the subsun will be stretched into a bright pillar.

It's a bit of a mystery to solve, but iridescence seems to be a common phenomenon in the clouds surrounding a partially eclipsed Sun. This image shows a crescent Sun with two arcs of brilliant colors in thin cumulus clouds.

Crepuscular rays are shadows of clouds cast upon the sky in the direction of the Sun. In the opposite direction, looking away from the Sun, the shadows converge toward the horizon, as in this example. Called anti-crepuscular rays, they are even more distinctive when combined with a rainbow.

This early morning fogbow is similar to a rainbow, but is formed in fog droplets rather than water droplets. Because the droplets in fog are much smaller than raindrops, the colors of the fogbow are smeared out by diffraction, leaving an arc with a white color.

Ice crystals in high-level cirrus clouds form a 22° halo around the Sun and a pair of sundogs, one of which is visible to the right of the halo. At the same time, water droplets in the low-level clouds give a brilliant iridescent tinge to the cloud edges.

This view of the aurora comes from directly below, a consequence of viewing from the high latitudes of northern Norway. The curtainlike structure of the aurora is more apparent from this viewpoint; more southerly observing sites see the curtains from the side unless the sky is particularly active.

CHAPTER 11

THE HISTORICAL FOUNDATIONS
OF METEOROLOGY

Meteorology has ancient roots.

The first forecasts come from the *Enūma Anu Enlil*, a collection of approximately 70 inscribed Babylonian cuneiform tablets containing over 6,000 omens that date from the second millennium BCE. The tablets (Figure 11-1) reveal a rich compendium of astronomical and meteorological portents that probably have their roots in even earlier times, back to the founding Sumerian civilization a thousand years before. The forecasts were based on simple sky signs: the presence of halos around the Sun and Moon, or darkening clouds in the morning, but often as not, an element of astronomy crept into the predictions. Thus, a dark halo around the moon suggested a cloudy or rainy month, which could be a tolerable forecast if applied in the right season.

With the passage of time, cuneiform writing and Babylonian omens were incorporated into cultures across Mesopotamia. Meteorological events and other "signs from the sky" were assimilated into a growing list of divinations, eventually leading to a comprehensive body of predictions that survived to be passed to the Greeks around 400 BCE. Astronomy and meteorology were intimately linked, but most associations were more in the nature of an almanac that linked seasonal climate—winter cold and summer winds—to the rising of stars and constellations.

OPPOSITE, FIG. 11-1. *Mesopotamian scribes recorded political changes, commodity prices, astronomical phenomena, and meteorological events in cuneiform script on clay tablets such as this.*

When Alexander defeated Darius at Gaugamela in 331 BCE, the Greeks became the keepers of the intellectual treasures (and the actual treasures) of Persia, eventually stamping the whole of the ancient world with a culture that valued observation and hypothesis rather than observation and omen. After its founding, the city of Alexandria became the leading intellectual center in the western world, bringing the knowledge of Babylon, Egypt, and Greece into one place, fostering its spread across the Mediterranean basin. The simple weather omens were given a stronger climatological foundation and greatly expanded in scope when the Greeks incorporated them into their own philosophical writings.

Some of the earliest writings on everyday meteorology came from the poet Hesiod around 700 BCE, in a work entitled *Works and Days*. Though mostly concerned with "good advice," the poem also emulates an almanac, relating a selection of important agricultural tasks, such as planting and harvesting, with the rising and setting of the stars according to the seasons, as in the following example:

> *When the Pleiades, daughters of Atlas, are rising, begin your harvest, and your ploughing when they are going to set.*
> *Set your slaves to winnow Demeter's holy grain, when strong Orion first appears, on a smooth threshing-floor in an airy place. (Evelyn-White 1914)*

At the time of the fall of Babylon to Alexander, Aristotle (384–322 BCE) was at his prime, living in Athens, where he had established his own school, known as the Lyceum. He was a prolific writer who, in his few years, laid a foundation for Western and Middle Eastern science that lingered for over a millennium. Aristotle established the study of weather as a scientific discipline in his treatise *Meteorologica,* which contained his thoughts and observations on earth sciences (Figure 11-2). The title of the book is derived from the Greek *meteoros,* meaning "high in the air," and Aristotle applied it to such diverse phenomena as clouds, winds, lightning, hail, and thunder, as you would expect, but also to earthquakes, the Milky Way, comets, and even meteors. In *Meteorologica,* Aristotle proposes a coherent model of the causes of each of the phenomena based on the proportions and mixings of four basic elements—earth, water, air, and fire—and their continual movement. The theories seem contrived and inadequate in the present day, but there are hints of observation and deduction. For instance:

> Both dew and hoar-frost are found when the sky is clear and there is no wind.
> . . . dew is found with south winds and not with north winds
> . . . rain is due to the cooling of a great amount of vapor
> Hail is ice, and water freezes in winter; yet hailstorms occur chiefly in spring and autumn and less often in the late summer, but rarely in winter and then only when the cold is less intense. (Webster 1923)

These are relationships that a modern meteorologist would have no trouble accepting.

We see in Aristotle's hypotheses an attempt to connect observed natural patterns with some sort of physical explanation. Greek science at that time was concerned with hypothesis and observation but not with experimentation. Aristotle was probably overly wedded to his ideas, and invented many contrivances to explain the natural world, but it was not until the maturation of experimental science many centuries later that Aristotle's stranglehold on natural philosophy was loosened. Though we now know that many of his insights were incorrect and even quaint, *Meteorologica* was the first work to treat the study of weather as a comprehensive subject.

After Aristotle, Greek meteorology was largely static, preferring the explanations of the old master rather than new philosophical explorations. Theophrastus, Ptolemy, Geminus, Aratus, and many others proposed extensions of Aristotle's work, but they were largely hampered by a lack of measuring instruments and an unwillingness to leave the library and go out into the real world.

Aristotle's pupil and successor to the Lyceum, Theophrastus of Eresus (372–287 BCE), also wrote widely on a multitude of subjects, some of which were his own and some derived from Aristotle. His extant works include *On Winds* and *On Weather Signs*. The second treatise contains hundreds of proverbs—80 signs of rain, 45 of wind, 50 of storms, and 24 of good weather—but Babylonian roots are still very much in evidence. The whole has a strong fortune-telling flavor about it, though it contains some useful public weather lore driven

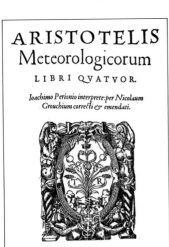

FIG. 11-2. *The frontispiece of a 16th-century translation of Aristotle's* Meteorologica.

by the experiences of farmers and fishermen who had an intimate association with the seasons and the weather. Evidence of such an early profound knowledge of local weather comes from Herodotus's (c. 484 BCE–c. 425 BCE) account of the Battle of Artemisium in 480 BCE:

> And when their fleet was stationed at Chalcis in Euboea and they realized that a storm was rising, or perhaps before this, they sacrificed and summoned Boreas [the north wind] and Oreithyia [the mountain wind] to help them and to destroy the ships of the barbarians . . .

In the ensuing battle, the already storm-ravaged Persian fleet was checked by a clever set of tactics by the Greeks, who used the offshore mountain wind to maneuver around the enemy's fleet.

The Followers of Aristotle

Just as Babylonian sciences survived and expanded under Assyrian, Akkadian, Persian, and Greek conquerors, so too did Greek knowledge diffuse across Europe and North Africa during the Roman Empire. Alexandria, with its magnificent libraries, made knowledge accessible, even into China. Science in Rome had a distinctly practical side—its mainstays were engineering, architecture, medicine, nature, transportation, water, plumbing, map making, astronomy, astrology, and alchemy. Meteorology, important to a seafaring, conquering nation, was especially useful. Greek weather sayings were copied and extended by Roman authors, who borrowed the Greek view of weather and heavens almost word for word. Pliny the Elder (CE 23–79), in his only extant work, *Natural History,* gave an explanation for wind that closely paralleled Aristotle, as his work was compiled from the writings of 472 other authors, two-thirds of them Greek, and so carried the musings of the past into the future.

Meteorology under the Caliphates

After the separation of the Roman Empire into eastern and western parts in the fourth century, the Byzantine Empire became the trustee of Greek and Babylonian art, literature, and philosophy, a role that it played until the fall of Constantinople in 1453. The works of the classical Greek authors were copied and preserved, translated into Syriac, Persian, Armenian, and eventually Arabic. The Ottoman Turks turned out to be receptive to the philosophical works of the ancient Greeks, and as the Muslim caliphates spread outward from their Arabic and Ottoman roots, they carried the works of Aristotle, Ptolemy, and the host of other Greek scholars west along the Mediterranean, eventually into Spain and Sicily.

The expansion of the several caliphates was accompanied by a periodic flourishing of science, technology, trade, and culture that added to the Greek and Mesopotamian bounty as successive Arabic scholars studied, critiqued, and expanded the old works. In general, however, the Arabic scholars were hindered by an overly fond respect for traditional teachings, and made only small adjustments on the philosophies inherited from the Byzantines. There were notable exceptions, especially in mathematics, astronomy, and medicine, but in meteorology, Arabic teachings would have been very familiar to Hesiod and Theophrastus.

Nevertheless, it was Arabic scholars who began to advance the science of meteorology away from the philosophical approach of the Greeks and into the study of the atmosphere.

The Arabic scholar leading this transition was Ibn al-Haytham (965–1035), more widely known as Alhazen, after the Latinized version of his name. Alhazen is considered to be one of the greatest Arabic scholars, an author of over 120 works on optics, number theory, geometry, astronomy, and the natural sciences. The translation of his major work, *Book of Optics*, was widely studied in Medieval Europe and inspired many great scientists that followed his generation, but his major achievement was the introduction of experimentation and testing to the study of nature, a process that evolved into what we call the scientific method. In this spirit, one of Alhazen's contemporaries,

FIG. 11-3. *A portrait of Avicenna taken from a silver vase at the Museum at the the BuAli Sina (Avicenna) Mausoleum in Hamadan, Western Iran.*

Ibn Mu'adh, calculated the depth of the atmosphere using the observation that the twilight glow ended when the setting sun was 19° below the horizon. The calculated height, around 53 miles (86 km), accords well with present-day measurements.

At about the same time, a Persian physician, philosopher, and natural scientist, Avicenna (980–1037), as he was known to European scholars (Figure 11-3), adopted a similar observational approach to science and natural philosophy. His *Encyclopaedia of Philosophy and Natural Sciences* devotes six chapters to meteorology, primarily discussing the mechanisms of clouds and rain, cloud reflections, rainbows, winds, thunder and lightning, and comets and meteors.

The greatest contribution of Arabic scholars to the study of meteorology and science in general was in the process rather than in discovery. While Babylonians had been content with determining patterns and omens, and while Greeks eschewed observation in favor of clever philosophy, Arabic scholars developed a focus on measurement and experimentation. The Islamic world put greater value on a link between theory and practice than had been accepted in classical Greece.

The development of measurement and instrumentation in Arabic hands and its adoption by European academics led to the great advances in meteorological sciences that began at the end of the Middle Ages. It was fortunate that after the tenth century, the center of Islamic science moved west into Spain and Sicily, where it became more accessible to Latin Europe. The mix of Muslims, Christians, and Jews in Moorish Spain, where religious tensions were relaxed for several centuries, fostered the translation of classical works from Arabic to Latin. The flowering of Iberian science was supported by capable scholars from the region, in particular Averroes (1126–1198), the last and perhaps greatest of the expositors of Islamic natural philosophy.

Instrument and Experiment

The Barometer

The invention of the barometer and the acknowledgment that air had weight began with experiments designed to study the vacuum. Giovanni Battista Baliani (1582–1666), a member of the Supreme Council of Genoa, wrote to Galileo Galilei (1564–1642) in 1630 describing the failure of a siphon constructed to bring water to the city. When the siphon was filled with water and one end opened, it was unable to lift water over the summit of a small hill. Galileo replied that he had discovered long before that a siphon could not lift water beyond 20 braccia (45 ft/14 m, but later corrected to 18 braccia). He ascribed this limit to resistance to the void (or vacuum, as we now call it). Galileo maintained that it was the vacuum that was responsible, and that at a certain height, the weight of water became too much for the vacuum to support. In spite of Galileo's reassurances, Baliani, who was a pretty good physicist himself, seems to have recognized the true implications of the 18-braccia limit—that it was related to the weight of air, not to properties of a vacuum.

In the small scientific world of fifteenth-century Italy, news of the experiments with pumps and vacuums quickly reached Evangelista Torricelli (1608–1647). The observations prompted Torricelli (Figure

FIG. 11-4. *Evangelista Torricelli from the frontispiece to* Lezioni accademiche d'Evangelista Torricelli . . . , *published in 1715.*

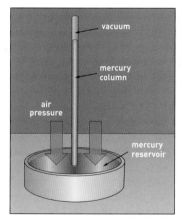

FIG. 11-5. *Berti's barometer. The weight (pressure) of air pressing on the reservoir elevates the column of mercury to the height at which the column's weight is equal to the air pressure.*

11-4), who had succeeded Galileo as Philosopher and Mathematician to the Grand Duke of Tuscany, to conduct the experiment with the heaviest liquid he could obtain—quicksilver, now called mercury. His letter to his friend Michelangelo Ricci (Middleton 1963), on June 11, 1644, explains the results:

> We have made many glass vessels . . . with tubes two cubits long. These were filled with mercury, the open end was closed with the finger, and the tubes were then inverted in a vessel where there was mercury . . . We saw that an empty space was formed and that nothing happened in the vessel where this space was formed . . . I claim that the force which keeps the mercury from falling is external and that the force comes from outside the tube. On the surface of the mercury which is in the bowl rests the weight of a column of fifty miles of air. Is it a surprise that into the vessel, in which the mercury has no inclination and no repugnance, not even the slightest, to being there, it should enter and should rise in a column high enough to make equilibrium with the weight of the external air which forces it up?

In this letter, he described how he had made several glass bowls and for each, a tube about three feet long, open on one end. When the tubes were filled with mercury, closed with a finger on the open end, and inverted into a reservoir of mercury in the bowl, an empty space formed on the closed end of the tube as the mercury drained partly into the bowl (Figure 11-5). Torricelli claimed that an external force stopped the mercury from draining completely into the bowl—a force he attributed to the weight of 50 miles of air above the vessel.

For these experiments, and for the conclusions that he describes, Torricelli is recognized as the inventor of the barometer. In this simple paragraph, we see the complete overthrow of Aristotelian philosophy. In it, Torricelli demonstrates the use of experimentation, hypothesis, and the publication of results—all characteristics of the modern scientific method outlined by Alhazen (and he uses Ibn Mu'adhs estimate of the depth of the atmosphere).

Torricelli also realized that the instrument he had constructed might provide more insights into nature. In the same letter he notes that the instrument that he had constructed to demonstrate the weight of air could also be used to show changes in the pressure of air as it varied in time.

> *I have already hinted to you that a philosophical experiment was being performed concerning the vacuum, not simply to produce a vacuum, but to make an instrument that might show changes in the air, which is now heavier and coarser, and now, lighter and more subtle.*

In this experiment, Torricelli launched meteorology as a modern science.

Barometers were suddenly all the rage among the scientific *cognoscenti,* and several curious experimenters took up the instrument. Among them were the father-and-son pair of Etienne and Blaise Pascal (Figure 11-6), who heard of Torricelli's work and decided to duplicate it. Aided by engineer Pierre Petit, the trio constructed a mercury barometer and, to their surprise and pleasure, reproduced Torricelli's measurements. They repeated their experiment in a series of spectacular public displays in early 1647, using water, wine, and combinations with mercury to show the creation of a vacuum.

Blaise Pascal carried out further experiments throughout 1647, using tubes of various shapes, syringes, bellows, various liquids, and even inserting and then withdrawing rope from the tube. About the summer of 1647, he began to suspect that it was an external force that limited the height of the liquids in the tube, an insight reinforced when he was informed of Torricelli's hypothesis concerning the role played by the weight of the atmosphere.

Toward the end of 1647, Pascal realized that if the weight of the overlying air was the source of the force supporting the liquid, then it should decline as a barometer was carried up a mountain. He wrote to his brother-in-law, Florin Périer, who lived in Clermont-Ferrand near Puy-de-Dôme (a dormant volcano in central France, Figure 11-7),

FIG. 11-6. *Blaise Pascal.*

FIG. 11-7. *Puy-de-Dôme, Auvergne, France.*

asking him to carry a barometer up the mountain and take measurements along the way. Périer was more than willing and assembled a collection of local notables and compatriots to make the trek to the top. In the opening sentence of his report to Pascal (Pascal 1648), he captured some of the initial excitement of the expedition:

> *The weather last Saturday, the 19th, around 5 o'clock in the morning, was changeable, nonetheless, the summit of Puy de Dôme was visible and so I resolved to go there for the adventure.*

What an adventure it must have been, too, as a crowd of local dignitaries and clergymen pressed to join the expedition and climbed with Périer that morning.

Before departing, Périer poured a quantity of mercury into two glass vessels and inserted glass tubes, sealed at one end, upright into each vessel, constructing a barometer in the manner described by Torricelli (Figure 11-5). The mercury levels in the barometric tubes were measured several times, overseen by the assembled company, and a baseline pressure level of "24 inches and 3½ lines" was established. The assembly of citizen scientists then began the climb to the summit, leaving one barometer behind to keep account of any changes in the pressure at the base of the mountain.

On reaching the summit, a height of 3,000 feet (915 m), Périer and his entourage remeasured the height of the mercury column, finding, to their delight, that the pressure had declined to "23 inches and 2 lines." After descending, they found that their barometer again agreed with the instrument left behind. Florin Périer was so entranced by the result that he repeated the experiment the following day, this time climbing to the top of the cathedral in Clermont, where he detected a smaller but definite drop in pressure.

When news of the experiment reached Pascal, then in Paris, he immediately arranged to make similar observations on the top of a high house and in the belfry of a church, Tour Saint-Jacques. He was so pleased with the results that he proposed the application of the barometer for measuring the relative height of places on the Earth. For Pascal's persistence in deciphering the mechanism of the barometer, the Système International unit of pressure is named after him: the pascal (Pa).

Further identification of the role of air pressure came from a clever experiment derived by Adrien Auzout (1622–1691), a French instrument maker, who placed a second barometer within a first. This "vacuum within a vacuum" demonstrated that mercury was suspended by air pressure and not the presence of the vacuum.

For about two decades, the mercury "siphon" remained a toy of amateur and professional scientists, though there were gradual evolutions in design. Scientific advances moved to England where Robert Boyle (1627–1691), who coined the name "barometer," conducted experiments that confirmed the role of atmospheric pressure by placing a barometer inside a closed container that was then evacuated with a pump; the experiment caused the mercury column to fall to a height of one inch. Boyle set up a barometer in his bedroom, where he could watch it from day to day. Over a period of five weeks, the barometer varied over a distance of two inches, rising in cold weather and falling in warm. The cause of the changes was a mystery to him, though he speculated about the role of the Moon and tides.

With his assistant, the also-famous English inventor Robert Hooke (1635–1703), Boyle designed a more portable U-shaped barometer. Hooke then built a wheel barometer, in which a lever arrangement moved a pointer on a dial, making it more convenient to read. Instrument makers seized on the design and began to offer dial "banjo" barometers as weather instruments for private homes in the 1670s. These became popular status symbols, encased in ornate cabinets for public show. Glass tubes took on many different shapes and were often combined with leather, iron, or wood cisterns. In the late 1690s, Dutch

FIG. 11-8. *Replica of a seventeenth-century Dutch alcohol-over-mercury barometer.*

designers invented an inverted barometer in which the mercury was at the top of one arm of a U-shaped glass tube (Figure 11-8). Sometimes the mercury in the column was combined with alcohol or other colored liquids to magnify the changes in level for more sensitive measurements. Over time, the barometer evolved to a sophisticated precision instrument with vernier scales and temperature corrections (Figure 11-9), but in recent decades, the task of measuring pressure has been given over to electronic sensors.

Mercury is a fussy liquid, requiring great care in its handling, as its weight can easily break the glass column. Around 1700, the mathematician Gottfried Wilhelm Leibniz (1646–1716) proposed an instrument that relied on changes of shape of a sealed bellows, but it was not until 1843 that such a barometer, called an aneroid, was built by the French scientist Lucien Vidie (1805–1866). Replacing mercury made the barometer into a very portable, inexpensive, and stable instrument, so that today an aneroid barometer can be found hanging in many homes.

The impetus for the use of a barometer for weather forecasting came as a result of the efforts of Robert Fitzroy during the mid-1800s. Fitzroy is best known as the commander of the *HMS Beagle,* the ship that carried Charles Darwin on his five-year voyage of discovery. In 1854, Fitzroy was appointed to head a department tasked with arranging the collection of weather data gathered at sea. Captains of ships were charged with providing the information, using instruments loaned for the purpose. He arranged that barometers be mounted at every port to warn of impending storms. A disastrous storm in 1859 inspired him to develop charts that he called "forecasting the weather" and later to write *The Weather Book* in 1863.

The Weather Book, while composed at an early time in our modern understanding of the weather, contains observations that are not out of place in the present day. We learn, for instance, that a rising barometer with a north wind presages drier (or less wet) weather, cooler temperatures, and a decline in the wind, circumstances that describe the approach of a high-pressure system behind a cold front. Fitzroy instigated the establishment of 15 weather stations spread around the English coast, each providing readings to him by telegraph at fixed times. Weather forecasts, published daily in *The Times,* were compiled beginning in 1860, and the following year, storm-warning signals were introduced at English ports. More than any other individual, it was Fitzroy who pushed the esoteric science of meteorology into daily forecasting.

Fancy instruments that measured barometric pressure were prized possessions of the moneyed classes, but a simple version known as a "weather glass" or "storm glass" became popular in the late eighteenth century. This device is a small glass container with a narrow spout,

LEFT, FIG. 11-9. *A modern mercury barometer.*
RIGHT, FIG. 11-10. *A weather glass. Lower external pressure causes the colored water to rise in the spout; higher pressure reverses the flow. The level stabilizes when the internal pressure is equal to that of the atmosphere. The tray beneath the glass catches overflow drops when the pressure is very low and the spout fills.*

looking much like a teapot, and half filled with water (Figure 11-10). The lower part of the spout joins the container below the water level. When air pressure drops, water is drawn up into the spout; when pressure rises, the liquid is forced back into the bottle. For this device, the reference pressure is that inside the bottle when it was first filled. Because the internal pressure is not a vacuum, the rise and fall in the spout is muted, and only a short tube is required to contain the water through its range of motion.

The Thermometer

The thermometer is an orphan or, at least, of uncertain parentage. While discussions of hotness and coldness were common in classical texts, there are no records of devices from that era that indicate the construction of temperature-measuring instruments. It was well

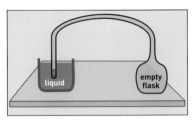

FIG. 11-11. *A schematic diagram of Philon's thermometer.*

within Greek technology, for both Philon (Philo) of Byzantium (c. 280–c. 220 BCE) and Heron (Hero) of Alexandria (c. CE 8–70) built wondrous mechanical devices, a few of which relied on the expansion of air, when heated, to force water along conduits and operate various mechanisms. Philon described a device in which a tube projecting from a hollow bulb is inserted into water; when the bulb is warmed, air is expelled from the bulb to form bubbles in the water; when allowed to cool, water is drawn up into the tube (Figure 11-11). Not only is this device very close to a modern thermometer, needing only a temperature scale to make it useful, but it is also the basis for a weatherglass barometer. Philon's experiment was likely incorporated into Hero of Alexandria's *Pneumatica,* from whence it made its way to Renaissance Europe through Arabic translation.

Galileo (Figure 11-12) claimed for himself the invention of the thermometer. His claim is controversial, as the question of inventor is laden with the politics of science and nationality. Galileo was familiar with *Pneumatica* and the classical experiments by 1594, and may have used an elementary form of thermoscope in his lectures at the University of Padua. His device was built following the description provided by Heron—a glass bulb with a long tail that extended into a reservoir of water. As the temperature varied, water rose and fell in proportion to the expansion and contraction of the air in the bulb. Support for Galileo comes from a number of sources, but primarily from his friend, the Venetian mathematician Giovanni Francesco Sagredo (1571–1620), who wrote in early 1613:

> *The instrument for measuring heat, which you invented, I have made in several convenient styles, so that the difference in temperature between one place and another can be determined up to 100 degrees. (Bolton 1900)*

This would place the manufacture of a true thermometer in the hands of Galileo in the early 1600s and perhaps in the late 1500s. Galileo himself cites "degrees" in descriptions of his own measurements, and we can only conclude that right from the start, the thermoscope was equipped with a scale and used for temperature measurements in Renaissance Italy. In the end, knowledge of the construction of the thermoscope was so widespread that it likely had many parents. Even credit for the first to place a scale upon the instrument is uncertain and probably of no great importance, since it is hard to image that a scientific investigator would not place reference marks upon the glass to show the magnitude of change right from the start.

The thermoscope is open to the air, and so responds to pressure as well as temperature changes—in effect, it was as much a barometer as a temperature-measuring device. To separate the two effects, the thermoscope has to be isolated from the environment. The first of these "closed instruments" to be designed, though probably not for that reason, was again by Galileo, and this time he has undisputed

FIG. 11-12. *Galileo Galilei by the sculptor Aristodemo Costoli, outside of the Uffizi Gallery in Florence, Italy.*

priority. The Galileo thermometer consists of a sealed glass cylinder containing a clear liquid and a series of submersed, labeled, glass balls whose densities are such that they rise or fall as the temperature and density of the surrounding liquid changes. The glass balls must be carefully adjusted so that they each begin to float at a particular temperature; the instrument is read by noting the highest value on the label of the floating spheres. It is not a very sensitive measuring device, but it is immune from atmospheric pressure within its glassy confines. Galilean thermometers are popular today as intriguing decorations (Figure 11-13).

The first modern-style thermometers were crafted at the Accademia del Cimento, an academic society established by Prince Leopold and Grand Duke Ferdinando II de' Medici (1610–1670) to conduct

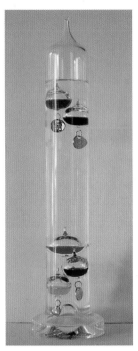

FIG. 11-13. *Galileo thermometer. The glass balls, each of which carries a temperature label, rise and fall according to the temperature (and density) of the fluid. The glass cylinder is sealed so that it does not respond to atmospheric pressure, which would also make the floating balls rise and fall.*

scientific investigations according to Galileo's methods. The Accademia engaged in extensive research into thermometer design, and its members became highly skilled in the manufacture of thermometers of reproducible dimensions (though with many different scales). These thermometers were graduated into 50, 100, or 300 degrees according to their size and used distilled, colored wine as the thermometric fluid. The instruments were roughly calibrated by the heat of the Sun and the cold of ice water, and every degree was marked on the tube by an enamel point. The craftsmanship in the smaller of the Florentine thermometers produced at the Accademia was exceptional, with measurements from different instruments providing remarkably uniform readings. Such characteristics made them popular, and the instruments were exported across Europe.

In the 1600s, nearly every manufacturer's thermometer was unique, even though attempts were made to control the industrial process and calibrate the final product. The lower calibration point was usually the temperature of an ice-water mix, as in the Florentine thermometers. The upper reference point, if used at all, varied according to the manufacturer and could include body temperature, the melting point of butter, or the temperature of a hot summer day. Scales were largely arbitrary and often inverted, with the freezing point at the top. In 1665, Christiaan Huygens (1629–1695), a Dutch mathematician and astronomer, suggested the use of the freezing and boiling points of water as standards, and in 1694, Carlo Renaldini, a member of the Accademia del Cimento, suggested using the same points as international standards. In October 1663, members of the Royal Society of London agreed to use one of the thermometers made by Robert Hooke as a standard, so that the readings of others could be adjusted to it.

Thermometers need a scale, and for this there were dozens of candidates—more than 35 measurement systems had been devised by the early 1700s. Many famous scientists got involved, but the system that caught on was that devised by Gabriel Daniel Fahrenheit (1686–1736).

Fahrenheit learned the art of making thermometers in 1708 and proceeded to develop his techniques and skills, eventually earning a reputation as one of the best thermometer manufacturers in Europe. Fahrenheit modified previous scales, increasing the number of divisions between freezing and boiling from 52 to 180 (from 32°F to 212°F). He described his calibration technique for thermometers that are used for observing weather in a 1724 paper in *Philosophical Transactions of the Royal Society* (Fahrenheit, 1724):

> *The division of the scale is based on three fixed points, which can be determined in the following manner: The first is placed at the lowest part of the beginning of the scale and is attained with a mixture of ice, water, and [sea salt]; if the thermometer is placed in this mixture, its fluid descends to a point that is marked zero. . . . The second fixed point is obtained if water and ice are mixed together without the above-mentioned salts. If the thermometer is placed in this mixture its fluid takes up the thirty-second degree, which I call the point of the beginning of congelation . . . The third fixed point is found at the ninety-sixth degree; and the spirit [or mercury] expands to this degree when the thermometer is held in the mouth, or under the armpit . . .*

Fahrenheit's other innovation, after 1717, was to use mercury as the thermometric fluid. The change provided several advantages: the bore of the thermometer stayed clean; the instrument could be used over a wide range of temperatures from the freezing point to the melting point of mercury; it responded quickly to temperature changes, as it was a metal; it was easily seen inside the bore; and the instrument was more portable. Other inventors had tried and abandoned mercury, because its expansion was so small that values were difficult to read, but Fahrenheit solved the problem by constructing instruments with a very narrow and even bore that magnified the rise of the column. Mercury thermometers are not at all useful for measuring very low temperatures, for the metal turns to a solid at –37.9°F (–38.8°C), so alcohol

thermometers (Figure 11-14) are substituted beginning at about –35°. In recent years, mercury thermometers have disappeared from public view, in part because of the toxicity of mercury and partly because of the development of more sensitive electronic temperature sensors.

Anders Celsius (1701–1744), a Swedish astronomer, did not invent the namesake temperature scale that is so ubiquitous in the world today and was not the first to propose that there be 100° between boiling and melting. Celsius's scale had zero at the boiling point and 100 for the melting point—upside down from the namesake Celsius scale we use today. His reputation instead rests on the careful experiments made to define the melting and boiling points of water to calibrate thermometers of his construction. In 1948, the centigrade degree was officially renamed "degrees Celsius" in recognition of those efforts to standardize the temperature scale. In the modern era, the calibration points have been modified to absolute zero (–459.67°F/–273.16°C) and the temperature of the triple point of water (where ice, water, and vapor co-exist, but essentially the melting point of ice). Under these new definitions, the melting point is 0.01°C (32.02°F) and the boiling point (at 1 atmosphere pressure) is 99.98°C (211.97°F).

For scientific calculations, an absolute temperature scale is needed rather than one based on arbitrary melting and freezing points as in the Celsius and Fahrenheit schemes. The solution was the Kelvin temperature scale, in which the zero point is set at absolute zero, where all molecular motion stops, and the triple point of water, designated as 273.16 K. This makes a kelvin the same size as a degree Celsius.

Measuring Humidity

Invention of a device to measure moisture in the air had to wait until the fifteenth century, and its origins lie in the marketplace rather than with scholars. This first hygrometer (as humidity-measuring instruments are called) was designed by Cardinal Nicholas de Cusa (1401–

1464) to resolve arguments between buyers and sellers of wool. Wool's weight (and price) changed with variations of humidity, increasing on humid days and declining on dry ones. The Cardinal's measuring instrument was the epitome of simplicity (Cajori 1899):

> *If you suspend from one side of a large balance a large quantity of wool, and from the other side stones so that they weigh equally in dry air, then you will see that when the air inclines toward dampness, the weight of the wool increases, and when the air tends to dryness, it decreases.*

After reading of de Cusa's observation, Leonardo da Vinci (1452–1519) redesigned the balance hygrometer using cotton as an absorber and noting that it could be used "to show when the weather is breaking." There was little interest in the device for another half-century.

Santorio Santorio, Galileo's friend and a physician with an analytical approach to medicine, seems to have employed the first practical hygrometer. Santorio built and used several hygrometers to determine optimum levels of humidity for healthy and unhealthy patients. One of these instruments consisted of a cord supporting a small weight that was suspended horizontally on a wall (Figure 11-15), a design later refined and made into handsome instruments by Francesco Folli (1624–1685) and others. As the length of the string changed in response to varying humidity, the weight's rise and fall could be measured against a scale attached to the wall. Santorio also experimented with a coiled string connected to a scale and with hygroscopic (water-absorbing) salts whose weight would change with humidity.

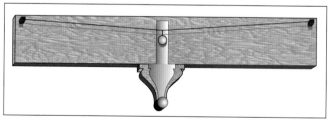

FIG. 11-15. *A schematic of one of the hygrometers constructed by Francesco Folli after a design by Santorio. The weight on the cord rises and falls according to the stretch in the string hanging between the posts; the stretch varies according to the humidity of the air.*

Shortly thereafter, the condensation hygrometer was invented by the Grand Duke Ferdinando II de' Medici and constructed by the artisans at the Accademia del Cimento. The instrument consisted of a pointed glass filled with snow or ice that was suspended over a small collection vial. Water droplets condensed on the surface of the ice-cooled glass and dripped into the collector. The amount of water gathered over a certain time was a measure of the humidity in the air.

In 1783, Horace-Bénédict de Saussure built the first hygrometer utilizing a human hair to measure humidity. Properly treated hair—one from which the oils are carefully removed—will change length by about 2 percent across a humidity change from 1 percent to 100 percent, with increasing humidity causing the hair to lengthen. In de Saussure's instrument, the hair was wound around a worm screw that allowed the tension to be adjusted. Hair hygrometers are most suited for environments that do not experience very low humidities. Response is relatively rapid, taking only a few minutes to respond to a sudden change in the air's moisture content. Hair hygrometers for household use are still sold today, though most national weather organizations ceased using them in the 1970s (Figure 11-16).

Humidity measurements came of age with the development of the psychrometer (from the Greek *psykhros* for "cold") by James Hutton (1726–1797) in the late 1700s. A psychrometer consists of two thermometers mounted side-by-side—a "dry-bulb" thermometer that measures conventional temperature and a "wet-bulb" thermometer that has its bulb encased in a muslin sleeve that is kept moist with distilled water (Figure 11-17). When the instruments are exposed to the atmosphere, usually in moving air of some sort, the dry-bulb thermometer indicates the normal "sensible" air temperature, while the wet-bulb shows a lower reading because of evaporation from the muslin sleeve (unless the air is saturated). The rate of evaporation and thus the difference in temperatures measured between the two thermometers is a reliable function of relative humidity.

FIG. 11-16. *A hygro-thermograph, used to measure and record humidity and temperature. Humidity is measured by the change in length of 12 strands of horsehair, seen here in their mounting within the right-hand opening.*

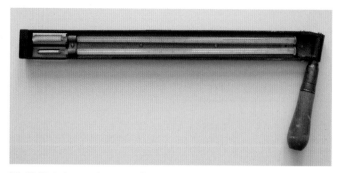

FIG. 11-17. *A sling psychrometer. The muslin sleeve on the top thermometer is moistened with distilled water and the whole instrument is swung around the handle to evaporate water from the sleeve. Evaporation cools the thermometer, and the difference in temperature between the dry-bulb thermometer and the wet-bulb thermometer can be used to calculate atmospheric humidity.*

These and other types of psychrometer were used by various national weather services up to the 1970s.

Another technique for determining humidity was to measure the dewpoint directly by cooling a surface until water began to condense on it. The instrument was first devised by English chemist John Frederic Daniell (1790–1845) in 1820 and improved by French chemist and physicist Henri Victor Regnault (1810–1878) in 1845. Regnault's device used the evaporation of ether as a cooling mechanism and a silver-coated thermometer on which the deposition of water vapor could be easily seen as a slight mistiness in the reflection.

Most modern weather observations rely on electronic sensors that do not require a human presence. For humidity, the most common sensor is the dew cell, in which a wire heater is wound over a wick containing a hygroscopic salt, lithium chloride. As the salt absorbs moisture, it becomes conductive. The heater is used to warm the salt, driving out the moisture until it no longer conducts electricity; the temperature at which this occurs is a measure of the moisture content of the air.

At a standard weather instrument site, thermometers and dew cells are housed in a ventilated white box known as a Stevenson screen (Figure 11-18). The Stevenson screen shields the instruments from solar radiation as "official" temperatures must be taken in the shade. The housing is typically ventilated by a fan so that the instruments within are in intimate contact with the surrounding atmosphere. For

FIG. 11-18. *A Stevenson screen. The louvered white box is topped by an intake vent through which environmental air is pulled into the enclosure by a fan to ventilate the thermometers. A ground-level anemometer can be seen in the background just above the screen.*

the most accurate readings, the Stevenson screen and any other instruments are placed in an open setting; in North America, the nearest obstruction should be at a distance of at least 10 times the height of the wind sensor (usually about 32 feet or 10 m).

Measuring Wind

In a quiet park near the center of Athens is a tall octagonal tower of uncertain age (Figure 11-19). Its construction is attributed to Andronicus of Cyrrhus in 50 BCE, but it may be much older, perhaps dating to 200 BCE. The eight sides contain carvings of the wind gods: Boreas (N), Kaikias (NE), Eurus (E), Apeliotes (SE), Notus (S), Livas (SW), Zephyrus (W), and Skiron (NW), and on the top there once stood a wind vane that pointed in the direction of the wind. Winds and weather were of critical importance to the nautical Greeks, but there is scant evidence of an attempt to measure wind speeds with some kind of anemometer (from *anemos,* meaning "wind"). Wind direction was another matter, and the basis of much weather lore, as the waters surrounding Greece have predictable winds at certain seasons—changes that often found their way into local proverbs and onto municipal walls.

The first mechanical anemometer is credited to Leon Battista Alberti in 1450. His device was the model of simplicity—a flat disk hung on a pivot, mounted on a weather vane, and set against a scale, so that the angle of inclination of the disk gave a measure of speed (Figure 11-20). His little anemometer was designed for use by sailors, so Alberti suggested calibrating the device using the distance that a boat could go in a certain interval while the board kept a certain angle.

As the design was fairly obvious, several others reinvented similar wind-measuring devices, among them Leonardo da Vinci in the 1400s and Robert Hooke, the English inventor and architect, nearly 200 years afterward.

Credit for the first cup anemometer—a design in widespread use today—goes to John Thomas Romney Robinson of Armagh Observatory in Northern Ireland. Robinson's anemometer (Figure 11-21), invented in 1846, consisted of four cups, each mounted on the end of a horizontal arm; the arms in turn were mounted on a vertical shaft. Airflow turned the cups in a manner that was proportional to the wind speed, and the speed could

FIG. 11-19. *Tower of the Winds in Athens.*

be determined by counting the number of revolutions in a fixed time interval. Robinson's design was not particularly efficient, turning at about one-third of the actual wind speed. Design improvements, by John Patterson in Canada in 1926 and by M. J. Brevoort and U. T. Joiner in the United States in 1935, greatly improved the response

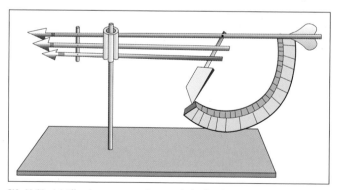

FIG. 11-20. *An Alberti anemometer. In a wind, the flat plate was deflected around its pivot on the upper arrow to give a reading on the scale at the right. The arrows pivoted to face into the wind.*

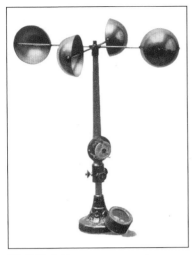

FIG. 11-21. *Robinson cup anemometer.*

of the cups, so that present-day anemometers capture 97 percent of the wind flow. Cup anemometers must be mounted with a companion weather vane in order to indicate wind direction.

Across the United States, present-day weather stations use propeller or windmill anemometers, a device that resembles a small airplane on the top of a tower. In this design, the wind turns a small propeller mounted on a rotating swivel. Propeller anemometers have the advantage of being able to measure both wind speed and wind direction with the same device.

To reduce the effect of the surface on the wind, the anemometer is typically placed on a pole 32 feet (10 m) above the ground (Figure 11-22).

Measuring Precipitation, Sunshine, and Clouds

In addition to the four major weather elements (pressure, temperature, wind, humidity), there are two more that are important in characterizing the climate of an area. Precipitation is especially important and is also very easy to measure—all that is required is a container to catch the rain or a ruler to measure snow depth. The earliest records of systematic rainfall measurement are found from ancient Greece around 500 BCE, from India about 100 years later, and from Jewish records from the Palestine region about 200 BCE. The standard rain gauge used in most modern weather services was developed in the early 1800s.

The tipping-bucket rain gauge, first developed by Christopher Wren in 1662 (though it was already known from much earlier times), funnels the rainfall into a small bucket mounted on a device similar to a teeter-totter. When the bucket is full (typically, around 0.01 inch or 0.2 mm), it tips over, spilling the contents into a larger collector and triggering a counting device. Tipping-bucket gauges are particularly useful, as they record rainfall rate as well as amount.

Recording precipitation in winter is more challenging than collecting rainfall in summer. Snow can blow over a rain gauge or stick in the collection mechanism, making the gauge susceptible to underreporting total amounts. In Canada, snow and other icy forms of precipitation are collected in a container of antifreeze and the amount of water is determined by weighing. The gauge is usually surrounded by a wind screen (Figure 11-23) to increase the capture efficiency. In remote terrain with large snow depths, water content is estimated using snow pillows. These are large, flat, partially inflated bags with a pressure sensor that responds to the weight of an overlying snow pack. And though it's not particularly accurate, precipitation rate and accumulation can also be measured crudely by radar.

FIG. 11-22. *A wind mast with an anemometer.*

Sunshine recorders measure the duration (not the intensity) of bright sunlight. Generally they are of two types: those that mark a track along some sensitive surface, or those that utilize photosensors. The simplest is the Campbell-Stokes sunshine recorder, invented in 1853, which consists of a glass globe that focuses the light of the Sun onto a paper chart, where it burns a track (Figure 11-24). The time scale on the track need only be measured with a ruler to determine the number of hours of sunshine for the day.

FIG. 11-23. *A snow gauge with a Nipher shield to help collect snow and prevent it from blowing across and out of the collection funnel.*

Clouds are a beautiful but perplexing part of the sky, and

FIG. 11-24. *A two-sided Campbell-Stokes sunshine recorder designed for high latitudes where the summer Sun shines through a 24-hour day.*

FIG. 11-25. *Clouds come in an infinite number of forms, but the classification system, based on shape and height, is simple and concise. From top left, clockwise: cirrus; altocumulus wave clouds; cumulonimbus (thunderstorm); altocumulus; altocumulus (lenticular clouds); altocumulus (mackerel sky).*

measuring the amount and type of cloudiness is an equally perplexing process. Certain types acquire distinguishing names—the thundercloud in particular—and can be traced in literature back to the Babylonians and Greeks. Others are, well, just clouds and seem to have escaped a precise nomenclature until 1802, when two natural philosophers turned their attention to defining them. One was the French naturalist Jean-Baptiste Lamarck (1744–1829); the other, Luke Howard (1772–1864), an English Quaker and amateur meteorologist. Lamarck's system never caught on, but that of Howard was more sensible and was quickly adopted. In his *Essay on the Modification of Clouds*, Howard (1804) laid out the main types:

- Cumulus (Latin for "heap"): convex or conical heaps, increasing upward from a horizontal base.
- Stratus (Latin for "layer"): widely extended horizontal sheets.
- Cirrus (Latin for "curl"): flexuous fibers extensible by increase in any or all directions (wispy).

Intermediate categories—stratocumulus, cirrostratus, cumulonimbus—were defined, and the prefix "alto" was added to distinguish mid-level clouds (altocumulus) from the higher cirrus types and lower stratus. Since Howard's time, these cloud names have been refined and additional adjectives attached to the main types to give more exact identities to the formations (Figure 11-25). In spite of these improvements, cloud type identification is often "in the eye of the beholder."

Measurements Aloft

The four fundamental meteorological measurements—pressure, temperature, wind, and humidity—are easily acquired from the surface, but the atmosphere is a three-dimensional entity, and these critical parameters must also be collected above the ground. The traditional method of doing this is to attach everything to a balloon, along with a transmitter, and send it aloft. Aeronautical meteorology began after the Montgolfier brothers demonstrated the first hot-air balloon flight in 1783 (Figure 11-26). After a few tethered practice flights, including one that sent aloft a sheep, a duck, and a rooster to prove that animals could survive the ascent, the Montgolfiers conducted the first free-floating ascent, though the balloon was kept very close to the ground.

FIG. 11-26. *The ornate balloon, similar to that employed by the Montgolfiers, used by Jean-François Pilâtre de Rozier and André Giroud de Villette in an ascent from Paris, October 19, 1783, reaching an altitude of 330 feet.*

At the same time that the Montgolfier brothers were proving their design, Jacques Alexandre César Charles (1746–1823), a member of the French Academy of Science, successfully tested a balloon that used hydrogen gas as the lifting mechanism. His first successful launch, on August 27, 1783, reached an altitude of about a half mile (1 km). A second launch, on December 1 of that year, carried Charles and his assistant along with a thermometer and a barometer. After a quiet voyage of 21 miles (33 km), the assistant left the balloon, and Charles ascended alone:

> When the barometer ceased to fall, I marked exactly
> 18 inches 10 lines (20.01 inches English), the mercury suf-
> fering no sensible oscillation. From this I deduce a height
> of 1524 toises (3,100 yards) or thereabouts, til I can be
> more exact in my calculations. In a few minutes more,
> my fingers were benumbed by the cold . . . I beheld, for a
> few seconds, the circumambient air and the vapors rising
> from the valleys and rivers. The clouds seem to rise from
> the earth and collect one upon the other . . . showed me
> that I was tacking about twice; and I observed certain cur-
> rents that brought me back again. I had several sensible
> deviations, and observed, with surprise, the effects of the
> wind and saw the streamers of my banners point upward
> . . . (Zahm 1911).

No wonder his hands were cold! His thermometer showed that temperatures declined from 15° above freezing at the ground to 12° below freezing at altitude, a bitter temperature for a Parisian. This flight has the distinction of being the first scientific balloon ascent.

Across Europe and North America, scientists, adventurers, and governments began making balloons and ascents to study the upper atmosphere. John Jeffries, an American physician, collected pressure, temperature, and humidity measurements in flights over London during 1784. In 1804, Joseph Louis Gay-Lussac (1778–1850) and Jean-Baptiste Biot (1774–1862) ascended with meteorological instruments to 13,000 feet (4 km); Gay-Lussac made a second ascent to 23,000 feet (7 km) later that year. In the latter half of 1852, John Welsh ascended to heights between 12,000 and 23,000 feet (3.6 to 7 km) in a series of four launches, measuring air temperatures and currents. However, the most adventuresome of the balloonists were James Glaisher (1809–1903) and

Henry Coxwell (1819–1900) in England, who made eight high-altitude flights in 1862 in an open, hot-air balloon equipped with two barometers, five thermometers, two hygrometers, magnets, ozone papers, and an air-sample container. One of these was an impressive ascent to nearly 29,000 feet (8,800 meters), during which Glaisher struggled to make observations of temperature and pressure in spite of periodic blackouts. While he never ventured so high again, Glaisher continued his meteorological flights into 1866, making 28 ascents in all.

American experiments began in 1871, when the pioneering meteorologist Cleveland Abbe (1838–1916) began making flights, and by the following year, over 50 sets of measurements had been collected and analyzed. The first purely scientific ascent for meteorology in America was made on the afternoon of January 15, 1885, from Philadelphia, the first of a series funded by the United States government. Forecasting was in its infancy at that time, and the conditions in the upper atmosphere, particularly the temperature gradients in high- and low-pressure systems, were recognized as critical for accurate predictions.

The modern radiosonde balloon traditionally carries three instruments: an aneroid barometer, a thermometer, and a humidity sensor (Figure 11-27). Winds are determined by tracking the radio signal of the balloon, or by transmission of the balloon's position determined by GPS receivers. Height above ground or sea level is usually determined by solving the hydrostatic equation, as the necessary information to do so is gathered along the way. The first primitive experiments with automated balloons began in 1924, under the auspices of the United States Army Signal Corps. The first modern radiosondes were launched in France in 1929 and in Russia the following year.

FIG. 11-27. *Release of a small helium-filled radiosonde balloon. The instrument package is visible as the small white box beneath the balloon.*

In North America, radiosondes are filled with helium, except in the Arctic regions, where the additional lifting power of hydrogen is needed to overcome the very cold temperatures. The balloons are of various sizes, but larger balloons are capable of reaching altitudes over 100,000 feet (30 km) in an ascent that takes from one to two hours. At maximum altitude, the balloons burst and fall to earth, usually without benefit of a parachute.

Meteorological Networks

Surface and upper-air weather observations at a single point, no matter how sophisticated, have a limited ability to reveal the larger state of the atmosphere. Single-point measurements can reveal the approach and passage of highs and lows, fronts, and storms, but forecasting requires upstream data in order to anticipate the arrival of weather systems. It is not surprising, then, that the development of measuring instruments was followed almost immediately by the establishment of ad hoc networks to decipher the larger state of the atmosphere.

The first observational networks, established in the seventeenth century around London, Paris, and Tuscany, were short-lived, localized, and produced little in the way of insights, but there were widespread sentiments that data should be shared and compared.

The earliest successful impetus for the establishment of meteorological networks came from James Jurin (1684–1750), who in 1723 published an invitation to establish a meteorological network in the *Philosophical Transactions of the Royal Society* of London. Fifteen observers, from India to North America, replied, providing diaries of their observations, which were then compiled and edited for the *Philosophical Transactions* by an English clergyman, William Derham (1657–1735). Unfortunately, much of the data collected were not useful for the larger purpose, as the instruments used had not been calibrated against each other or to a standard. Observers themselves were not particularly fastidious about collecting continuous runs of data, and there were many gaps in the data set that could not be replaced. The data collection continued until 1734, but its utility was much reduced by ongoing instrumental and observational problems and the lack of a reporting mechanism.

In spite of all these shortcomings, Derham and other meteorologists were able to characterize the climatology of many of the reporting stations and draw some preliminary conclusions about the meteorological linkages between neighboring locations. They found that warm and cold spells frequently coincided, separated by intervals that ranged from a half day to almost a week. While speculation suggested that the same weather system must be responsible, the evidence was weak, and Derham (1733) noted: ". . . the weather in both places was influenced by the same causes, whether the Alpine hills and the cold, or the influx of the moon. . . ." Some classical weather superstitions were proven to be correct: "a cold summer is commonly a wet one" or "western clouds bring much wind."

Observational meteorology progressed slowly through much of the 1700s, but by the end of the century, organized groups in France, Britain, and the United States had begun to build a sustainable network of observers, largely in support of agriculture and climatology. Instrumentation became more precise and calibrated, and observational procedures were formalized. Thermometers and barometers were made to higher standards and accuracy, transforming meteorology from a qualitative to a quantitative science. Data were comparable from place to place with the widespread use of the common temperature scales across Europe and America.

The growth of observational meteorology in the years after 1770 was, in part, due to the establishment of formal national programs under the control of learned societies in England and France (the Royal Society and Société royale de médecine). These agencies laid the groundwork for the present day, ensuring calibrated instruments, fixed times for observation, instrument exposure, data collection and archive, and the caliber of the observers. Other countries followed suit, and by 1775, weather events—a cold wave or a hailstorm, for instance—could be traced across Europe. A growing collection of weather observations and an expanding climatology of Europe brought meteorology to the brink of new mathematical theories and techniques. The new climatology was summarized in 1793 by the publication of *Meteorological Observations and Essays* by John Dalton (1766–1844).

The Napoleonic Wars put a pause into international collaboration, but when the wars ended in 1815, the pace of exploration and innovation picked up again, building on the foundations laid during the previous century. Discovery and bureaucracy went hand-in-hand: national agencies were formed as the importance and financial benefits of daily observations, regional climatologies, and warnings of severe weather were recognized. Most important of all was the invention of the telegraph in 1837, which made possible the dissemination of weather observations and weather forecasts in real time. The *Manchester Examiner* published the first weather report in 1847:

> *The weather having been lowering and occasionally wet in the neighbourhood of Manchester during the last two days, and still showery this morning, the anxiety of the commercial classes to know how the agricultural districts were affected, led us to inquire if the electric telegraph was yet extended far enough from Manchester to obtain information from the eastern counties. By the prompt attention of Mr Cox, the superintendent, inquiries were made at the following places; and answers were returned, which we append: Normanton, fine. Derby, very dull. York, fine. Leeds, fine. Nottingham, no rain, but dull and cold. Rugby, rain. Lincoln, moderately fine. Newcastle-upon-Tyne, half-past 12, fine. Scarborough, quarter to 1, fine. Rochdale, 1 o'clock, fair. (Roberts 2006)*

In the middle years of the nineteenth century, collection and dissemination of weather data were largely conducted by meteorological societies made up of members who maintained their own observation sites. Among the earliest was the Meteorological Society of London, formed in 1823, but it had an erratic history until replaced by the British Meteorological Society (now the Royal Meteorological Society) in 1850. Other countries in Europe—Austria, Switzerland, France, Prussia, Italy, Russia, and the Netherlands—had similar societies. The United States held a prominent place among such organizations with over 800 observers by 1860; English and Scottish societies numbered about 150 members; Austria, 108; and Switzerland, 83. These organizations maintained loose connections with one another, sharing data at infrequent intervals.

Weather is immune to international boundaries, and private societies, with their organizational fragility, made for haphazard studies of weather systems and greatly restricted the production of forecasts and warnings, where information has a shelf life of only a few hours. National institutions were needed, and so, in 1854, the United Kingdom Meteorological Office (the "Met Office") was established as a small department within the Board of Trade, with Admiral Robert Fitzroy as its first director. Fitzroy introduced a system of meteorological telegrams in which weather observations from coastal stations—pressure, temperature, wind, cloud, weather character, and sea state—were collected twice daily and forwarded to London for analysis and incorporation into forecasts.

Other countries did not stand idly by. Similar organizational activities were going on at weather services across Europe, and in Turkey and India. Urbain Jean Joseph Le Verrier (1811–1877), better known for successfully predicting the existence and position of Neptune, began offering weather services for France in 1855 and for Europe generally in 1857. More widespread weather services began across Europe in 1865.

The development of weather data collection and dissemination in the United States followed a different track, with government becoming involved at an early stage because of sparse populations and the large distances involved. Before independence, the only large-scale government department was the Post Office, and the Postmaster General of the time, Benjamin Franklin (1706–1790), made some efforts to collect data from postmasters and shipmasters for studies of weather systems. During the War of 1812, responsibility for the collection of weather data fell on military hospital surgeons, a practice that continued into the 1880s.

Military surgeons were not the only information gatherers in early America. Within the Signal Service, the Interior Department, the Smithsonian Institution, the American Philosophical Society, and some states and universities, networks were set up for the collection of weather information. Much of the work to establish a United States weather agency was the work of James Pollard Espy (1785–1860), who served as a meteorologist with the Navy and with the War Department until moving to the Smithsonian Institution. Espy established a small network of observers near Philadelphia in 1834 and, after considerable lobbying, expanded it to a corps of 110 by 1843. Until 1849, observations were tabulated on printed forms and mailed to the surgeon general's office, where they were plotted on daily weather maps (Figure 11-28).

Under the auspices of the Smithsonian Institution and its secretary, Joseph Henry (1797–1878), a coordinated effort was made in 1847 to establish observation sites across the United States, using the newly developed telegraph system to disseminate the reports. The first reports began moving along the lines two years later. Lobbying efforts in Congress continued for many more years, finally resulting in the

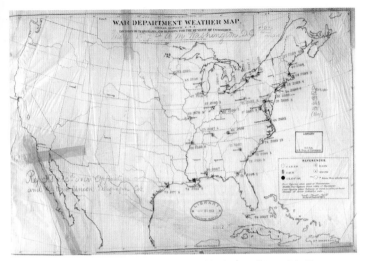

FIG. 11-28. *A weather map for May 1, 1887, issued by the United States War Department. At each station, the plot shows the temperature, pressure, and wind speed; the arrows through the station location indicate wind direction.*

passage of appropriations to create a Weather Bureau in 1870 with instructions to ". . . provide for taking meteorological observations at the military stations in the interior of the continent and at other points in the States and Territories . . . and for giving notice on the northern (Great) Lakes and on the seacoast by magnetic telegraph and marine signals, of the approach and force of storms" (NWS 2019). The Weather Bureau became a civilian agency in 1890 and was renamed the National Weather Service in 1967.

The growth of national institutions led to the formation of the International Meteorological Organization in 1873 to foster the exchange of weather information among countries. In 1953, those functions were taken over by the World Meteorological Organization, an agency of the United Nations. Today, meteorological data are widely shared among governments, even between countries with acrimonious relations. Data have acquired a value of their own, so while national weather services share with each other, the door for public access is often closed. In much of the world, detailed climatological and meteorological data can be had only at a price, though this barrier is gradually disappearing.

Conclusion

Here we come to the beginning. The writing is at an end, but we hope this is the beginning for you. We hope the sky will never look the same again; that the charts and scenes behind the TV meteorologist will now mean much more; that the internet's rich supply of satellite images and maps are now bookmarked on your home screen. We hope that you immerse yourself in the clouds and document your discoveries on your cell-phone camera. We hope you bore your

FIG. 11-29. *A tracking theodolite used to measure the angle toward a rising balloon in order to calculate the wind direction and speed or the height of a cloud base. The balloon was assumed to rise at a fixed rate, allowing its altitude to be determined by its time since launch.*

friends with impertinent comments about the colors in the sky and the shape of the clouds. We hope that you seek out the aurora and noctilucent clouds, even if you have to travel.

If you want to go storm chasing, there is much more to learn, but some of the first secrets of that cabal have been hinted at here. If you want to become a master of cloudscapes and sky scenes, you are well on your way.

Above all, look. Every sky on every day has something to say. Take your Merlin moments—those secret instants when you perceive and understand the physics of the atmosphere that those around you fail to see.

ATMOSPHERES OF PLANETS, MOONS, AND EXOPLANETS

Our Solar System

The Earth's weather systems are interesting on their own, but we can learn more about them by understanding weather on other planets, too. Though some planets and moons, such as Mercury and our own Moon, have negligible atmospheres, many of the others have substantial ones.

In this appendix, we will briefly discuss and illustrate the atmospheres of the planets Venus, Mars, Jupiter, Saturn, Uranus, and Neptune, and of the dwarf planet Pluto. We will also discuss the atmospheres of Saturn's moons Titan and Enceladus and Neptune's moon Triton. Further, astronomers are increasingly finding atmospheres around exoplanets, planetary objects orbiting stars other than our Sun.

Since wind and weather in our Earth's atmosphere are affected by the intensity of the Sun's incoming radiation and by our planet's rotation speed, scientists learn about the laws that govern atmospheric circulation in part by studying the atmosphere of other planets in which these parameters have different values. In that way, we can better understand the importance of being closer to or farther from the Sun and of rotating relatively quickly (in about 10 hours for Jupiter, for example) or slowly (in about 243 days for Venus).

Earth's neighbors, Venus and Mars, have atmospheres completely dominated by carbon dioxide (CO_2), but the density of Venus's atmosphere is thousands of times higher than that of Mars and the quantity of radiation-trapping carbon dioxide is correspondingly greater. From a meteorological point of view, Mars is the planet most like the

FIG. A-1. *Even from space and close-up, Venus's atmosphere shows little detail, except for a few hazy bands. In a small telescope, the planet is almost pure white.*

Earth, even though the atmosphere has a completely different composition and a density $\frac{1}{80}$ that of our home. A forecaster looking at Mars will see familiar cloud shapes and structures: rotating low-pressure storms, wave clouds, morning mists, upslope stratus, whirling dust devils, and even occasional precipitation from clouds in the higher layers of the atmosphere.

Venus

In some ways, Venus is our sister planet: it is about the same size and density of Earth, but its position in the solar system, 70 percent of our Earth's distance from the Sun, means that the solar radiation is much stronger there (Figure A-1). However, the planet is covered in dense yellowish clouds that reflect most of the incoming solar radiation. Venus's atmosphere wound up about 53 times denser than our own and is composed mainly of carbon dioxide, some 96 percent of its mass. If we were standing on Venus's surface, we would be oppressed by a pressure about 90 times higher than the pressure we feel on the Earth's surface.

The immense amount of carbon dioxide in the Venusian atmosphere blocks the outward flow of cooling infrared radiation to a much greater degree than here on Earth, a process known as the "greenhouse effect" (Chapter 1). The name is a bit mistaken, since actual greenhouses on Earth heat up mostly because the glass walls keep the air from circulating, rather than because they don't let the infrared out. Still, the name greenhouse effect is universally used. Our Earth's atmosphere also has a greenhouse effect, but a much smaller one than at Venus. Without it, Earth's average temperature would be about 60°F (33°C) colder. The greenhouse warming of Venus's atmosphere is much more, about 955°F (510°C).

Venus's clouds extend from about 28 to 40 miles (45 to 65 km) above the surface on the day side and up to 56 miles (90 km) on the night side. The high-level clouds are made of mainly sulfuric acid droplets but the composition of lower clouds is unknown, though water vapor and sulphur dioxide are also present in the atmosphere.

Mars

Mars's atmosphere is much thinner (less dense) than that of Earth by a factor of nearly 100. The atmosphere has been sampled and monitored by a series of spacecraft.

The low-density atmosphere of Mars (Figure A-2) is composed almost entirely (95 percent) of carbon dioxide with small amounts of carbon monoxide and water vapor. Nevertheless, Mars's atmosphere has enough water vapor to be able to form many of the types of clouds that are found on Earth, including mountain waves, fog, frontal clouds, and cirrus.

FIG. A-2. *A view of Mars from the* Mars Global Surveyor *showing blue-white clouds hanging over the 16-mile-high (25 km) volcanoes in the Tharsis region.*

Jupiter

When we look at Jupiter, we see the tops of its clouds, but it is clouds and atmosphere almost all the way down. Jupiter's weather isn't limited to a thin region on top of a solid surface, the way the atmospheres of Venus, Earth, and Mars are.

Jupiter, 11.2 times larger across than Earth, dominates the solar system, with 318 times the mass of our own planet. It orbits the Sun over five times farther out than Earth (meaning that the intensity of solar radiation reaching it is 25 times weaker) and takes 12 years to complete a single orbit.

Jupiter's chemical composition is largely hydrogen with about 10 percent helium and an admixture of the heavier elements, so it resembles the makeup of the Sun more than it does the composition of the rocky, inner planets like Earth. At the bottom of the atmosphere, the planet's gases liquefy; at the core is perhaps

FIG. A-3. *Jupiter's bands and zones, different levels of clouds of ammonia ice in this turbulent atmosphere, imaged in 2019 with NASA's/ESA's Hubble Space Telescope. The Great Red Spot, a giant storm, shows clearly.*

a repository of heavy elements that is thought to be much larger and about 10 times more massive than our whole planet.

Jupiter's surface cloud bands (Figure A-3) can be followed from Earth, most precisely on the occasions when it is observed with the Hubble Space Telescope or from spacecraft. Though Jupiter's surface rotates about every 10 hours—much faster than Earth's 24-hour rotation even though Jupiter's circumference is so much larger—it is a differential rotation in which bands of clouds at different latitudes rotate at slightly different speeds.

Saturn

Saturn, known especially for its beautiful rings (Figure A-4) that are visible even in small telescopes, is less than half the size of Jupiter, but when the ring diameter is included, only slightly smaller than its neighbor. Its diameter is 9.4 times Earth's and its mass is 95 times higher. Saturn's surface looks blander than Jupiter's, perhaps because, at its greater distance from the Sun, fewer chemical reactions take place in the outer atmospheric layers. As the planet orbits, its tilt with respect to the Sun changes in a seasonal manner. Sometimes Saturn's Southern Hemisphere gets more direct solar radiation than the Northern Hemisphere, and vice versa.

FIG. A-4. *Views of Saturn from the Hubble Space Telescope over a five-year period. We see how the angle of illumination of Saturn, which more or less matches our view from Earth, varies.*

Saturn, like Jupiter, rotates in about 10 hours. Its winds reach the great value of 1,000 miles per hour (1,800 km/h), four times faster than the maximum speed of Jupiter's winds.

Saturn's Moon Titan

Saturn's moon Titan is 40 percent Earth's diameter, half again larger than our Moon and larger than the Galilean satellites of Jupiter (the four moons of Jupiter discovered by Galileo). It has a thick atmosphere (Figure A-5). If you were standing on Titan's surface, you would find the air pressure to be half again larger than that we now feel on Earth.

Most of Titan's atmosphere is the molecular form of nitrogen, as is most of Earth's atmosphere. Methane, though only 1 percent or so, is

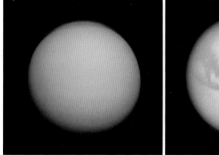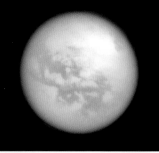

FIG. A-5. *Images of Titan from NASA's Cassini mission showed a relatively feature-less cloud deck in visible light (left), while infrared radiation (right) was able to see through the clouds to reveal some of the surface features. Blue haze layers above the upper limb can be seen in the visible-light image.*

important for most of the chemical reactions in the atmosphere. When we look at Titan from Earth, we see only a pinkish cover, which turns out to be a thick layer of photochemical fog.

Saturn's Moon Enceladus

Enceladus is only 300 miles (500 km) across, so small compared with Titan that it wasn't thought in advance of NASA's flybys to be very interesting. But even though it has only 0.1 percent of Titan's volume, it turns out to give off plumes (Figure A-6) of water vapor and ices, including organic compounds, from its interior that give the moon an atmosphere of 91 percent water vapor with smaller amounts of nitrogen, carbon dioxide, and methane. The low gravity of the planet means that the atmosphere

FIG. A-6. *Jets of water ice (bottom) with organics mixed in erupt in this backlit view of Saturn's moon Enceladus.*

is not retained for long and must be continually replenished by the plumes. The discovery of the plumes and their composition, which were sampled directly as *Cassini* flew through some of them, has put Enceladus at the top of the list of places in which scientists want to look for life in the solar system outside of Earth.

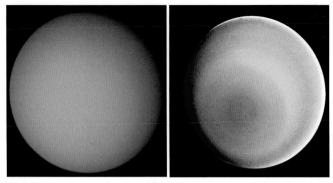

FIG. A-7. *Uranus's atmosphere from NASA's* Voyager 2 *spacecraft's flyby. The left image shows the appearance of the planet in visible light. The right-hand view, taken in ultraviolet and visible wavelengths, and with greatly enhanced contrast and false colors, shows some of the banded structure of the planet.*

Uranus

Uranus and Neptune are often called ice giants in contrast to the gas giants that categorize Jupiter and Saturn, though their atmospheres have a similar composition, mostly of hydrogen and helium. The name comes from other constituents in the atmosphere: ices such as water, ammonia, and methane. The high albedo (reflectivity) of these ices gives the planet a bland cloudiness. The views from NASA's *Voyager 2* had to be contrast-enhanced to see any structure at all (Figure A-7). The atmospheric layer we see is made of thick clouds of methane ice crystals, visible through a clear level of molecular hydrogen, with a bit of methane mixed in to explain the bluish/greenish color. The methane preferentially soaks up the orange and red wavelengths, leaving the blue-green to be reflected.

Uranus has been viewed from time to time with the Hubble Space Telescope, and when springtime comes to the planet, some activity can be seen in the clouds. It is just such discoveries as this one that make the scientific study of planetary atmospheres relevant to better understanding our own atmosphere, climate, and weather. Telescopes on Earth, using adaptive optics to minimize the distorting effect of Earth's atmosphere, can now track winds at the tops of Uranus's atmosphere.

Neptune

The ice-giant planet Neptune, in spite of being farther from the Sun than Uranus and therefore colder, has a more active atmosphere, driven, in part, by internal heat sources. Its blue color derives from small amounts of methane in the largely hydrogen and helium atmosphere. Indistinct bands of clouds surround the planet, punctuated with occasional bright, white wisps of high-level cirrus. When *Voyager 2* arrived at Neptune in 1989, it found an Earth-sized dark region superimposed on a deep blue atmosphere. By analogy with Jupiter's Great Red Spot, it was called the Great Dark Spot (Figure A-8), though in this case it seemed to be a large opening within an anticyclone in the upper haze layers.

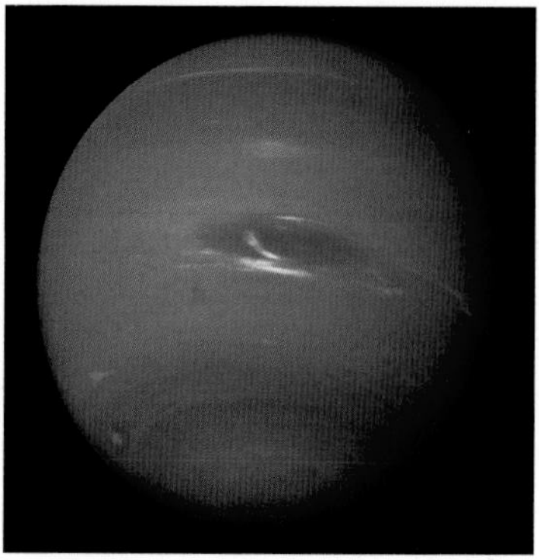

FIG. A-8. *Neptune, imaged from NASA's Voyager 2 spacecraft as it flew by in 1989, showing the Great Dark Spot (GDS) with its necklace of white methane-crystal clouds and the banded appearance of the lower-level clouds. The dark spot to the lower left, while similar to the GDS, has a bright core. Streaks of high-level cloud can be seen at the top.*

Voyager imaged clouds of ice crystals, the methane analogue to Earth's cirrus clouds, at the edge of the Great Dark Spot. These methane-ice crystals seem to have resulted from lower-level flow over the high-pressure Dark Spot, which forced methane-rich gas upward until it condensed into a white cloud. It was a surprise to discover the Great Dark Spot, and another surprise when the Hubble Space Telescope's image of Neptune a few years later showed that it had disappeared. Since we don't know when it formed, we have no idea of its longevity.

Neptune's Moon Triton

Triton, Neptune's largest moon, is just over half the size of Saturn's Titan, and 15 percent or so smaller than our Moon. *Voyager 2* skimmed over Triton as it finished its solar-system tasks, confirming that Triton had an atmosphere and that the atmosphere was transparent to the surface. Triton's atmosphere, like Earth's, is mostly nitrogen gas with trace amounts of methane. Even though its atmosphere is extremely thin, Triton has a troposphere, created by convection that extends to a depth of about 5 miles (8 km). Thin nitrogen ice clouds have been observed a few miles above the surface.

Triton's surface turned out to be highly varied. A solar ice cap,

FIG. A-9. *Triton's southern region, including its ice cap at the south pole, imaged by NASA's* Voyager 2 *in 1989. Several dark oval-shaped plumes can be seen toward the lower right and bottom.*

presumably of nitrogen ice, showed a lot of structure. It looked pinkish, probably because the methane in Triton's atmosphere and on its surface interacted with ultraviolet light and incoming particle radiation guided by Neptune's magnetic field. Elsewhere on Triton's surface, several dozen dark streaks attracted attention when the returning images were examined. They turned out to be erupting plumes from ice volcanoes (Figure A-9); the material from them had spread downwind and settled onto the surface.

One of us (Jay Pasachoff) participated in a study of Triton's atmosphere by watching how it affected starlight as the moon occulted a star. Our group's observations, attempted from the ground in Australia and then Hawaii and with the Hubble Space Telescope, revealed details of Triton's atmosphere. The atmosphere had warmed slightly, by a few degrees, since the measurements taken by *Voyager 2*. Punning on the analogy with Earth's atmosphere, we called our published paper with the results "Global Warming on Triton."

Pluto and Other Dwarf Planets

The majority type of planetary objects in our solar system turns out to be "dwarf planets" rather than the eight ordinary "planets." Many of these dwarf planets have atmospheres, so we consider them here. Pluto was long thought, starting with its 1930 discovery, to be a ninth planet of our solar system. But when its mass was reevaluated to be only 1/500 the mass of Earth, many scientists questioned whether it deserved planethood. Telescopic capabilities, and our abilities to use computers to help search and analyze sky images, turned up another object even farther out in the solar system, since named Eris. At first, Eris was thought to be bigger than Pluto, so it became difficult to maintain Pluto's status as a planet unless we became willing also to make Eris, and perhaps eventually another 100 objects out there, planets.

Because of the existence of Eris, the International Astronomical Union set up a new category of solar-system object known as "dwarf planet." (The term "dwarf" in astronomy is a common one: Normal stars, like our Sun, are "dwarf stars.") Pluto and Eris are in that category, as are perhaps a hundred such other objects in the outer solar system, two of which are named Haumea (from a Hawaiian goddess) and Makemake (from an Easter Island god). The criteria for being a dwarf planet is that the object both has to be massive enough to be approximately round under its own gravity, though not a moon, and that it has not "cleared its orbit"; regular planets, on the other hand, have to have "cleared their orbits," using their gravity to slingshot other objects away. The asteroids Ceres and Hygiea are also dwarf planets. (They are in the asteroid belt between Mars and Jupiter rather than beyond Neptune, where the other dwarf planets reside, among the Trans Neptunian Objects, TNOs.)

The status of dwarf planet can be considered a promotion for Pluto, not the demotion that many people think. Isn't it better to be prominent in a new category than to be the runt of the litter in an old one (planets)?

In any case, Pluto has a perfectly good atmosphere, though it is only 1/100,000 the density of Earth's. Pluto's atmosphere is mostly nitrogen and has an admixture of methane (in some sort of equilibrium with methane ice on Pluto's surface). When Pluto goes in front of (occults) a star, the starlight is bent by Pluto's atmosphere, and we see the starlight being extinguished gradually rather than abruptly, as it would be if Pluto had no atmosphere.

NASA's *New Horizons* mission flew closest to Pluto on July 14, 2015. Its close-up views and other measurements revolutionized our understanding of Pluto's atmosphere, surface, and interior (Figure A-10).

FIG. A-10. *After passing Pluto, the* New Horizons *spacecraft looked back, revealing several haze layers in the atmosphere shining above the dwarf planet's disk.*

Comets

Comets are made of rock and ices, and as they come close to the Sun in their elliptical orbits, about every 10 years one becomes visible to the naked eye (Figure A-11). As the solar energy turns the ices into their constituent gas and dust, the dust is left behind as a curving dust tail, while gas that sublimes from the ices is blown behind by the solar wind to make the bluish gas tail (Figure A-12).

FIG. A-11. *Comet NEOWISE was visible to Northern Hemisphere terrestrial observers for weeks in 2020. (Its name comes from NASA's Near Earth Object extension of the Wide-field Infrared Survey Explorer mission; its technical name is C/2020 F3.) Though a bright comet appears about every decade (here it is left of center near the top of the frame), dozens of faint comets are in the sky all the time, usually with extended orbits that take them out far beyond the planets' orbits, though with some coming to perihelion well within our Earth's orbit.*

Over the eons, much of the water on Earth and in our atmosphere may have been brought to us from afar by comets. How much water came from comets as opposed to asteroids can be assessed by the relative amount of heavy hydrogen (deuterium) to regular hydrogen, compared with terrestrial and interstellar values.

The Solar System As a Laboratory

Big worlds and little, dense atmospheres and thin, hot Sun and cool, our solar system provides us with an abundance of worlds and weather to explore. One can only imagine what other meteorological processes we might encounter in the thousands of exoplanets now being discovered by satellites and ground-based observations as these exoplanets tug the stars they orbit slightly toward or away from us, or block tiny amounts of the stars' light from reaching us. Studies of spectra as the exoplanets go in front of their stars even show us constituents in the exoplanets' atmospheres. In the not-too-distant future, we may be

FIG. A-12. *From a dark site (here from Arches National Park), with exposures tracking the stars, NEOWISE's two tails showed clearly and spectacularly: the blue gas tail and the yellowish dust tail.*

monitoring storms on steaming hot, giant planets around other stars or speculating about the precipitation on an Earthlike body attended by a pair of cool dwarf stars. Science fiction is now becoming our reality.

GLOSSARY

μm. The symbol for micron, also known as micrometer, equal to 1 millionth of a meter.

absolute zero. −459.67°F or −273.15°C.

adiabatic expansion (and compression). Expansion of a gas that takes place without an external source of energy. Instead, energy is taken from the expanding gas, causing its temperature to fall. Adiabatic compression releases energy and the gas temperature rises.

advection. The transport of some atmospheric parameter such as temperature or moisture by the wind.

advection fog. Fog formed when warm, humid air flows over a colder surface.

aerosol. A solid particle or liquid droplet suspended in the atmosphere.

airmass. A large (sometimes continent-sized) atmospheric volume with a similar temperature and humidity throughout.

air pressure. The weight of the overlying atmosphere.

albedo. A measure of the fraction of incident light that is reflected by a surface. A black surface that absorbs all incoming radiation and reflects none has an albedo of 0. A surface that reflects all incoming radiation has an albedo of 1.

Alberta Clipper. A fast-moving, cold-season storm that moves from Alberta eastward across the northern plains into the northeastern states or eastern Canada.

altocumulus. A modest mid-level convective cloud, forming as discrete masses or waves in sheetlike patterns.

altocumulus *castellanus*. A special form of altocumulus that forms in an unstable mid-level environment. It is often a portent of more severe convective weather later in the day.

altostratus. Uniform gray to white cloud formed at mid-levels of the atmosphere and arranged in a flat layer.

anemometer. A device for measuring wind speed and direction.

anticyclone. A high-pressure region.

anticyclonic flow. A flow around a high-pressure system: clockwise in the Northern Hemisphere and counterclockwise in the Southern Hemisphere.

aphelion. The Earth's farthest point from the Sun in its annual orbit.

Arctic Oscillation. A climate index that reflects the strength and pattern of the Arctic jet stream and the penetration of cold air southward into mid-latitudes. The AO is derived from the pattern of surface pressure anomalies between high and mid-latitudes.

aurora. A natural, colored, moving display of light in the upper atmosphere caused when incoming solar electrons and ions collide with atmospheric gases.

auroral oval. A band surrounding the geomagnetic pole where the magnetic field dips deepest into the atmosphere and where aurorae are most frequent.

axial tilt. The angle that a planet's rotational axis makes with its orbital plane; for the Earth, it is 23.4°.

banner clouds. Clouds that form on the lee side of isolated mountain peaks and blow downwind.

baroclinic. A region with a moderate to strong temperature contrast between warm and cold air, usually along a frontal boundary.

barometer. A device for measuring pressure.

barotropic. A region with a weak or no temperature contrast, for example, a region with no fronts.

beaver tail. A type of inflow cloud band with a broad, flat appearance that appears in strong thunderstorms. The beaver tail appears to attach to the side or bottom of the storm where it joins the general updraft region. Cloud elements move along the beaver tail toward the updraft region.

Bergeron-Findeisen process. The process by which ice crystals scavenge water molecules from water droplets in a cloud consisting of both types. Eventually almost all of the water will be converted to ice.

blackbody. A theoretical object that absorbs all radiation that strikes it and re-emits that radiation in a precise form that depends only on its temperature. The Sun is an approximate blackbody with a temperature of 5,800 K.

blizzard. A Great Plains winter storm characterized by low visibilities in blowing snow. The name has been adapted to other regions of the globe.

blocking. A long-lasting pattern in the upper-level flow that brings prolonged spells of similar weather: warm, cold, wet, or dry.

bora. A gusty north wind in the Adriatic Sea.

bow echo. A radar configuration of a squall line characterized by a section of the line that bows forward.

buoyancy. The tendency of a body to float upward when immersed in a fluid. In a liquid or gas, where pressure increases with depth, an object has a lower pressure on its upper side and a higher pressure on its lower. This tiny pressure difference exerts an upward force, but only objects that are less dense than the air or water around them will actually move upward. A human body will float in water, but in air, body weight is reduced by only about 0.1 percent by buoyancy. In a gas, a cold volume of air will sink if its density is higher than the surrounding fluid.

cap clouds. Stationary clouds that form on the peaks of mountains when air is forced upward to saturation. They often take a lenticular form and may be quite spectacular.

chinook. A local name for a foehn (or föhn) wind that arises when a warm, drying wind flows downhill along the slopes of North American mountains. It is usually associated with the western Canadian provinces and the U.S. Pacific Northwest.

chromosphere. The layer of the Sun's atmosphere just above the visible photosphere (actually composed of Texas-sized spikes known as spicules); it appears to have a brilliant red color, from its dominant hydrogen emission, though other emission spectral lines of other colors also contribute.

circumzenithal. A name for a feature that wholly or partly circles the zenith (the overhead point).

cirrocumulus. A high-level ice cloud in a region of modest instability. Cirrocumulus forms small discrete clouds and may be arranged in waves, ripples, or globular patterns.

cirrostratus. A hazy, semitransparent high-level ice cloud that forms in sheets.

cirrus. A feathery, high-level ice cloud.

cloud streets. Lines of stratocumulus clouds aligned along the wind, usually in a cold, blustery flow across a warm lake.

cold conveyor belt. A rising flow of air into a mature low (cyclone) that arises to the east of the storm and carries cool and moderately humid air into the storm.

cold front. The boundary of advancing cold air.

Colorado low. A strong cold-season storm that forms in or near Colorado and moves northeastward, usually toward the Great Lakes. Colorado lows can bring heavy snowfalls, freezing rain, and long-lasting blizzard conditions to north and central North America.

comma cloud. A mature low-pressure cyclone in mid-latitudes named for its commalike shape in satellite images.

condensation. The conversion of water vapor to liquid water when in contact with a liquid or solid surface. In a cloud, the "surface" is usually a cloud condensation nucleus.

condensation nuclei. Microscopic particles that act as a substrate on which water vapor can begin condensing in cloud droplets. Such cloud condensation nuclei (CCN) greatly increase the efficiency of cloud-making.

conduction. The transfer of heat (internal energy) through microscopic collisions of atoms, electrons, and molecules in a substance (solid, liquid, or gas), or between two substances in contact.

confluence. A coming-together of the wind field. Confluence may or may not result in convergence.

continentality. The climatic characteristics of a region insulated from the influence of oceans and large lakes, usually in the center of a large landmass. Continental climates typically have a large range in temperature between warm and cold seasons or from day to night.

contrail. A line of cloud that forms behind a high-flying aircraft when hot exhaust is mixed with cold, dry air aloft.

convection. The transfer of heat by the movement of a fluid between areas of different temperature. Convection can be caused by buoyancy or it can have an external cause; in meteorology, this second cause is typically mass transport caused by a wind.

convective cloud. A cloud of vertical development in an unstable environment.

convergence. A net inflow into a region or level in the atmosphere that results in an accumulation of mass. The addition of mass results in higher pressures at the surface and generates downward motion in the atmosphere. If at the surface, upward motion results.

Coriolis force. An apparent force that seems to act on an object moving across a rotating surface that causes it to deviate to the left or right according to an observer also on the surface. On the Earth, the Coriolis force causes air movements in the Northern Hemisphere to turn to the right; in the Southern Hemisphere, it is to the left.

corona. (a) The million-degree gas and dust that form the Sun's outermost atmosphere, above the chromosphere; especially visible at total solar eclipses as a pearly white, structured halo, or from spacecraft. (b) A colored halo formed around the Moon by diffraction of light in water droplets.

coronal mass ejection (CME). A large release of plasma (electrons and ionized atoms) and embedded magnetic field from the solar corona.

crepuscular rays. Shadows of clouds projected on the atmosphere in the direction of the Sun, made visible by suspended dust and smoke.

cumulonimbus. A deep convective cloud that usually produces thunder or lightning. Cumulonimbus clouds tend to form long downwind cloud streamers called anvils.

cyclogenesis. The formation of a low-pressure system.

cyclone. Various meanings: a low-pressure system at the surface; a tornado; a hurricane in the Indian Ocean or southwest Pacific.

cyclonic flow. Flow around a low-pressure system counterclockwise in the Northern Hemisphere and clockwise in the Southern Hemisphere.

density. The mass per unit volume of a substance (for example, pounds per cubic inch, grams per cubic centimeter).

derecho. A straight-line windstorm that contains periodic winds in excess of 58 mph (93 km/h) over a total distance of at least 240 miles (400 km).

dewpoint temperature. The temperature to which an atmosphere must be cooled in order for its water vapor to begin condensing (typically, as dew). At the dewpoint temperature, the atmosphere will have a relative humidity at or near 100 percent. Dewpoint temperature is related to the quantity of water in the atmosphere.

diabatic. A process in which heat is acquired from or given to the surroundings, such as cooling by contact with cold land or water, evaporation, condensation, and infrared emission to space.

diffraction. The spreading and apparent bending of light waves as they pass through a small opening or encounter an obstacle.

dispersion. The separation of light into colors as it is undergoing refraction.

divergence. A net outflow from a region or level in the atmosphere that results in a reduction in mass. The removal of mass results in lower pressures at the surface and generates upward motion in the atmosphere.

downburst. A downdraft, usually with damaging wind speeds.

downdraft. A descending wind from a thunderstorm that originates in mid-levels of the atmosphere and flows outward on reaching the ground.

drizzle. Precipitation of very small water droplets.

dry adiabatic lapse rate (DALR). The rate at which dry air cools as it rises in the atmosphere (5.5°F per 1,000 feet; 9.8°C per kilometer).

dry conveyor belt. A descending jet-stream-level wind flow that carries dry air into the cloud mass of a mature cyclone, giving the storm its comma shape.

dry slot. A descending intrusion of dry air into the cloud mass of a mature low-pressure system that subsequently gives the mass a comma shape as seen from satellite. The dry slot is caused by the jet-stream flow into the storm.

dryline. A quasi-frontal structure in which humidities change abruptly and significantly over a short distance. Drylines are usually found over western Texas and Oklahoma, derived from air flowing from the Southwest deserts.

dust devil. A rotating column of dust and sand formed when hot air from the surface rises rapidly upward. Under the right conditions, the warm updraft will begin to rotate as cooler air rushes in to replace the rising air.

EF scale (Enhanced Fujita scale). A modern version of the F scale that better assesses the range of damage caused by a tornado.

El Niño. The component of the ENSO circulation that is characterized by warm Pacific equatorial surface waters, declining easterly trade winds, and shifts in seasonal precipitation.

electromagnetic energy. Light in all its forms, from gamma rays to radio waves.

emission. The release of a photon of light when electrons make a transition from higher to lower energy levels within an atom or molecule.

ENSO (El Niño Southern Oscillation). The multiyear cycle of hydrological and meteorological changes in the equatorial Pacific that gives rise to El Niño and La Niña circulations.

entrainment zone (layer). The top of the planetary boundary layer where it meets the free atmosphere.

environmental curve. The measured temperature and humidity profile through the depth of the atmosphere.

evaporation. The escape of molecules or atoms from a liquid surface into the atmosphere. Because of the attractive forces between molecules, only those with higher kinetic energies can easily leave the liquid. The loss of these high-energy molecules cools the liquid.

evapotranspiration. The evaporation of water from vegetation after its movement through the plant from the ground to the leaf surface (a process known as transpiration).

exosphere. The Earth's highest atmospheric layer, lying above 620 miles (1,000 km) and fading into outer space.

F scale (Fujita scale). An older measure of the strength of a tornado based on the damage caused to a well-constructed home. The F scale is often used to estimate tornado wind speeds.

fallstreak hole. A circular opening that appears in a supersaturated mid-cloud layer when condensation nuclei are suddenly introduced into the cloud. The conversion of the cloud water droplets into ice and the subsequent precipitation leaves a hole in the original overcast layer. The ice nuclei often come from aircraft exhaust as the plane passes through the cloud layer or when ice-crystal virga from a higher layer seeds the lower cloud.

Ferrel cell. A mid-latitude global circulation that carries subtropical air northward and Arctic air southward to balance the energy flow of the planetary atmosphere.

fog. Cloud along the ground.

free atmosphere. The layer of the atmosphere above the boundary layer in which frictional drag from the surface is negligible.

freezing drizzle. Tiny supercooled water droplets that freeze on contact with a below-freezing surface. Freezing drizzle is similar to freezing rain, but does not require above-freezing temperatures aloft.

freezing rain. Raindrops that freeze on contact with a cold (below freezing) surface.

frontal wave. The wavelike shape formed by the intersection of warm and cold fronts in a low-pressure center.

front-flank precipitation. Precipitation that develops at the front of a supercell thunderstorm.

frontogenesis. The process in which a front forms or strengthens.

frontolysis. The process in which a front decays or weakens.

geomagnetic pole. The calculated position on the Earth's surface where the axis of a theoretical, planet-sized bar (dipole) magnet best matches the large-scale structure of the Earth's magnetic field. The auroral oval circles the geomagnetic pole.

glaze. A hard, transparent ice coating that forms when rain freezes slowly in below-freezing temperatures.

glory. A colored ring that can often be seen surrounding an aircraft shadow projected on clouds below.

gradient. The rate of change of a parameter (such as temperature) over a specified distance. On a contour map, the gradient is directly related to the separation or packing of the contour lines.

gradient flow. A wind flow that results from a balance between the pressure gradient force, the Coriolis force, and the centripetal force.

graupel. A snow pellet with a significant coating of frozen water droplets. Graupel is a more extreme form of snow pellet.

green flash. A small green appendage that appears on the edge of the Sun as it is setting or rising. The green color results from the absorption of blue and red wavelengths when the Sun is at the horizon, magnified by an inversion.

green rim. A very narrow green rim that appears on the edge of a setting or rising Sun caused by refraction and dispersion in the atmosphere.

gust front. The leading edge of a thunderstorm outflow.

gustnado. A dusty whirlwind that forms in the downburst outflow from a thunderstorm but which is not attached to the storm itself. Also known as a gust tornado.

Hadley cell. A global-scale circulation that distributes heat and moisture from equatorial regions to higher latitudes. At the equator, warm moist air rises in convective plumes, moves north and southward at higher levels, and descends into subtropical highs at about 30° latitude. From the mid-latitudes, the cycle returns to the equator in the trade-wind circulations.

hail. Precipitation of balls or irregular clumps of ice, usually from thunderstorms.

halos. Patterns of light formed by water droplets, ice crystals, and atmospheric gases due to the refraction, reflection, scattering, dispersion, and absorption of light.

Hatteras low. A winter-season storm that develops and moves along the Eastern Seaboard of the United States, past Cape Hatteras. Also called a nor'easter.

heat. Energy that is transferred from one system to another, typically from high temperature to low. Heat is not a property of a material—that should be referred to as "internal energy." Heat may be transferred by direct contact (conduction), emission and absorption of radiation, or by movement of an intervening fluid (convection). The transfer of heat usually results in changes in temperature.

heat capacity. See "specific heat."

heiligenschein. A bright halo around a person's shadow caused by the focusing and concentration of the Sun's rays by dew droplets on grass.

helicity. A mathematical unit that describes rotation present in the wind field.

high. A region of higher pressure at the surface of the Earth or a region of higher heights of a particular pressure level aloft. A high at the surface is known more formally as an anticyclone.

hurricane. A violent low-pressure tropical storm characterized by a circular shape, spiraling bands of thunderstorms, a central eye, and wind speeds in excess of 74 mph (119 km/h). The name "hurricane" is used to describe Atlantic and eastern Pacific storms; elsewhere in the world, they may be called cyclones or typhoons.

hydrogen bond. A weak electrostatic attraction between the positively charged side of one polar molecule and the negatively charged side of another similar, adjacent molecule. In meteorology, the polar molecule of most importance is the water molecule.

hydrostatic balance. The balance in the atmosphere between pressure and gravity.

hygrometer. A device for measuring humidity.

hygroscopic. Description of a substance that readily absorbs water from the surrounding atmosphere.

ice crystals. Tiny slivers of ice, often falling from a clear or nearly clear sky.

ice nuclei. Relatively large microscopic atmospheric particles that act as a platform on which water molecules can collect to form ice. Ice nuclei may form crystals from water vapor, from contact with supercooled water droplets, or from inclusion in a water droplet that subsequently cools to the freezing point.

ice pellets. Frozen raindrops or melted and refrozen snowflakes.

Icelandic low. A persistent low-pressure system situated over the Atlantic between Greenland and Iceland.

instability (or stability). A measure of the intrinsic buoyancy in the atmosphere given a certain combination of temperature and humidity. A stable atmosphere will resist vertical motion (upward or downward); an unstable atmosphere will allow movement of air upward and downward without significant impediment. Convective clouds form in an unstable atmosphere.

Intertropical Convergence Zone (ITCZ, ICZ). A low-pressure trough that moves back and forth across the equator with the seasons and which marks the convergence of wind flows from the Northern and Southern Hemispheres.

inversion. A layer in the atmosphere where temperatures rise or remain steady with height.

ionization. The removal of an electron from an atom to give it a net positive charge.

isobar. A contour line of constant pressure. Isobars are used to outline the pressure pattern of the atmosphere on a weather map.

jet stream. A ribbon of high wind speeds in the atmosphere, usually separating regions of warm and cold temperatures.

katabatic. A downslope flow of cold, high-density air.

Kelvin-Helmholtz (K-H) billows. A type of cloud that looks like a rolling ocean wave. K-H clouds form in the wind shear between two layers of the atmosphere.

kinetic energy. The energy of motion.

La Niña. The component of the ENSO circulation that is characterized by cool Pacific equatorial surface waters, strengthening easterly trade winds, and shifts in seasonal precipitation.

land breeze. A daily wind circulation in which winds blow offshore in response to temperature differences between land and sea, usually at night.

landspout. A tornado that forms from a pre-existing vertical rotating column of air when the column is caught up in a convective cloud.

lapse rate. The rate of change of temperature with height. Because temperature typically falls with altitude, a positive lapse rate indicates a declining temperature.

latent heat. Heat energy stored internally within the vibrations of an atom or molecule. In meteorology, latent heat is absorbed or released during phase changes as water freezes, melts, evaporates, or condenses.

lenticular clouds. Smooth-topped, lens-shaped clouds with a high degree of symmetry. Lenticular clouds form at the crest of atmospheric waves and are often stationary if the wave is generated by mountain terrain.

longwave radiation. Infrared radiation emitted by the Earth's surface and atmosphere, typically with wavelengths of 4 to 100 micrometers. Longwave radiation to space is sometimes called thermal infrared radiation.

low. A region of lower pressure at the surface of the Earth or a region of lower pressure heights aloft. A low at the surface is also known more formally as a cyclone.

low-level jet. A jetlike flow in the lower atmosphere, usually around 1 mile (1.5 km) above the surface.

macroburst. A thunderstorm-induced windstorm with dimension greater than 1.5 miles (2.5 km).

magnetic pole. The location on the Earth's surface where the planet's magnetic field points straight down. Because of local influences, this position is not coincident with the geomagnetic pole.

magnetopause. The boundary between the magnetic fields of the Sun and the Earth.

magnetotail. An extension of the Earth's magnetic field that stretches to considerable length in the anti-sun (night side) direction. The magnetotail is caused by pressure exerted by the solar wind.

mammatus. A form of udderlike cloud pouches that hang from the underside of other clouds, particularly thunderstorm anvils.

meridional flow. A meandering north-to-south wind flow in the upper atmosphere.

mesocyclone. The large-scale rotation contained within a supercell thunderstorm, often visible in Doppler radar.

mesopause. The upper boundary of the mesosphere, lying beneath the thermosphere.

mesoscale. A meteorological scale that encompasses small to medium-sized events such as thunderstorm complexes, sea-breeze circulations, and frontal systems. Mesoscale systems have lifetimes of several hours to a few days.

mesosphere. The third layer of the atmosphere, found at about 30 miles (50 km) altitude. It is the coldest layer of the atmosphere.

microburst. A thunderstorm-induced windstorm with a dimension less than 1.5 mile (2.5 km).

micron. A micrometer or 1/1000 of a meter. Its symbol is "μm."

mixed layer. A portion of the planetary boundary layer in which turbulence and convection mix the energy, moisture, pollutants, and aerosols upward from the surface.

monsoon. A seasonal cycle in the wind direction that is usually accompanied by changes in precipitation. Typically, the monsoon seasons are characterized as being wet or dry.

moonbow. A rainbow formed by the Moon.

multicell storms. An array of thunderstorms whose downdrafts interact to create long-lived mobile storm systems. Multicells may be in the form of storm clusters or lines (squall line).

nacreous clouds. Rare, brilliantly colored, high-level stratospheric clouds that can be seen in deep twilight.

nanometer. One-billionth of a meter.

noctilucent clouds. Pearly, translucent clouds that can be seen only in the deep summer twilight. Noctilucent clouds are the highest clouds produced in the atmosphere.

nor'easter. A strong, northward-moving, cold-season low that strikes the New England states and eastern Canada. A nor'easter gets its name from the northeast winds that announce its arrival. It is often an extension of a Hatteras low.

North Atlantic Oscillation. A climate index that reflects the strength and pattern of the jet-stream circulation over North America and the North Atlantic.

occluded front. A warm front that has been lifted off of the surface after being undercut by a faster-moving cold front.

opacity. A measure of an object's ability to transmit light. An opaque substance will block all light; partially opaque substances will have a lower opacity.

Pacific Decadal Oscillation (PDO). A climate index that reflects the pattern of long-term, warm and cold sea-surface temperature pools in the Pacific Ocean.

Panhandle low. A cold-season storm that moves from the Oklahoma Panhandle northeastward toward the Great Lakes or Upper Ohio Valley.

parcel. An imaginary volume used to evaluate the consequences of a movement of a sample of air in the atmosphere.

parcel curve. The calculated temperature and humidity profile followed by a theoretical parcel of air moving between two layers in the atmosphere. In most cases, the parcels are assumed to change temperature and humidity values at the dry and saturated adiabatic rates. Stability of the air column is determined by comparing the parcel curve with the environmental curve.

pascal (Pa). A unit of measurement for pressure.

perihelion. The Earth's closest point to the Sun in its annual orbit.

phase. In meteorology, the state of water in the atmosphere: liquid, solid (ice), or vapor.

photosphere. The visible surface of the Sun.

pileus. A caplike lenticular cloud that forms at the top of a growing thunderstorm or towering cumulus.

planetary boundary layer (PBL). The layer of the troposphere lying against the ground. It is a region where energy, moisture, pollutants, and aerosols are exchanged with the surface and where friction is important.

planetary scale. The largest of the meteorological scales, spanning systems with global dimensions and lifetimes of weeks to months or more. These include structures such as the trade-wind circulations, ENSO events, and semipermanent anticyclones and cyclones.

polar cell. A high-latitude hemispherical circulation that carries cold air southward to mix with warmer mid-latitude air.

polar molecule. An arrangement of atoms and electrons in a molecule that results in the molecule having a positive charge on one side and a negative charge on the other.

polarized light. A light beam in which the oscillations of its electric and magnetic components are not random, but oriented along some preferred direction or pattern.

pressure gradient force (PGF). The force that causes air to move from regions of high pressure to low. The force and the acceleration of the air depend on the rate of change of pressure (gradient) over a specific distance.

pressure height. The height of a specific pressure level in the atmosphere above mean sea level. A given pressure level will be lower in cold air than in warm.

psychrometer. A humidity-measuring device consisting of two thermometers, one with a wet cloth sleeve over the bulb and one left bare. The difference in temperature between the two (the wet-bulb and dry-bulb readings) is a measure of the rate of evaporation and thus the water content of the air.

quasi-stationary front. A boundary between cold and warm airmasses that is not moving or is moving very slowly.

radiation fog. Fog formed aboveground cooled by infrared radiation overnight.

radiosonde. An instrumented balloon that is sent aloft to measure temperature, humidity, wind, and other parameters in the atmosphere and relay the results to ground by radio.

rain. A falling water droplet larger than about 0.04 inch (1 mm).

rainbow. A circular arc of spectral colors formed by the refraction, reflection, and dispersion of light in a raindrop when illuminated by the Sun.

reflection. A term that describes light bouncing off of an object.

refraction. The bending of light waves as they move between transparent materials of differing density.

relative humidity. A measure of the amount of moisture in the air compared to the amount that could be held if the air were saturated.

residence time. The average length of time that a substance (water) will remain in a reservoir such as a glacier, a lake, the ground, or a cloud as it moves through a cycle.

residual layer. An elevated portion of the planetary boundary layer left over from the previous day's mixed layer. It is underlain by the stable boundary layer.

ridge. An elongated region of higher pressure or higher pressure height.

rime. A loose, crumbly, frozen raindrop.

Rossby waves. Planetary-scale meanderings in the upper-level flow that dictate the longer-term and large-scale character of the weather. Rossby waves are associated with the jet stream, the tracks of highs and lows, and separate regions of warm and cold temperatures.

Saffir-Simpson scale. A scale that represents the intensity of a hurricane based on its maximum wind speed.

Sahel. A 3,880-mile-long (6,200 km) ecoclimatic zone that marks the transition between the dry Sahara Desert to the north and the more humid African wood-and-grassland savannas to the south.

Santa Ana (wind). Strong, very dry, downslope wind that originates over the Great Basin of Nevada and flows downhill into coastal California, bringing exceptionally low humidity and strong surface winds. Santa Anas are notorious for the forest fires they help create.

saturated adiabatic lapse rate (SALR). The rate at which moist, saturated air cools as it rises in the atmosphere. The rate is variable according to the temperature and thus the moisture content of the rising air.

scattering. The deflection or diffusion of light waves by aerosol particles or surfaces.

sea breeze. A daily wind circulation in which winds blow onshore in response to temperature differences between land and sea, usually in the afternoon.

sensible heating. Heating that results in a rise in temperature.

shear. A change in wind speed or direction across a horizontal or vertical direction.

shelf clouds. A cloud line associated with the outflow winds of a strong thunderstorm. It is often stacked in layers, much like a shelf.

ship trails. Long, curving, and persistent cloud lines that form under oceanic high-pressure regions, frequently seen from satellite images. The lines are formed from ship exhausts, which provide condensation nuclei on which the cloud droplets can form in an otherwise pristine atmosphere.

shortwave. Electromagnetic radiation at the near-ultraviolet, visible, and near-infrared wavelengths.

showers. Occasional precipitation from convective clouds.

Siberian high. A persistent seasonal anticyclone that develops over the cold Arctic air of Siberia and Eastern Russia during the winter months.

sleet. Various definitions: precipitating, transparent, solid grains of ice (ice pellets); a mix of rain and snow; wet snow.

slope winds. Winds that form on the up-and-down slopes on the side of a valley or mountain in response to pressure forces generated by solar heating or nighttime cooling.

snow. An ice crystal that forms and precipitates from the atmosphere.

snow grains. A smaller version of snow pellets.

snow pellets. Snow crystals with attached, frozen water droplets.

snow pillow. An inflated bag that contains a pressure sensor used for measuring snowfall. The weight of snow on the bag causes a change in pressure that can be related to the accumulated snowfall.

solar corona. The outer atmosphere of the Sun, seen best during solar eclipses.

solar cycle. A quasi-regular variation in the Sun's magnetic activity that is most apparent as an 11-year cycle in the number of sunspots. The magnetic cycle is twice the sunspot cycle.

solar stripping. The loss of atmospheric gases at high levels by collision with charged particles flowing outward from the Sun.

solar wind. A stream of charged particles flowing outward from the Sun into the solar system.

Southern Oscillation Index (SOI). An index of the state and intensity of the ENSO circulation derived from the difference in surface pressure between Tahiti and Darwin, Australia. When the SOI is negative, pressures are below normal at Tahiti and higher than normal at Darwin—conditions usually associated with El Niño. The opposite relationship signifies La Niña conditions.

specific heat. The amount of heat required to raise the temperature of a unit mass of a substance by 1°. Also known as heat capacity.

spectrum. The range of electromagnetic wavelengths, ranging from high-energy gamma rays to low-energy radio waves. Visible light lies in the middle of the spectrum.

speed shear. A change in wind speed along or across the wind direction.

stable boundary layer. A shallow, cool layer lying above the ground that forms overnight and usually dissipates during the day.

stratiform clouds. Layer clouds that form in stable environments.

stratocumulus. A convective cloud that forms in an environment of weak, low-level instability.

stratopause. The boundary between the stratosphere and the mesosphere.

stratosphere. The second layer in the Earth's atmosphere, lying above the troposphere. Temperatures remain steady or rise with height in this layer. The stratosphere begins at an altitude of about 4 miles (6 km) at the poles and 12 miles (20 km) at the equator.

stratus. Flat, opaque, low-level cloud.

subsidence. The gradual downward movement or sinking of a column of air in the atmosphere.

substorm. A sudden increase in intensity of the aurora following the release of a large number of energetic electrons and ions into the atmosphere when containment in the Earth's magnetic field breaks down.

subtropical anticyclones. Semipermanent high-pressure cells that lie over the world's oceans at about 30° latitude in the descending branch of the Hadley circulation. The anticyclones move small distances north and south with the seasons.

suction vortex. A small but intense secondary tornadic circulation that rotates around a larger tornado column.

sunshine recorder. A device for measuring the duration and intensity of sunshine.

supercell. A thunderstorm with a rotating updraft that causes it to adopt a distinctive form. Supercell storms produce the most severe types of convective damage.

supersaturated. In meteorology, the condition in which the atmosphere contains more water vapor than is needed to produce saturation. When air becomes supersaturated, the relative humidity rises above 100 percent, though seldom by more than 1 or 2 percent.

surface layer. A small layer lying directly against the ground; it is cooled by the ground overnight and warmed during the day.

surface tension. A kind of "skin" that forms on the surface of a liquid, caused by the cohesive forces between molecules.

synoptic scale. A meteorological scale that encompasses structures and events that range in size from about 300 miles (500 km) to a few thousand miles. These systems include migrating high- and low-pressure systems, tropical storms (hurricanes), winter storms, and airmass regions. Synoptic-scale events typically have lifetimes of a few days to a week or more.

tail cloud. A sloping, quasi-horizontal cloud that extends from the wall cloud toward the heavy rain sector of a severe thunderstorm.

teleconnection. The association between weather patterns at one part of the globe and meteorological events at another.

temperature. A measure of the average kinetic energy of molecules in a substance.

Texas hooker. A cold-season storm that forms in eastern Texas and curves northward to move onto the Great Plains and across the Great Lakes. Also known as a Panhandle hook.

thermal escape. The loss of atmospheric gases from the upper atmosphere by solar heating.

thermal low (heat low). A low-pressure system that forms in the lower atmosphere over regions with intense solar heating. Thermal lows may be daily events or extend across a season.

thermometer. A device for measuring temperature.

thermosphere. The Earth's fourth atmospheric layer, lying from 300 to 620 miles (500 to 1,000 km) above the surface.

tipping-bucket rain gauge. A device for measuring rainfall rate and amount. Rain is collected and directed into a small container that tips over when a certain volume has been collected. The rainfall rate is determined by the frequency of the tips and the amount from the total number.

tornado. A narrow, rotating column of air attached to a convective cloud (usually a thunderstorm) and touching the ground. It is usually visible as a rotating cloud column.

towering cumulus. A deep convective cloud that is usually capable of producing rain, but not intense enough for lightning and thunder. Also called (rarely) swelling cumulus.

trade winds. Steady easterly subtropical winds that flow around the equatorial side of subtropical anticyclones.

tropopause. The boundary between the troposphere and the stratosphere.

troposphere. The lowest region of the Earth's atmosphere, containing most of the planet's weather. On average, temperature decreases with height in this layer.

trough (sometimes shortened to "TROF"). An elongated region of lower pressure or lower pressure height.

typhoon. A severe tropical storm that forms over the waters of the Northwest Pacific, west of the date line. A typhoon is a regional name for strong tropical storms; in other regions, they are called cyclones and hurricanes.

undular bore. A type of wave cloud, appearing as cloud rolls with an extended lifetime.

updraft. The rising air column in a convective cloud.

valley winds. Winds that flow up- and down-valley in response to pressure forces generated by solar heating or nighttime cooling.

virga. A streak of rain or snow falling from a cloud that evaporates before it reaches the ground.

von Kármán vortices. A chain of alternating "whirlpools" that forms in the lee of an island barrier when the low-level wind flow is blocked by the land.

vorticity. A measure of clockwise or counterclockwise rotation in the flow of the wind (or any fluid). Vorticity is positive if the flow contains anticyclonic rotation; it is negative if the rotation is cyclonic.

Walker circulation. A large east-west circulation in the atmosphere driven by the differences in heating between land and ocean.

wall cloud. A large semicircular cloud, sometimes rotating, that hangs beneath the rain-free area of a strong thunderstorm. Wall clouds mark the updraft region of the thunderstorm.

warm conveyor belt. A rising flow of air into a mature low (cyclone) that arises in low latitudes and supplies the storm with heat and moisture.

warm front. The boundary of advancing warm air.

waterspout. A tornadic circulation over water, similar to a landspout over land. The waterspout usually dissipates upon reaching land.

wave cloud. Any cloud that occurs in waves or billows, but typically reserved for those formed downwind of a mountain barrier, where they are called lee waves.

window region. A region in the electromagnetic spectrum where energy from the Earth can pass through the atmosphere to escape into space.

work. A mechanical change in a system caused by the expenditure of energy such as heating or cooling.

zonal flow. A more-or-less west-to-east flow in the upper atmosphere.

REFERENCES

Bender, James A. 1962. "Ukichiro Nakaya" (obituary). *Arctic* 15, no. 3 (September 1962): 242–243.

Bentley, Wilson A. 1902. "Studies Among the Snow Crystals During the Winter of 1901–2 with Additional Data Collected During Previous Winters." *Monthly Weather Review* 30:607–616.

Bolton, Henry Carrington. 1900. *Evolution of the Thermometer, 1592–1743*. Easton, PA: Chemical Publishing Company.

Bostock, John, and H. T. Riley. 1855. *The Natural History of Pliny*. London: Henry G. Bohn.

Buratti, Bonnie J. 2017. *Worlds Fantastic, Worlds Familiar: A Guided Tour of the Solar System*. Cambridge and New York: Cambridge University Press.

Cajori, Florian. 1899. *A History of Physics in Its Elementary Branches*. London: Macmillan and Co.

Dalton, John. 1793. *Meteorological Observations and Essays*. London: W. Richardson, J. Phillips, W. Pennington.

Dampier, William. 1697. *A New Voyage Round the World*. London.

Derham, William. 1733. "An Abstract of the Meteorological Diaries, Communicated to the Royal Society, with Remarks upon Them." *Philosophical Transactions of the Royal Society* 38, Issue 429. London: Royal Society.

Dunlop, Storm. 2017. *Weather: A Very Short Introduction* (Very Short Introductions). Oxford: Oxford University Press.

Evelyn-White, Hugh G., trans. 1914. *Hesiod, Homeric Hymns, Epic Cycle, Homerica*. Vol. 57 of *G. Loeb Classical Library*. London: William Heinemann.

Fahrenheit, Daniel Gabriel. 1724. "Materiarum quarundam gravitates specificæ, diversis temporibus ad varios scopes exploratæ a D. G.

Fahrenheit, R. S. S." *Philosophical Transactions of the Royal Society* 33, Issue 383. London: Royal Society.

Feynman, Richard. 1964. "Conservation of Energy." *The Feynman Lectures on Physics,* Vol. 1, Chapter 4. https://www.feynmanlectures.caltech.edu/

Hall, Charles F. 1879. *Narrative of the second Arctic expedition made by Charles F. Hall: his voyage to Repulse bay, sledge journeys to the straits of Fury and Hecla and to King William's land, and residence among the Eskimos, during the years 1864–69.* Washington: Government Printing Office.

Harrison, R. G., G. Pretor-Pinney, G. J. Marlton, D. G. Anderson, D. J. Kirshbaum, and R. J. Hogan. 2017. "Asperitas—a Newly Identified Cloud Supplementary Feature." *Weather* 72, no. 5.

Hlad, C. J., Jr. 1944. "Stability-Tendency and Mammatocumulus Clouds." *Bulletin of the American Meteorological Society* 25:327–331.

Howard, L. 1804. *On the Modifications of Clouds.* London: J. Taylor.

Ingersoll, Andrew P. 2013. *Planetary Climates.* Princeton: Princeton University Press.

Middleton, W. E. K. 1963. "The Place of Torricelli in the History of the Barometer." *Isis* 54, no. 1: 11–28.

Millikan, R. 1919. "Some Scientific Aspects of the Meteorological Work of the United States Army." *Monthly Weather Review* 47:210–215.

National Weather Service. 2019. Introduction to the National Weather Service. Retrieved from https://www.weather.gov/jetstream/nws_intro.

Pasachoff, Jay M., 2021. *A Field Guide to the Stars and Planets,* 4th ed., 2021 printing, Boston: Houghton Mifflin Harcourt.

Pascal, Blaise. 1648. *Recit de la grande experience de l'Equilibre des liqueurs. Projectée par le Sieur B. P. Pour l'accomplissement du traicté qu'il a promis dans son abbregé touchant le vuide. Et faite par le Sieur F. P. en une des plus hautes montagnes d'Auvergne.* Paris: Chez Charles Savreux.

Roberts, Steven. 2006. *Distant Writing, A History of the Telegraph Companies in Britain between 1838 and 1868.* Retrieved from https://distantwriting.co.uk/companiesandweather.html.

Vasquez, Tim. 2009. *Storm Chasing Handbook.* Garland, TX: Weather Graphics Technology.

Walker, G. T. 1923. "Correlation in Seasonal Variations of Weather, VIII: A Preliminary Study of World-Weather." *Memoirs of the Indian Meteorological Department* 24 (Part 4): 75–131.

Walker, G. T. 1924. "Correlation in Seasonal Variations of Weather, IX. A Further Study of World Weather." *Memoirs of the Indian Meteorological Department* 24 (Part 9): 275–332.

Webster, E. W. 1923. *Works of Aristotle Translated into English: Meteorologica*. Oxford: Clarendon Press.

Woodcroft, Bennet. 1851. *The Pneumatics of Hero of Alexandria*. London: Taylor Walton and Maberly.

Zahm, Albert F. 1911. *Aerial Navigation*. New York and London: D. Appleton and Company.

Website Suggestions

College of DuPage Next Generation Weather Lab: weather.cod.edu. This site is a favorite with storm chasers and includes satellite imagery, numerical model output, and radar displays.

EUMETSAT: https://eumetview.eumetsat.int/static-images/MSG/. Satellite image portal for the European satellite agency. This site provides access to the Meteosat geostationary satellites that cover Europe, Africa, the Middle East, and much of the Indian Ocean. Many specialized products are available.

Government of Canada weather portal: https://weather.gc.ca/. A portal to Canada's meteorological agency and its weather data.

NASA Worldview: https://worldview.earthdata.nasa.gov/. This NASA site provides daily, high resolution satellite images of the globe stretching back to the turn of the century.

National Weather Service (NWS): https://www.weather.gov/. A portal to the U.S. weather service with links to forecasts, warnings, satellite and radar imagery, station reports, and other data.

NOAA *GOES* Image Viewer: https://www.star.nesdis.noaa.gov/GOES/index.php. A NOAA site for satellite image display. A large number of wavelength bands are available for the Western Hemisphere.

NOAA National Hurricane Center: https://www.nhc.noaa.gov/. NOAA's hurricane forecast and tracking center for the Atlantic and Eastern Pacific.

Spaceweather: https:spaceweather.com. A comprehensive site for auroral predictions from NASA, solar activity, commentary, and aurora, atmospheric, and astronomical photos.

A large number of other weather sites are available across the globe from both government and private agencies and can be found with appropriate terms in a search engine.

All photos by Jay Anderson except as listed.

Fig. 7-45: *Data provided by the NOAA/ESRL Physical Sciences Division, Boulder, CO, from their website at www.esrl.noaa.gov/psd/*

Fig. 7-48: *Data: provided by the NOAA/ESRL Physical Sciences Division, Boulder, CO, from their website at www.esrl.noaa.gov/psd/*

Fig. 7-49: *Data: provided by the NOAA/ESRL Physical Sciences Division, Boulder, CO, from their website at www.esrl.noaa.gov/psd/*

Fig. 7-50: *Data: provided by the NOAA/ESRL Physical Sciences Division, Boulder, CO, from their website at www.esrl.noaa.gov/psd/*

Fig. 7-51: *Image data: provided by the NOAA/ESRL Physical Sciences Division, Boulder, CO, from their website at www.esrl.noaa.gov/psd/*

Fig. 7-52: *Data provided by the NOAA/ESRL Physical Sciences Division, Boulder, CO, from their website at www.esrl.noaa.gov/psd/*

Fig. 7-55: *Data: BOM, Australia*

Fig. 7-56: *Source: NASA*

Fig. 7-57: *Image: NASA*

Fig. 7-60: *Image: NASA*

Fig. 7-63: *Data: Environment Canada*

Fig. 7-69: *Image: NASA*

Fig. 8-3: *Image: NASA*

Fig. 8-5: *Image: NASA*

Fig. 8-7: *Image background: NASA*

Fig. 8-8: *Source: NASA*

Fig. 8-10: *Image: NASA*

Fig. 8-13: *Image: NASA*

Fig. 8-16: *Image: NASA*

Fig. 8-17: *Source: Satellite Training Course Notes (Roger Weldon), NOAA*

Fig. 8-18: *Data: NCAR*

Fig. 8-20: *Background image: NASA*

Fig. 8-21: *Image: NASA*

P. 334: *Image: NASA*

Fig. 9-3: *Image: Sheila Wiwchar*

Fig. 9-7: *Data: Storm Prediction Center*

Fig. 9-8: *Image: NOAA*

Fig. 9-9: *Data: Storm Prediction Center*

Fig. 9-11: *Image: NOAA*

Fig. 9-12: *U.S. data: Storm Prediction Center*

Fig. 9-14: *Image: Dave Carlsen*

Fig. 9-17: *Image: Pat McCarthy*

Table 9-1: *Source: Storm Prediction Center*

Table 9-2: *Source: Storm Prediction Center*

Fig. 9-26: *Image source: NOAA*

Fig. 9-27: *Image: NASA*

Fig. 9-30: *Image: NASA*

Fig. 9-31: *Image: NASA/GSFC/MODIS*

Table 9-3: *Source: Storm Prediction Center*

Fig. 9-33: *Image: USCG*

Fig. 9-34: *Image: NOAA NESDIS*

P. 385 (top): *Image: Scott Gottilla*

P. 388 (top): *Source: NOAA/NWS*

P. 388 (bottom): *Image: NOAA/Charleston Weather Forecast Office*

P. 389 (top): *Source: NOAA/ NWS*

P. 389 (bottom): *Source: NOAA*

Fig. 10-21: *Image: Jennifer West*

Fig. 10-22: *Image: Jay Pasachoff*

Fig. 10-33: *Source: Mila Zinkova*

Fig. 10-35: *Judy Anderson*

Fig. 10-37: *Data: NOAA Space Environment Center*

Fig. 10-38: *Image: NASA/NRL/ESA*

Fig. 10-40: *Image: NASA Earth Observatory image by Jesse Allen and Robert Simmon, using VIIRS Day-Night Band data from the Suomi National Polar-orbiting Partnership (Suomi NPP) and the University of Wisconsin's Community Satellite Processing Package*

Fig. 11-2: *Source: NOAA Central Library*

Fig. 11-3: *Image: Adam Jones, PhD*

Fig. 11-4: *Source: NOAA*

Fig. 11-6: *Image: Fotolia*

Fig. 11-7: *Image: Fotolia*

Fig. 11-12: *Image: Fotolia*

Fig. 11-16: *Image: Pat McCarthy*

Fig. 11-21: *Source: NOAA Photo Library*

Fig. 11-24: *Image: Alan Sim*

Fig. 11-26: *Source: Library of Congress*

Fig. 11-28: *Image: NOAA*

P. 478: *Image: Jay M. Pasachoff, Allen B. Davis, and Vojtech Rusin, with computer compositing by Miloslav Druckmüller*

P. 480: *Image: NASA*

P. 483: *Jay M. Pasachoff (Williams College) and Ron Dantowitz (Clay Center Observatory, Dexter Southworth School); Williams College Transit of Venus Expedition, with support of the Committee for Research and Exploration of the National Geographic Society*

P. 494: *Image: NASA*

Fig. A-1: *Image: NASA*

Fig. A-2: *Image: NASA*

Fig. A-3: *Image: NASA, ESA, A. Simon (Goddard Space Flight Center) and M. H. Wong (University of California, Berkeley)*

Fig. A-4: *NASA and the Hubble Heritage Team/ STScI/AURA; Richard G. French (Wellesley College), Jeff Cuzzi (NASA's Ames Research Center; Luke Dones (Southwest Research Institute), and Jack Lissauer (NASA's Ames Research Center)*

Fig. A-5: *NASA/JPL-Caltech/Space Science Institute*

Fig. A-6: *Image: NASA/JPL-Caltech/Space Science Institute*

Fig. A-7: *Image: NASA/JPL-Caltech*

Fig. A-8: *Image: NASA/JPL-Caltech*

Fig. A-9: *Image: NASA/JPL-Caltech, reprocessed by U.S. Geological Survey*

Fig. A-10: *Image: NASA/Johns Hopkins University Applied Physics Laboratory/Southwest Research Institute*

Fig. A-11: *Image: Jay Pasachoff*

Fig. A-12: *Image: Cameron Zucker*

ADDITIONAL
FIGURE CAPTIONS

Page i: *Hoarfrost bejewels a snowy park on a quiet winter morning.*

Page ii-iii: *Fair-weather cumulus clouds reflect from a quiet prairie lake while a distant grain elevator punctuates the horizon.*

Page vi: *A sunset rainbow, tinted in red, promises clearing skies overnight.*

Page viii: *An ominous, towering thunderstorm cast in gloom by the late afternoon sun.*

Page x: *A late spring snowstorm dresses this calendula in a gown of fluffy snow crystals.*

Page xv: *Pouches of mammatus clouds descend from the anvil of a departing thunderstorm.*

Page xvi: *Low, medium, and high clouds display the atmosphere in three dimensions.*

Page 12: *Mammatus clouds beneath a thunderstorm reflect the red tones of sunset.*

Page 96: *Mid-level lenticular clouds decorate the sky above a small hilltop.*

Page 144: *An ominous wall cloud beneath a thunderstorm warns of severe weather and a possible tornado.*

Page 186: *A spreading collar at the top of this towering cumulus cloud suggests that the updraft is near its maximum altitude and will soon begin to decay.*

Page 212: *Three stately thunderstorms, carefully avoided by the pilot, line up outside the aircraft window. These three were part of a dangerous line of wind-producing storms.*

Page 304: *A time exposure of an approaching line of thunderstorms reveals the twisting path of a lightning strike.*

Page 336: *A snaking tornado touches down beneath a supercell thunderstorm, raising a distant plume of dust and debris.*

Page 390: *Colorful light pillars shine upward as falling ice crystals reflect city lights toward the observer.*

Page 478-79: *The Sun in total eclipse, showing the spreading wings of the corona above the intense red of its lowest atmospheric layer, the chromosphere. The hourlong gradual and then abrupt darkening under the lunar shadow, a factor almost a million in the solar insolation, has important effects on Earth's atmosphere. These* include a fall in temperature, dissipation of smaller convective clouds, subtle atmospheric pressure waves, formation of surface temperature inversions, and a decrease in atmospheric turbulence. One of us (J.M.P.) working with an international team, measured temperature drops with shielded sensors in 2015 in Svalbard from –23°F to –28°F (–19°C to –21.5°C); 120°F to 115°F (49°C to 46°C) in the Middle East in a pair of annular eclipses in 2019 and 2020; and from 90°F to 60°F (32°C to 15°C) in Oregon during the 2017 total solar eclipse.

Page 480: An Earth-trained meteorologist would find many familiar features on Mars, but one of the most surprising would be the enormous number of dust devils that form in the afternoon heat. This image, taken by NASA's Mars Reconnaissance Orbiter, shows a 12-mile-high (20 km) dust devil spinning across one of the Martian plains in late spring.

INDEX

Index page references in *italics* refer to text graphics.

wet monsoon, 251–52, *251*, *252*, *253*, 254–56, *255*

India Meteorological Department, 251, 266

indices and meteorologists, 282
    See also specific indices

interference with light/waves, 392–93, *393*

International Geophysical Year (1951–52), 267

International Meteorological Organization, 476

International Space Station/images, *16*, *26*, *148*, *153*

Intertropical Convergence Zone (ICZ/ITCZ), 241–42, *241*, 246, *246*
    anticyclones, 242, 246, *246*
    descriptions, 241–42, *241*
    monsoons, 250, 259, 264, *264*

inversions
    Arctic airmasses, 309
    chinook/foehn winds, 298, *299*
    clouds/fog, 106, 108, 117, *132*, *192*, *195*, 247, *247*
    cloud streets/streamers, *174*, *192*
    cold/warm fronts, 22, *22*
    high pressure systems, 22
    overview, 21–22, *22*, *23*
    planetary boundary layer (PBL), 19–21, *19*
    saturation/fog, 20, *20*
    ship trails, 172

ionization, 26, 431

iridescent clouds, 409–10, *409*, *439*

isobars, 217, *218*

ITOS (weather satellites/Improved TIROS Operational Satellite), 201

Jeffries, John, 470

jet streams
    blocking patterns, 236
    cyclogenesis, 328–29, *329*, 335
    descriptions, *141*, *142*, 212, 229–30, *230*, *232*
    effects/images, *141*, *142*
    extreme weather, 338, 352, 358–59, 360, *360*, 361, *364*, 367, 378

    locations, 229–32, *230*, *231*, *232*
    names, 230
    overview, 229–32, *230*
    polar jet cross section, 231
    storm direction, 123
    temperature, 229–30, *230*
    zonal flow, *230*

Joiner, U. T., 465–66

Jupiter, 483–84, *483*

Jurin, James, 472

katabatic/anabatic winds defined, 289

Kelvin-Helmholtz (K-H) billow clouds/waves, 164–66, *165*, *182*

Kelvin, Lord, 164

Kelvin temperature scale, 460

kinetic energy, 40, *41*, 42

Landsat series (weather satellite), 203

land/sea breezes, 283–88, *285*, *287*, *288*, *289*

landspout tornadoes, 348–49, *348*, *349*

La Niña. *See* ENSO (El Niño Southern Oscillation)

lapse rate, 159

latent heat
    description, 7, 53–55, *54*
    phase changes, 7, 53–55, *54*
    water vapor to precipitation, 73–75, *74*

layers in atmosphere
    boundary between layers, 14–15, *15*
    overview, 14–16, *15*
    temperature, *15*
    See also specific layers

lee/mountain waves, 148–50, *149*

"lee trough," 331

Leibniz, Gottfried Wilhelm, 454

lenticular clouds, 23, 120, *121*, 123, *136*, *139*, *149*, 151–53, *151*, *152*, *153*, *179*, *181*

Leopold, Prince, 457–58

Le Verrier, Jean Joseph, 475